"This will be go-to book before I plunge into a verse-by-verse study of any of our four Gospels. Schreiner provides an excellent overview of each book's content, examines important connections to the Old Testament, and unfolds the Gospel's theological themes and emphases. Use of this book will enrich any expositor's handling of the biblical text."

—**Daniel L. Akin**, president, Southeastern Baptist Theological Seminary

"Patrick Schreiner has done us a great favor with his concise, clear, comprehensive textbook *The Four Gospels*. In marvelously readable style, he overviews what a Gospel is and how to read the Gospels. For each of the four, he reviews the background issues and provides an insightful interpretative overview before turning to connections with the Old Testament and the gospel. He concludes with life connections. This is an outstanding resource for committed followers of Jesus to begin their study of the Gospels."

—**Gerry Breshears**, professor of theology, Western Seminary

"Patrick Schreiner has gifted Christians with a handy primer on the Gospels. In addition to overviews of the four Gospels, he highlights their key themes, their reliance on the Old Testament, and the ways they illuminate the (singular) gospel. Schreiner considers the Gospels at their core to be 'discipleship texts' and concludes each chapter with 'life connections' to help readers consider ways to apply the Gospels to their own discipleship. An inviting and engaging volume."

—**Jeannine Brown**, David Price Professor of Biblical and Theological Foundations, Bethel Seminary

"Patrick Schreiner's *The Four Gospels* will serve students well. It is crisp, concise, and crystal clear. The key questions are addressed, and the four Gospels are treated succinctly. This well-written book can serve as a stand-alone textbook or as supplementary text. If you teach the Gospels, you'll want *The Four Gospels*."

—**Craig A. Evans**, John Bisagno Distinguished Professor of Christian Origins, Houston Christian University

"For many Christians, the easy familiarity of the four Gospels masks their rich depth. With clarity and accessibility, Schreiner lifts the veil for those ready to go deeper in their study of these foundational texts. The reader is not only given a brisk and well-informed survey of the Gospels but is treated to a host of rich connections between the Gospels and the Old Testament, the four Gospels and the one gospel, and the Gospels and life in the world today."

—**Peter Gurry**, associate professor of New Testament, Phoenix Seminary, and director of Text & Canon Institute

"Patrick Schreiner effectively 'rips out the page between the two testaments' in *The Four Gospels* and displays the continuity between the Old and New Testaments for modern Christian readers. Written in a manner accessible to all, Schreiner lucidly conveys that the Gospels do not just record the beginning of a new story, but that they are the indispensable continuation of a preexisting narrative. Schreiner's close and nuanced readings of the Gospels skillfully illustrate how the stories of Jesus, and even his very words, interact with the preceding testimony of Israel. *The Four Gospels* is graced with helpful outlines, judicious sidebars, and specific life connections valuable for students and seasoned scholars alike. This book brings Matthew, Mark, Luke, and John to life as discipleship texts that are utterly applicable to readers in modern times."

—**Dominick S. Hernández**, associate professor of Old Testament and Semitics, Talbot School of Theology, Biola University

"Patrick Schreiner is a prolific and insightful young scholar. Both students and teachers will benefit from his accessible and thorough introductory textbook to the Gospels."

—**Robert L. Plummer**, Collin and Evelyn Aikman Professor of Biblical Studies, The Southern Baptist Theological Seminary

THE
FOUR GOSPELS

Gary Edward
Schnittjer
AND
Mark L. Strauss
SERIES EDITORS

THE
FOUR GOSPELS

— JESUS, THE HOPE OF THE WORLD —

Patrick

Schreiner

SCRIPTURE CONNECTIONS

B&H
ACADEMIC
BRENTWOOD, TENNESSEE

The Four Gospels: Jesus, the Hope of the World
Copyright © 2024 by Patrick Schreiner

Published by B&H Academic
Brentwood, Tennessee

ISBN: 978-1-0877-4636-4

Dewey Decimal Classification: 226.1
Subject Heading: BIBLE. N.T. GOSPELS \ JESUS CHRIST \ CHRISTIANITY

Unless otherwise noted, all Scripture quotations are taken from the Christian Standard Bible®, Copyright © 2017 by Holman Bible Publishers. Used by permission. Christian Standard Bible® and CSB® are federally registered trademarks of Holman Bible Publishers.

Scripture quotations marked ESV are taken from The Holy Bible, English Standard Version. ESV® Text Edition: 2016. Copyright © 2001 by Crossway Bibles, a publishing ministry of Good News Publishers. Used by Permission. All Rights Reserved.

The web addresses referenced in this book were live and correct at the time of the book's publication but may be subject to change.

Cover design by Derek Thornton / Notch Design and Emily Keafer Lambright. Cover image: Jesus washes his Disciples' Feet, sourced from Wolfgang Diederich / Alamy Stock Photo. Additional images by Rubanitor/Shutterstock and Balefire/Shutterstock.

Printed in China

29 28 27 26 25 24 RRD 1 2 3 4 5 6 7 8 9 10

CONTENTS

A Note to Professors from the Editors   ix

Introduction to the Gospels   1

1   Matthew   17

2   Mark   67

3   Luke   109

4   John   157

Subject Index   203

A NOTE TO PROFESSORS
FROM THE EDITORS

The textbooks in the Scripture Connections series feature somewhat shorter page counts than many traditional survey texts. Professors in traditional courses can use these textbooks to provide room in their courses for other targeted readings. Professors teaching courses in more concise formats can assign the entire textbook. In sum, the short page count is meant to offer maximal flexibility in course design.

Professors who adopt this book as a required text are welcome to access its supplemental professor's materials at no cost. Please go to bhacademic.com/requests.

Gary Edward Schnittjer, editor of Old Testament
Mark L. Strauss, editor of New Testament

INTRODUCTION TO THE GOSPELS

Every story needs a resolution. Every lock needs a key. Every symphony needs a final movement. And every dark night is pierced by the dawn.

In many ways the Old Testament is a dark story. After only two pages humanity has fallen. The rest of the story is a downward spiral involving murder, hate, tears, grief, and division. Though God calls a people, they too fail again and again. Though there are glimmers of light, darkness and shadows cloud the narrative.

But the darkness can't thwart the light. As the Gospel of John says, "That light shines in the darkness, and yet the darkness did not overcome it" (1:5). The Gospels are the light of the Bible. In them we finally meet Jesus. Here the story finds a resolution. Here we find the key and the final movement to all the Scriptures, Christ himself. Here the veil is lifted, and we behold the glory of God in the face of Jesus Christ.

The Gospels are the center of the Bible, the climax of the Scriptures. It is here we meet our Savior, our Shepherd, our Servant. It is here our King rides before us. It is here we see the Suffering Servant languish at Calvary. It is here we see the tomb empty. It is here we see he is the son of David, the son of Abraham, the son of Adam, and most important, the Son of God. The Gospels are where the rest of the story falls into place, the shadows depart, and the light shines. In the Gospels we finally see Jesus: the resolution, key, final movement, the light. Jesus is the hope of the world.

I will prepare you for reading the Gospels by (1) arguing the Gospels are the center of the Scriptures, (2) asking why the Bible has four Gospels and who chose them, (3) examining three lenses that help us read the Gospels, (4) retelling the story that led to the Gospels, (5) explaining Jesus's main message and action in light of the preceding story, and (6) maintaining the Gospels are discipleship texts. All of these provide pathways for readers who wish to interpret the Gospels more faithfully and see Jesus more truly.

The Importance of the Gospels

People tend to overlook the four Gospels because they seem to tell the same story again and again. But the Gospels are the center and climax of the Scriptures. Below are five reasons we need the Gospels.[1]

First, we need the Gospels because in them *we get a direct sense of the Bible's great story line.* At its core the Bible is a narrative of God's work in the world. This story focuses on Israel because they were chosen to represent God. But because Israel failed, they needed someone to come and make things right. Jesus is Israel's longed-for Messiah who resolves the plot. Unlike the Letters, the Gospels bring this story to completion.

Second, we need the Gospels because *the Old Testament leans toward the Gospels.* Everything in the Old Testament bends toward a coming new prophet, priest, king, seed, Israel, and servant. The Old Testament asserts that God must intervene for his people and that one will come who will make all things right. Each book of the Old Testament ends with lingering questions: Are things about to be put right? Who will fix this? Who will redeem Israel? The Gospels answer all these questions in the person of Jesus.

Third, we need the Gospels because *the rest of the New Testament presupposes and builds on the Gospels.* Even though the Gospels were written after some of the Epistles, the Jesus traditions are the source material for the written Gospels. The story of Jesus and his teachings is the reason we have letters to the churches scattered around the Mediterranean Sea. The stories of the Gospels come before the Epistles and set the stage for them. The life of Jesus functions as the basis for apostolic preaching. Though some people might be drawn toward the propositional formulations of the gospel in the Epistles, it's the *story* that produces these propositions.

Fourth, we need the Gospels because *they have been central for the church both in their liturgy and declarations of faith.* The Gospels were read and used more consistently than any other part of the Scriptures in the early church because they understood the importance of this section of Scripture. The Gospels were also central to the early creeds as the church defined the boundaries of the Christian faith. The creeds

---

[1] The following points are dependent on Jonathan Pennington, *Reading the Gospels Wisely: A Narrative and Theological Introduction* (Grand Rapids: Baker Academic, 2012), esp. 36–49.

confess the nature of the triune God, and at the center of these creeds is the revelation of Jesus's ontology—the nature of his being.

Fifth, we need the Gospels because *in the Gospels we meet Jesus*. Jesus is Israel's Messiah, but he is more than the Messiah. He is the Son of God. As the Nicene Creed confesses, Jesus is "the only-begotten Son of God, begotten of the Father before all worlds; [God of God,] Light of Light. Very God of very God, begotten, not made, being of one substance with the Father, by whom all things were made."[2] The one through whom all things were made, the one who upholds the universe by his word, the one who is one with the Father, has now come to earth. The Gospels are the stories of what this God-man said and did. Jesus is not only God but the life we are to emulate. Nothing could be more important than God taking on flesh. Erasmus puts it this way:

> If someone exhibited a print made by the feet of Christ, how we Christians would prostrate ourselves, how we would adore! Why, then, do we not rather venerate his living and breathing image, preserved in these books? If someone displayed the tunic of Christ, would we not fly to the ends of the earth to kiss it? But even if you were to produce every possession he owned, there is nothing that would show Christ more clearly and more truly than the written Gospels. Through our love of Christ, we enrich a statue of wood or stone with jewels and gold. Why do we not rather adorn these books with gold and jewels and anything more precious, for they recall Christ to us more vividly than any little statue. A statue shows only the appearance of his body—if indeed it shows anything of that—but these books show you the living image of his holy mind and Christ himself, speaking, healing, dying, rising to life again. In short, they restore Christ to us so completely and so vividly that you would see him less clearly should you behold him standing before your very eyes.[3]

The point Erasmus makes is illustrated in church history at the council of Ephesus in 431 CE. At that meeting, Cyril of Alexandria formally opened the council by enthroning the four Gospels in the center of the church. The Gospels were a symbol of Christ's living presence among them.

---

[2] Nicene Creed, in *Creeds of Christendom, with a History and Critical Notes*, vol. 1, *The History of Creeds*, 6th ed., ed. Philip Schaff (Harper & Row, 1919); Christian Classics Ethereal Library, https://www.ccel.org/ccel/schaff/creeds1.iv.iii.html.

[3] Desiderius Erasmus, *Paraclesis* (*Collected Works of Erasmus* 41:422), in Jason K. Lee and William M. Marsh, eds., *Reformation Commentary on Scripture: Matthew* (Downers Grove, IL: IVP Academic, 2021), 1.

Why Four, and Who Chose Them?

Why do we have four Gospels? And further, who chose these four? Both of these questions deal with the question, Why are we reading what we are reading? Most simply, we are reading these four Gospels because they are in our canon. The canon refers to the books the church views as authoritative Scripture. The concept of canon is bound up with the question of authority. The canon establishes the boundary of authority. But this raises the question of who chose what goes in our canon.

A variety of proposals exists for how certain books arrived in the Christian Scriptures.[4] First, some argue the community was the key factor. In this view, the canon was established by the church as they selected the books to be in the Bible. Second, others look to history. Many argue the books we have in our canon are based on "criteria for canonicity" such as apostolicity, orthodoxy, and usage. The books need to have come from an apostle or someone closely connected to an apostle. The books need to teach orthodox doctrine, and they need to have been widely used in the early church.[5]

ANCIENT CONNECTIONS I.1. THE HISTORICAL DEVELOPMENT OF THE GOSPELS

- **Historical event:** The Gospels assert that they recount historical events of what Jesus said and did. Some of his followers probably used notebooks to aid in remembrance and transmission of Jesus's teaching. Some of Jesus's sayings were probably memorized.
- **Oral tradition:** These stories of Jesus were passed around for more than thirty years as oral stories about Jesus. But as noted earlier, the relationship between orality and textuality was fluid. Some of these stories were tightly controlled, and in others the details could be shifted slightly (Acts 20:35; 1 Cor 9:14; 11:25).
- **Social memory:** Passing along the Jesus tradition involves selectivity and subjectivity. Social memory asserts that past memories are reconstructed in

---

[4] These categories come from Michael J. Kruger, as found in his *Canon Revisited: Establishing the Origins and Authority of the New Testament Books* (Wheaton, IL: Crossway, 2012).

[5] For a helpful overview of the criteria for canonicity, see chapter 1 in Andreas J. Köstenberger, L. Scott Kellum, and Charles L. Quarles, *The Cradle, the Cross, and the Crown*, 2nd ed. (Nashville: B&H Academic, 2016), esp. 9–11.

- light of present needs. That means these stories were not always told simply as data but were molded for present needs.
- **Written Gospel:** The Evangelists researched, recalled, collected, and composed the Gospels as biographies of Jesus. They used each other and other eyewitnesses as sources (Luke 1:1–4).

The third proposal is the books themselves asserted their own authority on the church. This is what some mean when they call the canon *self-authenticating*. While there is some truth to the first two proposals, the problem is they ground the authority of the canon in something outside the canon itself (community or history). Divine revelation is necessarily self-authenticating because God himself is the source of authority. Neither the community nor history creates the Word; rather, the Word creates the community and directs history. However, the self-authenticating model provides the grounds for considering the other models. This allows one to affirm some aspect of each but ground it in the authority of the canon in the books themselves because these are the very words of God.

So, who chose the Gospels? Most fundamentally, the Gospels imposed themselves as canonical upon the church. They were authoritative because they were written under the inspiration of the Holy Spirit and were part of God's authoritative words from the start. The community recognized which books were authoritative, and we can retroactively note these books were closely tied to apostolic testimony, cohered with orthodox doctrine, and were widely used in the early church. In this sense, God chose the Gospels.

But why do we have four? Most fundamentally because these four set out the theological content of the gospel unlike the noncanonical Gospels. However, the church fathers also asserted there are four because that number has a sense of completeness. One Gospel could not have adequately summarized the ministry of Jesus. We needed four different perspectives on Jesus's life. Irenaeus (130–202 CE) says the following about why we have four:

It is not possible that the Gospels can be either more or fewer in number than they are. For, since there are four zones of the world in which we live, and four principal winds . . . For the cherubim, too, were four-faced, and their faces were images of the dispensation of the Son of God. For, [as the Scripture] says, "The first living creature was like a lion," symbolizing His effectual working, His leadership, and royal power; the second [living creature] was like a calf, signifying [His] sacrificial and sacerdotal order; but "the third had, as it were, the face as of a man," an evident description of His advent as a human being; "the fourth was like a flying eagle," pointing out the gift of the

Spirit hovering with His wings over the Church. And therefore the Gospels are in accord with these things, among which Christ Jesus is seated. . . . For the living creatures are quadriform, and the Gospel is quadriform, as is also the course followed by the Lord.[6]

ANCIENT CONNECTIONS I.2. THE OTHER GOSPELS?

It can be surprising to learn there are other gospels besides the four in the Christian canon. The early church never gave special place to these other gospels because they do not share key theological elements that distinguish the four canonical Gospels.[7] The noncanonical gospels seem to have been written for small sectarian circles in the early church. They have been labeled pseudepigraphal, falsely attributed works whose claimed author is not the true author.

- *Gospel of Thomas*: A gnostic gospel written in Coptic (an Egyptian dialect) in the second century. It's a collection of Jesus's sayings, and about half of the sayings have parallels in the canonical Gospels.
- *Gospel of Peter*: Also written in the second century, this gospel focuses on Jesus's passion, is dependent on the canonical Gospels, and appears to be pseudepigraphal.
- The *Secret Gospel of Mark*: Clement mentions this gospel in a letter discovered in 1958, known as the Mar Saba letter, and quotes from two passages where Jesus raised a rich young man from the dead in Bethany. Some think it was written by Mark, author of the Second Gospel; others argue it was written in the second century; and finally, some think it is a modern forgery.
- **Gospels of the Ebionites, the Hebrews, and the Nazarenes:** The early church fathers preserved within their writings fragments of three Jewish Christian gospels. These reflect the interests of believers to maintain their Jewish identity.

Others include the *Gospel of Marcion*, the *Gospel of Truth*, the *Gospel of Philip*, the *Gospel of Judah*, and the Coptic *Gospel of the Egyptians*.

---

[6] Irenaeus, *Against Heresies* 3.11.8, in *Ante-Nicene Fathers*, vol. 1, ed. Alexander Roberts, James Donaldson, and A. Cleveland Coxe; trans. Alexander Roberts and William Rambaut (Buffalo, NY: Christian Literature Publishing, 1885). Revised and edited for New Advent by Kevin Knight, http://www.newadvent.org/fathers/0103311.htm.

[7] See Simon J. Gathercole, *The Gospel and the Gospels: Christian Proclamation and Early Jesus Books* (Grand Rapids: Eerdmans, 2022).

Irenaeus's logic may seem strange to us. There are four Gospels because there are four zones of the earth, four winds, and four cherubim? However, this is more of an aesthetic argument after the four had presented themselves as authoritative. Additionally, his logic goes deeper than you might imagine. Irenaeus recognizes Jesus is the One who sits on the throne, and the cherubim witness to him. When Ezekiel and John see the four living creatures surrounding the throne, they witness to the glory of Jesus (Ezek 1:10; Rev 4:7). Jesus is the One seated on the throne (John 12:41).

In the same way, four Gospels surround the Son's throne. In the four we have an inclusive biography of our Savior. All four Gospels say something unique about the Son, and they are all necessary for faith and practice.

Three Lenses for Reading the Gospels

If the Gospels are this important, it is vital to read them wisely. Because all the Gospels are narratives, many of the skills one needs to read the Old Testament also apply to the Gospels. Three lenses help in reading the Gospels.[8]

First, we need to read the Gospels according to their *historical context*. Jesus was a Jew living in the first century in the land of Israel. The practices, languages, and customs of the time were very different from our own. We cannot assume similarity in cultures. For example, the house was not a place of privacy for the nuclear family. It usually included multiple generations and was a place out of which many did their business. Men and women interacted differently at this time. The literacy rate was very low. Most letters would be read to people and were expensive to produce. Travel was dangerous, long, and laborious. The division between the rich and the poor was extreme, and most of the population lived hand to mouth. Politics and religion were not distinguished. Rome ruled over Israel. Polytheism ruled the day. Slavery was ubiquitous. Temples to various gods dotted the cities. Patronage and reciprocity was the system by which people interacted. Honor and shame were central at that time. It is easy for us to project our culture onto the Gospels when reading them, but we must be aware of the historical context of the Gospels.

---

[8] One of the most important skills in reading the Gospels is seeing how they interact and advance the Old Testament story. One of the best books on this topic is Richard Hays, *Echoes of Scripture in the Gospels* (Waco, TX: Baylor University Press, 2017).

ANCIENT CONNECTIONS I.3. THE GOSPELS AS BIOGRAPHIES

The Gospels can be categorized into the ancient form of a biography, or what was called *Lives* (Latin, *vita*; Greek, *bios*). A *bios* was a book about a recent historical person and may have developed out of funeral orations. Plutarch wrote the largest and most famous collection of *Lives*. Laertius composed a series of *Lives of Eminent Philosophers*. Philostratus wrote the *Life of Apollonius of Tyana*, and Philo wrote *Life of Abraham, Joseph, and Moses*. Most *Lives* are shorter than most modern biographies. Authors regularly arranged their material topically, did not always start with a person's childhood, and often paraphrased material in their own words. They wrote them to promote a way of life or to encourage emulation.

Second, we need to read the Gospels according to their *literary context*. The Gospels are examples of Greco-Roman biographies; they are centered on one principal figure.[9] In the Gospels, that figure is Jesus. Every story is primarily about him. Even the secondary characters reveal something about Jesus. Sometimes readers grab whatever they like from the narrative and make it the major point. However, if these are narratives, we must follow the best practices for narrative analysis. This includes paying attention to the structure, setting, point of view, characters, and plot. Each story has a form that readers need to follow to get the main point.

Related to the literary context, we need to read the Gospels in *the context of the whole book*. Each Gospel was meant to be heard as a whole. Although there are individual stories, they are also tied together into a larger canvas. Each episode is carefully placed. To put this another way, we need to read books, not verses. This means discovering the significance of repeated words and ideas across various stories. This means paying attention to characters, settings, responses, titles, phrases, and actions. Each Gospel has the same subject, but each Gospel also tells its story differently, and we must follow the flow of each story. This means moving away from the harmonization of the four Gospels and seeking the unique voice of each one. As Richard Burridge puts it, "By opting for four pictures rather than one . . . the early Fathers provided a

---

[9] The classic work for the Gospels mirroring ancient biographies is Richard A. Burridge, *What Are the Gospels?: A Comparison with Graeco-Roman Biography*, 25th anniversary ed. (Waco, TX: Baylor University Press, 2020).

spur to the production of new images of this person in every generation. By selecting only four, they mapped out the ballpark where those who wish to remain in the tradition must play."[10] We purposively have four Gospels; they all testify differently to the one Jesus.

READING THE GOSPELS AS STORIES

- **Setting:** the backdrop against which the story unfolds, including the time and location.
- **Point of view:** the perspective from which the narrative is told. First person uses *I* and *we*. Second person uses *you*. Third person employs *he*, *she*, *it*, and *they*.
- **Characters:** the people in the story. Are they the protagonists, antagonists, or side characters? What do they contribute to the story? Do they reappear later in the story?
- **Plot:** the chain of events that make up a story, usually including the following:
  — **Rising action:** an event or speech that sets the story in action
  — **Climax:** the peak point of tension
  — **Falling action:** where the story begins to move toward conclusion
  — **Resolution:** the end of the story, where it resolves either happily or tragically, or moves the larger narrative forward

Third, we need to read the Gospels in the *context of the Bible as a whole*. Jesus didn't appear out of thin air. He was born in a real historical town that had prophecies of a messiah connected to it. Most of what Jesus does interacts with the story that precedes Jesus in the Old Testament. This means maybe the first thing to do when reading the Gospels is to rip out the page dividing the two testaments in your Bible. Jesus came in fulfillment of the expectations of Israel, so most of his actions relate in some way to their previous story. Your ear should be carefully attuned to the Old Testament story and how Jesus either shifts or imitates what came before. The Bible is one story, and it all leads to Jesus.

---

[10] Richard A. Burridge, *Four Gospels, One Jesus?: A Symbolic Reading*, 3rd ed. (Grand Rapids: Eerdmans, 2014), 177.

The Story Continues

To assist us in reading the Gospels in the context of the Bible as a whole, we can now overview the story that led to the Gospels.

The Gospels don't start a story; they continue one. This story begins back in the garden of Eden. God made the world and everything good. All was in harmony. But the serpent tempted Adam and Eve to rebel against God. They did so, and the harmony existing at creation broke. God's relationship with humans was fragmented, humans fought among themselves, and concord with creation was crushed. However, though the seed of the serpent and the woman would feud, God promised one day this story would be resolved. A wise Victor would arise.

In the meantime, sin spread like gangrene. Humanity fought, killed, and was separated into nations. God revealed he would rescue humanity through the family of one man: Abraham. He called this descendant of moon worshipers to a new place and promised Abraham a great family that became known as Israel. Israel didn't grow quickly, but they began to grow more rapidly when they sojourned to Egypt because of a famine. Pharaoh became frightened by their multiplication, so he enslaved them. However, God redeemed his people by the hand of Moses. He brought them through the sea and gave them his law on Mount Sinai. This law was Israel's marching orders for how to relate to him and the world. Central to this was the practice of meeting with God and offering sacrifices for their sins.

Israel finally entered the land as God had promised Abraham, but they didn't cleanse it of temptations completely. They continually forsook God. Israel asked for a king, like the other nations, and God granted their request. Most of their kings were wicked, like the people, but one king was after God's own heart. King David was promised an heir who would sit on Israel's throne forever. However, David's descendants forsook the Lord and split the nation into north and south. The north (Israel) was especially disloyal to Yahweh and was exiled in 722 BCE by Assyria. The south (Judah) was later conquered and brought into exile by Babylon in 597 BCE.

During the time of the monarchy and exile, the prophets attempted to call Israel back to the covenant they had made with God. They were largely unsuccessful. They also predicted that a time would come when God would again redeem his people, as he did out of Egypt. A new leader would arise and lead them out of exile and back into their land. The temple would be rebuilt, and Israel would worship their God in their own home. The prophets also predicted other nations would arise, such as the Babylonians, Medes, Persians, Greeks, and finally Rome.

After Babylon lost power, the Persian rulers allowed many Israelites to return to their land, and they began to rebuild their temple. However, things were not as the prophets predicted. Israel was still under foreign oppression, their throne was empty, and God's presence did not return like before.

Four hundred years of prophetic silence commenced (usually called the intertestamental period, from 400 BCE to 25 CE). When the silence began, Persia was still in power. But at the opening of the New Testament, Rome is on the scene. Many Bible readers don't know what happened between Malachi and Matthew, because it is not recounted in the Scriptures. However, it is an important part of the story.

As noted earlier, the Persians allowed Jews to practice their customs with little interference. Israel was even allowed to rebuild their temple. However, Alexander the Great arose and defeated Persia (331 BCE). He spread Greek culture and language to various regions (a process known as *Hellenization*) and is the reason we have a Greek New Testament and the Septuagint (i.e., Greek Old Testament).

Alexander did allow religious freedom for Jews, even though he strongly promoted Greek lifestyles. When Alexander the Great died, the region of Israel was divided under different rulers (323 BCE). Eventually, the Jewish people came under the rule of the Seleucids, a Greek state. Under this regime Antiochus IV (Epiphanes) began his campaign to force the Jewish people to take on Greek practices. He overthrew the proper Jewish line of priesthood and desecrated the temple, defiling it with unclean animals and a pagan altar.

Antiochus's actions stirred up a rebellion called the Maccabean Revolt (167 BCE). A priestly family arose and rebelled against their Greek lords, demanding religious freedom. Eventually, they gained their freedom through guerilla warfare. This freedom lasted almost eighty years until Rome ascended and claimed Jerusalem as a Roman colony under Pompey (63 BC). Rome appointed Herod, a corrupt half-Jewish king, to rule directly under Rome's authority. Rome allowed some freedom but taxed and controlled Jews while Herod did what was best for his own reputation.

Into this context Jesus was born. Some Jews had returned to their land, but God's promises had not been fulfilled. Israel longed for freedom and their own ruler. The Gospels writers assert Jesus is the Jewish Messiah. However, he doesn't do what the Jewish people expect.

Jesus's Main Message and Action

This history is essential for understanding Jesus's message and actions. Too often we divorce Jesus from his context. Jesus speaks into the hopes of Israel, but he comes in both an expected and unexpected way. While we sometimes get sidetracked concerning Jesus's main message, all the Synoptic Gospel writers assert Jesus announced the kingdom of God, while John transposes this concept into the phrase "eternal life."[11] The kingdom is the umbrella under which Jesus operates. Jesus begins his ministry announcing the kingdom of God is at hand. Too often when evangelicals speak about the gospel, they abandon the language of kingdom.

THE KINGDOM OF GOD AND ETERNAL LIFE

While the Synoptic Gospels speak of the salvation Jesus brings primarily as the arrival of the kingdom of God, the Gospel of John references this same concept with the phrase "eternal life." John relegates kingdom language to three verses (3:3, 5; 18:36). Eternal life speaks more to images of creation, rebirth, resurrection, and philosophy. Kingdom, on the other hand, is more concrete and conjures images such as authority, rule, and empire. Kingdom insinuates political hopes, while life has more philosophical and symbolic resonances.

However, the kingdom *is* the content of the good news and the longing of Israel.[12] Yet confusion still reigns about what the kingdom is. Different descriptions arise from different quarters. Some have equated the kingdom with heaven, affirming Jesus was saying, in so many words, "The kingdom is the place you go when you die." Others have understood the kingdom as referring to the church. Still others have equated the kingdom with social justice. Evangelicals in particular are prone to reduce the kingdom to God's rule or reign. In more popular evangelical circles, the kingdom becomes a shorthand for the rule of God in one's heart.

However, the kingdom is the summary label for Israel's expectations. By declaring the arrival of the kingdom, Jesus announces he is Israel's King, who has come to rescue his people and restore their home. It is the announcement of a new era in which God's true King would reign on his throne, defeat Israel's enemies, restore their land, and reestablish the right practice of the Torah and the temple. The kingdom therefore is not an abstract concept or merely a spiritual reality. It is concrete and concerns Israel's

---

[11] The following is based on my book *The Kingdom of God and the Glory of the Cross*, Short Studies in Biblical Theology (Wheaton, IL: Crossway, 2018).

[12] This view is influenced especially by George Eldon Ladd, *The Presence of the Future* (Grand Rapids: Eerdmans, 1974); "Kingdom of God-Reign or Realm," *Journal of Biblical Literature* 81, no. 3 (1962): 230–38.

land and their practices. The kingdom most simply can be described as the King's presence over the King's people in the King's place.

Jesus's announcement of the kingdom is expected. What is unexpected is how this new era bursts onto the scene. Surprisingly, the cross and resurrection are the mechanisms by which the kingdom comes. This is not to neglect Jesus's ministry, as his healings, exorcisms, and teachings are proleptic signs of the new era.

However, all the Evangelists spend the most amount of space on Jesus's last days. This was typical for ancient biographies. A hero's death either confirmed his philosophy of life or refuted it. In Jesus's case, he taught about self-giving love. This was climactically enacted in his death. When Jesus said take up your cross, he was speaking literally. The kingdom would not come by power and strength; rather it came by weakness and suffering.

Israel expected a king, but they didn't expect their king to die. That is why Peter rebukes Jesus for saying he will suffer at the hands of the Romans. Like Peter, we are tempted to either speak of the kingdom or the cross, unintentionally driving a wedge between the two. However, Jesus says the two must come together. The kingdom will be accomplished by a shameful death and a glorious resurrection. If the kingdom is the *goal* of Jesus's campaign, then the cross and resurrection are the *means*.

The Gospels and Christian Formation

Many times, when it comes to the Gospels—or any part of the Bible, for that matter—the emphasis is on history. These reconstructions are valuable, as they engender greater accuracy and faithfulness to the subject of the text. Jesus was a historical figure, and the Christian faith is historical to its core. However, these are not mere historical facts. To think so is to miss the point of the Gospels.

The highest purpose of the Gospels is to introduce us to Jesus so that we might trust him and be formed into his likeness. The purpose statement for John, the Fourth Gospel, is a good summary of the purpose statement of all of them: "But these are written so that you may believe that Jesus is the Messiah, the Son of God, and that by believing you may have life in his name" (20:31).

The Gospels are discipleship texts. They are meant to lead us to practice the way of Jesus. In the Gospels, Jesus is put forward as a Savior to trust (faith), a King whose return we long for (hope), and a wise teacher to emulate (love). If we don't grow in these virtues while reading the Gospels, we have not understood them at all. Virtue is not only what the Gospels are to produce but how we are to approach the Gospels.

Gregory of Nyssa says virtue is not simply part of the application of the text. Rather, it is a prerequisite for good reading.[13]

First, the Gospels introduce us to our Savior, who died for our sins. The Gospels tell the story of Jesus to compel faith. The greatest need of Israel, the greatest need of humanity, was that their sins needed to be forgiven. Sin causes chaos and separation; it produces violence and pain. Sin is like a disease; it corrodes and destroys all it touches. Sin devastates the purpose of creation: shalom, the state of well-being. Therefore, Jesus came to restore shalom by triumphing over sin. He lived without sin, always trusting his Father, always doing what was right, always loving everyone. However, people still hated him. They nailed him to a cross, though he had done nothing wrong. The Gospel writers tell this story so that you would trust not in yourself for salvation but in him. He is the way, the truth, the life. If you don't leave reading the Gospels with greater awareness of your own sin and greater faith in Jesus, then you haven't read them as they were intended.

Second, the Gospels introduce us to our King, whose return we long for. The Gospels tell the story of Jesus that we might have hope. Our hope is not merely for the future but in the present. We can have hope because Jesus has done what is necessary. The King has arrived and conquered, and now he empowers us to practice his way. When we read the Gospels, we remember there is hope in the present. Our hope is also in the future. We long for Jesus to return and set all things right. Though the kingdom has come in part, we await the time when heaven and earth will unite completely. Jesus sits on the throne in heaven, and we wait for his throne to come to earth. Then all sadness, sickness, oppression, and hate will cease. The Gospels remind us that our King has come and is coming back. Any reading of the Gospels that does not spawn hope is a poor reading.

Finally, the Gospels introduce us to our wise teacher, whom we emulate. The Gospels tell the story of Jesus so we might grow in love. Though the tendency is to focus either on Jesus as our substitute or our example, the Scriptures affirm both are true. He is our sacrificial Davidic King and our Solomon-like wisdom Truth-Teller. The stories and teachings of Jesus are meant to capture our imagination and compel us to live like Jesus. When Jesus eats with tax collectors and sinners, we should be induced to reach out to those who most need the words of Christ. When Jesus speaks to the Samaritan woman, we also should be invigorated to reach out to the marginalized. When Jesus speaks the truth in love, we too should be refreshed to be

---

[13] Hans Boersma, *Embodiment and Virtue in Gregory of Nyssa: An Anagogical Approach* (Oxford: Oxford University Press, 2013), 19.

truth-tellers in an age of lies. Jesus teaches his followers that to be one of his disciples, they must love everyone, even their enemies.

The greatest command is to love God and neighbor. While faith and hope will cease to be when Jesus returns, love will continue. In a true sense, love is the greatest and most important virtue. If you don't come away from the Gospels with a greater sense of love for God and for others, you have missed the point entirely.[14]

---

[14] This is a reworking of Augustine's statement, "So anyone who thinks that he has understood the divine scriptures or any part of them but cannot by his understanding build up this double love of God and neighbor, has not yet succeeded in understanding them." Saint Augustine, *On Christian Teaching*, trans. R. P. H. Green (Oxford: Oxford University Press, 1997), 76.

1

Matthew

Outline[1]

1. Introduction: Jesus's birth (1–2)
2. Narrative: Jesus's preparation and ministry (3–4)
3. Teaching: The Sermon on the Mount (5–7)
4. Narrative: Healings (8–9)
5. Teaching: The sending of the disciples (10)
6. Narrative: Opposition to Jesus (11–12)
7. Teaching: Kingdom parables (13)
8. Narrative: Jesus establishes his church (14–17)
9. Teaching: Household instructions (18–20)
10. Narrative: Jesus enters Jerusalem (21–22)
11. Teaching: Jesus judges Jerusalem (23–25)
12. Conclusion: Jesus's death, resurrection, and commission (26–28)

---

[1] Matthew is unique among the Evangelists in having a clear narrative-discourse outline. Others plot Matthew either geographically (1:1–4:11; 4:12–16:20; 21:1–28:20) or in terms of the narrative (1:1–4:16; 4:17–16:20; 16:21–28:20). Yet these bury the narrative-discourse structure that makes Matthew distinctive.

MATTHEW IN THE NEW TESTAMENT

- Matthew (also called Levi) is one of the twelve disciples of Jesus (Matt 10:3; Mark 3:18; Luke 6:15).
- He is introduced as a former tax collector (Matt 9:9; 10:3; Mark 2:14).
- In all of the Synoptic Gospels, Matthew hosts a banquet for Jesus at his house with other tax collectors (Matt 9:9–13; Mark 2:13–17; Luke 5:27–32).

Author, Date, and Message

The Gospel typically attributed to Matthew is officially anonymous. However, it is likely that people knew the author from the start and unlikely that the manuscript circulated without a name attached for long. Most scholars suppose it was quickly grouped with other biographies of Jesus and distinguished by its source. All the manuscripts we have assign some role to Jesus's disciple and the former tax collector Matthew. Additionally, the early church evidence from Papias, Irenaeus, Clement, and Origen all point to Matthew as the author.

ANCIENT CONNECTIONS 1.1. EARLIEST TITLE OF MATTHEW

The earliest surviving manuscript containing the title of Matthew (or any Gospel title) is a fragment from the flyleaf found with $\mathfrak{P}^4$. The manuscript probably dates to the late second or early third century and reads "Gospel according to Matthew" (*euangelion kata mathaion*).

The first canonical Gospel identifies a certain Matthew as a tax collector (9:9; 10:3), while Mark 2:14 and Luke 5:27 call the tax collector Levi. Matthew might be the name Jesus gave Levi. The name Matthew means "gift of Yahweh," which is particularly appropriate for a tax collector chosen for discipleship. Tax collectors were despised and viewed as traitors to the Roman Empire. They were notorious for inventing new taxes so they could increase their own profits. They were viewed as ritually unclean because of their frequent contact with Gentiles. We see a unique emphasis and specificity on taxation in Matthew's Gospel (9:9; 10:3; 17:24–27). Matthew's occupation may have had some impact on his Gospel being the most structured of the four. Additionally, Matthew could have had scribal skills because of his profession (Matt 13:52). Despite Matthew's occupation, Jesus still calls him. Matthew is among the apostles of Jesus (Matt 10:3; Mark 3:18; Luke 6:15; Acts 1:13).

Many also recognize Matthew's work as the most Jewish of the Gospels. His knowledge of Jewish law, customs, traditions, and Semitic language is apparent throughout. As far as we know, Matthew's work has always stood at the head of the four Gospels, and of the entire New Testament canon, because of its direct and not-so-subtle connection to the Old Testament.

Some argue against Matthean authorship because they believe Matthew was not likely literate. A disciple would not have needed to use an eyewitness as his source, and it seems clear that Matthew used Mark. However, Matthew likely would have been literate because he was a tax collector who had to take notes. Additionally, Mark relied on Peter, who was a part of Jesus's inner circle, and therefore Matthew would have trusted Peter's testimony. Because of the early testimony of the church, the manuscript evidence, and the lack of internal evidence contrary to this testimony, it is reasonable to move forward with Matthean authorship.

ANCIENT CONNECTIONS 1.2. THE AUDIENCE OF THE GOSPELS

People have tended to associate the Gospels with a specific audience.

- Matthew = Antioch
- Mark = Rome
- Luke = Theophilus
- John = Ephesus

If these associations are correct, each Gospel reveals issues in each community. However, the Gospels, unlike the Epistles, give us very little information about the community to which they are written. *Lives* (Greco-Roman biographies) were written to more broad communities. While the Evangelist's historical context is important, the needs of the Christian community as a whole seem to be the focus of the Gospels.

Matthew does not identify when or to whom his Gospel was written, and all reconstructions are tenuous.[2] The early church asserted Matthew was written first, but modern scholars have defended Mark's priority. Scholars usually suggest either

---

[2] Richard Bauckham, *The Gospels for All Christians: Rethinking the Gospel Audiences* (Grand Rapids: Eerdmans, 2013).

an early (late 50s or early 60s) or later date (after 70). Three events are used to date Matthew's Gospel: the publication of Mark, the separation of the Christian church from the synagogue, and the fall of Jerusalem.

A later Mark dating (early to mid-70s) would mean a later Matthew dating. Matthew also distinguishes between "their" and "your" synagogues and scribes (4:23; 7:29; 9:35; 10:17; 12:9; 13:54; 23:34), which may suggest Matthew's audience has separated from the Jewish synagogue. And since Jesus refers to the destruction of Jerusalem in Matthew 24, some assume it already happened.

However, one can argue for an earlier Markan date (late 50s or early 60s), the separation from the Jewish synagogue is not clear, and many believe Jesus could have spoken true things beforehand as a prophet and Son of God. Irenaeus, living just under a hundred years after the apostles, even states Matthew published when Peter and Paul were preaching the gospel in Rome, in the late 50s or early 60s. In summary, the date of Matthew is inconclusive, but a mid-60s date is possible based on the date of Mark and Irenaeus's statements.

UNIQUE MATERIAL IN MATTHEW[3]

Genealogy (1:1–17)
Birth of Jesus (1:18–25)
Visit of magi (2:1–12)
Flight to Egypt (2:13–21)
Sermon on the Mount (portions)
Mission to Israel (10:5–6)
Invitation to rest (11:28–30)
Parables (portions)
Peter tries to walk on water (14:28–31)
Blessing of Peter (16:17–19)
Peter pays the temple tax (17:24–27)
Church discipline (18:15–20)
Peter asks about forgiveness (18:21–22)
Parable of the unforgiving servant (18:23–35)

---

[3] Adapted from Mark Alan Powell, *Introducing the New Testament: A Historical, Literary, and Theological Survey*, 2nd ed. (Grand Rapids: Baker Academic, 2018), 108. See also David A. deSilva, *An Introduction to the New Testament: Contexts, Methods & Ministry Formation* (Downers Grove, IL: IVP, 2004), 243.

Parable of the vineyard workers (20:1–16)
Parable of the two sons (21:28–32)
Prohibition of titles (23:8–12)
Denunciation of Pharisees (23:15–22)
Parable of the ten virgins (25:1–13)
Description of last judgment (25:31–46)
Death of Judas (27:3–10)
Pilate washes his hands (27:24–25)
Dead saints rise (27:52–53)
Guard at the tomb (27:62–66; 28:11–15)
The Great Commission (28:16–20)

The message of Matthew is one of fulfillment. Many argue Matthew puts his signature in the middle of the book. "Every teacher of the law who has become a disciple in the kingdom of heaven is like the owner of a house who brings out of his storeroom treasures new and old" (13:52).[4] Matthew is the trained scribe who brings out treasures both new and old. He points to the bridge between the new and the old; that bridge is Jesus. Matthew writes to show Jesus is the answer to Jewish hopes. "Christianity" is authentic Judaism, not deviant apostasy.[5] Jesus does not diverge from the Jewish story; he completes it. Yet he also looks ahead to a new and expanding future. Jesus is the Messiah who inaugurates the kingdom of heaven, fulfills the Torah in his teaching, establishes the new people of God, and sends them out to bless the world (28:16–20).

Because of the Jewish character of Matthew, most stories have some quotation, allusion, or echo of an Old Testament text or story. Jesus is the new David, Moses, Abraham, and Jeremiah. In fact, Matthew is well known for his twelve "fulfillment quotations" and five teaching discourses from Jesus. These indicate his purpose concerning how Jesus satisfies the Old Testament story. This is not the beginning of a new story but a continuation of an old one. Yet Matthew seems to claim even more than this. He asserts Jesus is Immanuel—Israel's God in the flesh. At numerous places in his Gospel, he attributes actions to Jesus only associated with Yahweh (8:23–27; 9:1–8; 10:1).

---

[4] Patrick Schreiner, Charles Quarles, and Charles Nathan Ridlehoover, "Jesus and Matthew: Matthew as a Discipled Scribe," in *Jesus as Teacher in the Gospel of Matthew*, Library of New Testament Studies (London: Bloomsbury, 2023).

[5] Some of the content in this book has been adapted with permission from my book *The Visual Word: Illustrated Outlines of the New Testament Books* (Chicago: Moody, 2021).

Without Matthew, we would not have explicit mentions of the church in the
Gospels (16:18; 18:17). Without Matthew, we would not have the Sermon on the
Mount or a Gospel focused on the "Teacher" Jesus. We wouldn't have a Gospel in
which Peter functions so prominently. We wouldn't have the stories of the wise men,
or Herod seeking to destroy Jesus, or Joseph's perspective on Jesus's birth. Matthew,
more than any other Gospel, is more concerned with the "facts" than storytelling,
emphasizes Jesus's human frailty less, shows the disciples exhibiting more potential
for leadership than in Mark, and has Jesus vehemently denounce the religious leaders. Matthew has been characterized throughout history as a Christian Pentateuch,
a manual of discipline, or an ecclesiastical handbook. The purpose of Matthew is an
invitation to follow Jesus; it is a discipleship text.[6] Matthew summons people into the
kingdom of heaven by telling the story of Jesus.

Interpretive Overview

Like the other Gospel writers, Matthew tells the story of Jesus largely in chronological order: birth, life, death, and resurrection. However, this can be deceiving, for
Matthew structures his work alternating between narratives and teachings from
Jesus. He arranges things topically to show how different sections and stories connect
with one another. In this way, Matthew's Gospel is highly cohesive. Matthew's work
has often been called "the teacher's Gospel" because it focuses so heavily on Jesus
as a teacher. But as Mark Allan Powell notes, it can also be called the "accountant's
Gospel" because he is so interested in keeping track of things and putting them in
similar sections.[7]

"FULFILL"

Matthew uses *plēroō* ("to fulfill") or a form of it sixteen times in his Gospel
compared to twice in Mark and nine times in Luke. Lexically, Bauer and Danker
give at least three options for the gloss of the term: (1) to make full; (2) to complete a period of time, or that which was already begun; (3) to finish, complete,
or bring to a designated end. To make full is a spatial metaphor, like filling a cup.

---

[6] Michael Wilkins, *Discipleship in the Ancient World and Matthew's Gospel*, 2nd ed. (Grand
Rapids: Baker, 1995).

[7] Powell, *Introducing the New Testament*, 119.

To complete a period of time is a temporal comparison, such as when a person reaches a certain age. To bring to a designated end is a logical metaphor. All of these can be at play in the employment of the word, but the temporal reality is especially highlighted in the New Testament.[8]

Although Matthew spends only a few short chapters on Jesus's birth, this section contains some of Matthew's most distinct material. Then he alternates between narratives *concerning* Jesus and discourses *from* Jesus. The narratives paint Jesus as the Jewish Messiah who heals and has all authority. In the discourses Jesus is the new Torah teacher like Moses. Matthew devotes seven chapters to Jesus's last week. He slows down the narrative for his dramatic conclusion. While Mark lingers on Jesus's suffering, Luke on Jesus's innocence, and John on Jesus's exaltation, Matthew focuses on Jesus's kingship. Jesus is a political threat whose death has cosmic implications. After Jesus's resurrection, he commissions his disciples to go to all ethnicities, teaching and baptizing people into the name of the triune God.

Introduction: Jesus's Birth (1–2)

Matthew opens his Gospel with his convictions fully exposed. He answers the question of who Jesus is and where he is from. Chapter 1 focuses on Jesus's origins by giving a royal lineage, and chapter 2 concerns where he is from with a geographical emphasis. Though Matthew largely follows Mark's order, he adds two chapters on Jesus's birth and childhood, which is highly significant for Matthew's purposes. In chapter 1, Matthew begins by confirming Jesus is the Christ, "the Son of David, the Son of Abraham" (1:1).

To claim Jesus is the Messiah is an honorific. It states Jesus is God's anointed figure who will defeat Israel's enemies, establish them in their land, follow the Torah, and rebuild their temple. But Jesus will do so in the most unexpected way. Matthew doubles down on the kingly imagery, not only referring to him as an anointed figure, but saying he is the Son of David (1:1). This makes Jesus the heir to David's throne, who will build the temple and reign forever (2 Sam 7:13, 16). It also paints Jesus as the wise king in the vein of David's son Solomon.

---

[8] F. W. Danker et al., *A Greek-English Lexicon of the New Testament and Other Early Christian Literature* 3rd ed. (Chicago: University of Chicago Press, 2000), s.v. πληρόω.

Jesus is also the Son of Abraham. Abraham was promised a large family and land and that all nations would be blessed through him (Genesis 12). By labeling Jesus the Son of Abraham, Matthew indicates God's family will be established through him. Additionally, just as Abraham's son Isaac willingly went up on the temple mountain with Abraham as a sacrifice (Genesis 22), the new kingdom and new family will only come by the sacrifice of the firstborn.

The genealogy then divides into three sections of fourteen, matching the gematria of David's name. There are six sevens, and then the perfection of the seventh seven comes. Matthew's penchant for organization is immediately evident. The first section largely concerns the founders of Israel's faith, tracing the line from Abraham to David (1:2–6a). The second section, from David to the exile, focuses on the kings of Judah and the descent of the kingdom (1:6b–11). The third section covers exile to the birth of Jesus (1:12–16) and looks at the less than satisfying return to the land of Israel. The people listed are tied to the rebuilding of the temple. Matthew's forty-two generations go from patriarchs to kings to temple themes. Placing the exile as one of the only events in a list of names indicates Jesus comes to end the exile.

MATTHEW'S GEMATRIA

Gematria is a numerological reading whereby Hebrew letters correspond to numbers. Most argue Matthew divides his genealogy in sections of fourteen because it matches the gematria of David's name in Hebrew. In Hebrew, *David* consists of three letters and has the numeric value of fourteen:

$$dalet\ [4] + waw\ [6] + dalet\ [4]$$

Surprisingly, some in Jesus's family are Gentile women with checkered sexual pasts, who nonetheless uniquely preserved the line of Judah when the line was in danger. Tamar, Rahab, Ruth, and Bathsheba ("Uriah's wife") are all listed.[9] All of them, with maybe the exception of Ruth, suffered under sexual exploitation, but they are all characterized by tenacious fidelity to Yahweh. Their reputations paved the way

---

[9] Rahab and Ruth were explicitly Gentiles (Josh 2:1; Ruth 1:4). Tamar, according to Jewish tradition, was a Gentile (*Jubilees* 41:1; Judah 10:1; Philo, *De Virtutibus* 221–22). It is also unclear whether Bathsheba was a Gentile; she was married to Uriah the Hittite (2 Sam 11:3, 6), possibly indicating she was also a Hittite.

for Mary, who will be questioned the rest of her life about the birth of Jesus (1:16; John 7:27). However, Matthew's genealogy isn't primarily about people but about a child and God himself. God carries along this family line despite their failures. The genealogy implies the exile will end, the temple will be rebuilt, and God's people will be regathered. Jesus truly is the Messiah who comes from the line of David. He is the King—indeed, the King of kings.

ANCIENT CONNECTIONS 1.3. MESSIANIC HOPE

Israel longed for a Messiah (Christ). "Messiah" simply means an anointed figure. Kings, priests, and prophets were anointed. This Messiah was to be associated with the Davidic dynasty and would bring God's blessings to Israel and even the world.

- Genesis asserts the ruling staff will not depart from Judah until the obedience of peoples belongs to him (49:10).
- Numbers speaks of a star and scepter arising out of Jacob (24:17).
- Micah says this figure would be born in Bethlehem (5:2).
- Isaiah speaks of a child who will sit on the throne of David forever and will judge with equity (9:6–7; 11:1–5).
- Jeremiah asserted that the Lord would raise a Righteous Branch for David who would execute justice (23:5–6).
- Ezekiel promises a Davidic shepherd (34:23–24; 37:24–25).
- Psalm 2 speaks of God's Anointed, God's Son, who will rule over Israel and possess the nations.
- Isaiah tells of a coming servant who will suffer for the nation but will be rewarded because of his sacrifice (52:13–53:12).

If the genealogy shows Jesus is the Son of David and Abraham, the birth narrative displays Jesus as the Son of God (1:18–25). The birth narrative explains how Joseph is not the father of Jesus, for Jesus is conceived by the Holy Spirit. However, Joseph names him according to the angel's command, thereby adopting him. Matthew highlights the names of Jesus, explaining he is Immanuel (God with us) and Jesus (save his people from their sins). The Immanuel statement is the first of Matthew's fulfillment quotations from Isa 7:14. The name *Jesus* is the same Hebrew name for Joshua, who led Israel into the promised land (Josh 1:1–5:12). Jesus is the greater Joshua who will save his people not from their political enemies, but from their sins, by being God among them (Exod 14:30).

Matthew 2 transitions to *where* Jesus is from. Providential acts permeate the narrative, and the dreams of Jesus's adopted father, Joseph, echo the dreams of an earlier Joseph (Gen 37–50). Matthew shows that the places where Jesus is from fulfill Old Testament texts. First, Jesus is born in Bethlehem, the city of David (Matt 2:1–12). But another king already exists, so Jesus and his family must flee. Herod is a tyrant (like Pharaoh) who acts violently against his people. Mary's child will be a Shepherd-King, leading his people to quiet waters (Ps 23:2; Ezek 34:15, 23–24). Here we learn magi from the east are the first to worship Jesus. Gentiles already seek this Jewish Messiah and will later be included in the mission (Matt 28:19–20).

Second, Joseph and Mary take Jesus to Egypt, and he lives there for about three years (2:13–15). Like Israel, Jesus must flee into Egypt for safety, but he and his people will come out of exile (Hos 11:1). This point is further reinforced by a reference to Ramah (Matt 2:16–18). Ramah was the place Israel departed for exile (Jer 40:1). Now Rachel weeps for her children who are killed by Herod, but Jeremiah 31 sees Israel's children returning to their land with joy.

Finally, Jesus is from Nazareth, north of Galilee. No prophet says the Messiah will be from Nazareth, but Nazareth derives from the word *branch* in Hebrew (*netzer*) and therefore fulfills the promise of a Davidic branch (Isa 11:1; Jer 23:5; 33:15; Zech 3:8). All these places prove Jesus is Israel's long-awaited Shepherd-King.

ANCIENT CONNECTIONS 1.4. NAZARETH

Nazareth is in Galilee and largely separated from the southern region (Judah) by several factors. Racially, it had a more mixed population. Geographically, it was removed because it was detached from Judea by the non-Jewish territory of Samaria. Politically, both Galilee and Judea were under Herod the Great, but the rulers resided in Judea. Culturally, Judeans looked down on their northern neighbors because of their lack of Jewish sophistication and their openness to Hellenistic influence. Linguistically, Galileans spoke in a different Aramaic accent that was immediately noticeable (Matt 26:73). Religiously, the Judean opinion was that the Galileans were lax in the observance of proper ritual, though there were pious Jews in Galilee.

Narrative: Jesus's Preparation and Ministry (3–4)

Matthew 1–2 is a prologue. Now Matthew leaps ahead in time to Jesus as an adult as he begins his ministry. The emphasis continues to be on the identity of Jesus. John the Baptist is introduced as Jesus's forerunner. The Baptizer calls people to the Jordan River to be purified. The imagery paints the Baptizer as a prophetic figure who washes Israel clean from their covenant disloyalty as they prepare to enter their new land. Surprisingly, Jesus also wants to go through the water.

In being baptized, Jesus identifies with John's message and links himself to Israel's story. It marks a turning point in his life and foreshadows his coming death, burial, and resurrection. The baptism marks Jesus out for his anointed task. Jesus explains his baptism as fulfilling all righteousness. Though we think of "righteousness" in individualistic terms, Matthew employs it here to indicate Jesus completes all the obedience God requires of his people. He submits to the Father's will for him and sets things right according to God's character.

The heavens open and the Spirit comes down on Jesus like a dove when Jesus is baptized (Ps 144:5; Isa 64:1; Ezek 1:1). The dove symbolizes the new creation and the new age (Gen 8:8–12; Isa 32:15–16). A voice from heaven, the voice of the Father, declares Jesus as his beloved Son with whom he is well pleased. This language recalls both Ps 2:7 (king) and Isa 42:1 (servant). Jesus is the Lord, but he will also become King by acting as the Suffering Servant. Importantly, Jesus's baptism indicates this liberation plan is not only the work of Jesus but of the triune God.

After Jesus goes through the water, he is driven into the wilderness to be tempted by the devil like Israel and Adam (Matt 4:1–11; Gen 3:1–7). Jesus has been declared the Son, and now he will be tested as the Son. Jesus fasts for forty days and nights, and the tempter gives him three tests. In each one, the accuser entices Jesus to take another route to kingship, questioning whether he is truly the Son. Jesus responds by quoting from Deuteronomy 6–8, which reminds Israel of their forty years of wilderness wandering. Jesus remains faithful where Israel failed. He will not shy away from his cross-shaped throne even though the devil entices him. He will be obedient to the Father's will, unlike Israel and Adam (Hos 6:7).

ANCIENT CONNECTIONS 1.5. HONOR AND SHAME

Greco-Roman culture was an honor-shame culture, which refers to the attribution or loss of esteem from one's peers. This was based on several factors (e.g., wealth,

education, skill, family, social status). Matthew may have written in part to honor
Jesus, since Christians were a minority group that was constantly tempted to be
pulled back into a more accepted group (Judaism or Roman culture). Matthew
displays Jesus's nobility by his ancestors, parents, race, and city of birth. Jesus's
fame spreads as he performs deeds and teaches. Matthew shows Jesus's death is
not deserved, thereby honoring him. A voluntary death was viewed as admirable.[10]

Between the two mountains of Jesus's temptation and the Sermon on the Mount
is the valley of Jesus's return to Galilee, which functions as a snapshot of his Galilean
ministry. While Jesus was designated as the messianic figure at his baptism, in Matt
4:11–25 we see where and how Jesus will accomplish this task. First, we learn he spends
his time in the northern regions of Israel, namely Galilee. Zebulun and Naphtali were
the first two tribes to go into exile. Jesus restores what was first destroyed—northern Israel—and he reverses the exile. Second, we see a summary of Jesus's message
and ministry: "Repent, because the kingdom of heaven has come near" (4:17, 23–25).
People need to turn from their sin because God's kingdom, his presence and rule,
has come near. This language, "come near," may recall priestly imagery indicating the
presence of Jesus is the presence of God (Exod 24:2; Lev 10:3; 21:21, 23). Jesus also
will enact God's presence by healing. Finally, between these two summaries, Jesus calls
his disciples to his side. He reconstitutes the people of God as the twelve join him.
We see in this section the three elements that will make up Jesus's ministry: preaching
and teaching, healing, and calling people to follow him. The rest of the narrative will
examine these in more detail.

Teaching: The Sermon on the Mount (5–7)

Now Jesus goes up on a mountain and teaches his disciples, but the crowds also listen
(7:28). This mirrors Exodus, where the nation of Israel stays at the base of Sinai while
only a few leaders go up the mountain (Exodus 19; 24:1). Jesus is the greater Moses;
he will bring his people out of slavery to sin, lead them to a new mountain, and medi-
ate a new covenant so that God may dwell with them. The sermon, like the Torah, is
concerned about what it means to flourish, be whole, and be blessed in God's creation
(Psalm 1).[11] Jesus argues this comes by having an all-encompassing righteousness,

---

[10] See deSilva, *An Introduction to the New Testament*, 280–90.

[11] Jonathan Pennington, *The Sermon on the Mount and Human Flourishing: A Theological Commentary* (Grand Rapids: Baker Academic, 2018).

both inward and outward. The Torah was always meant to regulate human hearts, but it could not because of people's sin. The sermon begins with an introduction and then focuses on three major themes: Jesus and the law (Matt 5:17–48), piety or participation in the new temple (6:1–18), and justice issues (6:19–7:12).

ANCIENT CONNECTIONS 1.6. BEATITUDES

Two different Hebrew and Greek words can be used for the English term for "blessing." *Brk* (Hebrew) and the corresponding *eulogētos* (Greek) refer to divine blessings. *Aśry* (Hebrew) and *makarios* (Greek), the term Matthew uses, more commonly refer to the happy state of those who live wisely. *Eulogētos* refers to an act of God, while *makarios* refers to a state of being. While the two cannot ultimately be separated, Jesus's "blessings" in Matthew should be understood as comforts (rather than conditions) for those who are already living in these states of being because they are the wise ones.[12]

Jesus begins with words of comfort for those in exile, words now known as the Beatitudes (5:1–12). He offers them the upside-down kingdom. The kingdom of heaven is for those who are down and out, for those who are peacemakers. Matthew goes back and forth from the present and future tenses, showing these blessings will be fulfilled now *and* in the future. These beatitudes are reminiscent of Moses's final blessings in Deut 33:29 and the proverbs of Solomon. Jesus also says his disciples are salt and light. Salt is a preservative, and light is a metaphor for people who manifest the glory of God to the nations (5:13-16; Isa 9:1–2; 60:1–3).

Then Jesus gives his thesis: he came to fulfill the Torah and to teach about greater righteousness (Matt 5:17–20). Jesus will challenge the pharisaical interpretation of the law, but Jesus is not against the law, nor is he even raising the bar; he simply clarifies the Torah's true meaning. His disciples' righteousness must surpass the scribes' and Pharisees'. Jesus goes on to explain this greater righteousness in three different sections. He examines six specific issues in 5:21–48—murder, adultery, divorce, oaths, retaliation, and love—arguing that though they have heard man-made traditions about these commands, he will tell them the true interpretation. In each of these he shows them they have misunderstood the Torah's purpose. Jesus wants more than behavioral modification; he wants heart change. Murder and anger go together;

---

[12] See Pennington, *The Sermon on the Mount and Human Flourishing*.

adultery and lust are linked; strife and hate are inseparable. The inside of the cup must be clean like the outside of the cup (23:25).

Then Jesus applies his teaching to three Jewish pietistic rituals associated with the temple: almsgiving, prayer, and fasting (6:1–18). Again, Jesus says outward actions only go so far. The Father in heaven sees the disciples' hearts. He teaches them how to pray, focusing on the coming of God's kingdom and how we treat others.

Finally, Jesus looks to how the Torah defines justice (6:19–7:12). God will provide for them, so they should not be greedy or seek their own comfort but seek first the kingdom of God. They shouldn't judge other people too harshly and forget their own faults. Jesus summarizes the commands of the Torah in the phrase "Whatever you want others to do for you, do also the same for them" (7:12).

Jesus closes his sermon with a warning: the disciples can take two paths, follow two prophets, and build on two different foundations (7:13–29). Like the wisdom tradition, one path means life, the other death. They must build their lives on the words of Jesus because they are a solid foundation against any storm. When Jesus finishes his teaching, the people are amazed at his authority. He speaks with power, unlike their scribes. He is not only the new Moses but the ultimate Lawgiver himself, Yahweh enfleshed.

Narrative: Healings (8–9)

Jesus has spoken of the kingdom; now he enacts the kingdom through his deeds. To put this another way, "Chapters 5–7 disclose *what* is required of those living within the kingdom, whereas chapter 8 reveals *who* is admitted to the kingdom."[13] Jesus is not only a teacher but one who heals. Ultimately, this paints him as the Suffering Servant who gives his life for and welcomes the least likely into the kingdom (Isa 52:13–53:12). Jesus brings heaven to earth by the touch of his hand.

ANCIENT CONNECTIONS 1.7. MORAL AND RITUAL IMPURITY

In the Old Testament, moral impurity was inherently sinful, while ritual impurity was not. Sometimes these categories would be combined. The three major sources of ritual impurity were genital discharges of blood or semen, leprosy, and

---

[13] Benjamin L. Gladd, *Handbook on the Gospels* (Grand Rapids: Baker Academic, 2021), 30 (italics original).

corpses (Leviticus 12–15; Numbers 19). Jesus seems opposed to the sources of impurity because they were linked to death, not the rituals themselves.

Ten miracles occur, many of them matching and reversing failures of the wilderness generation (Num 14:22). These ten failings in the wilderness can be described as two at the Red Sea, two for water, two for food, two for flesh, one for the idolatry of the golden calf, and one for the spies. In a similar way Jesus will deal with water, flesh, nature, disciples, and idolatry.

First, Jesus comes to the marginalized: a man with leprosy, a centurion's servant, and Peter's mother-in-law (Matt 8:1–17). He heals the man with leprosy, dealing with the flesh. Elisha also healed Naaman of leprosy, a connection that paints Jesus as a great prophet. Jesus also pronounces a centurion has a place at his table, confronting ethnocentrism. He heals Peter's mother-in-law, showing he cares intimately for his friends.

Each healing has its own significance. Three lepers are healed in the Old Testament directly by God (Exod 4:6–9; Num 12:10–15; 2 Kgs 5:1–19). It was generally recognized that healing a leper was a miracle only God could perform (2 Kgs 5:7, 15), and the healings of leprosy took time in the Old Testament. But Jesus heals the leper immediately. By healing the leper in this way, Jesus indicated he is the Greater Priest (Lev 14:7). The healing of the centurion's servant highlights the theme of table fellowship because Jews would not share the table with Gentiles. But Jesus said Gentile followers would dine with Abraham (Isa 25:6).

Matthew summarizes Jesus's healings with a fulfillment quotation from Isa 53:4: "He himself took our weaknesses and carried our diseases" (Matt 8:17). Jesus was not only removing suffering; he bore it. Jesus is the Suffering Servant not only in his death but in his life (20:28). Then Jesus calls others to follow him, but many view it as too costly (8:18–22). They are not ready to give up all for Jesus (1 Kgs 19:19–21). The Son of David will sit on the throne, but he will be homeless on the earth.

Three more miracles occur, displaying Jesus's power over the chaotic forces of nature, the supernatural, and sickness (Matt 8:23–9:8). Jesus stills a storm. Matthew 8:24 in the Greek refers to the storm as a "shaking" (*seismos*), a term connected to Jesus's crucifixion and resurrection when the earthquakes strike (27:54; 28:2). In Revelation this term indicates judgment, and Matthew employs the term to indicate Jesus will now judge the chaotic and demonic forces. Jesus rebukes the waves and the sea as God does in the Old Testament (2 Sam 22:16; Ps 18:15; 104:7; 106:9; Isa 50:2; Nah 1:4; see especially Ps 107:23–30). The Greek word for "rebuke" is also used when

Jesus castigates demons (Matt 8:26; 17:18). Jesus is the divine warrior, but the enemy is chaos sourced in the satanic forces. Jesus brings order to creation.

After Jesus and the disciples cross the water, Jesus again shows his power over the supernatural realm. He heals two demon-possessed men who come out of the tombs. Like David, Jesus has the power to drive out evil spirits (1 Sam 16:14–23). Jesus also has authority over sickness. Death is in the air as a paralytic man lies on a stretcher. However, Jesus not only forgives the man but heals him. In Matthew's mind, the physical and spiritual aspects of healing intertwine. The scribes are incensed, but the people glorify God. Again, the narrative pauses as Jesus calls Matthew to come and follow him, contrasting Matthew's response with those who refused earlier (Matt 9:9–17). Jesus affirms he came to call sinners, not the righteous (9:13).

Three final healings show Jesus's authority over disease, death, and demons (9:18–34). Jesus has healed those who have some form of death on them, and now he raises the dead. He raises a ruler's daughter, touching what is unclean but making her alive. He also allows a sick and unclean woman to touch his robe. Then Jesus opens the eyes of two blind men who call him the Son of David. Another demon-possessed man who can't speak comes to Jesus, and Jesus heals him with a touch. Both the first miracle in this larger section (leprosy) and the last one (the mute man) are performed with a simple touch of Jesus's hand. The Pharisees think Jesus does these miracles by the power of Satan, but Jesus continues to heal and teach. Matthew ends this section with another summary statement of Jesus's work (4:23; 9:35). But now, Jesus prepares to send out the disciples. He recognizes the harvest is ripe but that more workers are required (9:37; Num 11:29; John 4:35–38).

Teaching: The Sending of the Disciples (10)

When Christians think of commissioning texts in Matthew, most run to chapter 28. However, readers get a longer discussion of mission in chapter 10 than in 28. In Matthew 8–9, Jesus calls some of his disciples. Now, in chapter 10, Jesus sends out the twelve disciples. The narrative answers the prayer of 9:37–38 for more workers and mirrors the conquest of the Promised Land from the Old Testament (Num 13:17; Josh 1:2–6). Jesus affirms that their calling will mean power over demonic spirits, but it will also mean persecution.

First, Jesus identifies the messengers (Matt 10:1–4). He emphasizes the number twelve by stating it three times in five verses and listing out all the twelve (10:1, 2–4, 5). The narrative ends with Jesus returning to the number (11:1). This indicates the disciples are symbols of the renewed and reunited Israel, but it also points forward to the new people of God. Jesus grants authority to his disciples. They are to be strong and courageous (Josh 1:6). They will carry Jesus's message both while he is alive and when he is gone.

Surprisingly, the disciples are not to go to Gentiles or Samaritans but to the lost sheep of the house of Israel (Matt 10:5). The mission to the Gentiles would be a gradual one, and it was important to reach Israel first since it was through Israel that God would bless the world. Some even think "lost Israel" not only refers to those who have been led astray (Jer 50:6), but specifically to northern Israel. The disciples' message is to be the same as that of Jesus and John the Baptist (Matt 3:2; 4:17). They also will perform the same miracles as Jesus (9:35). Mercy and evangelism are inseparable ministries. They are not to take items along with them, for God will provide for them. Their shoes will not wear out, like Israel's garments did not wear out during the forty years in the wilderness (Deut 8:3–4).

Jesus then identifies the responses his followers will receive. They are to go into the land and let their shalom (peace) fall on houses who welcome them but judgment upon those who don't (Matt 10:11–15). When they enter the land, they will face persecution (vv. 16–42). They will be delivered over to courts, but they should not be anxious. God will teach them what to say. Family division will occur, but they are to endure to the end. They will be maligned, but they are to have no fear. Ultimately, if they acknowledge Jesus, he will acknowledge them. If they lose their life, they will find it. They are to be the Servant's servants. Jesus closes with strong words about hospitality. If people welcome Jesus's followers, they welcome Jesus; if they reject them, they reject Jesus.

Narrative: Opposition to Jesus (11–12)

Matthew 11–12 is about the various responses to Jesus, most of which are negative. Jesus has finished telling his disciples they will be rejected, and now he exemplifies this. These negative responses come primarily from Israel and pave the way for Jesus's teaching on the mystery of the kingdom in Matthew 13. The Jewish leaders' rejection of Jesus is made explicit when they begin planning to kill him.

References to "this generation" tie these chapters together thematically as Jesus laments Israel's response to him. Three patterns make up these chapters. First, Jesus is questioned on various issues. Second, in response, he defines his true identity. Third, Jesus clarifies and redefines his true family. In all these, Matthew shows the responses to Jesus from Israel are not what readers might expect.

The questions about Jesus begin with John the Baptist asking if Jesus is the Messiah or if they should be expecting someone else (11:2–19). John likely wonders why Jesus hasn't been more forthright about his mission or made bigger moves to overthrow the Roman Empire. He also doesn't understand how the arrival of the new creation coincides with suffering and imprisonment. The narrative section begins with this story to signify that people have a choice to make about Jesus's identity, whether to trust in him as Messiah or to reject him as a false prophet. The Pharisees also question Jesus about not following the Sabbath, but their question is negative and accusatory (12:1–14). After Jesus's answer, the Pharisees decide they want to kill him (12:14). This culminates in the Pharisees declaring Jesus heals by the hand of the prince of the demons—Satan himself (12:22–37). They have made their decision about Jesus, and opposition to Jesus grows each day.

Jesus responds to all these questions and accusations by clarifying his true identity. To John the Baptist, Jesus quotes from Isaiah, showing he is working from Isaiah's script concerning God's plan. The blind receive their sight; the lame walk; the lepers are cleansed (11:4–6; Isa 26:19; 29:18–19; 35:5–6; 42:7, 18; 61:1). Jesus came to redeem Israel, to lift up the downtrodden. In fact, John the Baptist is the Elijah-type forerunner to Jesus, but the kingdom will not come by violence (11:7–15). To the Pharisees' accusations about the Sabbath, Jesus responds by indicating he adheres to the deeper sense of the Sabbath. Like David, Jesus is the true Priest-King and knows the Sabbath was meant to be life-giving, not life restricting. Jesus is the Lord of the Sabbath (12:8). Jesus makes his superiority crystal clear when he heals on the Sabbath, showing that the Sabbath is about fullness of life. Matthew's longest quote from the Old Testament occurs at this point, when he employs Isa 42:1–4 to identify Jesus as Yahweh's servant who has the Spirit. Jesus is not here to argue or shout. Rather, he comes to gather the weak, proclaim justice to the nations, and lead forth in showing justice (Matt 12:18–21). Jesus is not doing the work of Satan. In fact, he binds Satan by his actions.

Finally, Jesus condemns those who will not listen to him and redefines his true family. Israel doesn't recognize their Messiah even though he has come to them. Jesus therefore pronounces woes upon the town where his miracles were performed but the people did not repent (11:20–24). He says those who are against him deny the Holy Spirit (12:32), calls the religious leaders bad trees and a den of vipers, and condemns those who seek a miraculous sign when the Son of Man is about the give the most compelling sign. Ultimately, Jesus says he comes for the least expected: the little children to whom he will give rest (11:25–30), the Gentiles who hope in God (12:15–21), and those who do the will of his Father (12:46–50). These people are his true family; it was more than a matter of simply flesh and blood. Some are stumbling on the rock; others are building on it (Ps 118:22; Dan 2:34–35).

Teaching: Kingdom Parables (13)

The third discourse is in the center of Matthew and contains parables on the mystery of the kingdom. It follows directly from the rejection Jesus has received and answers the question about the nature of his kingdom. Jesus answers the question of why some of Israel has not embraced their Messiah. The term *mystery* originates in the book of Daniel, where it concerns the judgment of the nations and the establishment of God's kingdom. But Jesus corrects misunderstandings of how this kingdom will come to be. The parables can be divided into three sections: responses, growth, and the value of the kingdom. The response to Jesus is less than impressive, but the kingdom will grow, and seeking after the kingdom is of ultimate value.

ANCIENT CONNECTIONS 1.8. THE HOPE FOR A KINGDOM

The parables of the mystery of the kingdom only make sense against the backdrop of Israel's hope for a restored kingdom. The prophets had promised Israel the following:

- **A new King:** Isaiah says a child of Jesse will arise (Isa 11:1), be given the sevenfold spirit of God (11:2), delight in the Torah (11:3), and judge justly (11:4).
- **The retrieval and bounty of Israel's land:** The prophet Isaiah speaks of God changing the land from a wilderness to a forest (Isaiah 35).
- **Regathering Israel:** Jeremiah prophesied that God would gather his people and allow them to be fruitful and multiply. Shepherds will care for them (Jer 23:3–4).
- **Rebuilt temple:** Ezekiel has a vision of a new temple that will be built in the last days (Ezekiel 40–48).
- **Foreign nations overcome:** Daniel speaks of God's kingdom being established, conquering every other kingdom, and standing forever (Dan 2:44).
- **The nations will look to Yahweh:** Isaiah says the temple of Israel will be the highest temple and the nations will stream to it (Isa 2:2–3).

Jesus's kingdom parables indicate things will not proceed as expected. The promises still stand, but the means and timing by which they come will be unexpected.

Jesus begins by giving a parable about parables: the parable of the sower (Matt 13:1–23). Not all of Jesus's words will be accepted. Some of his words will fall on paths, rocky ground, or thorns. Only some fall on good ground and produce fruit. This parable helps explain the negative responses in Matthew 11–12. The language of word, correlated with fruit or creation, echoes the Genesis narrative where God created all things by his word. Jesus doubles down on the various responses by quoting Isa 6:9–10, saying Israel's ears have become shut and their eyes closed. The parables further harden those who already won't accept Jesus's message; they open the eyes of those who seek and are ready to accept. In short, the result of Jesus's ministry is not a mistake. He speaks in such a way that both welcomes and hardens people.

However, in case people are disheartened by the negative response to the kingdom, Jesus reassures them, affirming the growth of the kingdom (Matt 13:24–43). He compares the kingdom of heaven to a man who sowed good seed but plants and weeds appeared. With this parable Jesus sustains the kingdom will grow, but evil will exist in its midst. It won't be as pure and spotless at the beginning as some suppose. Though Daniel prophesied the other kingdoms would fall, this does not happen now.

ANCIENT CONNECTIONS 1.9. JESUS AS A DANIEL FIGURE

The term *mystery* is used especially in Daniel. Jesus is like Daniel in that he interprets eschatological mysteries (Daniel 2, 4, 7, 8, 10–12). In addition, when Jesus asks if the disciples have "understood" these things in Matt 13:51 and the disciples reply with "Yes," this mirrors Daniel 11 and 12 concerning the "wise ones" who understand the nature of God establishing his kingdom (Dan 11:35; 12:3, 10).

Finally, Jesus presents parables about the value of the kingdom (Matt 13:44–50). Even though the kingdom has not come the way people expect, it is to be cherished. The kingdom is like a treasure hidden in a field that is worth giving up everything for. It is like a large net thrown into the sea collecting every kind of fish, but these fish will be separated at the end of time.

Jesus closes all the parables by describing an ideal disciple and scribe, pointing forward to the new community he is forming. He asks the disciples if they have understood. They reply they have. For Matthew, the disciples' understanding is a key theme (13:51). Every scribe who has been discipled by Jesus is like an owner of a house who brings out of his abundance treasures both old and new (Ps 19:10; Prov 3:13–15). In other words, disciples of Jesus will teach both what is old and new. Though some have rejected Jesus, he also has followers who understand.

Narrative: Jesus Establishes His Church (14–17)

In the last few sections we have seen how Israel rejects Jesus and his explanation of the varied responses. In Matthew 14–17 Jesus continues to spread his kingdom, and now he establishes his church. Though the response has been negative, Jesus gathers a new community. This section and the next one are the only sections in Matthew, and all the Gospels, in which the term *church* occurs (16:18; 18:17). Jesus will build his church on the confession that he is not only the Jewish Messiah (16:13–20) but also the Son of God (17:1–13).

The narrative begins at the end of chapter 13 with Jesus being rejected in his own hometown. Nazareth confirms the point of Jesus's parables; the least expected will accept his message, and he is building a new family. After Nazareth a dark scene occurs. Matthew inserts the story about John the Baptist's gruesome death to foreshadow Jesus's similar future (14:1–12; 21:33–44). The previous section began with John in prison, and now he is killed. The tension is growing. The rejection of Jesus will reach a fever pitch; blood will be spilled. This brings the rejection of Jesus to a preliminary climax. But Jesus's response is to feed his people as Yahweh and Moses did in the wilderness and to walk over the waters (14:13–33; Exodus 16). Jesus not only provides in the wilderness but walks on water. The point of these narratives is that Jesus will establish a new covenant community that is like the old covenant community yet also different.

The Pharisees and scribes ask Jesus a question because they are not ready for this new era. They question him as to why his disciples break the traditions of the elders, but Jesus turns the question around on them (15:1–20). He asks why they break the commandments of God for their own traditions. Jesus quotes from Isa 29:13, confirming the religious leaders have outward righteousness, but their hearts have not changed. Then, Jesus explains where true defilement comes from. It is not what goes into a person or what they touch on the outside but what comes from inside them. Jesus's new community will be the true Torah followers.

Jesus then goes to Gentile territories (Tyre and Sidon), indicating his family and church is expanding to other nations. A Canaanite woman comes to him crying for her daughter to be healed (Matt 15:21–28). The term *Canaanite* was not even in use at this time, and therefore to label her a Canaanite indicates she would have been viewed as Israel's enemy and puts her in sharp contrast to the Jewish leaders. Jesus replies that his mission is to the lost sheep of the house of Israel. But the woman shows great faith, and Jesus heals her daughter. Readers should remember another Canaanite woman is listed in Jesus's genealogy: Rahab (Matt 1:5). One's loyalty to Jesus is the only determining factor in Jesus's new family (Gal 3:28). Then Jesus performs a Gentile feeding by feeding 4,000 rather than the 5,000 (Matt 15:29–39). The number four symbolizes the four corners of the earth (Dan 7:2; Zech 2:6; Rev 7:1).

Additionally, Isaiah told of the day when the nations will stream to the mountain of the Lord (Isa 2:2; Mic 4:1–4). Though Jesus's mission is to Israel, Gentiles will taste the benefits of his reign. This causes the Pharisees and Sadducees to again test Jesus by asking for a sign (Matt 16:1–12). This word for "test" is used when the devil comes to Jesus in the wilderness (4:1, 3), and thereby Matthew indicates who their father truly is (John 8:44). Jesus says they are a wicked generation, again pointing to the sign of Jonah. He warns his disciples about the teaching of these religious leaders.

Jesus has been revealing who he is, but at Caesarea Philippi heaven finally reveals to Peter that Jesus is the Messiah, the Son of the living God (Matt 16:13–28). It is around this confession that Jesus will build his new community, making this episode central to chapters 14–17. Jesus blesses Peter and appoints him as an authority figure. He gives Peter (and implicitly the church; 18:18) the keys to the kingdom of heaven. They have authority from heaven. But Jesus also clarifies his messianic vocation includes suffering. Peter doesn't accept this part of Jesus's mission, so Jesus rebukes him and says the Messiah must go to the cross. The disciples must follow Jesus in this suffering.

ANCIENT CONNECTIONS 1.10. PETER'S CONFESSION

Many details are included in the narrative of Peter's confession that are easy to overlook. For example, before the Roman conquest, Caesarea Philippi was known to the Greeks as the spot to worship Pan, a fertility deity. Sanctuaries were found here, and it was a hub of pagan worship. Some think this may be why

Jesus refers to gates of Hades, which refers to the realm of the dead. Additionally, keys were symbols of authority. The god Hecate was thought to hold the keys to the underworld. Finally, in Greek, *Petros* (Peter's name) was used interchangeably with *petra* (rock), indicating Jesus was doing a play on words. Different traditions debate why Jesus blesses Peter. Is it the content of Peter's confession, Peter's character, or Peter's mode of knowledge? Likely, all these elements are at play. These details support the importance of this narrative for Matthew as a whole, and chapters 14–17 particularly, indicating Jesus will form a new community that is built around the Messiah and the spiritual forces will have no power over them.

Another revelatory scene occurs in the mold of Peter's confession, showing that despite the coming suffering, Jesus is God's chosen One (17:1–27; 3:17). After six days, Jesus takes Peter, James, and John up to a high mountain and is transfigured before them.[14] The time stamp of "after six days" is unusual for Matthew, because he typically uses more general terms (3:1; 13:1). This indicates a seventh-day theology, recalling when Moses went up to Sinai on the seventh day (Exod 24:15–16). Elijah and Moses appear next to Jesus, and a voice from heaven repeats the words from Jesus's baptism: "This is my beloved Son, with whom I am well pleased. Listen to him!" (Matt 17:5). This is the same command Moses gave the people in Deut 18:15 when he said, "The Lord your God will raise up for you a prophet like me from among your own brothers. You must listen to him." Jesus stands both as the prophet and the Son from Psalm 2, the one who fulfills all the Law and the Prophets.

Matthew 14–17 is all about Jesus establishing his new community, what he calls the church. Though the disciples think this will mean earthly glory, Jesus corrects them and tells them it will include suffering. The transfiguration reminds them glory will come, but only through the cross.

Teaching: Household Instructions (18–20)

The fourth discourse provides instruction for Jesus's new community. If in the last section Jesus has separated those who will follow him from those who won't, in this one he teaches his followers about how to act in this new community. As Benjamin Gladd

---

[14] See Patrick Schreiner, *The Transfiguration of Christ: An Exegetical and Theological Reading* (Grand Rapids: Baker Academic, 2024).

says, the fourth discourse "unpacks how kingdom citizens *relate* to one another."[15] Through Jesus's visionary words, he establishes, teaches, and orders his church. The new community has its own structures of authority and the presence of God to enforce standards. The text is a household code for Jesus's new community, where Jesus instructs them to be peaceable, forgive, and care for one another.

In chapter 18 Jesus challenges God's new people to be servants and peacemakers. When the disciples ask who will be the greatest, they display worldly wisdom. They are to become like children in humility (18:1–6). Only those who consider themselves the least will enter the kingdom of heaven. In fact, they need to care especially for little ones, making sure they don't stumble or stray from the flock (18:10–14). The disciples are also instructed to be peacemakers and care for one another, seeking reconciliation (18:15–35). People in the new community will sin against one another, but a process needs to be in place so offenses do not get out of hand. The goal is to be reconciled and forgive one another. Peter even asks how many times they should forgive; Jesus says their forgiveness should have no parameters.

In chapter 19 Jesus instructs his followers on domestic ethics: divorce (19:3–12), children (19:13–15), and wealth (19:16–30). The Pharisees question Jesus about divorce, and Jesus brings them back to Genesis, showing the ideal for marriage is a lifelong one-flesh union. Moses permitted divorce because of sin, but the creation story indicates lifelong companionship. Next, Jesus again reiterates that in his community children are welcome. Rather than making them last in line, Jesus brings them to the front and says the kingdom is for the least. Finally, Jesus challenges his followers on wealth. A rich man asks Jesus how to obtain eternal life, and Jesus says to keep the commandments. However, Jesus says he must also give up all his wealth to the poor. The young man is sad, for he cannot bring himself to give up his possessions. Jesus affirms that those who give up everything will have rewards in heaven. Following Jesus is worth giving up everything, for in doing so you will gain everything.

Chapter 20 sums up the community's vocation as Jesus's body. His followers are to be last rather than first (20:1–16). Jesus tells a parable about workers who go out into the vineyard and work. Though people come in to work at different times, the landowner gives them all the same amount. This is a parable that follows the salvific progression of Jews to Gentiles. Even though Gentiles come into God's kingdom later, they will receive the same reward. Jews should not be jealous of Gentiles, for they all will receive the same. The narrative ends the same way it began (20:17–34). This larger section started with the disciples asking if they could be the greatest in the

---

[15] Gladd, 62 (italics original).

kingdom (18:1–6). Now the mother of James and John comes to Jesus and asks if they can sit on Jesus's right and left in the kingdom. Jesus affirms that ruling and service are not at odds. They must become slaves and serve like Jesus.

The vocation and identity of Jesus's new community is clear. He has taught his followers about their status in his kingdom; how they are to act; and even on divorce, children, and wealth. The new community is being discipled in the way of Jesus.

Narrative: Jesus Enters Jerusalem (21–22)

Matthew 21 marks a definite shift in the story. The narrative slows dramatically as Jesus enters Jerusalem. Though Jesus has given hope to his remnant, from here onward, he is the "judging prophet" like Jeremiah. He enters Jerusalem for the first time since Matthew's introduction and is questioned, responds with parables, and provides his own answers. The narrative tension explodes as Jesus condemns the people for corrupting what is most precious to them and God: the temple. Jerusalem is not yet God's righteous hill where the nations will stream (Isa 2:2). Only one is righteous; he will establish God's house (Ps 127:1).

The narrative begins with three symbolic actions from Jesus. First, Jesus enters Jerusalem on a donkey (Matt 21:1–11). Matthew explicitly asserts that this humble entrance fulfills the prophecy from Zech 9:9. This appearance is Jesus's royal procession into his city. The crowd goes ahead of him, shouting that Jesus is the Son of David and the one who comes in the name of the Lord (Matt 1:1; 9:27). "Son of David" is one of Matthew's favorite titles, appearing nine times in his Gospel. By singing Psalm 118, the people identify Jesus as the coming deliverer. This psalm and Psalms 113–118 were sung to remember Israel's release from Egyptian captivity. However, Jesus also arrives in all humility. He rides on a donkey and not a warhorse (Rev 19:11). He brings no sword. It is his royal procession but an unexpected one.

Second, Jesus condemns the corruption of the temple (Matt 21:12–17). Jesus is not anti-temple, but the Jewish temple has become corrupt, and a new era has come. Jesus's body is the new temple. Messianic figures were thought to enter the temple and reestablish its centrality for the nation, but Jesus enters the temple and turns over the tables declaring that it has become a den for robbers rather than the house of God. This mirrors Jeremiah's condemnation of the temple (Jer 7:11). Third, Jesus curses a fig tree (Matt 21:18–22), which stood for Israel. This confirms Jesus's condemnation of the temple (Jeremiah 24; Hos 9:10). Jesus censures Israel for producing no fruit (Isaiah 5). These actions drop like a bomb on Israel's cultic playground and will ultimately lead to his death.

ANCIENT CONNECTIONS 1.11. TEMPLES IN THE ANCIENT WORLD

Temples in the ancient world were viewed as the earthly home of a divine being, with many symbols indicating this place connected the two realms. Conquering nations destroyed temples to indicate they had defeated the god of the local region. A renewed or rescued people usually rebuilt their temple to honor their gods and reestablish their identity. Temples were not only religious centers but political, economic, and social hubs.

The elders of the people respond by asking what authority Jesus possesses to do this. However, Jesus will not play their game. He stumps them with his own question about John the Baptist and his authority (Matt 21:23–37). Jesus baffles them again at the end of this section when he asks about David's Lord from Ps 110:1 (Matt 22:41–46). Between these passages Jesus tells three critical parables about Israel and then responds to three questions about the hottest issues of the day.

The first parable is about two sons (21:28–32). One said he would work in the field based on his father's request but changed his mind. The other said he would not but changed his mind. Jesus points out that the one who ended up working is the one who did his father's will. With this parable Jesus slyly censures Israel's leaders. Those who act and do not give lip service will enter the kingdom (Jas 1:22). The second parable is about a landowner who plants a vineyard (Matt 21:33–46). The landowner cares for this vineyard, but when he sends his servants to harvest fruit, the farmers refuse to let them reap the owner's reward. Therefore, he sends his son, but the tenant farmers kill the son and try to take the inheritance. The point is obvious. While the parable speaks of an owner and vineyard, the owner is the heavenly Father, the vineyard is Israel (Isaiah 5), and the farmers are the elders of the people. The elders are stealing from the Father. Even worse, they will kill the Father's Son. The vineyard will be torn from them and given to another. The final parable concerns a wedding banquet (Matt 22:1–14). The king invites many guests, but few come. Therefore, he goes out and invites those on the margins of society. Many are called, but few are chosen. All these parables indicate that Israel's leadership has forfeited their role and inheritance; their reward will be removed (Ezekiel 34).

The religious leaders understand these parables and the scathing rebuke that comes with them. Jesus must be stopped, so they try to trap him in his words by asking him about politics, eschatology, and the interpretation of the Old Testament

(Matt 22:15–40). Their goal is not to learn from Jesus; it is to ensnare him. The Pharisees and Herodians ask whether they should pay taxes to Caesar. Basically, they want to know if Jesus is a Zealot or a compromiser. Jesus responds by saying that foreign governments are legitimate, but they sit under God's ultimate authority. Jesus's opponents don't know what to say in response. The Sadducees then ask him about marriage in the resurrection. Jesus confounds them by saying that we won't marry in heaven and affirms the reality of the resurrection of the dead. Finally, a scribe asks him about the most important commandment in the Old Testament. Jesus says the commandments can be summed up by loving God and loving others (Lev 19:9–18).

ANCIENT CONNECTIONS 1.12. JEWISH SECTS

At least four Jewish sects are identified in Jewish literature: Pharisees, Essenes, Zealots, and Sadducees. Pharisees sought to be faithful to the Torah by enforcing and embodying its commands. Sadducees made peace with Rome and focused on religious rituals. Essenes withdrew from the corrupt temple system and empire. They lived holy lives as separatists. Zealots desired to overthrow Rome, sometimes with violence, and would not tolerate pagan practices.

The section ends with Jesus not answering a question but asking one (22:41–46). In so doing, he proves his authority as their teacher, leader, and interpreter. Jesus asks about the Messiah and whose son he is. Jesus's opponents reply that he is David's son. Then Jesus stumps them by alluding to Ps 110:1, asking how David can call him Lord if he is also his son. No one can retort. Jesus is the new Solomon abounding in wisdom, but he is also more than Solomon. Jesus has now entered Jerusalem, condemned the temple, and withstood the tests through which they ran him. Jerusalem is not pleased with their own Messiah. Only one last resort remains: to kill him.

Teaching: Jesus Judges Jerusalem (23–25)

In the final discourse, Jesus castigates the Jewish leaders not only with his actions but with his words. Jesus has enacted his judgment and now speaks more plainly about the lack of fruit he finds in Jerusalem (Matthew 23). Jesus then foretells the destruction of the temple and the end of the ages, encouraging vigilance for his own people considering the looming destruction (24–25).

In 23:1–12, Jesus speaks of false and true ways of leadership. The scribes and Pharisees have a certain authority. They sit on Moses's seat. However, their lives don't match their teaching. They are false shepherds. True shepherds will be servants, not masters. Then Jesus pronounces woes upon them, the opposite of beatitudes (23:13–36). The scribes and leaders have false enthusiasms, emphases, exteriors, and traditions. They are blind guides who should not be followed. They have always killed God's prophets. While Jesus has harsh words for them, he laments the fate of Jerusalem (23:37–39). He longs to gather his people to his side, but they will not come to him. The Babylonian captivity taught them nothing. Their house will be left empty.

ANCIENT CONNECTIONS 1.13. HOSPITALITY IN THE FIRST CENTURY

Hospitality was a chief virtue in Mediterranean society. Jesus says those who do something kind for the least of these do so for Jesus (Matt 10:40; 25:45). This may allude to the tradition of theoxenies, where the unknown guest is later revealed as God in disguise. In these cases, it would be representatives of God himself.[16]

The language of "house" allows Jesus to transition to his words about the last days, what some have called the "Olivet Discourse." Jesus looks at the temple and predicts its destruction (24:1–2). The glory of the Lord is leaving the temple as Ezekiel prophesied (Ezekiel 10), and the temple will be destroyed. Many people wonder whether Jesus speaks here about the last day or the destruction of the temple. He speaks of both. The end of the temple would be the end of an era for Jews. When the temple is destroyed it confirms the last days have been inaugurated. Both are described in apocalyptic terms. Matthew seems to go back and forth between both. First, he speaks of the last day for the world and the temple (Matt 24:4–14), then focuses on the last day for Israel (24:15–28), and back to the return of Jesus (24:29–35). The last day (end times) and the destruction of the temple were so correlated for Matthew, as it was for the Old Testament prophets, that it is difficult to determine when he speaks of one or the other.

---

[16] See Christine D. Pohl, *Making Room: Recovering Hospitality as a Christian Tradition* (Grand Rapids: Eerdmans, 1999).

The last day and the temple's destruction should compel vigilance and sober-mindedness for true Jesus followers (24:36–25:46). Jesus tells three parables about the appropriate response. First, he speaks of the faithful and the unfaithful servants (24:46–51). Those who think the master is delayed and begin to neglect their task will be punished, while those who are ready will be rewarded. Second, Jesus tells the parable of the ten virgins who go to meet the groom (25:1–13). Some were prepared and brought extra oil for their lamps, but some were not prepared, so when the groom was delayed, they fell asleep. When the groom finally came, some were ready, and some were not. Finally, Jesus speaks of a master who entrusts his servants with his possessions (25:14–30).

The destruction of the temple and the last day are coming. Disciples of Jesus must be ready for the return of the King (24:36–25:30). He will be a judging Shepherd when he returns, separating the sheep from the goats (25:31–46; Rev 20:11–15). Jesus has condemned the current generation. Now he will go and die for them.

Conclusion: Jesus's Death, Resurrection, and Commission (26–28)

Matthew's introduction covered Jesus's birth and early days. His conclusion looks to Jesus's death and last days. The narrative can be broken down into five sections: preparation for Jesus's death, arrest and trials, crucifixion, resurrection, and commission.

The narrative begins with an emphasis on the calendar. All this took place during the Passover (Matt 26:17–19). This is important because it allows Matthew to paint Jesus as the sacrificial Lamb of God who will rescue his people from oppressive forces (Exod 12; John 1:29; 1 Cor 5:7). However, Jesus clarifies these oppressive forces are Satan and his hordes. Jesus also presses into the Exodus imagery by celebrating the Passover with his followers. He reinterprets the bread and wine as his body, and they eat of him (John 6:52–59). A new covenant is coming. Jesus enters the garden and prays he would not have to endure this suffering but accepts the Father's will. Unlike Adam, Jesus conquers in the garden (Rom 5:17, 19).

The next section covers Jesus's arrest and trials (26:47–27:26). Matthew especially focuses on Jesus's control of the circumstances and therefore his kingship in his last days. Jesus is betrayed by Judas (26:47–56; Ps 41:9), but Jesus knows before Judas arrives that he will come. As his disciples' commander, he forbids violence from them. He asserts he could call more than twelve legions of angels to his aid, but all this happens so the Scriptures might be fulfilled. Jesus is brought for trial before the Sanhedrin, who accuse him of threatening to destroy the temple, and they present false witnesses (26:57–75). Jesus keeps silent until they ask if he is the Messiah, the Son of God. Jesus answers them by speaking the words of Dan 7:13 and Ps 110:1: the Son of Man will be seated at the right hand of Power and coming on the clouds of heaven (Matt 26:64). The leaders accuse Jesus of blasphemy and call for his death, while Peter denies he ever knew Jesus. Jesus is faithful to his task; Peter falters. The scene fulfills the parable of the wicked tenant farmers who kill the owner's son (21:33–46).

Because they don't have the authority to kill Jesus, the Jewish leaders bring him before the Roman governor, Pilate (27:1–26). The episode is filled with signs of Jesus's innocence (27:14, 23, 24; Isa 53:7; 1 Pet 2:22). Judas says he has sinned by betraying innocent blood and hangs himself. Pilate knows Jesus is innocent. But Pilate wants to please the people, so he washes his hands of Jesus's blood. The people scream that they want Jesus's blood on their own hands (Matt 27:25). While this verse has been used to justify anti-Semitism, we must remember Matthew himself was a Jew; this is only a subset of Jews, and Matthew had no right to condemn his entire nation for their deeds. Additionally, there might be an ironic note in this scream for they will only be forgiven through Jesus's blood covering them.

The actual crucifixion is described briefly (27:27–56). Matthew spends more time on the events leading up to it. Irony fills the scene as Jesus is mocked as a king. He is adorned with a purple robe, a crown, and a staff; and a battalion of soldiers surround him, kneeling. Finally, they bring Jesus to a high place and lift his body on the cross. Above his head reads a sign: "This is Jesus, the King of the Jews" (27:37). In crucifying him, they enthrone him. The mocking continues as the criminals crucified with Jesus taunt him, and those who pass by him deride him and claim he cannot save himself or others (Ps 25:2; 30:1; 35:19; 38:19; 41:5; 89:51; 102:8). Salvation is precisely what he performs as the King.

ANCIENT CONNECTIONS 1.14. CRUCIFIXION IN THE FIRST CENTURY

Crucifixion was a distinctly Roman execution (though Persians did it before Romans). It was used as a punishment for rebels of the state or those who were considered a threat to the peace of the empire, and it served as an example to people who might consider following their actions. There may have been many forms of crucifixion, but death came by asphyxiation, not nail piercing. Some think the arms were nailed to the crossbeam (John 20:25), legs bent, and twisted to one side, and a single nail passing through both the left and right heel bones. Other evidence shows no nails in the arms (maybe the arms were tied) and the legs straddled the cross with the nail going in the side.

Then an apocalyptic sign occurs. Darkness covers the earth, and the curtain of the temple is torn in two. An earthquake occurs, tombs are opened, and dead bodies come alive. The darkness symbolizes a great evil. However, it more prominently symbolizes a new era (Exod 10:22; Joel 2:10; Matt 24:24). As in Genesis and Exodus, the darkness marks a transition to a new day. The curtain of the temple represented the cosmos and the panorama of the heavens, and therefore the tearing of it indicates shockwaves and an opening between heaven and earth. The earthquake with dead bodies coming to life can be confusing, but Ezekiel prophesied the dead would come to life (Ezekiel 37). Jesus has gone to Sheol to release the righteous dead who were held captive. Here the bodies of the saints anticipate Jesus's abundant resurrection life. Climatically, a centurion and those with him recognize what has happened and declare Jesus is the Son of God (Matt 27:54; see also 3:17; 17:5), the new king.

Death cannot stop innocent blood. While the authorities try to seal the tomb, they cannot halt resurrection life; darkness has no power over light. The resurrection vindicates Jesus. After the Sabbath, Mary Magdalene and the other Mary go to view the tomb, and again, a violent earthquake shakes the earth. An angel of the Lord descends from heaven. The women are afraid, but the angel declares Jesus has risen. He tells the women to proclaim the good news to the disciples. While the religious authorities commission the soldiers to spread lies and deceit about someone stealing Jesus's body, Jesus commissions his female followers to tell the truth (28:1–15).

This leads to a more formal commission from Jesus to his eleven disciples in Galilee (28:16–20). Jesus asserts that like the Son of Man in Daniel, all authority in heaven and earth has been given to him. Satan tried to promise Jesus this in his temptation, but Jesus followed God's will. Jesus commands them, in light of his universal sovereignty, to make disciples of all nations. Jesus is the King of the universe, and new followers must be baptized in the name of the triune God. Though Jesus has largely restricted his mission to Israel now that he has been crowned as Lord of all, he tells his disciples to build a new temple with Jews and Gentiles. But how can they do this?

Jesus promises he will always be with them. He is, after all, not only the new King, but Immanuel: God with them (1:23).

Matthew's message is now complete. Jesus's birth, life, death, and resurrection fulfill all expectations in the Old Testament. A new era has come. The new covenant has begun. A new temple will be built. Gentiles will be a part of God's house. And Jesus will return to finish what he started.

Old Testament Connections

Matthew is explicit in his use of the Hebrew Bible. Whereas some authors are more subtle in their allusions, Matthew frequently marks his Old Testament citations with formulas. Many scholars look only to the fulfillment quotations or to Jesus as the new Moses in Matthew's use of the Old Testament, but this is far too narrow and incomplete. While Matthew's fulfillment quotations are large signposts, he also sequences his narrative to track Israel's story as a whole.[17] Thus, Matthew's use of Scripture contains different dimensions and patterns. Matthew's entire Gospel is parallel to the Hebrew Bible and the story of Israel.

The Story of Israel in Matthew

Matthew tips readers off to Israel's story as a whole by the way he frames his beginning, middle, and ending.[18] He begins with two important Greek words: *biblos geneseōs* (the book of the offspring). The explicit phrase occurs in the LXX in only two places: Gen 2:4 and 5:1. Genesis 2:4 is about the origin of heaven and earth, while 5:1 concerns the origin of Adam and Eve.

- Genesis 2:4: "These are the records [*biblos geneseōs*] of the heavens and the earth, concerning their creation."
- Genesis 5:1: "This is the document containing the family records [*biblos geneseōs*] of Adam."

---

[17] Peter Leithart has already argued a form of this in the introduction to his Matthew commentary, *The Gospel of Matthew through New Eyes: Jesus as Israel*, vol. 1 (Monroe, LA: Athanasius Press, 2017), esp. 15–22.

[18] For a more thorough argument for the structure of Matthew following the Hebrew Bible, see chapter 7 in Patrick Schreiner, *Matthew, Disciple and Scribe: The First Gospel and Its Portrait of Jesus* (Grand Rapids: Baker Academic, 2019).

These echoes suggest Matthew begins with a new creation, which now arrives in Jesus Christ, the new Adam. Of all the four Gospels, Matthew and John most clearly open their narratives with the themes of the new creation. The form of Matthew's opening—a genealogy—also alludes to Genesis because Genesis itself is structured around genealogies. It could even be argued that the entire Old Testament is centered around genealogies (Gen 3:15).

ANCIENT CONNECTIONS 1.15. THE GENEALOGIES IN GENESIS

- Genealogy of heaven and earth (2:4–4:26)
- Genealogy of Adam (5:1–6:8)
- Genealogy of Noah (6:9–9:29)
- Genealogy of Noah's sons (10:1–11:26)
- Genealogy of Terah (11:27–25:11)
- Genealogy of Ishmael (25:12–18)
- Genealogy of Isaac (25:19–35:29)
- Genealogy of Esau (36:1–36:43)
- Genealogy of Jacob (37:1–50:26)

The end of the Gospel also mirrors the end of the Hebrew Bible (2 Chronicles in the Hebrew ordering). Matthew closes with Jesus's commission to go and make disciples of the nations (28:16–20). In many ways, Jesus tells his disciples to go and rebuild their temple with people. Second Chronicles also ends with a note about the restoration project looming in the future. Cyrus gives a commission, for Israel to go up to Jerusalem to rebuild the temple. Cyrus, the king of Persia, says, "The LORD, the God of heaven, has given me all the kingdoms of the earth, and he has charged me to build him a house at Jerusalem, which is in Judah. Whoever is among you of all his people, may the LORD his God be with him. Let him go up" (2 Chr 36:23 ESV).

Cyrus speaks of his universal authority, the source of his authority, and his commission to go. Jesus lists the same three elements. He has all authority in heaven and on earth, given to him by his Father, and he tells his disciples to go. Both Matthew and 2 Chronicles end with a construction project. Matthew begins with echoes to Genesis and closes with allusions to 2 Chronicles, thus framing his Gospel with references to the Hebrew Bible.

ANCIENT CONNECTIONS 1.16. THE HEBREW OLD TESTAMENT

Though the ordering of the books of the Hebrew Bible is diverse, one of the earliest attestations to the ordering of the Hebrew Bible comes in Baba Batra (or Bava Batra). Baba Batra (c. 450–550 CE) is the third of the three Talmudic tractates in the Babylonian Talmud. The Talmud is the central text of rabbinic Judaism and the source of Jewish religious law (*halakha*). The Talmud is made up of the Mishnah (the oral Torah) and Gemara (commentary on the Mishnah). Baba Batra 14b–15a states the ordering of Prophets and the Writings, placing Chronicles at the end of the writings.

In the middle of his Gospel, Matthew has Jesus giving kingdom parables that mirror the wisdom tradition (Matthew 13). Toward the end of chapter 12, Matthew indicates Jesus is a Solomon-type figure (12:42). In chapter 13 Jesus speaks in parables and in poetic form like David (Psalms) and David's son Solomon (Proverbs). Matthew explicitly quotes from the Wisdom literature, saying that these words fulfill the line "I will open my mouth in a parable; I will utter dark sayings from of old" (Ps 78:2 ESV; Matt 13:34–35). A key fulfillment quotation gives a clue to where readers are in the history of Israel. In all of chapter 13 Jesus is opening his mouth to speak in parables as in the Wisdom literature. However, not only the fulfillment quotation helps readers see the connection with Wisdom literature in chapter 13. The word *parable* is employed twelve times in this chapter, indicating the completeness of the parable tradition. The Wisdom books are thus summed up in this new Son of David, who showers the people with wisdom and truth. Matthew even explicitly says the people are astonished at Jesus's "wisdom" immediately after he delivers his kingdom parables (13:54)

Matthew's beginning, middle, and ending give readers license to look for similar sequencing in the rest of his work. What readers find is the continuation of the tracing of Israel's story.

Jesus as the New Moses and Israel

After the Genesis echoes, Matthew wastes little time before he introduces Mosaic themes. In Matthew 2, Jesus is born in a land where a jealous and anxious king resides. The parallels between Moses's birth and Jesus's birth are unmistakable and not coincidental.

Table 1.1: Parallels between Jesus and Moses

Moses	Jesus
Moses is born as a helpless child under Pharaoh's reign.	Jesus is born as a helpless child under Herod's reign.
Pharaoh (labeled as "king" in Exod 1:15, 17, 18) seeks to kill the male Hebrew children.	King Herod seeks to kill the male Hebrew children in Bethlehem.
Moses is preserved by faithful servants and Yahweh's sovereign hand.	Jesus is preserved by faithful servants and Yahweh's sovereign hand.
God sovereignly preserves his redeemer.	God sovereignly preserves his Redeemer.

Matthew portrays Jesus as walking in the same footsteps of both Israel and Moses. Jesus represents both the nation and the leaders of the nation. After Matthew's introduction, Jesus goes through water in his baptism like Israel went through the Red Sea (3). Then he goes into the wilderness for his temptation like Israel (4). But unlike Israel, he does not fail.

Matthew 5–7 then mirrors Sinai. The account that Jesus "went up on the mountain" reads similarly to Exod 19:3, which describes Moses as ascending Mount Sinai to receive the law. Matthew also describes the obscure mountain Jesus ascends as *the* mountain. Matthew invites a comparison with the most prominent mount in the Old Testament. Matthew also describes Jesus as sitting down to teach. This recalls Moses's stance when he received God's law on Mount Sinai. Although the verb in the Hebrew is debated, references in the Talmud show that Jewish interpreters regarded Deut 9:9 as meaning that Moses sat down on the mountain. Finally, the content of Jesus's sermon is largely an explanation, or interpretation, of the Torah. Matthew's point is that Jesus comes as the new Moses and new Israel.

Jesus as the New Joshua

Jesus enacts the law in chapters 8 and 9 through healings, reversing many of the wilderness events. Some even propose these ten miracles in the two chapters may mirror the ten rebellions of Israel in the wilderness (Num 14:22).[19] Then Matthew 10 recalls the sending of spies into the land of Canaan. The Missionary Discourse is bracketed by a reference to Jesus's "twelve disciples" in 10:1 and 11:1. Matthew 10 mirrors both

---

[19] Leithart, *Gospel of Matthew through New Eyes: Jesus as Israel.*

the sending of the twelve spies into the land and the commissioning of Joshua as Moses's successor (Numbers 13; 27). The picture presented by this discourse is one of taking territory for the kingdom of God, much like the conquest. Jesus is also the new Joshua.

Jesus as the New David and Solomon

Matthew 11–13 follows the story of the monarchy. Jesus is the new David and new Solomon. Matthew's first descriptions of Jesus are that he is the Messiah, the Son of David (1:1). The inaugural images function as the threshold through which readers are required to pass before entering the house of Matthew's Gospel. After Matthew announces Jesus is the Davidic King in 1:1 he takes readers on a journey to see how Jesus becomes King. Jesus is first exiled by Herod's antagonism and must be raised in Nazareth of Galilee (northern Israel). Jesus conducts his ministry in Galilee, but as he returns to his hometown and the city of the King he suffers as the wise servant. Finally, Jesus is enthroned on the cross as the King of the Jews.

While Davidic imagery is in the whole Gospel, chapters 11–13 uniquely focus on Davidic and Solomonic imagery. Jesus offers to give the people Sabbath rest as David did (11:25–30), but the people quarrel about what Jesus is doing on the Sabbath rather than accepting the rest he offers to them. Jesus also speaks of himself as greater than the temple (12:6), which refers to the Solomon era. Jesus is the new and greater David and Solomon, who can enter the temple and eat the bread (1 Sam 21:6). In the middle of chapter 12, Matthew employs the longest fulfillment quotation in his Gospel: "Behold, my servant whom I have chosen, my beloved with whom my soul is well pleased. I will put my Spirit upon him, and he will proclaim justice to the Gentiles" (12:18 ESV). While this quotation is from Isaiah, the text reaches back to David. The title *servant* is applied to David more than any other figure. The key servant of Yahweh is David.

Jesus as the New Elijah, Jeremiah, Ezekiel, and Isaiah

Just as Matthew 13 mirrors the wisdom tradition, Matthew 14–17 has certain resemblances to the divided kingdom. Although many Jews reject Jesus, he still holds out the promise of life to them like the Prophets. In this section he is the new Elijah who performs a food miracle (1 Kgs 17:14) and a water miracle (1 Kgs 18:41; 2 Kgs 2:8); goes to a woman outside of Israel (1 Kgs 17:9); with whom the people explicitly identify with Elijah (Matt 16:14); and next to whom Elijah appears (17:3). As in Elisha's day, Jesus shows that a remnant is left within Israel, though the nation is divided (1 Kgs 19:18). The prophets give hope to the remnant and warn Israel of the flesh. Jesus is the new Jeremiah, Ezekiel, and Isaiah.

Matthew 18–20 continue prophetic themes centering on the people of God, the remnant. Like Ezekiel, Isaiah, and Jeremiah, Jesus provides instructions for the covenant community (18:4, 21–22; 19:3, 21; 20:16, 26; Isa 2:2; 66:2; Jer 5:1; 11:4; 31:34; Ezek 22:29). Through his visionary words, he establishes and teaches his *ekklesia* (church). The people of God, like Israel of old, are to remember the Torah and the instructions about humbling themselves before God and caring for the down-and-outs (Matt 18:1–14). They are to become like children in humility (18:1–6) and care for little ones (18:10–14). Likewise, they are instructed to be peacemakers (18:15–35) and care for one another.

In Matthew 21–25, Jesus is the judging prophet. He enters the city of Jerusalem, but rather than coming into the city as the conquering Messiah, he acts as the condemning prophet by attacking the temple and cursing the fig tree. Jesus's language even mirrors Jeremiah's as he calls the temple a "den of robbers" (21:13 ESV; Jer 7:11). Jesus then condemns the religious leaders in Matthew 23–25, matching the condemnation by the major prophets, Isaiah, Jeremiah, and Ezekiel (Isaiah 5; Jer 2:8; Ezek 2:3–7). Jesus describes the false leadership of the religious leaders as he declares seven woes (Matt 23:1–39) and predicts the destruction of the temple (24:1–2). The glory of the Lord is leaving the temple, as Ezekiel witnessed (Ezekiel 10). The apocalyptic language employed in this fifth discourse is eerily similar to Isaiah's prophetic apocalyptic condemnation of Babylon in Isaiah 13.

At the end of chapter 23, Jesus says God has sent Jerusalem these prophets so that "the blood of righteous Abel to the blood of Zechariah" might come on them (Matt 23:34–35). He links Abel and Zechariah through righteous blood, which reveals Matthew is aware and thinking of the larger story line of the Hebrew Bible. Abel is the first in the Hebrew Bible whose blood is spilled (Gen 4:10), and Zechariah is the last prophet whose violent death is reported (2 Chr 24:20–21). In essence, Matthew is saying that the blood speaks from cover to cover, from Genesis through Chronicles.

The concept of blood leads into chapters 26–28. If Matthew is following the history of the Old Testament, the next thing that should happen is the destruction of the temple and the exile. Blood should fill this section as the people of Israel are attacked and destroyed by their enemies as in the Old Testament. But a twist occurs in the passion. The blood of Israel *is* spilled, but it is innocent blood. The blood turns out to be not only the cue for the exile of the true Israel but also the prompt for the rebuilding of the temple and the return from exile. Jesus's blood is both spilled and it redeems. Blood is both the curse and the blessing, and it lies at the center of Israel's future.

Overall, Matthew's narrative follows Israel's history. Jesus is Israel embodied in one figure. He fulfills not only the role of Moses but the role of the nation. He is all that the Old Testament points to.

Table 1.2: Israel's Story in Matthew[20]

Matthew	Matthew Section	Old Testament Allusion
1–2	Genealogy and birth	Genesis and early Moses story
3–4	Beginning of ministry	Israel's story and continued Moses theme
5–7	Sermon on the Mount	Mount Sinai: Exodus–Deuteronomy
8–9	Healings	Law enacted: Exodus–Deuteronomy
10	Sending of the Twelve	Conquest
11–12	Reactions to the king	Monarchy
13	Kingdom parables	Wisdom literature
14–17	Divided reactions to Jesus	Divided kingdom: Elijah and Elisha
18–20	Instruction for the church	Prophets' hope: establishment of a new community
21–25	Clash of the kingdoms	Prophetic condemnation: castigation of current leadership
26–28	Death, resurrection, commission	Exile, return from exile, rebuilding the temple

Gospel Connections

Considering gospel (good news) connections in most of the Bible usually means looking either forward or backward. However, the Gospels uniquely contain *the*

---

[20] This table is taken from Schreiner, *Matthew, Disciple and Scribe*, 233.

gospel. The Gospels are the gospel. The Greek word for "gospel" is the compound form of the adverb *eu* ("well") and the noun *angelos* ("messenger") and has its Hebrew corollary in the term *basar*. It is a media term—a message of good news. We will first consider how the Gospels are the gospel more broadly (thus not distinct to Matthew) and then turn to some distinctive emphases from Matthew on the gospel.

The Gospels as the Gospel

When most Protestant evangelicals define the gospel, they run to Paul. Paul has more propositional statements about the gospel, so it is easier for us to summarize the points of the gospel from him or another epistle writer. However, this is the wrong starting point, even if many of the epistles were written before the first Gospel was penned. Paul builds his theology on the reality and story of Jesus—not the other way around. In Jesus, we see the embodiment, fulfillment, and explanation of the gospel. Paul and the other disciples rightly explain the implications and even content of this gospel, but these reflections are founded on the arrival of Jesus. Three arguments support the contention that the Gospels are the gospel.

First, the Gospels are called "the Gospels." This should tip readers off concerning their content. The Evangelists are not writing as disinterested historians but as heralders of the gospel. Even though the titles are not original, Mark, our first Gospel writer, describes his work as a "Gospel" in 1:1: "The beginning of the gospel of Jesus Christ, the Son of God." The gospel is an oral proclamation of a beneficial report. However, Mark uses the term to describe his written report that details the sacrifice and victory of Jesus the Messiah. This means early Christians understood the Gospels as *the* gospel. All four of the books are summaries of the gospel.

Second, the Gospels define the gospel because of the narrative structure of the Bible. Most of the Bible—including 60 percent of the Old Testament—is made up of narrative. It is a story that carries readers along the Bible's narrative path, the other genres breaking the flow of the narrative but also further supporting it. The Gospels, unlike many of the other New Testament books, directly step into this story and continue it. If the Old Testament is about the gospel promised, the Gospels announce that the gospel has come in Jesus Christ. The Gospels therefore uniquely and centrally describe the gospel.

Third, the Gospels define the gospel because the audience of the Gospels is broader than that of the Epistles. Most of the Epistles are occasional, but the Gospels seem less occasional and were written for all Christians.[21] This is not to say that the Epistles were not also written for all Christians, but they were written to specific communities and the particular issues with which they dealt. They therefore intentionally deal with more narrow and specific issues. This does not make them less valuable, but it does mean they speak to us at a different level. Though some still argue for specific communities for the Gospels, it is difficult to tie the content to specific communities. The earliest textual evidence confirms this as well, given that the fourfold Gospel codex circulated quickly and widely throughout the ancient world. This makes the Gospels central to the large plotline of the Bible.

Fourth, and finally, the Gospels introduce us to Jesus. Jesus is the gospel. He is the long-awaited good news, the one for whom John the Baptist prepares the way. The whole Bible has been leaning forward toward Jesus. He has been promised, but in the Gospels we finally meet him. Jesus explicitly announces "the good news of the kingdom" (Matt 4:23; 9:35). These texts summarize Jesus's message in Matthew. Jesus preaches the good news and heals every disease. Matthew's point is that Jesus's entire ministry was the "gospel."

Every act Jesus performs has to do with the good news of the kingdom. This culminates rightly in his death and resurrection, but we tend to overlook Jesus's life. The good news begins, according to Jesus, before his death. Yet it also cannot be separated from Jesus's death. In Matt 11:5 Jesus says in response to John, "The blind receive their sight, the lame walk, those with leprosy are cleansed, the deaf hear, the dead are raised, and the poor are told good the news." Notice how Jesus parallels the good news with the blind receiving their sight and the lame walking. Jesus's miraculous acts are part and parcel of the gospel.

The Gospels give us the gospel. So do the Epistles, Revelation, and the rest of the Old Testament. However, there is a unique sense in which everything in the Old Testament has led to the Gospels and all the letters draw out implications from the life, death, resurrection, and ascension of Jesus. The Gospels are not unique because of their authors. They are unique because of their subject. No other biographers have ever told the story of a figure who defeated death and is still living. His biography remains unfinished.

---

[21] Richard Bauckham, ed., *The Gospels for All Christians: Rethinking the Gospel Audiences* (Grand Rapids: Eerdmans, 1998), esp. 9–48. Alternatively, see Craig Blomberg, "The Gospels for Specific Communities and All Christians," in Klink, ed., *The Audience of the Gospels: The Origin and Function of the Gospels in Early Christianity*, Library of New Testament Studies (London: T&T Clark, 2010), 111–33.

The Gospel as Fulfillment

In the Old Testament, promises are made. In the New Testament, promises are kept. Matthew reminds readers that the gospel can be understood through the lens of fulfillment. The previous analysis might tempt you to think the gospel is not found in the Old Testament. This is not true. The gospel is *foreshadowed* in the Old Testament and *revealed* in the New Testament.[22] This section will look at some of the ways Matthew sees the concept of fulfillment as essential to the gospel.

First, Matthew sees Jesus as fulfilling the hope for an offspring who will crush the serpent. Genesis 3:15, the *protoeuangelion* (the first gospel), predicts there will be a certain progeny who will strike the serpent's head but take a blow to his heel. Some may wonder if this theme is present in Matthew, but a few arguments prove it is. Most fundamentally, Matthew is about a person: Jesus the Messiah. All the scenes are primarily about this hero. It appropriately begins with his birth. A new offspring has arrived, one for whom the Old Testament has been waiting.

Additionally, Matthew's Gospel appropriately begins with a genealogy, more than hinting at this offspring theme. Genesis and the Old Testament trace the hope for a new child through genealogies. Numbers is named such because it lists out the people and tribes who come out of Egypt. In Joshua, the different tribes are listed and are allotted land showing that this seed theme continues. Ruth 4:18–22 reminds readers that Ruth and Boaz's faithfulness are part of the story for how we get a good king. Second Samuel 7 promises that a son of David will sit on the throne forever. Ezra 7 provides a genealogy of those who came back from exile. And in 1 Chronicles 1–9 many of the previous genealogies are brought together. All the genealogies point to Jesus.

Matthew gives the most space to Jesus's last days: his death on the cross. Genesis promises Satan's defeat, but it will come at a sacrifice. In many ways, all of Matthew is about Jesus's sacrifice that leads to victory. This fulfills the promise of Genesis 3. Matthew shows his readers that the hopes for the victorious child are now realized. The gospel is that a child has been born who will trample the serpent but die in the process.

Second, Matthew sees Jesus as fulfilling the hope of a good shepherd. The good news is that we have a Good Shepherd, as the Old Testament foreshadowed and predicted. Yahweh is described as the shepherd of Israel. Jacob speaks of God as his shepherd (Gen 48:15) and later uses the imagery again when he prays to the "Mighty One, . . . the Shepherd, the Rock of Israel" (49:24).

---

[22] Though see Gal 3:8 where Paul affirms the gospel was preached to Abraham.

Not only is Yahweh portrayed as a shepherd, but also the leaders who guide Israel are considered under-shepherds. Early in Genesis, Abel and Jacob are described as shepherds (4:2; 30:31). Three of the most prominent figures in the Old Testament are described as shepherds. Abraham is depicted as a shepherd who obtains many flocks and herds (Gen 12:16; 13:2, 7; 20:14; 24:35). Moses is described as a shepherd while he lives in Midian (Exod 3:1). While Moses is shepherding, God meets him in the burning bush. In Num 27:16–17 Moses prays that God will provide a shepherd for Israel. Later the psalmist describes the role of Moses: "You led your people like a flock by the hand of Moses and Aaron" (Ps 77:20). But the most prominent under-shepherd in the Hebrew Scriptures is King David. The first time a reader meets David is as the shepherd of his father's flock, when Samuel comes to Jesse to anoint one of his sons as the future king. This task transforms when David becomes the shepherd of Yahweh's people (2 Sam 5:1–2; 7:5–17).

However, the prophets longed for another shepherd for Israel (Isa 13:14; 63:11; Jer 3:15; 12:10; 23:1–4; Ezekiel 34). Their current shepherds mistreated them, and even the good ones ultimately failed them. They still waited for the Good Shepherd. Jesus is born as the Good Shepherd. Matthew begins by describing Jesus as the Son of David and the Son of Abraham. He is fonder of describing Jesus as the Son of David than any other Gospel writer, and he consistently paints Jesus in Mosaic robes. When Jesus arrives in Jerusalem as a child, the scribes read that a ruler will come who will shepherd God's people (2:6; Mic 5:2). Matthew sees Jesus's arrival as fulfilling Micah's hope. Rather than exploiting God's people, the Messiah will serve God's people.

Jesus's shepherding is again seen as he teaches and heals the people. In fact, Jesus views Israel as sheep without a shepherd, so he cares not only for himself but enlists his disciples to help (9:36). He is the shepherd not only to Israel but to the nations as he shows mercy to a Canaanite woman (15:24). Jesus acts as the judging shepherd throughout the Gospel, separating the sheep from the goats for the good of his community (25:31–46). Finally, Jesus acts as the sacrificial shepherd who is struck and the sheep scatter (26:31). He is the Good Shepherd who will rescue and protect his sheep by dying for them.

According to Matthew, the gospel message is that a new shepherd has appeared. He will not only shepherd Israel but the nations (Ps 28:9). He will care for people and lead them to the land flowing with milk and honey (23:1–6). He will do so by his sacrificial death. Without a good shepherd, God's people have no hope and will die in the valley of the shadow of death (80:1).

Third, Matthew sees Jesus as fulfilling the *Mosaic-prophetic* hope. The Lord promised the people he would raise up a prophet for them in the form of Moses

(Deut 18:15). God also promised this prophet would lead them on a new exodus. In Hosea, Yahweh gave assurance he would speak tenderly to Israel and would come again out of the land of Egypt (Hos 2:14–15; 11:1, 11). Other prophets speak of Israel's future redemption in similar terms (Jer 23:7; Mic 7:14–15). According to Matthew, the gospel is that a prophet has arrived who will provide liberation.

In Matthew 1–2, we find Jesus is the prophet who is preserved. Like Moses, Jesus is spared from a tyrant king who wants him dead. He then goes through the water and into the wilderness. Matthew even quotes from Hos 11:1, showing that Jesus is Israel, and he likewise is called out of Egypt (Matt 2:15). This foreshadows how Jesus will bring his people out of Egypt. The five discourses of Matthew also portray Jesus as the prophet who delivers the new Torah, and they likely mirror the five books of the Torah.[23] In the first discourse Jesus is painted as the new Moses who delivers the Torah.

Jesus is also a miracle worker like Moses who redeems his people from sickness and death. He is a mediator who meets with God on a mountain and shows the goal of the law. When Jesus is transfigured before his disciples, his face becomes like Moses's after he came down from Mount Sinai. The goal of the law is to see the face of God and be transformed. Jesus also explains the terms of the new covenant and installs a new era at the Last Supper like Moses did at Sinai.

In all these actions, Jesus liberates his people. He is preserved so that he might bring them to a new place. He instructs them and heals them so they will follow him. He dies for them so that they might enter the new land. For Matthew, the gospel is liberation from all who might oppress us. Jesus is the new prophet who brings freedom.

The Gospel as Seeing God

One of the most important aspects of the gospel according to Matthew is that Jesus is not only the Davidic Messiah, the son of Abraham, but he is God in the flesh. Jesus is Immanuel: God with us. According to the Christian tradition, the goal of the gospel is to see God, also known as the *beatific vision*. Too often we focus on how we enter a relationship with God and forget about the end goal: being with God and seeing him face-to-face. In Jesus, this future is previewed.

Jacob speaks of seeing God "face to face" but not dying (Gen 32:30). The Scriptures say the Lord spoke to Moses face-to-face after he went up on the

---

[23] B. W. Bacon, "The Five Books of Matthew Against the Jews," *Expositor* 15 (1918): 56–66.

mountain (Exod 33:11; Deut 5:4; 34:10). The rest of Israel must stay at the base of the mountain and wait for Moses to come down. The biblical storyline is a promise for those who keep God's covenant that they will see God. Jesus says the pure in heart will see God (Matt 5:8).

According to Matthew, Jesus is God in the flesh, and through him we see God. Yet three specific texts make it more explicit. First, Matt 1:23 quotes Isaiah, saying, "Behold, the virgin shall conceive and bear a son, and they shall call his name Immanuel (which means, God with us)" (ESV). The second text is in Matt 18:20, where Jesus promises that when two or three gather in his name, he is present with them. The third text is in Matt 28:20, the last verse of the Gospel, where Jesus assures his disciples he is with them to the end of the age.

In Matt 1:23 Matthew affirms that Jesus is the fulfillment of God's presence predicated in Isa 7:14. In Isaiah 7, Ahaz (king of Jerusalem) was in turmoil because Rezin (king of Syria) and Pekah (king of Israel) were mounting an attack against Jerusalem. Therefore, the Lord sent the prophet Isaiah to meet Ahaz to tell him not to fear because he resided in the "house of David" (7:13). Ahaz was given the Immanuel sign to comfort him. Immanuel, the presence of God, was the promise of salvation.

MATTHEW'S USE OF THE OLD TESTAMENT

Some of Matthew's fulfillment quotations have troubled interpreters. Isaiah 7:14 is one such example, with some arguing there is a double fulfillment both in Isaiah (8:8; 36:1) and Jesus (Matt 1:23) or a single fulfillment in Christ and therefore Isa 7:14 is typological and pointing beyond itself. The two options are not necessarily mutually exclusive. The text is partially fulfilled in Isaiah (double fulfillment) but not completely (typology). A true virgin would later give birth to the true Immanuel.

Matthew asserts this promise is fulfilled in Jesus Christ. That is why he says his name is Jesus (Yahweh saves) and Immanuel in Matt 1:18–25. God will save his people not from the foreign nations but from their sins by coming to them in the flesh. Now God has done so in the person of Jesus. In the Old Testament the presence of God was their salvation (or judgment if they forsook him). God's presence was located in the tabernacle and temple. It was their protection and safety. Now this temple presence was in their midst again, but in a person. Jesus is the incarnate Word, the living temple.

Matthew 18:18–20 also speaks directly to the presence of Jesus, and this time the emphasis is on his presence with his people: "Truly I tell you, whatever you bind on earth will have been bound in heaven, and whatever you loose on earth will have been loosed in heaven. Again, truly I tell you, if two of you on earth agree about any matter that you pray for, it will be done for you by my Father in heaven. For where two or three are gathered together in my name, I am there among them."

Jesus affirms that the two spaces (heaven and earth) converge *through* his presence. What is bound or loosed in heaven is done on the earth because Jesus's presence is with his people. This indicates God's presence is not only for their salvation, but their salvation includes the unity of heaven and earth. God's presence with his people on earth brings heaven down to earth and brings earth up to heaven. Matthew shows his readers Jesus's project was much larger than simply saving Israel. The story of Israel was about the cosmos, which means the gospel is about the cosmos.

The Great Commission promise also contains a phrase about the presence of Jesus with his people. Jesus tells his disciples, "Behold, I am with you always, to the end of the age" (28:20 ESV). The presence of Jesus is spoken of in relation to empowerment for mission. As Cyrus sent Israel to rebuild their temple, so now Jesus commands Israel to build his spiritual house (2 Chron 36:23; Matt 28:19). This house will include Jews and Gentiles who are spiritual stones built on the cornerstone, Jesus Christ.

The Gospel ends with a beginning: the disciples are to go into the whole world and make disciples. Jesus promises his presence because he knows they will be persecuted. If the first statement about presence was about salvation and the second about the unity of heaven and earth, this one emphasizes the presence of Jesus as an emboldening reality. The gospel is an oral proclamation that Jesus is God with us, but it is also a mission to be fulfilled. People need to hear this message, and Matthew says Jesus's presence will be with his people forever.

The gospel has a goal. For Matthew, this goal is seeing God. Matthew beheld God in the face of Jesus Christ. Now Jesus is gone, so we long for him to return. In the meantime he has granted his people his presence so that they can unify heaven and earth and go forth proclaiming the reality of Jesus come in the flesh. If Matthew has a gospel emphasis, it is not only how we are saved but the hope of God's presence.

Life Connections

The Gospels are discipleship texts. Though many points could be discussed, my focus will be on what it means to follow Jesus as a Solomon-like wisdom teacher. According to Matthew, to be a disciple of Jesus is to listen to the teacher of wisdom, interpret the law rightly, and practice the law.[24]

The book of Job asks, "Where can wisdom be found?" (28:12). Matthew asserts that wisdom is found in Jesus. We must come to Matthew with a receptive and humble posture, ready to listen to our teacher of wisdom. Our temptation is to only hear what we want to from Jesus, or only what we already agree with, but Matthew shows us we must attend to all his words. We must listen to him (17:5). Jesus's commands are clear. He tells us if we have gazed on a woman with lust, we have committed adultery with her in our heart (5:28). He tells us to not lie and to be people of our word (5:37). He tells us to love our enemies (5:44). These are hard commands, but they are the path to life.

Second, a disciple is one who interprets the Old Testament law rightly. It is easy to dismiss the Old Testament or criticize it for its dissimilarity to our culture. What are we to do with commands that include killing those caught in adultery (Lev 20:10)? Jesus affirms the Old Testament but also asserts a new era has arrived. The law was good and functioned as a babysitter for Israel for a time, but now that Jesus has come, he shows the true interpretation of the Torah. God's people are no longer under the law in the same way because Jesus has set them free. A disciple is one who realizes Jesus affirms the old but also completes it (Matt 13:52). They know Jesus fulfills the law, his yoke is easy, and he has come to welcome all those who have faith in him.

Finally, a disciple is someone who practices justice and mercy—not hypocrisy. Our call is not merely to interpret the law rightly but to live it rightly; this is wisdom. Jesus says, "A good person produces good things from his storeroom of good, and an evil person produces evil things from his storeroom of evil" (12:35; 7:15–23). A disciple performs their righteousness not to receive praise from others, but to receive a reward from their Father in heaven. They don't neglect "the more important matters of the law—justice, mercy, and faithfulness" (23:23). As Ulrich Luz asserts, the definition of discipleship in Matthew can be summed up in the phrase "doing the will of God" (12:50).[25]

Matthew forms disciples of Christ by urging them to listen to Christ, who is our new wisdom teacher like Solomon, follow in his interpretive footsteps, and practice the deeds of Jesus. The call in Matthew is to listen and obey. This might not be popular in our culture, but obedience is the pathway to true freedom.

---

[24] Some might question why I don't speak of "faith" in this section. I reserve a discussion of faith for the end of Mark.

[25] Ulrich Luz, "The Disciples in the Gospel according to Matthew," in *The Interpretation of Matthew*, 2nd ed., ed. Graham Stanton, Studies in New Testament Interpretation (Edinburgh: T&T Clark, 1995), 123.

Interactive Questions

1.1. What makes Matthew unique compared to the rest of the Gospels?

1.2. How does Matthew structure his Gospel, and how does that inform your view of the content?

1.3. Why do you think the early church put Matthew first in the canonical ordering even if it was not written first?

1.4. What is Jesus's view of the Old Testament law in Matthew?

1.5. How does Matthew characterize Jesus in his Gospel?

1.6. Where do we see echoes of Moses in Matthew?

1.7. What is the kingdom of heaven according to Matthew?

1.8. What are some main Old Testament echoes that you find in Matthew?

1.9. Why is Matthew called a "manual for discipleship," and how can it be used in this way?

Recommended Resources

Modern Commentaries

Blomberg, Craig L. *Matthew: An Exegetical and Theological Exposition of Holy Scripture.* Vol. 22. The New American Commentary. Nashville: Broadman Press, 1992.

Brown, Jeannine K., and Kyle Roberts. *Matthew.* Grand Rapids: Eerdmans, 2018.

Bruner, Frederick Dale. *Matthew: A Commentary.* 2 vols. Revised and expanded. Grand Rapids: Eerdmans, 2004.

Carson, D. A. "Matthew." In *The Expositor's Bible Commentary*, edited by Tremper Longman III and David E. Garland, 23–670. Vol. 9. Rev. ed. Grand Rapids: Zondervan Academic, 2010.

Davies, W. D., and D. C. Allison. *Matthew.* 3 vols. International Critical Commentary. New York: T&T Clark, 2004.

France, R. T. *The Gospel of Matthew.* The New International Commentary on the New Testament. Grand Rapids: Eerdmans, 2007.

Garland, David E. *Reading Matthew: A Literary and Theological Commentary.* Reading the New Testament. Macon, GA: Smyth & Helwys, 2001.

Keener, Craig S. *The Gospel of Matthew: A Socio-Rhetorical Commentary.* Grand Rapids: Eerdmans, 2009.

Leithart, Peter J. *The Gospel of Matthew through New Eyes.* 2 vols. Monroe, LA: Athanasius Press, 2017–18.

Luz, Ulrich. *Matthew.* 3 vols. Hermeneia. Edited by Helmut Koester. Translated by James E. Crouch. Minneapolis: Fortress Press, 2001–7.

Early Commentaries

Augustine. *Saint Augustine: Sermon on the Mount; Harmony of the Gospels; Homilies on the Gospels.* A Select Library of the Nicene and Post-Nicene Fathers of the Christian Church. Vol. 6. Edited by Philip Schaff. Grand Rapids: Eerdmans, 1956.

Hilary of Poitiers. *Commentary on Matthew.* The Fathers of the Church. Translated by D. H. Williams. Washington, DC: The Catholic University of America Press, 2013.

Isho'dad of Merv. *The Commentaries of Isho'dad of Merv, Bishop of Hadatha.* Translated by Margaret Dunlop Gibson. Cambridge: Cambridge University Press, 2011.

Jerome. *Commentary on Matthew.* The Fathers of the Church. Translated by Thomas P. Scheck. Washington, DC: The Catholic University of America Press, 2014.

John Chrysostom, *Homilies on the Gospel of St. Matthew.* 2 vols. Edited by Paul A. Böer. Washington, DC. Veritatis Splendor Publications, 2012.

Theophylact. *The Explanation by Blessed Theophylact of the Holy Gospel According to St. Matthew.* Translated by C. Stade. House Springs, MO: Chrysostom, 1992.

Special Studies

Allison, Dale C. *The New Moses: A Matthean Typology.* Eugene, OR: Wipf and Stock, 1993.

———. *Studies in Matthew: Interpretation Past and Present.* Grand Rapids: Baker Academic, 2012.

Bauer, David R. *The Gospel of the Son of God: An Introduction to Matthew.* Downers Grove, IL: IVP Academic, 2019.

Brown, Jeannine K. *The Disciples in Narrative Perspective: The Portrayal and Function of the Matthean Disciples.* Vol. 9. SBL Academia Biblica. Leiden: Brill, 2002.

Donaldson, Terence L. *Jesus on the Mountain: A Study in Matthew.* Sheffield, UK: Sheffield Academic Press, 1987.

France, R. T. *Matthew: Evangelist and Teacher*. Eugene, OR: Wipf and Stock, 2004.

Kingsbury, Jack Dean. *Matthew: Structure, Christology, Kingdom*. Philadelphia: Fortress Press, 1989.

———. *Matthew as Story*. 2nd ed. Philadelphia: Fortress Press, 1988.

Konradt, Matthias. *Israel, Church, and the Gentiles in the Gospel of Matthew*. Baylor-Mohr Siebeck Studies in Early Christianity. Translated by Kathleen Ess. Waco, TX: Baylor University Press, 2014.

Kupp, David D. *Matthew's Emmanuel: Divine Presence and God's People in the First Gospel*. Society for New Testament Studies Monograph Series 90. Cambridge: Cambridge University Press, 1996.

Luz, Ulrich. *Studies in Matthew*. Grand Rapids: Eerdmans, 2005.

———. *The Theology of the Gospel of Matthew*. New Testament Theology. Translated by J. Bradford Robinson. Cambridge: Cambridge University Press, 1995.

McKnight, Scot. *Sermon on the Mount*. The Story of God Bible Commentary. Edited by Tremper Longman III and Scot McKnight. Grand Rapids: Zondervan, 2013.

Neyrey, Jerome H. *Honor and Shame in the Gospel of Matthew*. Louisville: Westminster John Knox Press, 1998.

Pennington, Jonathan T. *Heaven and Earth in the Gospel of Matthew*. Grand Rapids: Baker Academic, 2012.

———. *The Sermon on the Mount and Human Flourishing: A Theological Commentary*. Grand Rapids: Baker Academic, 2017.

Schreiner, Patrick. *Matthew, Disciple and Scribe: The First Gospel and Its Portrait of Jesus*. Grand Rapids: Baker Academic, 2019.

Stanton, Graham N. *A Gospel for a New People: Studies in Matthew*. Louisville: Westminster John Knox Press, 1992.

2

Mark

Outline

1. The way of authority (1–8:21)
   a. Preparation (1:1–13)
   b. The authority of Jesus (1:14–3:6)
   c. The family of Jesus (3:7–6:6)
   d. The expanding mission of Jesus (6:7–8:21)
2. The way of suffering (8:22–16:8)
   a. Peter's confession and the revelation of suffering (8:22–10:52)
   b. Jesus confronts Jerusalem (11–13)
   c. The suffering of Jesus (14–15)
   d. The victory of Jesus (16)

MARK IN THE NEW TESTAMENT

- Mark (also called John or John Mark) is first introduced as the son of an apparently wealthy woman named Mary in whose home Christians gathered for prayer (Acts 12:12, 25).

- John Mark joins Paul and Barnabas on their first missionary journey but abandons them halfway (Acts 13:5, 13; 15:37–39).
- Mark is likely the person mentioned in 1 Pet 5:13 as being with Peter in Rome.
- Paul refers to a man named Mark who is the cousin of Barnabas (Col 4:10).

Author, Date, and Message

Like all the Gospels, Mark is officially anonymous. However, the early church attributes this Gospel to John Mark, the cousin of Barnabas (travel companion of Paul) and a close acquaintance of the apostle Peter. Papias, as quoted in Eusebius's *Ecclesiastical History*, identifies Mark as "Peter's interpreter" (3.39.15). Unlike Matthew and John, Mark was not a disciple of Jesus but likely wrote to preserve the eyewitness testimony of Peter.

While the early church believed Matthew was the first Gospel written, most modern scholars (since the late nineteenth century) argue the Gospel of Mark was written first. This view is called Markan priority. It arose from studying the literary relationships between Matthew, Mark, and Luke.

ANCIENT CONNECTIONS 2.1. PAPIAS ON MARK

Papias, a second-century Christian, says the following about the Gospel of Mark:

> Mark, who had been Peter's interpreter, wrote down carefully, but not in order, all that he remembered from the Lord's sayings and doings. For he had not heard the Lord or been one of his followers, but later as I said, one of Peter's. Peter used to adapt his teaching to the occasion, without making a systematic arrangement of the Lord's sayings, so that Mark was quite justified in writing down some things just as he remembered them.[1]

Irenaeus and the Anti-Marcionite Prologue claim Mark was written after Peter's death (mid-60s), but Clement and Origen say it was written while Peter was still

---

[1] Eusebius, *Ecclesiastical History* 3.39.15.

alive. Internal evidence is also debated. Some point to the theme of suffering in Mark and tie it to Caligula (41 CE) or Nero (64 CE). The reference to "wild animals" in 1:13 has caused some to wonder if this is a veiled reference to Nero's persecution. Mark 13:14 also speaks of the "abomination of desolation," which could refer to the destruction of the temple by Titus in 70 CE. Some therefore date Mark after 70, but these words are equally intelligible before 70 than after. This is also true of Jesus's words about raising the temple in three days.[2] A later date would thus be between 65 and 73, and the deaths of certain apostles may have prompted Mark to put the life of Jesus into writing. An earlier date would be in the 50s. I lean toward an earlier date, but certainty is elusive. What seems most likely is that Mark's Gospel is before Matthew based on analysis of the "Synoptic Problem."

THE SYNOPTIC PROBLEM

Scholars recognize Matthew, Mark, and Luke as having some sort of literary relationship because of shared stories, sayings, sequence, and even sometimes agreement in wording. However, scholars disagree on how they relate to one another. Three theories have presented themselves as most plausible.

- **Augustinian hypothesis:** Matthew wrote first and was used by Mark, both of whom were used by Luke.
- **Griesbach hypothesis:** Matthew wrote first and was used by Luke, both of whom were used by Mark.
- **Farrer/Goulder hypothesis:** Mark wrote first and was used by Matthew and Luke.
  - This is broken down into a two-source (Mark and Q) or four-source hypothesis (Mark, Q, M, L). Q, M, and L are lost sources.

Most New Testament scholars hold to Markan priority because of his (1) briefness, (2) grammar, (3) harder readings, (4) lack of Matthew–Luke verbal agreements against Mark, (5) lack of Matthew–Luke agreements in order against Mark, (6) omissions and wording, and (7) the argument from redaction.[3]

---

[2] Jonathan Bernier, *Rethinking the Dates of the New Testament* (Grand Rapids: Baker Academic, 2022).

[3] See Robert H. Stein, *The Synoptic Problem: An Introduction* (Grand Rapids: Baker, 1987), 7, 45–88.

Mark's original audience seems to be Christians in Rome, though the audience of the Gospels is also much wider than one specific community. Mark's Greco-Roman audience is evident in several ways. First, unlike Matthew, Mark quotes relatively infrequently from the Old Testament. Second, he provides parenthetical explanations of Jewish customs unfamiliar to his readers (7:3–4; 12:18; 14:12; 15:42). Third, Mark also translates Aramaic and Hebrew phrases by their Greek equivalents (3:17; 5:41; 7:11, 34; 10:46; 14:36; 15:22, 34). Fourth, Mark incorporates several Latinisms (Latin words borrowed by another language). Finally, early church tradition assumed Mark wrote this Gospel for Rome. Though we can't be certain, these realities point toward a Greco-Roman audience for Mark's Gospel. Therefore, while I was especially attuned to the Old Testament in Matthew (and this method should still be followed for Mark), more resonances with Greek and Roman culture are apparent.

Not only is Mark the most Roman of all the Gospels, but it is also the briefest. As Mark Allan Powell has noted, if we were to put together a greatest hits compendium of Jesus's teaching and deeds, much of what we would list is not found in Mark. No Sermon on the Mount, parable of the good Samaritan or prodigal son, Lord's Prayer, or even the golden rule.[4]

UNIQUE CONTENT IN MARK

- Parable of the seed growing secretly (4:26–29)
- Healing of the deaf and dumb man (7:31–37)
- Healing of the blind man of Bethsaida (8:22–26)
- Flight of the young naked man in the garden (14:51–52)

This does not mean Mark's storytelling suffers. Mark's style is full of color and fast-paced action. His account is gritty and unrelenting. His narrative surges with urgency, repeatedly using the word *immediately* and the historical present to give readers a vivid and realistic view of the action. One gets a sense Jesus is not merely a figure of the past but a person who still addresses us today. Mark has Jesus running around, breathlessly healing those around him. While his style is colloquial and common, Mark is also a master storyteller. Sometimes the stories end in predictable ways; other times they are full of suspense and surprise. Mark writes as an observer who watches

---

[4] Powell, *Introducing the New Testament*, 125 (see chap. 1, n. 3).

things from the outside but wants his readers so close to his stories that they can smell the characters.

> ## MARK'S HISTORICAL PRESENT
>
> Mark, more than any other Gospel writer, employs the historical present (Mark, 151 times; Matthew, 93 times; Luke, 11 times). The historical present is a present-tense verb used to describe a past action, which gives the narrative a vivid and realistic feel.

Mark's message displays Jesus as the powerful and victorious Messiah, yet also as the rejected and suffering Servant. Mark gives no lofty or philosophical view of Jesus as in John, or a high-minded teacher as in Matthew, or as the savior of the poor and oppressed in Luke. Cosmic conflict takes center stage as the demons submit to Jesus. Jesus is an exorcist and wonder worker in Mark. Around 27 percent of Mark deals with miracles. But Jesus is also very human in Mark's Gospel, and Mark's descriptions often match and even exceed the other Evangelists' descriptions of Jesus's humanity: he gets hungry (11:12) and tired (6:31); does not know everything (13:32); and exhibits pity (1:41), anger (3:5), sadness (3:5), wonder (6:6), compassion, (6:34), indignation (10:14), and anguish (14:34).

Mark also centers on the cross. A greater percentage of Mark's Gospel, compared to the other Synoptic Gospels, is devoted to Jesus's passion.[5] The plot to kill Jesus is mentioned quite early (3:6), and much of Mark's story is filled with dread and foreboding. For Mark, Jesus did not primarily come to exorcise, heal, or teach, but to die for the sins of his people (10:45). While Matthew emphasizes the fulfillment of Scriptures in Jesus's passion, Luke displays his innocence, and John manifests his glory, Mark indicates Jesus dies all alone. The disciples abandon Jesus, and even the Father has forsaken him. Many view Mark 10:45 as a central and thematic verse when Jesus says, "For even the Son of Man did not come to be served, but to serve, and to give his life as a ransom for many." Jesus is the Son of God and Messiah who conquers through suffering, and if anyone is to follow him, they must deny themselves and take up their cross.

---

[5] If we include the narratives about Jesus's resurrection and passion, 34 percent of Matthew is devoted to it (21–28), 37 percent of Mark (11–16), 24 percent of Luke (19–24), and 37 percent of John (12–20). This is based on words (not the chapters) in the NA28 Greek text (including the textual variants) according to the Accordance search.

Interpretive Overview

The Gospel of Mark is episodic. He writes in more of a TikTok video style than the tight bunching of material like Matthew. Mark interweaves, repeats, and reiterates his themes. The first half introduces a theme, such as Jesus's works of power, and then interweaves other themes while continually looping back to Jesus's powerful deeds. This makes it harder to determine Mark's structure. However, Mark seems to be structured thematically or perhaps even theologically while following a general geographical and chronological pattern.

ANCIENT CONNECTIONS 2.2. MARK'S GOSPEL OUTLINE AND PETER'S PREACHING

If Mark is Peter's interpreter, it is interesting to note that Mark follows Peter's outline for Jesus's life found in Acts 10:34–43. Peter speaks of God sending good news to Israel beginning in Galilee through Jesus, how Jesus was anointed with power, and how Jesus was killed on the cross in Jerusalem. This matches Mark's thematic and basic geographical outline.

Mark is framed around two questions: Who is Jesus? (1–8:21), and How will he become king? (8:22–16:8). In the first section Jesus exorcises, heals, teaches, and forms a new community. He displays his sovereign power as Israel's king. But this also causes conflict. The kingdom of God has arrived, but many are not ready. In the second section Jesus unexpectedly conquers by donning the crown of thorns. This is the way of suffering. The disciples still misunderstand that Jesus's power and suffering are paired, like the two halves of Mark. To become king, Jesus must bear the cross.

The Way of Authority (1:1–8:21)

Unlike Matthew and Luke, Mark does not include Jesus's birth narrative, genealogy, the wise men, and the shepherds. He begins with John the Baptist and the identity of Jesus. Then Jesus goes around Galilee performing miracles, gathering a community, and teaching. This constantly raises the question from those watching, "Who is this figure?"

The first section sets up the narrative by designating Jesus as the Messiah (1:1–13). John the Baptist prepares the way for Jesus, and Jesus is baptized and tempted. Next Jesus displays his power as he announces and enacts the kingdom of God (1:14–3:6).

Jesus then forms his new family (3:7–6:6), and the mission of Jesus expands to various towns and people groups (6:7–8:21). Jesus's authority is on full display as he spreads the kingdom of God.

PREPARATION (1:1–13)

Mark immediately thrusts readers into three wilderness events in rapid succession that reveal Jesus's mission and identity: John the Baptist is identified as Jesus's forerunner (1:2–8), Jesus is baptized (1:9–11), and Jesus has cosmic conflict with Satan (1:12–13). All these events display the identity of Jesus: he is the Christ, the Son of God.

John the Baptist is introduced through the words of Isa 40:3: a messenger will prepare the way for the Lord to bring his people out of exile. This messenger is tasked with purifying Israel. To return to Yahweh, Israel must go through purification waters.

Jesus himself is baptized by John, which recalls Israel passing through the waters at the exodus (Exodus 14). Jesus, like Israel, is declared to be God's Son as the heavens are torn open and a dove descends on him. This work of redemption is not the Son's alone, but each person of the Godhead is involved. The Father planned this liberation, the Son will accomplish it, and the Spirit will empower and apply it. The descent of the dove not only points to the new creation but is a Roman symbol of Jesus's kingship. The flight of the birds was the surest of all omens in Rome. Eagles denoted power and authority and established a candidate's claim to the throne. The descent of the dove was Jesus's royal inauguration, but the dove revealed it was antithetical to Rome's domineering power. The dove is a sign of peace; the eagle, of war. A truly different kingdom had arrived.

THE SON OF GOD IN MARK

In contrast to Matthew, not a single human being openly calls Jesus the "Son of God" until nearly the end of Mark (15:39). The demons seem to be the only ones who see this. Peter's confession in Matthew includes him affirming Jesus is God's Son, but this is absent in Mark (Matt 16:16; Mark 8:29). Additionally, in the baptism Matthew recounts the Father saying, "*This is* my beloved Son" (3:17, italics added), maybe indicating an announcement to the world. In Mark the voice says, "*You are* my beloved Son" (1:11, italics added), signifying a more personal address directed to Jesus. All of this may imply that Mark employs *Son of God* in a more exalted and trinitarian sense.

Jesus is then driven into the wilderness to combat Satan. The event frames the entire Gospel as a cosmic conflict. The heavenly Son will battle the hordes of hell. Jesus is not here to deal with Rome but with Satan and sin. Mark doesn't even recount Jesus's victory because either it is implied or the rest of the Gospel will detail Jesus's victory. Mark also includes a unique line about Jesus being with the wild animals (Mark 1:13). Some see echoes of Eden here (Gen 2:19–20). Others think it gives hope to Roman martyrs who also encounter wild beasts in the coliseums.[6] Both are true. Jesus tames these animals as Isaiah predicted, giving hope and a picture of the new creation (Isa 11:6–9).

Though Mark reveals Jesus's identity in the introduction, these themes will be expanded as the Gospel continues. Each major section of Mark has a revelation story that confirms Jesus's identity and vocation, especially as the Son of God.

Table 2.1: Revelatory Scenes in Mark

Baptism (1:9–11)	Transfiguration (9:1–13)	Crucifixion (15:21–41)
Heavens "torn" (Greek, *schizo*) Dove descends	Garments turn white Cloud descends	Sanctuary veil "torn" (Greek, *schizo*) Darkness spreads
"Voice" from heaven	"Voice" from cloud	Jesus's "loud voice"
"You are my beloved Son."	"This is my beloved Son."	"Truly this man was the Son of God!"
John the Baptist as Elijah (cf. 1:6)	Jesus appears with Elijah	"He's calling for Elijah."

THE AUTHORITY OF JESUS (1:14–3:6)

Who is Jesus? Mark has already let readers know through his introduction, but now he will press this point home by Jesus's powerful and authoritative actions in Galilee (Mark 1:14, 16–17, 21, 39; 2:5, 13). Jesus acts with the authority of God himself. Mark, more than any other Gospel writer, portrays Jesus as a miracle worker with great power. In the first eight chapters of Mark, 47 percent of the verses concern Jesus's miracles.

---

[6] Ignatius (Romans 4–5) repeats the same word ("wild beasts") six times with reference to his martyrdom by wild beasts in Rome. James R. Edwards, *The Gospel according to Mark*, The Pillar New Testament Commentary (Grand Rapids: Eerdmans, 2002), 41–42.

As Jesus's ministry begins, he gives a summary of his gospel: the kingdom of God is at hand—repent and believe (1:14–15). Jesus's message generates a new community. Interspersed through the narratives are community or calling texts (1:16–20; 2:13–27; 3:13–19, 31–35; 6:7–13). Jesus calls the brothers Peter and Andrew, and James and John. Peter will lead the church, James will be killed by a future Herod (Acts 12:2), and John is the disciple Jesus loved (John 21:7). Three of these disciples will form the inner ring. The call of the disciples takes place by the sea. Jesus's followers are called out of the chaotic waters to build a new Eden on dry land. Like Israel, God's new community is formed by the water.

After Jesus summarizes his message and calls his disciples, he enters Capernaum, where he teaches and drives out an unclean spirit (Mark 1:21–28), followed by healings in the same region (1:29–34). A man with an unclean spirit in the synagogue cries out to Jesus. An unclean spirit in the synagogue indicates that Jewish religion had been corrupted and needed cleansing. The forces of darkness know a great power has arrived on the earth, and they call Jesus "the Holy One of God" (1:24). The demonic forces recognize Jesus's identity as God himself. Jesus rebukes the spirit and casts him out. Jesus thus fulfills the role of a priest in protecting holy places from anything impure and foreshadows Jesus's purification of the temple (11:15–17). Everyone is amazed at Jesus's authority; the news begins to spread. Jesus continues to show his power when he goes into a house, where he raises up Peter's sick mother-in-law (1:29–31). This is a resurrection scene. Jesus came to bring life to those under the power of the evil one.

ANCIENT CONNECTIONS 2.3. THE HOLY ONE OF GOD

The language "Holy One of God" hails from Isaiah, where Yahweh is called "the Holy One of Israel" (or of Jacob) (1:4; 5:19, 24; 10:17, 20; 12:6; 17:7; 29:19, 23; 30:11–15; 31:1; 37:23; 40:25; 41:14–16; 41:20; 43:3, 14–15; 47:4; 48:17; 49:7; 54:5; 55:5; 60:9, 14), but actually may originate from Leviticus, where Yahweh says, "Be holy because I, the LORD your God, am holy" (19:2). The demons associate Jesus with Yahweh.

Jesus then goes to a deserted place and prays (1:35–38). He needs rest and time with his Father before his ministry continues. In a similar way, Elijah goes into the wilderness for guidance (1 Kgs 19:9–18). Mark includes another healing story, this time concerning a man with leprosy. Jesus is angry (some translations say Jesus has compassion) that suffering has spread so far; he willingly heals the man. Jesus touches an unclean man, showing that impurity does not cling to him but that purity goes out from him. This is proof of both his prophetic and priestly office (2 Kgs 5:7–8; Num 12:9–16). Jesus is not against the Jewish rituals—he tells the leper to show himself to the priest—Jesus is against the deadly powers associated with impurity.

ANCIENT CONNECTIONS 2.4. JESUS AND PURITY LAWS

In the Old Testament, moral impurity was inherently sinful, while ritual impurity was not. To be profane meant something was not to be used for ritually holy things, which is distinct from being impure. The three major sources of ritual impurity were genital discharges of blood or semen, leprosy, and corpses (Leviticus 12–15; Numbers 19). In Mark, Jesus touches the ritually impure: he touches a leper (1:40–45) and a girl's corpse (5:41), and he is touched by a woman with a flow of blood (5:25–34). Jesus also does not guard against defilement by eating with tax collectors, and not all his disciples perform ritual washing. He also does things that break Sabbath law, according to his opponents. Was Jesus unconcerned with ritual purity? Though Jesus's opponents thought so, Mark seems to communicate that Jesus opposed the sources of impurity that were signs of death, not the rituals themselves. Leprosy was a signal of death on the skin, an abnormal menstrual discharge indicated a dead womb, and a corpse had no life in it. Jesus redefined purity around himself. He is pure because the Spirit dwells within him.[7]

Jesus's popularity grows because of his miracles, but so does the conflict. Five controversy stories develop the tension that Jesus's continued authority instigates (Mark 2:1–3:6). Five questions occur in this section, and all the stories begin or end with a healing—a sign of the coming kingdom.[8]

---

[7] See Matthew Thiessen, *Jesus and the Forces of Death: The Gospels' Portrayal of Ritual Impurity within First-Century Judaism* (Grand Rapids: Baker Academic, 2021).

[8] Anthony Le Peau, *Mark through Old Testament Eyes: A Background and Application Commentary* (Grand Rapids: Kregel, 2017), 60–61.

Table 2.2: Five Questions in the Controversy Stories

Passage	Questioner	Question	Issue
2:1–12	Teachers of the law	"Who can forgive sins but God alone?"	Forgiveness
2:13–17	Teachers of the law	"Why does he eat with tax collectors and sinners?"	Eating
2:18–22	People	"Why do your disciples not fast?"	Eating and fasting
2:23–28	Pharisees	"Why are they picking grain on the Sabbath?"	The Sabbath
3:1–6	Jesus	"Which is lawful on the Sabbath: to do good or to do evil, to save a life or to kill?"	The Sabbath

In the first controversy story, after Jesus has healed a paralytic man and forgiven his sins, the teachers of the law ask, "Who can forgive sins but God alone?" (2:1–2). Jesus has asserted the paralytic man is forgiven of his sins, so the scribes are incensed. Jesus asks them which is easier to do: forgive sins or heal. He tells the man to get up and walk. This story indicates Jesus came to deal with more than their bodies; he came to make them right before God. The healings are a picture of the wholeness Jesus brings.

If the first controversy story was about the forgiveness of sins, the next four concern Jewish traditions: table fellowship and the Sabbath. Jesus calls Levi and then eats with sinners and tax collectors (2:13–17). Levi, also known as Matthew, is a tax collector who took money from the Jewish people and gave it to their Roman lords. Many tax collectors took more than their share. But when Jesus saw Matthew at his tax booth, Jesus said, "Follow me" (1:14). Matthew immediately obeys. Jesus goes to Levi's house and eats with tax collectors and sinners. The scribes and the Pharisees are shocked Jesus would do such a thing. The Pharisees prioritized purity, and eating with sinners was defilement.

The third story also concerns eating, but this time it is about Jesus's disciples, not fasting (2:18–22). Jesus answers with assertions about wedding guests and a groom, old garments and new garments, new and old wine. In all of these he shows the new age has arrived in himself. His miracles have already proved this. His disciples won't fast when their Savior is with them because fasting is a sign of mourning (1 Sam 31:13; Neh 1:4; Est 4:3). They will fast when he is gone. Jesus uses a salvation historical argument to indicate that his arrival shifts how they are to practice these traditions.

The final two controversy stories concern the Sabbath. The Pharisees question Jesus about why he does unlawful things on the Sabbath, for his disciples are picking heads of grain and eating them (Mark 2:23–28). Jesus replies with a story from the Scriptures introduced with "Have you never read . . . ?" or a similar phrase (2:25; 12:10, 26). He tells the story of David entering the temple and eating the Bread of the Presence (1 Sam 21:1–6). Jesus's point is that another priest-king is here; he is greater than the Sabbath. If Jesus is the true temple, he is also the true Sabbath rest. Jesus fulfills the Sabbath, and David's actions pointed to a greater reality than the Sabbath.

In the final controversy narrative, after healing a man with a withered hand on the Sabbath, Jesus asks whether it is lawful to do good or to do evil, to save life or kill it, on the Sabbath (Mark 3:1–6). The question foreshadows Jesus's own death at the hands of the religious leaders, because they will soon do evil to him by killing him (9:31; 10:34; 12:7; 14:1). At this point the Pharisees begin to plot with the Herodians about how they might kill Jesus (3:6).

THE FAMILY OF JESUS (3:7–6:6)

Mark has been answering the question, Who is Jesus? This next section especially focuses on Jesus's new community, his new covenant family. This expansion is indicated in 3:7 as Jesus withdraws to the lake and a large crowd follows him, attracted by his authority.

The previous section began with Jesus calling four of his disciples (1:16–20), and now Jesus appoints the twelve (3:13–19). They will be his "sent ones." Jesus commands his disciples to bless the nations as God told Abraham, and Moses instructed Israel, long before. Jesus recognizes that the kingdom task is too expansive for him, so he enlists their service in ministry.

While many people want to get to Jesus, this popularity also causes some to hate him. Climactically, the scribes claim Jesus is in league with dark powers (3:20–29). Irony fills the scene, for these are the very powers Jesus came to defeat. Jesus responds by pointing out that joining Satan's side is irrational based on his actions. Why would the prince of darkness drive out his own horde? Jesus has come and bound Satan (the strong man), and now he plunders his house (3:27; Isa 49:24–26). Jesus is growing his family by defeating Satan. Jesus's mission is to conquer Satan's household, not unite with him. Jesus warns them that if they claim he drives out demons by the power of Satan, they commit the eternal sin of denying that Jesus comes from God and attributing his work to Satan rather than the Spirit. It is blasphemy to attribute Jesus's authority to the wrong source. The division between those who accept and reject Jesus has been written in the sand.

In the face of opposition, Jesus defines his true family (Mark 3:31–35). Though people assume Jesus's family is blood-based, he claims his family is united by doing God's will. From a narrative viewpoint, Jesus's comments on his family might also be an indictment upon the Jewish leaders. Ethnic ties do not define his family; faith and doing God's will does. This text also gives evidence for the diverse nature of Jesus's followers: brothers, sisters, and mothers are all welcome. Men and women, young and old, are all called to follow Jesus. No one gets a VIP pass into his family. Loyalty to the King is all that is required.

The largest block of teaching in the early chapters of Mark occurs in Mark 4. Jesus defines his new family by explaining why some reject him. This chapter explains why some will be insiders and other outsiders. The mystery of the kingdom will only be given to his disciples. Jesus begins with the parable that explains how all parables work: the parable of the sower. Jesus's word is like seed that falls on different types of soil. Some respond to the word, but many don't. This does not mean the kingdom is stagnant; it is only not what they expected. He then quotes from Isa 6:9–10, explaining why he speaks in parables. Mark, more than any other Gospel writer, emphasizes that Jesus tells parables *so that* they may not understand. The concealing function of Jesus's teaching receives prominence because Jesus wants to define his own ministry and community. Jesus separates insiders from outsiders. These parables contain profound judgment. However, Jesus also affirms he came to reveal, not to conceal (Mark 4:22). Lamps are meant to shine. Parables also reveal. Much of hearing depends on those willing to listen carefully (4:24–25). Jesus continues with more parables on the kingdom, saying it will grow slowly and its presence is mysterious.

After Jesus teaches in parables, he continues his cleansing mission by conquering both the sea and land, providing a safe place for his new community. First, he calms the storm at the sea (4:35–41). The sea was a place of chaos and death and represents the hostile forces that marshal themselves against Jesus (Ps 74:13–14; Ezek 32:2; Dan 7:2). The terms *be still* and *obey* occur in exorcism stories (Mark 1:25; 4:39), implying Jesus exorcises the demons from creation. Second, Jesus shows his power over the land by casting out a legion of demons (5:1–20).

The supernatural power of Jesus and the nature of his community continues to be displayed as a synagogue ruler comes and begs for the life of his daughter (5:21–43). As Jesus is on his way to heal her, a woman with a lifelong illness touches his garment and is healed. According to Lev 15:25–28, the woman would have been perpetually unclean, but Jesus makes her clean. Then people from the ruler's house come and state his daughter has died; Jesus no longer is needed. This girl would have been unclean since she was now a dead corpse (Num 19:11). Nevertheless, Jesus comes and raises her from the dead. Jesus welcomes all, especially those who recognize death is all around them.

Mark 6 recounts the mounting hostility toward Jesus, again pointing to the insider/outsider theme. When Jesus comes to Nazareth, he goes into the synagogue and begins to teach (6:1–6). This is his hometown, but the response is unexpected; the people take offense at him. Jesus does not perform a miracle here as he did in Capernaum (1:23–26; 6:5).[9] Those closest to Jesus cannot see who he truly is. Jesus's family is not necessarily his blood relationships or even those from his own hometown. It is those who do his will.

This section of Mark (3:7–6:6) continues to emphasize Jesus's power and authority, thus proving his identity, but it also focuses on Jesus's new community. The insider/outsider theme takes center stage of this section, which concerns Jesus's teaching on parables. Those who are against Jesus claim he is in league with Satan. However, for those with eyes to see, Jesus rescues people from Satan's abusive power to a new reality called the kingdom of God.

THE EXPANDING MISSION OF JESUS (6:7–8:21)

Now that Jesus has displayed his authority and established his family, his mission begins to expand. This is immediately indicated as Jesus calls the Twelve to him and gives them authority to enlarge his kingdom (6:7–13). However, paired with the expanding mission is continued opposition. The fate of John the Baptist is narrated, displaying the cost of following Jesus (6:7–13, 14–21, 30–31).

As the mission expands, Jesus continues to clarify who he is. When the disciples are on their way to Bethsaida on the sea, Jesus comes to them, walking on the water (6:45–52). Mark includes this odd phrase; that he "wanted to pass by them" (6:48). They think it is a ghost, but Jesus says, "It is I" (*ego eimi*), perhaps paralleling Exod 3:14. Jesus identifies himself with Yahweh. Job 9:8 speaks of Yahweh as the one who "alone stretches out the heavens and treads on the waves of the sea." Then Job says, "He does great and unsearchable things, wonders without number. *If he passed by me*, I wouldn't see him; if he went by, I wouldn't recognize him" (Job 9:10–11, italics

---

[9] Gladd, *Handbook on the Gospels*, 141 (see chap. 1, n. 13).

added).[10] This is also the same language used when God *passes by* Moses and Elijah (Exod 33:19, 22; 1 Kgs 19:11).

Jesus is now in Gennesaret. Though a Gentile focus does not officially begin here, the narrative about defilement prepares readers for the expanding mission of Jesus (Mark 7:1–23). Some Pharisees and scribes come from Jerusalem and witness the disciples eating food with unwashed hands. This makes the disciples ritually impure according to their oral tradition. Jesus cites Isa 29:13, saying these leaders honor God with their outward actions but not with their hearts. He tells his disciples that the teachers are hypocrites (Mark 7:6–8), prop up their traditions rather than God's command (7:9–13), and misunderstand what actually defiles people (7:14–23). It is not the outside that defiles a person, but rather that which comes out of them. Readers have already seen corruption on the earth from demonic powers, and now we see another source of defilement: the human heart. The Jewish leaders are condemned for impurity in their hearts. This paves the way for others to enter the kingdom.

The explicit Gentile focus begins in Tyre (7:24–8:21). Jesus tries to escape notice, but a woman whose daughter has an unclean spirit comes and falls at his feet. She is a Syrophoenician woman, a woman from the Roman province of Syria (explicitly identifying her as a Gentile). While Jesus affirms his mission is to Jews, he recognizes her great faith and grants her request. Jesus is like the new Elijah and Elisha who go outside of Israel. Jesus again has compassion on the crowd that follows him, so he now feeds 4,000 Gentiles. This time seven baskets are left over, evidencing the completeness of his feeding. The narrative section closes with another story about food and the corruption of the Pharisees and Herod, linking to the beginning of chapter 7 (8:14–21). Jesus tells them to beware of their teaching, but the disciples are slow to understand what Jesus speaks of. This statement characterizes how Jesus's teaching has been received. Some see the truth, but most are sluggish in comprehending. Jesus reveals his identity, but it takes time for people to truly see him. He points to the twelve baskets and then the seven, asking them, "Don't you understand yet?" (8:21).

This question is also put to readers of Mark. The first eight chapters of Mark thrust us into the active ministry of Jesus. Readers are confronted with the power and authority of Jesus over the demonic forces, nature, and illness. Jesus heals, provides food, calms the sea, and walks on water. He establishes his new family and expands his mission. Mark wants people to ask, "Who is this figure with so much authority?"

---

[10] Hays, *Echoes of Scripture in the Gospels*, 72 (see intro., n. 7).

The Way of Suffering (8:22–16:8)

If the first half of Mark was about Jesus's authority, the second half especially focuses on Jesus's suffering. Mark continues to reveal who Jesus is, but he reframes how the kingdom will come. Jesus's messianic vocation means glory but only through suffering and death. Jesus is the true Servant-King.

The first section centers on Peter's confession as well as Jesus's three predictions of his death, which sets the tone for the rest of the narrative (8:22–10:52). When Jesus arrives in Jerusalem, Mark slows down the narrative to a snail's pace. Jesus first confronts the leaders of Jerusalem by entering the city, declaring the practices in the temple as corrupt, and predicting the downfall of the temple (11–13). Then Jesus is arrested, goes to trial, and is crucified (14–15).

Jerusalem is where Jesus should be crowned king—and he is—but on a Roman cross, not a throne. This is God's victory. Jesus is rejected by his own people, who are not ready to accept the suffering Messiah. What Jesus's opponents mean for evil, God means for good. Jesus's death and resurrection will save his people.

PREDICTIONS OF DEATH TIED TO DISCIPLESHIP

- Three times in 8:22–10:52 Jesus predicts his death (8:31–32; 9:31–32; 10:32–34).
- Three times the disciples respond with pride and misunderstanding (8:32–33; 9:33–34; 10:35–41).
- Three times Jesus teaches about servant leadership (8:34–38; 9:35–37; 10:42–45).

PETER'S CONFESSION AND THE REVELATION OF SUFFERING (8:22–10:52)

The healing of the blind man is transitional (8:22–26). In one sense, it closes off the previous narrative about who Jesus is, but it also evidences how comprehension of Jesus is still blurry. Blindness depicts Israel's inability to see God's revelation (Deut 29:4). Jesus spits on the blind man's eyes. The man can see but only partly; the people look like trees walking. People don't quite understand who Jesus is or how the kingdom will come.

The blinders are taken off in Caesarea Philippi when Peter confesses Jesus is the Messiah. Though readers already know this from Mark's narrative prologue (1:1), now a human character proclaims Jesus is the Messiah. People *in* the narrative are starting to understand who Jesus is. Caesarea Philippi was known for its pagan roots. It was an imperial cultic location and a site of worship for pagan deities. In this pagan powerhouse, Peter claims Jesus as Yahweh's anointed figure who will rescue his people, defeat the forces of darkness, and reign over them as king.

However, Jesus tells them not to spread this news because some might not understand. In fact, he shows them the Son of Man (the reigning one from Daniel 7) must suffer before he is enthroned. Three times in 8:22–10:52 Jesus predicts his death, three times the disciples misunderstand, and three times Jesus teaches about servant leadership. This is the tenor of the second half of Mark: Jesus is the powerful King, but he will also suffer.

Peter rebukes Jesus for saying he must suffer, but Jesus claps back. He castigates Peter for his lack of understanding. Though Peter has confessed Jesus as the Messiah, his attempt to prevent Jesus from going to the cross is satanic. Jesus turns this into a discipleship lesson. Followers of Jesus must also take up their crosses. If they are only following him for power, they have it all wrong. Even though Jesus will suffer, he tells them that some standing there will see the kingdom come in power (9:1).

ANCIENT CONNECTIONS 2.5. THE MESSIANIC SECRET

Jesus tells people not to spread news about him, an act that has been called the "messianic secret." Though scholars like William Wrede have argued that the messianic secret is an ahistorical addition to the narrative by Mark, three compelling reasons might explain why Jesus would have truly commanded silence in this regard. First, the narrative raises the tension around the theme of Jesus's identity. Second, historically, Jesus's identity was likely to be misunderstood, so he hid his identity so that he could define his messianic mission on his own terms. Third, it could also be a way of mimicking the Greco-Roman emperors who received more honor for refusing honor (*recusatio*).

The next scene fulfills Jesus's statement about seeing the kingdom come in power. Though Jesus must first suffer, his destination is glory. Peter, James, and John are taken to a mountain. Mountains are places of revelation and theophanies. God walked with Adam and Eve on the mountain of God (Eden; Ezek 28:12), and Moses met with God on Mount Sinai. Now Jesus is transfigured before them on the mountain. They see Jesus's glory, majesty, and power like Moses and Elijah saw on Mount Sinai. The glory of Jesus indicates both his preexistent glory and his future glory as the Messiah.

Jesus's clothes become dazzling white as someone in the presence of God (Dan 7:9; Matt 28:3; Mark 16:5; John 20:12; Acts 1:10). Elijah and Moses—prophets who had mysterious departures from this world and were rejected by their own people—appear next to him. A voice from heaven declares that Jesus is God's Son to whom the disciples must listen (1:11; Deut 18:15). Jesus is not only the Messiah but the Son of God. While this label can be synonymous with God's ruler, the scene paints a more exalted understanding. He is not only the Messiah but God's own heavenly Son. Again, Jesus commands silence until he has risen from the dead (Mark 9:2–10).

As they come down the mountain, the disciples reveal they are still confused about the timing of the kingdom. They wonder how the appearance of Elijah fits with the timetable. Jesus reminds them Elijah has already come (John the Baptist), and he was killed. The Son of Man will suffer like John. The three disciples then come off the mountain and find the other disciples having trouble with an exorcism (9:11–29). Off the mountain it is clear the kingdom has not come in fullness. When they leave that place, they make their way through Galilee, and Jesus reinforces that the Son of Man must suffer. But they still misunderstand his words. In fact, the disciples argue about who will be the greatest in the kingdom. They still do not comprehend that if they want to be first, they must be last (9:30–37).

Jesus has now entered Judea. Here, nearer to Jerusalem, the antagonism toward Jesus heightens. The Pharisees, wanting to trap Jesus in his words, ask him if it is lawful for a man to divorce his wife. A rich young ruler then asks what he must do to inherit eternal life. Jesus says to follow the commands of the Torah, but he also tells the man he must sell all his possessions (10:1–12, 17–22; Deut 15:11). As they get nearer to Jerusalem, Jesus reminds the disciples for a third time that he will be handed over and suffer at the hands of the religious leaders. But for the third time, the disciples are dense. James and John ask to sit on Jesus's right and left hand when he enters his glory. Jesus rebukes them and claims they do not know what they are asking. They will go through suffering like him. Jesus says the world wields power as tyrants. The disciples authority should be different; their power should be marked by servanthood. Jesus is not only their example but their substitute. He came not "to be served, but to serve, and to give his life as a ransom for many" (10:45; Isa 53:10–12).

This section of Mark ends as it began: the healing of a blind man (10:46–52). A blind beggar sits by the road as Jesus passes by, and the beggar calls out, "I want to see" (10:51). The blind man calls out to Jesus as the Son of David. Earlier Jesus has silenced those who spoke of him in such a way, but now he accepts it. Jesus is the Son of David, the Messiah, the Son of God. He heals the blind man, saying his faith has saved him. Unlike the first healing, this one is immediate. The messianic secret is over. Now Jesus will enter Jerusalem as the Messianic King.

Jesus Confronts Jerusalem (11–13)

Jesus enters the Holy City not on a warhorse but a colt, indicating the type of king he is (11:1-10; Gen 49:10–11; Zech 9:9). When Jesus enters the city, the people spread their clothes and branches on the road, welcoming a new dignitary and singing praise songs. It is an atypical royal entry and sets the stage for the standard images to be turned upside down.

However, while Jesus is humble, he won't tolerate corruption. He confronts Jerusalem's apostasy. This reality is immediately evident when Jesus curses the fig tree. The fig tree symbolizes Israel, but Jesus condemns it for not producing fruit (11:12–14; Isa 5:1–7; Jer 24:5; Hos 9:16; Mic 7:1). Then he enters the temple, and rather than restoring it as the Messiah should, he overturns tables and drives people out. In Mark this verb *drive out* usually refers to exorcisms, implying that the people of the temple have become corrupt. By extension the temple has become a den of robbers where the leaders cheat and steal from the people. Jesus comes as a condemning prophet like Jeremiah (Jer 7:11). The chief priests and scribes now seek a way to kill Jesus, who has critiqued their most prized landmark, and this action propels the antagonism to Jesus to new heights. Mark's message is clear. Before the kingdom can come, a cleansing of Israel must take place (Mark 11:15–19). The Baptizer was sent to purify Israel; now Jesus will complete this act.

The religious leaders want Jesus's body in a bag, so they seek to trap him in his words. They ask him by what authority he does these things. Readers should remember much of Mark concerns Jesus's authority, and now again they ask about the source of Jesus's authority. But Jesus responds with a question of his own, indicating that his authority comes from God, but they will not answer him because they seek the approval of people (11:27–33).

Jesus responds by speaking in parables, a repeat of Mark 3–4, confirming Jesus is the wise Messiah (Isa 11:1–3). He condemns the religious leaders for their failure to follow Jesus in the parable of the master and his vineyard. The prophet Isaiah also speaks about Israel as a vineyard whom God has cultivated but that did not yield fruit (Isa 5:1–7). Jesus employs the same imagery, saying this vineyard (Israel) is well cared for, but when the master of the house (God) sends out servants (prophets) to collect fruit, the hired hands (religious leaders) send him away without anything. He sends another and another, but they kill and beat them. Finally, he sends his son (Jesus), thinking they will listen to him, but they think they will receive the inheritance if they kill him. Therefore, the master of the house kills the farmers and gives the vineyard to others. Jesus closes the parable by quoting Psalm 118, saying the rejected stone has become the cornerstone. Jesus has covered all of Israel's history, condemned the leaders, and predicted his fate in this short parable (12:1–12).

The religious leaders know this parable is about them, so they seek to arrest Jesus. They again try to trap him in his words by asking a politically charged question, a theological question, and a question about the law. Jesus escapes all their traps. He affirms the role of secular governments but subordinates them under God's rule. He asserts there will be no marriage in the resurrection and summarizes all the law in two commands. Jesus's opponents are silenced by his wisdom.

Jesus responds to these tests by pointing to Ps 110:1 and asking his own question: If the Messiah is David's son, how can he call him Lord? The leaders are confounded because Jesus is both David's Lord (as the Son of God) and his son (from the line of David). The identity of Jesus is the primary issue they do not understand or accept. For this they will be condemned (Mark 12:13–40).

Chapter 13 is part of this condemnation as Jesus predicts the end of the temple. It is called "The Olivet Discourse" because Jesus and his disciples sit on the Mount of Olives and look out over the temple (13:3). As Jesus is leaving the temple, a disciple remarks on its beauty. Jesus responds by predicting not one stone will be left on another. The disciples ask two questions: (1) When will these things happen? and (2) What will be the sign when these things are about to be accomplished? Jesus answers both of their questions. He predicts the end of the temple period and correlates it with the end of the ages. The two events are similar. The destruction of the temple is part of the last days but not *the* last day.

First, Jesus speaks about the destruction of the temple. He says there will be wars, earthquakes, and famines. God's people will be delivered over to courts and witness for Jesus before them. The Holy Spirit will give them the words to speak, and the gospel will go to all nations. There will also be division in families over this message. This all sounds very much like what happens in Acts. Then Jesus speaks about the "abomination of desolation" (13:14). At that point they should not try to stay and fight for the temple. They should flee. Those on the housetop should run. Those in the field must not go back for their coats. God's judgment has come upon the corrupt temple, and they must not try to protect it.

ANCIENT CONNECTIONS 2.6. THE
ABOMINATION OF DESOLATION

The phrase "abomination of desolation" comes from Dan 9:24–27 and refers to Antiochus Epiphanes, who built a pagan altar in the temple in 167 BCE. This action became programmatic for a foreign ruler who conquers and defiles Israel's temple. Titus will also come with the Romans, walk into the temple, and then destroy it (70 CE). The abomination of Titus is likely what Jesus refers to in Mark.

In 13:24, Mark makes a slight but not complete transition. He speaks of the days after the tribulation, which still speak of the destruction of the temple but also look forward to the end of time. For the Jews, the destruction of the temple was the end of an era, so Jesus correlates these two events. After the days of trouble, other things will happen. Apocalyptic signs will occur: the sun will be darkened; the moon will not give light; the stars will fall. Debate still exists as to how literal this language is. In the Prophets, this was cosmic dissolution imagery (Isa 13:10; 34:4). It describes the destruction of a city or a temple, but it foreshadows something greater as well.

At this point, Jesus says they will see the Son of Man coming in the clouds with power and glory, and he will gather his elect from the four ends of the earth (Mark 13:26–27). Debate exists concerning what this refers to. It could be about the ascension. In Daniel, the Son of Man appearing before the Ancient of Days is an upward movement toward the heavens. Additionally, gathering his elect could refer to Pentecost. However, this entire text has been about the destruction of the temple, which took place forty years after the ascension. Jesus could be correlating the events, seeing the destruction of the temple as a climactic confirmation of what had happened. However, it is better to see this as the Son of Man returning on the clouds of heaven to earth in the Second Coming. If he goes up to receive authority, he must come back down to establish that authority on the earth. The angels in Acts 1:11 affirm Jesus will return in the same way he leaves. The Scriptures correlate Jesus's ascension and return, so a sharp division is not necessary, but the emphasis in this context seems to fall on his return. On the last day Jesus will send out his angels to gather his elect (Isa 43:6; Rev 14:18).

Jesus closes the discourse by telling his hearers to read the signs of the times. He even says, "This generation will certainly not pass away until all these things take place" (Mark 13:30). This might refer to the temple's destruction, but the reference to "this generation" could be qualitative rather than temporal. The Old Testament and the Gospels speak of "this generation" in reference to a rebellious group across time. There will be rebels to Jesus until the end of time. Jesus says no one knows the hour of "that day" except the Father (13:32). Jesus speaks of his limited knowledge in his human nature, not his divine nature. Jesus's imperative is that his followers need to be ready. They must not fall asleep. They must be alert. If they are found sleeping, they won't be among those gathered.

THE SUFFERING OF JESUS (14–15)

The darkness deepens. Betrayal, desertion, rejection, and death fill the story. It begins two days before the Passover, imagery that paints Jesus's death as an act of redemption but only through death. The first scene is in Bethany, where a woman anoints Jesus for his burial. In contrast, Judas Iscariot goes to the chief priests and agrees to betray Jesus. He sells out his Savior for silver while the woman lavishly anoints Jesus (14:1–11). Mark returns to the Passover imagery as the disciples prepare to celebrate the festival meal. Mark explicitly names the "sacrifice [of] the Passover lamb" (14:12).

At the meal, Jesus is with the Twelve (14:17–26). This is appropriate because a new covenant ceremony is about to take place. The new Israel is being formed. Jesus takes the bread and breaks it, saying it is his body. Then he takes the cup and gives thanks and has them drink it. As Moses sprinkled blood on the people in the old covenant, now Jesus has them ingest his own blood symbolized by the wine. The Passover lamb is Jesus. This is a shocking scene because Jews don't eat anything with blood in it. Jesus affirms he will not drink from the fruit of the vine until the realization of the kingdom of God. The meal not only points backward, it points forward to the coming messianic banquet.

The darkness swells as Jesus and the disciples go out to the Mount of Olives, and Jesus quotes from Zech 13:7, identifying himself as the rejected shepherd. When he is struck, the sheep will scatter. In Mark, Jesus's last days are characterized by abandonment. Jesus remains faithful while his disciples are faithless. Peter speaks up, saying he will never abandon Jesus, but Jesus predicts Peter will deny him three times. At Gethsemane, Jesus asks Peter, James, and John to stay awake while he prays. He prays that he might not have to endure the cross but that he will submit to the Father's will. Jesus faces a test and a tree; he follows God's plan, unlike Adam. When he returns, he finds Peter sleeping. The disciples are not only physically tired; they are spiritually slothful (Mark 13:27–42).

Judas arrives with a mob to capture Jesus. He betrays him with a kiss, as a friend would greet him. Those closest to Jesus forsake him. The guards take hold of Jesus and arrest him. One of the disciples draws his sword and cuts off the ear of the high priest's servant. Some still think the kingdom will come by violence and force. But Jesus has already told them it will come by suffering and death. Then they all desert Jesus and run from him (14:43–50); the sheep scatter. Jesus is led away for trial. The religious leaders look for a reason to put Jesus to death, but they can't find any. Jesus is innocent. Therefore, they bring false witnesses, but even their testimonies don't agree. The Torah explicitly says not to spread a false report or give false witness (Exod 23:1), and David lamented the false witnesses who rose around him (Ps 27:12). The high priest questions Jesus and asks if he has a reply, but Jesus remains silent, fulfilling Isa 53:7: "He was oppressed and afflicted yet he did not open his mouth."

Again, the high priest asks Jesus if he is the Messiah, the son of the blessed one. Now Jesus answers with a simple, "I am." Though this is the normal way to say, "I am he," Jewish readers might think of Exod 3:14, where Yahweh tells Moses that his name is "I AM WHO I AM." Jesus is more than the Messiah. He says they will see the vision from Dan 7:13–14—the Son of Man riding on the clouds. Jesus's enthronement begins at the cross, continues with his resurrection, and will climax at his ascension. When the high priest hears Jesus's words concerning the Son of Man, he tears his clothes and charges Jesus with blasphemy. Jesus has claimed something no human figure could assert: the authority of God himself. They begin to mock and mistreat Jesus as a counterfeit king. All have abandoned Jesus: Judas, his disciples, and his own people (Mark 14:53–65).

Jesus has been tried and found guilty before the Jewish leaders, but they can't put him to death. Rome is in charge. Pontius Pilate, the Roman governor, asks Jesus if he is the king of the Jews. Pilate is concerned about rebellion during a festival week and is shocked Jesus won't answer. A tradition during the festival was to release one prisoner, so Pilate asks the crowd if they want Jesus or Barabbas released. Barabbas is a rebel, likely some form of a Zealot who sought to overthrow Rome by violence. Barabbas is put next to Jesus as a foil character. Jesus doesn't seek to unseat Rome like Barabbas; he desires her heart. The chief priests stir up the crowd and call for Barabbas to be released. Pilate knows Jesus has done nothing wrong, but he bows to the will of the people. He hands Jesus over to be crucified (15:1–15).

The next scene recounts Jesus's crucifixion (15:16–39). Jesus's road to the cross is his death parade. Yet it was also Jesus's Roman triumph.[11] If we look through the lens of a Roman triumph, we see with new eyes Jesus on the road to the cross. Jesus is led by the soldier inside the palace, the *praetorium* (15:16). The praetorium is the Roman military headquarters and a word that described the emperor's bodyguard who would have been present at a Roman triumph. At the praetorium a whole battalion of Roman soldiers gathers. The battalion would have been a military unit numbering 600 soldiers. This is Jesus's escort. These soldiers also adorn the victor with a purple garment and a crown of thorns but in jest. They then mock Jesus as the King of the Jews and strike him with a reed (a fake scepter), spit on him (rather than kiss his feet), and kneel. When they lead Jesus out, they compel Simon of Cyrene to carry his cross. This mirrors the Roman official who carried a double-bladed ax over his shoulder, ready to slay the bull. Paradoxically, Jesus is both the triumphator and the bull.

ANCIENT CONNECTIONS 2.7. A ROMAN TRIUMPH

A Roman triumph was a parade that functioned to honor and celebrate a victorious Roman general or emperor for military success. In Rome, these military heroes were called *triumphators*. The triumphator would dress in kingly garb (sometimes purple), have a laurel placed on his head, and hold a branch in his right hand. As he passed, people would kiss his feet. A bull, designated for sacrifice, was in the procession. Next to the bull walked a Roman official who carried a double-bladed ax over his shoulders. The animal trudged next to the weapon that would end its life. Upon entering the city, they were escorted to the Roman Forum. The triumphator would give an order to take his captives to prison and execution. Then he would ride up to the Capitol. Here he performed rites and made offerings. He would be offered wine, but it was customary to refuse. Then, the bull was sacrificed. At the end of the ceremony, the triumphator was often elevated above the ground. Sometimes he was elevated alone, but many examples exist where he was flanked by two people on the right and left. When evening came, he would be escorted home, accompanied by flutes and pipes.[12]

---

[11] Adam Winn, *Reading Mark's Christology Under Caesar: Jesus the Messiah and Roman Imperial Ideology* (Downers Grove, IL: IVP Academic, 2018), 81–85.

[12] See Mary Beard, *The Roman Triumph* (Cambridge, MA: The Belknap Press of Harvard University Press, 2007).

Jesus is led to Golgotha, the place of the skull (15:22). It is far from coincidence that Roman triumphs would end at the Capitolium, a word derived from the Latin for "head" (*caput*). They offer Jesus wine, but he refuses (15:23). Then they perform their ritual sacrifice. They elevate the triumphator through crucifixion, lifting him up between two robbers. Above him is a sign that reads, "The King of the Jews" (15:24–27). Those who pass by him do not praise him. Instead, they deride him, saying he cannot even save himself (15:29–32). Darkness covers the whole land. Jesus utters a loud cry and breathes his last. While the other Gospels have multiple sayings from the cross, Mark only has one: "My God, my God, why have you abandoned me?" (15:34). This finalizes Jesus's abandonment. Even the Father has forsaken Jesus.

A centurion, who would have been familiar with the proceedings of a Roman triumph, recognizes what has happened. The one who pledged loyalty to Caesar looks on Jesus's battered, bloody, and dead body and declares, "Truly this man was the Son of God" (15:39). The cry of this centurion confirms Jesus's identity is revealed through his suffering. The Son of Man gave his life as a ransom for many, even for those who have crucified him.

THE VICTORY OF JESUS (16)

The Servant-King has now suffered and died. It would be a tragedy if the story were over. But death does not have the last word. Unlike the other Gospels, Mark's resurrection account is filled with mystery and fear. The same women who witnessed the crucifixion bring spices to anoint Jesus's body. On the first day of the week at sunrise they go and visit. A new creation is about to burst forth. When the women arrive, they find the stone has been rolled away. An angel declares Jesus has risen, but they do not see Jesus. They flee, trembling and astonished; they are afraid (16:1–8). This strange ending invites readers into Mark's story to imagine how they would react. Mark seems to be asking, "How will you respond to this powerful yet suffering resurrected king?"

The next verses either have brackets around them or are in italics in most Bibles because they are not a part of our earliest manuscripts (16:9–20), but the King James Version includes them. Later scribes viewed Mark's sudden ending as worthy of additional material. They recount how Jesus appeared to many. Jesus gives them a commission to drive out demons, speak in tongues, and pick up snakes and not be hurt by poison. Jesus then ascends into heaven, and his followers go out preaching and doing many miracles. Most of the material aligns with what we have in the other Gospels.

MARK 16:9–20

The reason Mark 16:9–20 is included in most English Bibles is because the evidence for these verses includes 1,600 Greek manuscripts, though most early translations of Mark do not have it. Irenaeus quotes from Mark 16:19 as Scripture in *Against Heresies* (3.10.6). However, most do not think it is original. Two early and important Greek manuscripts do not include these verses: Sinaiticus (01) and Vaticanus (BO3), both from the fourth century. In addition, Mark does not use many of the words in this section elsewhere in his Gospel, the style is different from the rest of Mark, the transition from verse 8 to 9 is awkward in Greek, and another shorter ending is given in some manuscripts. For all these reasons, the longer ending of Mark does not seem original but is still included because so many manuscripts contain it.

However, the earliest manuscripts of the Gospel do not include vv. 9–20. In modern times they have not been held to be canonical or from the hand of Mark, but most translations have kept this longer ending in our Bibles. The verses are undeniably early and have been considered part of the Scripture throughout most of church history. This means the words have been part of the transmission of the text but not its inspiration.

Old Testament Connections

Every Gospel is filled with allusions to the Hebrew Bible. Though Mark does not quote from the Old Testament as much as Matthew, it would be misguided to think Israel's story was not the backbone of his story. Mark's deft and allusive use of Scripture fits his enigmatic writing, but readers must work a little harder to see how Mark employs the Jewish story.[13] Because Mark is less direct, he re-narrates the story of Israel in a subtler way than Matthew. Though there are many ways to examine Mark's use of the Old Testament, I will look at one theme Mark highlights: the new exodus. While this theme appears in the other Gospels, it is also uniquely important to Mark and runs through his entire work.

---

[13] Hays employs this language to describe Mark's use of Scripture. Hays, *Echoes of Scripture in the Gospels*, 15.

THE OLD TESTAMENT IN MARK

Though Mark is not as explicit as Matthew with his use of the Old Testament, Mark also points to the connections between the ministry of Jesus and the Old Testament. Following are the more explicit Old Testament references in Mark.

- 1:2–3 (Isa 40:3; Mal 3:1)
- 1:11/9:7 (Ps 2:7)
- 4:12 (Isa 6:9–10)
- 7:6–7 (Isa 29:13)
- 9:11 (Mal 4:5)
- 9:12 (unspecified)
- 12:10–11 (Ps 118:26)
- 13:26; 14:62 (Dan 7:13)
- 14:21 (unspecified)
- 14:27 (Zech 13:7)
- 14:49 (the Scriptures)
- 14:62 (Ps 110:1)
- 15:23–36 (Psalm 22)
- 15:34 (Ps 22:1)

The New Exodus in the Prologue

Mark's Gospel should be viewed under the banner of Isaiah's promised new exodus (Isaiah 40–55). Isaiah promised a new exodus was on the horizon. This was partially fulfilled in Israel's return from exile in Babylon but not fully achieved. Rikki Watts has argued Mark portrays Jesus as the servant leader of a new liberation.[14] Mark's prologue supports this new exodus theme.

Mark's first three verses set up his entire story and Jesus's vocation as enacting a new exodus release. Mark draws together three texts from the Old Testament—Exodus, Malachi, and Isaiah—to explain John's role as a forerunner to Jesus: "As it is written in Isaiah the prophet: 'See, I am sending my messenger ahead of you; he will prepare your way. A voice of one crying out in the wilderness: Prepare the way for the Lord; make his paths straight!'" (Mark 1:2–3).

---

[14] The following three sections on the new exodus are dependent on Rikki Watts, *Isaiah's New Exodus in Mark*, Biblical Studies Library (Grand Rapids: Baker Academic, 2012).

Mark says the quotation comes from Isaiah, but a conglomeration of texts stands behind this passage. Verse 2 draws from Exod 23:20 and Mal 3:1, which speak of a messenger preparing the way for the Lord.

Table 2.3: The Old Testament in Mark 1:2–3

Exodus 23:20	A messenger will prepare the way for Israel to enter the land (if they listen).
Malachi 3:1	A messenger will purify Israel so the Lord can return and dwell with them.
Isaiah 40:3	A messenger commands Israel to prepare the way of the Lord.

In Exodus 23 the Lord reminds Moses of Israel's covenant obligations. Verse 20 focuses on the presence of an "angel," or as more accurately translated from the Greek, a "messenger" with Israel. Israel will be sent a messenger who will (1) protect them on the way and (2) bring them into their land. God's people are to listen to him, for Yahweh's name is in him (23:21), but if they do not listen, they will be punished.

Malachi 3:1 builds on the themes found in Exod 23:20. Israel is disappointed even after returning from exile because things are not as they expected. Malachi argues it is not Yahweh who has been unfaithful; Israel has been adulterous. Malachi 3 tells of a time when a messenger will be sent. He will clear the way for the Lord by purifying Israel. Some will be punished. The emphasis falls on judgment, but God cleanses his community to dwell with them.

Mark takes the past reference (Exodus 23) and the future reference (Mal 3:1) and puts both under the banner of the return from exile promised in Isa 40:3. In Isaiah 40 God tells Israel a voice will cry out in the wilderness and prepare the way for the Lord. By combining all these Old Testament texts in a prologue, Mark indicates that John is the prophesied messenger who prepares the way for God's rescue. Jesus, the new exodus servant, will bring salvation and judgment. Some will be cleansed willingly; others will refuse purification.

"IMMEDIATELY" IN MARK

Mark uses the term *immediately* (Gk., *euthys*) more than any other Gospel writer to give his story a sense of urgency. However, perhaps he uses it to indicate John and Jesus are doing their jobs well, because a form of *euthys* occurs in 1:3 as "straight." Mark seems to be telling his readers that Jesus does things "straightly." He leads them on the straight highway (Isa 40:3), thus further pointing to new exodus themes.

This new exodus theme continues as John baptizes people in the wilderness at the Jordan River (Mark 1:4–5). As the prophets said, the arrival of the new exodus would mean God's people would need to be cleansed. This is the new water-crossing and cleansing moment Israel had been waiting for. Jesus is then baptized by John, identifying with his message (1:9–11). The heavens are torn open, fulfilling the hope that God would come again as he did at Sinai (Ps 144:5; Isa 64:1, 3). The rending of the heavens and the descent of the Spirit fulfill the hopes of Yahweh's long-awaited arrival (Isa 63:7–64:12). God visits his people in the person of Jesus Christ. Jesus is called God's Son, whom he loves. Isaiah 42:1 says, "This is my servant; I strengthen him, this is my chosen one; I delight in him. I have put my Spirit on him; he will bring justice to the nations."

After Jesus's baptism he is tempted for forty days in the wilderness like Israel in the wilderness. But unlike Israel, Jesus conquers Satan. He provides a way in the wilderness. They will not be bitten by the snake (Num 21:9). Mark includes a line about the wild animals being with Jesus, which fulfills Isaiah's promise that wild beasts will live peacefully alongside humans in the new creation (Isa 11:6–9). Jesus turns the wilderness into a garden.

In the final moment of the prologue Jesus announces the good news of the kingdom of God. Mark's use of "gospel" (1:1, 14) is best understood in terms of the Isaianic announcement of comfort (Isa 40:9; 41:27; 52:7: 60:6; 61:1).[15] Isaiah speaks of a messenger publicizing the good news of the arrival of God (40:9), speaking of God's reign (52:7), and proclaiming good news to the poor (61:1). Jesus says this kingdom has "come near" (*eggizō*; Mark 1:15). *Eggizo* occurs in Isaiah and is primarily linked to the promise of the nearness of God's righteousness and, therefore, the inbreaking of God's reign (Isa 46:3; 51:5; 56:1).

The prologue sets the stage for the new exodus theme in the rest of Mark's Gospel. Every scene is set in the wilderness, and each one indicates Jesus is God's servant who has come to liberate his people.

---

[15] Watts, *Isaiah's New Exodus in Mark*, 119.

The New Exodus in Mark's Structure

Mark's new exodus theme is also evident in his structure. The first section paints Jesus as the new Liberator and Shepherd who brings his people out of slavery, the middle section reveals the way to the cross, and in the final section Jesus redeems and cleanses his people by his blood like the Passover lamb in the exodus. The entire new exodus structure of Mark can be viewed this way.[16]

Table 2.4: The New Exodus in Mark's Structure

The New Exodus in Mark	The Exodus in the Old Testament
The Liberator arrives (1:1–8:21)	Moses arrives to liberate Israel (Exodus 1–15)
The way to the cross (8:22–10:52)	The journey to the Promised Land (Exodus 16–40; Numbers; Deuteronomy)
Conquest in Jerusalem (11:1–16:8)	The conquest of Zion (Joshua)

Jesus acts as a powerful liberator in Mark's first section. He is Yahweh's warrior and healer. As the warrior Jesus fulfills the hopes of Isa 40:10–11: "See, the Lord GOD comes with strength [*ischyos*], and his power [*kyrieias*] establishes his rule. His wages are with him, and his reward accompanies him. He protects his flock like a shepherd; he gathers the lambs in his arms and carries them in the fold of his garment. He gently leads those that are nursing."

As seen in the summary, the first part of Mark especially focuses on Jesus as a wonder worker. For example, Jesus enters Capernaum and drives out an unclean spirit (1:21–28), who calls him the "Holy One of God" (1:24; Isa 41:14, 16, 20). In a key text Jesus says he entered "a strong man's" (*tou ischyrou*) house, tied him up, and now plunders his goods (3:27; Isa 49:24–26). In Mark 5 Jesus casts out a demon whose name is Legion. Like Pharaoh and his army, the demons are drowned in the sea. Jesus has come with strength. He not only liberates the land, but he conquers the sea. He quells the chaotic storm and even later walks on the sea. In the Bible the sea symbolizes hostility toward God's people but also the source of their redemption out of Egypt (Ps 74:13–14; Ezek 32:2; Dan 7:2).

Jesus is not only a warrior but God's healer and shepherd. Jesus heals the broken-hearted (Mark 1:29–34; 2:1–12), cleanses the leper (1:40–45), and declares himself

---

[16] Le Peau, *Mark through Old Testament Eyes*, 18.

God's true rest (2:23–28; Isa 63:4). In Mark 2, when a group of friends lowers the paralytic into the presence of Jesus, he declares that man's sins are forgiven. Isaiah ties in the theme of forgiveness with making a way in the wilderness.

> Look, I am about to do something new; even now it is coming. Do you not see it? Indeed, I will make a way in the wilderness, rivers in the desert. . . . I am the one, I sweep away your transgressions for my own sake and remember your sins no more. (Isa 43:19, 25)

> And none there will say, "I am sick." The people who dwell there will be forgiven their iniquity. (33:24)

Jesus also feeds his people in the wilderness and heals the mute, lame, and blind. The feeding of the 5,000 takes place at a deserted place where they find rest (Mark 6:31). Isaiah 32:16 is the only place in the entire Old Testament where these words—*deserted place* and *rest*—occur. Isaiah predicts the Spirit will descend on the cursed ground and bring the new creation. Isaiah asserts, "The LORD's justice will *rest* in the *deserted place*" (32:16, author's translation). The verses before this in the Isaiah scroll speak of the desert becoming an orchard and the orchard becoming a forest (32:15).

In Mark 7:31–37 Jesus goes to the Decapolis and heals a deaf and mute man. He uses a term for the deaf man—*mogilalon*—which only occurs at one other place in the Greek Old Testament. Isaiah 35:5–6 speaks of the reversal of curses at the new exodus: "Then the eyes of the blind will be opened, and the ears of the deaf unstopped. Then the lame will leap like a deer, and the tongue of the mute [*glossa mogilalon*] will sing for joy, for water will gush in the wilderness, and streams in the desert."

The middle section of Mark focuses on the way (*hodos*) Jesus travels to the cross (8:22–10:52). A reference to the *hodos* occurs seven times in this section (8:27; 9:33, 34; 10:17, 32, 46, 52) and only seven times in Mark outside this section. It harkens back to the prologue when Mark spoke of Isaiah's "*hodos* of the Lord." The way becomes programmatic for understanding Jesus's mission in Mark.

Along this way Jesus reveals he is the suffering Messianic King. He is the predicted Suffering Servant (10:45; Isa 52:14–53:12). Jesus must die (8:31–32; 9:31–32; 10:32–34). Three times the disciples respond with pride, showing they are blind (8:32–33; 9:33–34; 10:35–41). Isaiah predicts God will lead his blind people as Jesus does in this section of Mark: "I will lead the *blind* by a *way* they did not know; I will guide them on *paths* they have not known. I will turn darkness to light in front of them and rough places into level ground. This is what I will do for them, and I will not abandon them" (Isa 42:16, italics added).

Jesus is Isaiah's Suffering Servant who leads blind Israel. The middle of Mark appropriately begins and ends with the healing of blind men (8:22–26; 10:46–52). The phrase "on the way" occurs in both healing narratives (8:27; 10:52 ESV), and Isaiah promised the eyes of the blind would be opened (Isa 35:5; 42:7).

In the final part of Mark, Jesus warns and judges Israel in the language of Isaiah. When Jesus enters Jerusalem, he goes into the temple and drives out those buying and selling (11:15–19). God is concerned with restoring his house (Isa 60:7). Jesus quotes both Jeremiah and Isaiah, saying the temple will be a house of prayer for all nations and they have made it a den of robbers (11:17; Isa 56:7; Jer 7:11). Isaiah 56 speaks of how the temple will become a rallying point for the nations. Instead, the temple had become a stumbling block to the nations. Jesus must literally clear the way so the nations can come into the temple.

Jesus then appropriately tells the parable of the vineyard owner, which illustrates how a vineyard can be rented to farmers but the tenants can try to take it over from the master (12:1–12). The owner sends servants and finally his son to try to recover it, but they kill both the servants and the son. The Old Testament background is Isaiah 5, where God also plants a vineyard (5:1), the vineyard fails to produce a harvest (5:2), and God removes the vineyard (5:5–6). The Jewish leaders think the inheritance is theirs, but Jesus must remove them from the vineyard. Only a fruitful field will return from exile. In Mark 13 Jesus pronounces final judgment on Israel's temple. He associates its downfall with warfare and cosmic disturbance (Isa 13:10; 34:4). As the Passover begins, so begin Jesus's final hours. The next section will examine Jesus as the new exodus Lamb.

Overall, Mark's structure communicates that Jesus is the one to bring about the new exodus. He acts as Yahweh's liberator in the first half. He casts out demons, calms the storm, and comes to Israel as their Shepherd and Healer. In the middle section, Jesus reveals he is Isaiah's Suffering Servant who will bring redemption. In the final section Jesus warns Israel in Isaiah's dialect. However, Jesus's final act is not to warn but to give his life to accomplish the mission of the Suffering Servant.

The New Exodus in Jesus's Death

Mark's Gospel ends with the accomplishment of the new exodus in Jesus's death. The three passion predictions Jesus provides contain a note of divine necessity (8:31; 9:31; 10:33–34). The first prediction makes it the most explicit with the phrase "it was necessary" (8:31), but the others follow this same sense: Jesus *will* be betrayed, he *will* die, and he *will* rise. According to Mark, Jesus's death is not an accident; it is part of a providential plan. No single Old Testament verse reveals why Jesus must suffer and die, but several texts construct the new exodus picture behind Mark's presentation.

The cross is necessary because Jesus must fulfill the Passover lamb imagery. The miracles in Egypt were not enough; a sacrifice needed to be made. While in Egypt, Israel was commanded to take an unblemished sheep or goat and slaughter the animal. They were then to take the blood and put it on the doorposts of their houses so that the Lord would "pass over" them when he came to execute judgment on Egypt (Exodus 12). In the same way, Jesus will redeem his people by covering them with his blood. His blood is the new Passover, the means by which they are liberated.

Isaiah picks up this image and applies them to the Suffering Servant who will sprinkle the nations with blood (Isa 52:15), bear the sickness of God's people (53:4), and be slain for Israel's sins (53:5). This servant is led like a lamb to the slaughter, and his blood cleanses God's people, thus making a new covenant.

Mark employs this Isaianic image to elucidate Jesus's death. Regarding timing, Jesus's death occurs in and around the Passover festival, painting him as the Passover lamb (Mark 14:1–16). The images in Mark's crucifixion scene also correlate him with the Suffering Servant. Before Pilate, Jesus is silent (15:5; Isa 53:7). A substitution scene occurs (Mark 15:6–15; Isa 53:4–6, 11). Jesus is beaten (Mark 15:15; Isa 52:14), mocked (Mark 15:17–20, 29–32; Isa 53:3), and exalted (Mark 15:24; Isa 52:13); counted among the rebels (Mark 15:27; Isa 53:12); crushed by his Father (Mark 15:34; Isa 53:10); and buried (Mark 15:46; Isa 53:9).

Additionally, the two explicit texts that interpret Jesus's death do so in the mold of the Suffering Servant and Passover lamb. In Mark 14:24, at the supper, Jesus points forward to his death when he says, "This is the blood of the covenant, which is poured out for many." The first half alludes to Exod 24:8, which recounts Moses taking blood and splattering it on the people, saying, "This is the blood of the covenant." In both Exodus and Mark, a journey was followed by a blood-of-the-covenant meal at the mountain of God. The second phrase from Mark 14:24, "which is poured out for many," describes both *how* the new covenant is ratified and on *whose* behalf. Isaiah 53:12 asserts the servant "willingly submitted to death" and "bore the sin of many." Jesus pours out his life on behalf of his people.

The second text that interprets Jesus's death is Mark 10:45, which also indicates that Jesus is the Suffering Servant who opens a new exodus way: "For even the Son of Man did not come to be served, but to serve, and to give his life as a ransom for many." Though it does not quote Isaiah verbatim, many conceptual links exist. Both texts refer to the many who will benefit from this servant's death. Both speak of either a ransom or redemption (Isa 51:11; 52:3; 62:12). Two of Jesus's passion predictions include the phrase Jesus will be "handed over" as the Suffering Servant is handed over (10:33; Isa 53:6, 12). Jesus also references those who will mock him and spit on him (Mark 10:34; Isa 50:6).

In summary, the timing of Jesus's death (Passover), the picture of the passion (silence, substitution, mocking, counted among the rebels, buried), and the explicit explanations of Jesus's death (10:45; 14:24) all describe Jesus as the Suffering Servant and Passover Lamb of the new exodus.

Gospel Connections

While harmony between the Gospels exists in their presentation of the gospel, each Gospel has its unique emphases. As the most Roman Gospel, Mark portrays the gospel as a political victory in contrast to Roman ideology. However, Mark is even more interested in presenting the gospel as a supernatural victory over the forces of darkness. This can only come about because, according to Mark, Jesus pays the penalty and is the substitute for people's sins. For Mark, the gospel is multifaceted. It is a political announcement, but the main enemy is not Rome; rather, it is sin, death, and the spiritual forces. Jesus defeats their reign of death by death.

The Gospel as Political Victory

What is the gospel? The answer is debated more than might be expected. Some emphasize the personal side of this good news, while others look to the cosmic story of the Scriptures. Some run to Paul's short descriptions of the gospel and neglect the Gospels' presentation of the gospel. Mark clearly has a vested interest in helping us see the complexity, depth, and beauty of the gospel Jesus announces.

While the Old Testament background to the term *gospel* is key, the wider Greco-Roman culture also serves as helpful context for understanding the term. In the larger culture, the gospel was a media term for the announcement of victory or kingship. For example, the news of a ruler's birth, the coming of age, enthronement, speeches, decrees, and acts are all put under the banner of "good news."[17] A calendar inscription from 9 BCE in Priene (the ancient city of Ionia) speaks of the birth of the emperor

---

[17] Moisés Silva, ed., *New International Dictionary of New Testament Theology and Exegesis*, 2nd ed. (Grand Rapids: Zondervan, 2014), 2:307.

Augustus, who "made war to cease and . . . put everything in peaceful order; and whereas . . . the birthday of our God [Augustus] signaled the beginning of Good News for the world because of him."

One inscription states that the day when a son of Augustus takes on the toga is "good news for the city."[18] A papyrus letter from an Egyptian official in the third century CE uses the term in connection with the accession of Emperor Julius Verus Maximus. And an inscription at Amphiareion of Oropos from around 1 CE mentions the "good news of Rome's victory."

Plutarch speaks of how the Spartans would give a reward to the man who brought good news of victory.[19] He notes General Quintus Sertorius spoke of military victory in terms of good news.[20] The Roman general Pompey was given the news of the death of his adversary under the umbrella of good news.[21] The Jewish writers Josephus and Philo, who were conversant with the Greco-Roman tradition, wrote of the good news in terms of imperial power. Philo speaks of Gaius Caligula's accession to the throne as "good news."[22] Likewise, Josephus reports Vespasian's accession to the throne saying, "Every city celebrated the *good news* and offered sacrifices on his behalf."[23]

As one can see, the cultural understanding of "gospel" was fully political. When Mark writes of Jesus's gospel, readers would think of a political announcement of victory. In declaring a gospel Jesus announces his sovereignty and the eventual demise of every earthly kingdom. His message is an implicit challenge to Caesar; Jesus is claiming the highest throne.

However, the political nature of the gospel can easily be misunderstood, for Jesus did not see Rome or Caesar as his primary enemy. Jesus's political message brings him before a Roman governor (Mark 15:1–15). Pilate asks him, "Are you the king of the Jews?" It's a political question. This charge of being king of the Jews was a hot topic. Therefore, when Jesus, in response to Pilate's question, says, "You say so," the tension is thick (15:2). Jesus essentially says Pilate uses the right words but wrong associations. He cannot understand the nature of Jesus's kingship. Pilate thinks Jesus is innocent, and he claims Jesus has done nothing wrong.

---

[18] S. R. Llewelyn, *New Documents Illustrating Early Christianity* (Grand Rapids: Eerdmans, 1978), 3:12.

[19] Plutarch, *Moralia* 347D.

[20] Plutarch, *Sertorius* 11.4.

[21] Plutarch, *Pompeius* 66.3.

[22] Philo, *Ad Gaium* 231.

[23] Josephus, *Jewish War* 4.618.

This is not because Jesus's message was not political, but because Jesus was not after Pilate's or Caesar's throne. Jesus's kingdom has a different nature. His good news victory is obtained through sacrifice and submission, not by sword and spear. Therefore, when Jesus answers Pilate by asserting, "You say so," he is not sidestepping politics; he asserts a different kind of politic. His kingdom does not follow earthly rules. Its character is otherworldly.

After the rulers of this age crucify Jesus, a centurion looks up to Jesus and declares he is the Son of God. This was a title given to Caesar Augustus. The centurion recognizes a new ruler has been enthroned. His loyalty has now shifted to a new ruler.

In one sense, Jesus poses no threat against the empire. In another sense, his death is the final stroke against all empires standing against God. According to Mark, the gospel is fully political, but the means of accomplishing it and its nature are unique.

The Gospel as Supernatural Victory

When we think of the gospel we typically think of our relationship with God. This is not wrong, but it is incomplete. Mark shows us there are other players on the pitch. As we saw in the previous section, some of these other players are the rulers of the world. But if you look through Mark carefully, the rulers of the world do not explicitly come into Mark's sights often. Rome does not seem to loom large in Mark's imagination.

The same cannot be said of the dark supernatural forces. They are consistently on Mark's mind. The dark forces seek to quell the announcement of this victory, but Jesus indicates he came with a message of victory precisely over these powers. The gospel, according to Mark, demonstrates the preeminence of the Lord Jesus as he drives out all other gods and their minions.

For Mark, the gospel not only counters Rome's imperial ideology but, more importantly, conquers the forces of darkness. While Mark glances toward Rome, he stares at the forces of darkness, indicating the gospel concerns supernatural victory. Mark, unlike the other Gospels, has a unique focus on Jesus's miracles. Almost one-third of Mark's Gospel is taken up by miracles: twenty miracle stories or summaries of miracles stories occur. It is not as if the miracles are appendages to Jesus's teaching; they are part and parcel of his announcement of the gospel. Mark magnifies Jesus's miracles because they reveal the identity and vocation of this man from Nazareth.

After Jesus announces the gospel of the kingdom and calls his disciples, his first public appearance is an exorcism (1:21–28). Jesus drives out an unclean spirit in Capernaum. This action is not subsidiary to the gospel but at its core. After another healing, Mark says the whole town of Capernaum gathers, and he drives out many demons (1:34). When Jesus sends out his twelve apostles, he gives them authority to drive out demons (3:14).

Later, the scribes claim Jesus is in league with Satan, but Jesus refutes their logic (3:20–30). He says his kingdom is opposed to Satan's. Jesus explains his ministry in terms of entering the strong man's house (earth), plundering his possessions (people), and tying up the strong man (defeating Satan). For Mark, the kingdom of Satan is at odds with the kingdom of Jesus. That is why the first half of his gospel concentrates on Jesus as an exorcist and miracle worker.

The longest story in the first half of Mark's Gospel concerns Jesus's encounter with the demons who call themselves Legion (5:1–20). They recognize Jesus as the Son of the Most High God, indicating they agree with Mark's assessment of Jesus (1:1). Jesus's gospel mission is to clear the land of corruption, and he enacts this victory by telling them to "come out" of the man who lives in the tombs (5:8). These demons are placed in pigs and thrown into the sea, symbolizing their demise.

Not only do the dark forces appear in explicit texts, but in the time of Jesus people thought demons were the cause of illness. For example, in Mark 9, a boy who would fall on the ground and foam at the mouth (maybe a form of epilepsy) is brought to Jesus. Mark explicitly says a "spirit" was in the boy who made him do this from a young age (9:20). Those in the first century saw malevolent forces behind most physical sufferings, while modern people tend to relegate explanations to biological factors. The Scriptures combine them. The same reality is at play when Jesus calms the storm, walks on water, and even feeds the people.

Reading Mark reminds readers the gospel has a supernatural element. When Jesus is nailed to the cross, Satan is defeated. Paul says when Jesus is nailed to the cross, he "disarmed the rulers and authorities and disgraced them publicly; he triumphed over them" (Col 2:15). At the cross, the devil is defeated, and his horde is scattered. Jesus is victorious over the powers of this world.

The Gospel as Substitution

We have seen how the gospel has various forces aligned against it: Rome and the dark forces. However, to only speak of these would present an incomplete picture. For Mark, the gospel is good news because Jesus came to forgive people's sins. Sin and death are the enemies of the gospel. Jesus forgives people's sins by becoming their substitute. Victory over the enemy powers is the goal, but substitution is the means.

At the beginning of Mark, John the Baptist is introduced as one who baptizes for the forgiveness of sins. People come out confessing their sins (1:4–5). In chapter 2 Jesus looks at a paralytic and says, "Son, your sins are forgiven" (2:5). But the religious leaders balk, saying, "Who can forgive sins but God alone?" (2:7). Not only does this raise the question of the identity of Jesus but also the question of how God will forgive sins. In Mark 2:17 Jesus then affirms he has come to call not the righteous but the sinners. Yet good Bible readers know sinners must become righteous, so it raises the question about how sin will be nullified.

This sin discourse guides readers toward the cross, where Jesus strikes the decisive blow to sin. Though Mark doesn't spend a lot of time on the mechanics of the cross, both Mark 10:45 and 14:24 give a peek into Mark's theology of atonement.

> For even the Son of Man did not come to be served, but to serve, and to give his life as a ransom *for many*. (10:45, emphasis added)

> He said to them, "This is my blood of the covenant, which is poured out *for many*." (14:24, emphasis added)

Both Mark 10:45 and 14:24 end with the important phrase "for many." These words encompass a world of theology. The word *for* signifies Jesus does this on behalf of others, in their stead, or in exchange for them. Jesus takes the place of sinners as a substitutionary offering. The sacrificial system shows how this works. An animal is slain as a substitute for the people. Its blood, the life blood, covers Israel's sins, so they are acceptable to God. This is why Jesus speaks of his blood of the covenant in 14:24. His blood cleanses and covers them so that they can commune with God. In Mark the good news must start with the bad news. Both Israel and the nations are under the power of sin. Jesus comes to release them from sin. He does so by becoming their sacrificial substitute. Without substitution, there is no gospel at all.

The second word is also important: *many* (*pollōn*). Jesus is the substitute for all who accept him. Jesus dies not for one but for many. He can do so because, like Adam, he stands as a covenantal head. A leader of a nation may stand in and speak for the nation as a whole. In the same way, Jesus dies in the place of many because he is chosen by God to stand in for all who seek him. Mark 14:24 links the inauguration of the covenant with substitution.

For Mark, the theology of the cross must include substitution. Jesus takes the place of sinners on the cross. The Barabbas scene right before the cross illustrates this (15:6–15). Pilate offers the people one prisoner who may go free. The people have their pick between Jesus and Barabbas. They condemn Jesus, and Barabbas goes free. He suffers instead of, or in the place of, Barabbas. This story illustrates that rebels go free; the innocent one is condemned. The beating heart of the gospel is substitution.

Life Connections

The purpose of Mark's Gospel is to show us Jesus is the Messiah, the Son of God. And one of the primary goals of Mark's presentation of Jesus's identity is to encourage faith—or trust—in Jesus. To be a disciple of Jesus is not only to be a learner under an apprentice, but to submit to Jesus. This means trusting him with every part of our lives.

We need this trust because Mark reiterates again and again that following Jesus won't be easy. There will be more times than not when we think that following Jesus seems backward, that there must be a better way. The call of the disciples shows we must be ready to leave everything to follow Jesus. The disciples leave their profession; they lay down all to walk with Jesus (1:16–20). The rich young ruler decides it is not worth it (10:17–31). He does not trust Jesus. The question for us is whether we too are willing to lay aside all for his sake. This might be your reputation, your friends, your family, or your wealth.

This trust in Jesus is also necessary because the path of Jesus will be filled with suffering and self-denial. Jesus continually tells his disciples that they too must take up their cross and follow him. They too must make themselves servants of all. This might mean that people hate them, think they are not in step with society, or have hateful beliefs, but they are to continue to love those who might hate them. There might come a time where people might also hate you because you are a follower of Jesus. However, Jesus said it would be this way. If they hated him, they will also hate those who follow him.

Ultimately, this trust centers on the cross. We are to have faith because we cannot save ourselves. The tendency is to think we can do enough works so that God might save us, but Mark shows us the opposition is too strong for us. The world, the flesh, and the devil stand against us. Only one as strong as Jesus could conquer them. What looks like weakness in Jesus is actually strength. What looks like death is actually the path to life. Jesus's plan is better than ours, and we must follow him in all things, no matter how hard it might seem.

Mark's Gospel poses the following question to all readers: Whom will you believe? The world promises power, peace, and wealth. Jesus says his way is different. He also promises life to us, but it will come through suffering. Will we trust him? Will we follow him? Or will we run in fear?

Interactive Questions

2.1. What makes Mark unique compared to the rest of the Gospels?

2.2. How does Mark's style differ from Matthew's?

2.3. How does Mark characterize Jesus in his Gospel?

2.4. What are some main Old Testament echoes readers find in Mark?

2.5. How does Mark portray Rome?

2.6. How do the supernatural forces function in Mark?

2.7. How does Jesus interact with Jewish purity laws in Mark?

2.8. What is Mark's theology of the cross?

2.9. How does Mark portray the disciples?

Recommended Resources

Modern Commentaries

Edwards, James R. *The Gospel according to Mark.* The Pillar New Testament Commentary. Grand Rapids: Eerdmans, 2001.

France, R. T. *The Gospel of Mark.* The New International Greek Testament Commentary. Grand Rapids: Eerdmans, 2014.

Garland, David E. *Mark.* The NIV Application Commentary. Grand Rapids: Zondervan Academic, 1996.

Gombis, Timothy G. *Mark.* The Story of God Bible Commentary. Grand Rapids: Zondervan Academic, 2021.

Hooker, Morna D. *The Gospel according to Saint Mark.* Black's New Testament Commentary. Peabody, MA: Hendrickson, 2009.

Le Peau, Andrew T. *Mark through Old Testament Eyes: A Background and Application Commentary.* Grand Rapids: Kregel Academic, 2017.

Spencer, F. Scott. *Reading Mark: A Literary and Theological Commentary.* Macon, GA: Smyth & Helwys, 2023.

Stein, Robert H. *Mark.* Baker Exegetical Commentary on the New Testament. Grand Rapids: Baker Academic, 2008.

Strauss, Mark L. *Mark.* Zondervan Exegetical Commentary on the New Testament. Grand Rapids: Zondervan Academic, 2014.

Early Commentaries

Ambrosiaster, *Questions and Answers on the Gospel of Mark*, Patristic Bible Commentary, accessed April 19, 2023, https://sites.google.com/site/aquinasstudybible/home/genesis/ambrosiaster-questions-and-answers-on-genesis.

Gregory the Great. *Forty Gospel Homilies.* Translated by David Hurst. Collegeville, MN: Liturgical Press, 1990.

Saint Augustine. *St. Augustine: Sermon on the Mount; Harmony of the Gospels; Homilies on the Gospels.* A Select Library of the Nicene and Post-Nicene Fathers of the Christian Church. Vol. 6. Edited by Philip Schaff. Grand Rapids: Eerdmans, 1956.

Special Studies

Blackwell, Ben C., John K. Goodrich, and Jason Maston, eds. *Reading Mark in Context: Jesus and Second Temple Judaism.* Grand Rapids: Zondervan Academic, 2018.

Bolt, Peter G. *Jesus' Defeat of Death: Persuading Mark's Early Readers.* Society for New Testament Studies Monograph Series. Book 125. Cambridge: Cambridge University Press, 2008.

Bond, Helen K. *The First Biography of Jesus: Genre and Meaning in Mark's Gospel.* Grand Rapids: Eerdmans, 2020.

Garland, David E. *A Theology of Mark's Gospel: Good News about Jesus the Messiah, the Son of God.* Biblical Theology of the New Testament. Grand Rapids: Zondervan Academic, 2015.

Henderson, Suzanne Watts. *Christology and Discipleship in the Gospel of Mark.* Society for New Testament Studies Monograph Series. Book 135. Cambridge: Cambridge University Press, 2006.

Malbon, Elizabeth Struthers. *Mark's Jesus: Characterization as Narrative Christology.* Waco, TX: Baylor University Press, 2014.

Moloney, Francis J. *Mark: Storyteller, Interpreter, Evangelist.* Peabody, MA: Hendrickson, 2004.

Rhoads, David, Joanna Dewey, and Donald Michie. *Mark as Story: An Introduction to the Narrative of a Gospel.* 3rd ed. Minneapolis: Fortress, 2012.

Winn, Adam. *Reading Mark's Christology Under Caesar: Jesus the Messiah and Roman Imperial Ideology.* Downers Grove, IL: IVP Academic, 2018.

3

Luke

Outline

1. Introduction (1–4)
   a. Prologue (1:1–4)
   b. Birth stories (1:5–2:52)
   c. Jesus introduced and tested (3:1–4:13)
2. Galilee (4:14–9:50)
   a. Good news for the poor (4:14–44)
   b. Jesus establishes his family (5:1–6:49)
   c. Revelation, parables, and the Twelve (7:1–9:50)
3. Journey (9:51–19:27)
   a. Discipleship 101 (9:51–13:21)
   b. Warnings (13:22–17:10)
   c. Readiness (17:11–19:27)
4. Jerusalem (19:28–24:53)
   a. Jesus confronts Jerusalem (19:28–21:38)
   b. The passion (22:1–23:56)
   c. Exaltation (24:1–53)

LUKE IN THE NEW TESTAMENT

- Luke's name only occurs three times in the New Testament (Col 4:14; 2 Tim 4:11; Phlm 24). In each of these instances, Luke is placed with Paul in prison.
- Colossians 4:14 affirms Luke was a physician, and his interest in traveling was consistent with itinerant doctors at the same. Luke may have traveled with Paul to care for him, but this is not certain.
- Acts indicates Luke was a travel companion of Paul by using the first-person plural reference *we* (16:10–17; 20:5–15; 21:1–18; 27:1–28:16).
- Luke asserts he was not an eyewitness to the events in Jesus's life (Luke 1:1–4).

Author, Date, and Message

The early historical evidence points to Luke, a doctor and a friend of Paul, as the author of the Third Gospel. Papyrus 75 (175–225 CE), the earliest manuscript of the Gospel, has at the end *Euangelion kata Loukan* (Gospel according to Luke). Irenaeus (*Against Heresies* 3.1.1; 3:14.1) identifies Luke as the author of both Luke and Acts.

Internal evidence also supports Luke as the author. In Luke 1:1–4, Luke portrays himself as someone who did not walk with Jesus but who had contact with eyewitnesses of Jesus. Luke also uses the first-person plural pronoun *we* at significant points in Acts, indicating he was a travel companion of Paul. Though Luke names Paul's other travel companions, he never names himself, which is curious because we know from other sources in the New Testament that Luke traveled with Paul.

Luke may have been a Gentile God-fearer, and Col 4:14 seems to put him among the uncircumcised of Paul's companions. If he was a Gentile, Luke and Acts are likely the only books of the Bible written by a Gentile. However, others argue he was a Diaspora Jewish Christian who was a part of the Hellenist (Greek) mission. Luke's references to Israel, the emphasis on fulfillment, the positive portrayal of the Torah, and the depiction of Paul as a missionary to Jews first may indicate he is a hellenized Jewish Christian. The evidence ultimately is inconclusive but leans toward Luke being a Gentile.

ANCIENT CONNECTIONS 3.1.
GOD-FEARERS AND PROSELYTES

Jews could associate with two types of Gentiles. God-fearers believed in Yahweh but did not tie themselves to Jewish rituals or laws. Proselytes worshipped Yahweh, were circumcised, and bound themselves to keeping the Mosaic law. They could therefore participate in some Jewish rituals.

The date of Luke is closely bound with the dates of Mark and Acts. Most argue Luke used Mark, so Luke would be dated later than Mark. In addition, many think Acts has a sudden ending because Luke had recounted Paul's mission to his present imprisonment in Rome. This would put Luke at least before 60–62 CE. However, the reason for the sudden ending of Acts is not entirely clear. Luke is the most specific of the Synoptic Gospels on the destruction of Jerusalem, which makes some think he wrote after 70 CE. Based on the dating of these other two works, an early date would be the early 60s, while a later date would be roughly 80.

Luke states his purpose in his prologue. He writes an orderly sequence of the things that have been fulfilled among his audience "so that [they] may know the certainty of the things about which [they] have been instructed" (Luke 1:1, 4). The narrative itself, the ordering, provides certainty about the fulfillment of God's promises. But what was this uncertainty, and what was fulfilled?

Some help comes when Luke employs the same language ("know" and "certainty") and the concept (fulfill) in Acts 2:36. At the end of Peter's Pentecost sermon, he tells the crowd, "Let all the house of Israel *know* with *certainty* that God has made this Jesus, whom you crucified, both Lord and Messiah" (italics added). Additionally, the same word for "certainty" resurfaces once more in the judicial context of Acts, where Paul argues that Jesus is the Messiah (21:34; 22:30; 25:26).

Therefore, at the highest level Luke writes an ordered narrative to provide assurance that God has fulfilled his promises to Israel and the nations by sending and installing Jesus as the Savior and Messiah. As the Messiah, Jesus is the one on whom the Spirit rests, and he "judge[s] the poor righteously and execute[s] justice for the oppressed of the land" (Isa 11:4). Jesus stands as a banner for all peoples, and even the nations look to him for guidance (11:10). The Messiah establishes the temple and mountain of God as the center of the world.

LUKE'S USE OF MARK

Luke groups Mark's material into three main sections: Luke 3:1–6:1; 8:4–9:50; and 18:50–24:11. He does not include any material from Mark 6:45–8:26, sometimes called the *great omission*, but we do not ultimately know what Luke had at his disposal and whether this copy of Mark was the same as ours.

Without Luke, we do not have the stories of the shepherds, the baby in the manger, the Magnificat by Mary, Jesus's presentation in the temple, Jesus's announcement of good news to the poor, the emphasis on women who followed Jesus, the focus on the Spirit, or the story of the ascension.

LUKE'S UNIQUE MATERIAL[1]

Dedication (1:1–4)
Birth stories of John and Jesus (1:5–80)
The visit of shepherds (2:1–20)
Presentation in the temple (2:21–38)
Childhood visit to Jerusalem (2:41–52)
John's reply to questions (3:10–14)
Genealogy of Jesus to Adam (3:23–38)
Good news to the poor (4:14–30)
Miraculous catch of fish (5:1–11)
Raising of Nain's widow's son (7:11–17)
Encounter with homeless woman (7:36–50)
Parable of two debtors (7:40–43)
Women disciples (8:1–3)
Rejection by Samaritan village (9:51–56)
Return of the seventy (10:17–20)
Parable of the good Samaritan (10:29–37)
Mary and Martha (10:38–42)
Parable of friend at midnight (11:5–8)
Parable of the rich fool (12:13–21)
Parable of severe and light beatings (12:47–48)

---

[1] Adapted from Powell, *Introducing the New Testament*, 151 (see chap. 1, no. 3).

Parable of the barren fig tree (13:1–9)

Healing of the crippled woman (13:10–17)

Healing of a man with dropsy (14:1–6)

Two parables for guests and hosts (14:7–14)

Counting the cost (14:28–33)

Parable of the lost coin (15:8–10)

Parable of the prodigal son (15:11–32)

Parable of the dishonest manager (16:1–12)

Parable of the rich man and Lazarus (16:19–31)

Cleansing of the ten lepers (17:11–19)

Parable of the widow and judge (18:1–8)

Parable of the Pharisee and the tax collector (18:9–14)

Story of Zacchaeus (19:1–10)

Jesus weeps over Jerusalem (19:41–44)

Reason for Peter's denial (22:31–32)

Two swords (22:35–38)

Jesus before Herod (23:6–12)

Pilate declares Jesus's innocence (23:13–16)

Sayings associated with Jesus's death (23:28–31, 34, 43, 46)

Emmaus road (24:13–35)

Jesus appears to disciples (24:36–49)

Jesus's ascension (24:50–53)

Interpretive Overview

Luke's message is good news for the poor. Jesus is presented in Luke as the Savior of the world: this includes Israel, women, the socially underprivileged, and the ethnically marginalized. Luke has a particular interest in the upside-down nature of the kingdom. Jesus announces Jubilee release for the poor and oppressed and continually reaches out to the "lessers" in society. Unlike Mark, who has Jesus rushing about, Luke writes an orderly account in which Jesus moves deliberately toward his goal—the cross. Jesus is declared innocent by Rome, yet he is still crucified. His passion and exaltation install him as the Savior of the world.

The most distinctive aspect of Luke is Jesus's long journey to Jerusalem. In fact, over 35 percent of Luke's Gospel is taken up with this journey (chapters 9–19). Within this section, readers encounter some of Luke's most famous stories: the parable of the prodigal son, the story of Zacchaeus, and the parable of the good Samaritan.

Luke begins in the temple, telling the birth of both John and Jesus and stories of Jesus's childhood (Luke 1–2). Jesus is then baptized and tempted as the Son of God, as was Adam (3–4). Jesus's ministry begins in Galilee, with Jesus proclaiming Jubilee for the oppressed and revealing His identity (4:14–9:50). Luke's largest section concerns Jesus's long and slow journey to Jerusalem (9:51–19:27). Finally, Jesus enters Jerusalem as the sacrificial animal. It is necessary for him to die, rise, and ascend to be the Savior of the world (19:28–24:53).

Introduction (1–4)

Unlike the other Gospels, Luke introduces Jesus through the paired birth stories of John the Baptist and Jesus. Joy fills the prose because God is turning the world upside down through these children. Jesus appears as lowly to exalt the lowly. He is born in Nazareth and shepherds, not magi, first visit Jesus. A series of temple stories fill out the narrative of Jesus's early years, signifying God is fulfilling his promises.

Luke continues pairing Jesus with John when Jesus is baptized by John. Luke positions the Baptist's ministry in the context of a new exodus, but he is the only Gospel writer to include the line "and everyone will see the salvation of God" (3:6). Jesus came not only for Jews but for Gentiles and the poor. Jesus is the Savior of all humanity, so Luke traces Jesus's genealogy back to Adam. This new Adam is tempted in the wilderness to abandon his sacrificial task as the Son of God, but he withstands the onslaughts (4:1–13).

PROLOGUE (1:1–4)

Luke is a chronicler of salvation history. His preface declares his aims and sources. Luke is the only Synoptic Gospel writer to provide a preface to his work, but this was quite common in Hellenistic historical accounts. He explains that many have written about Jesus's life, indicating he knew of other Gospels, but he also wants to add his voice. In the same way, the Holy Spirit adds another human voice to give a needed additional perspective of Jesus. Luke admits he was not an eyewitness to the Jesus events, but he carefully investigated these things. As a companion of Paul, he put events together based on the stories he heard from eyewitnesses. Those in the first century prioritized eyewitness testimony (Acts 4:20; Heb 2:3; 1 Pet 5:1; 2 Pet 1:16; 1 John 1:1).

SOURCE CRITICISM

Luke asserts he knows of other Gospels (many have undertaken to compile a narrative). Source criticism attempts to determine the sources the Gospel authors used. The most widely held view is that Mark wrote first, and Matthew and Luke used Mark and maybe a common sayings source (Q). The existence of Q is questioned by some scholars because no hard evidence of this document exists. Most of Mark is found in either Matthew and Luke, and Matthew and Luke seem to smooth over less-polished Greek in Mark. When Matthew departs from Mark's order, Luke follows Mark, and when Luke departs from Mark's order, Matthew agrees with Mark. John is usually not included in this discussion. However, some argue there is evidence that John knew some of the Synoptics and especially Mark (John 3:24/Mark 1:13–14; 11:2/Mark 14:3–9).

The eyewitnesses handed down these stories. This phrase can mean it was "traditioned" from the apostles. Luke is writing a new and old story. It is new in that no one has put it together like this. It is old in that he is following the tradition he received. Therefore, Luke writes an orderly account of the events that have been fulfilled among them. He does this so his readers might have certainty about the things they have been taught. To no surprise, derivatives of "fulfill" appear no fewer than fifteen times in the first four chapters of Luke, and they continue to occur throughout Luke and Acts. Luke writes for the initiated, for the community of faith. The Gospel of Luke is meant to be a word of assurance and encouragement for God's people.

Birth Stories (1:5–2:52)

Luke begins with two paired conception stories (Luke 1:5–80). Patterned birth stories were important occasions in the Old Testament, signifying God was at work (Gen 16:7–12; 17:1–21; 18:1–15; Judg 13:3–21; 1 Sam 2:1–10). In many of them angels appear (usually to a barren woman), a response is recorded, and sometimes a sign accompanies the announcement. Birth stories also push readers back to the promise of a child from Gen 3:15. Luke's story begins not with the prediction of Jesus's birth but John's (1:5–25). Zechariah is in the temple serving as a priest, and an angel appears to him, telling him his prayer has been heard and Elizabeth will give birth to a child. This child will be a prophet like Elijah and prepare the way for the Lord (1:17; Isa 40:3).

ANCIENT CONNECTIONS 3.2.
PATRONAGE AND RECIPROCITY

Greco-Roman culture operated under a system called *patronage and reciprocity.* "'Patronage' refers to a system in which access to goods, positions, or services is enjoyed by means of personal relationships."[2] A patron would have protection, money, or access and provide these to a client. The client would reciprocate with loyalty, thanks, or allegiance. All the Gospel writers operate in this context, but Luke especially emphasizes God's favor or grace (*charis*; 1:25, 28, 30; 2:40, 52; 6:32–34). God's patronage is not directed toward the elite or worthy in Luke but to those who are poor and sinners but acknowledge their unworthiness.[3]

A matching story occurs but this time with Mary (Luke 1:26–38). Readers should note the similarities and differences between the narratives. Gabriel appears to both. John's parents are from priestly lineage. They are in Jerusalem and even more centrally in the temple. Nothing is said of Mary's background, and she resides in the quiet, no-name town of Nazareth. Zechariah is a priest; Mary is a teenage girl. Zechariah's wife is old and barren; Mary is young and a virgin. Both are asked to believe God's messenger about a child. They both ask questions (1:18, 34), but Mary is portrayed as believing while Zechariah doubts. Elizabeth's child will be a prophet, but Mary's will be the Son of the Most High, the Son of David, and his kingdom will have no end. This language recalls the Lord's promise through Nathan that God will establish David's kingdom and establish his throne forever (2 Sam 7:12–14).

Mary's praise to God for this child is filled with scriptural echoes but especially imitates Hannah's song and therefore paints Jesus as a kingly prophet (1 Sam 2:1–10). She rejoices in her Savior because he has raised the downcast (2:7–8), his mercy is forever (Exod 34:6–7), and with his mighty arm he has scattered the proud and mighty (6:1) and exalted the lowly and hungry (1 Sam 2:7). Zechariah also praises God for his redemption (Exod 3:16), the salvation he has provided through the house of David (2 Sam 7:13–14). He speaks of the prophet who prepares the way of the Lord (Isa 40:3). He says the dawn will visit them and shine on those in darkness (Luke 1:78–79). This last line is pulled from Isaiah 60, where God's light shines on the world: "Arise, shine, for your light has come, and the glory of the LORD shines over you. For look, darkness

[2] David A. deSilva, "Patronage and Reciprocity," *Ashland Theological Journal* 31 (1999): 32.
[3] See deSilva, *An Introduction to the New Testament,* 334–37 (see chap. 1, n. 3).

will cover the earth, and total darkness the peoples; but the LORD will shine over you, and his glory will appear over you. Nations will come to your light, and kings to your shining brightness" (60:1–3).

Overall, the first chapter of Luke recounts the joy at the conception of both John and Jesus. God fulfills his promises to Israel. John will be a prophet and forerunner; Jesus will be the Davidic King.

ANCIENT CONNECTIONS 3.3. ROMAN EMPERORS CORRELATED WITH PALESTINIAN RULERS

Roman Emperors	Palestinian Rulers	Biblical References
Pompey/Caesar (63–31 BCE)	Herod the Great (37–4 BCE)	*Herod the Great:* Matt 2:1–19; Luke 1:5
Augustus (31 BCE–14 CE)	Archelaus (4/2 BCE–6 CE) Herod Antipas (4/2 BCE–39 CE) Philip (4/2 BCE–34 CE)	*Archelaus:* Matt 2:22 *Herod Antipas:* Matt 14:1–12; Mark 6:14–22; 8:15; Luke 3:1, 19–20; 9:9; 13:31; 23:7–15 *Philip:* Luke 3:1 *Augustus:* Matt 22:17–21; Mark 12:14–17; Luke 2:1; 20:22–25; 23:2; John 19:12, 15
Tiberius (14–37)	Pontius Pilate (26–37)	*Tiberius Caesar:* Luke 3:1 *Pilate:* Matthew 27; Mark 15; Luke 3:1; 13:1; 23:1–52; John 18:29–19:38
Gaius Caligula (37–41)	Herod Agrippa I (39–44)	*Herod Agrippa I:* Acts 12:1–24
Claudius (41–54)	Fadus (44–46) Tiberius Alexander (46–48) Cumanus (48–52) Herod Agrippa II (53–73) Felix (52–59)	*Felix:* Acts 23:24–25:14 *Agrippa II:* Acts 25:13–26:32
Nero (54–68)	Festus (60–62) Albinus (62–64) Florus (64–66)	*Festus:* Acts 24:27–26:32 *Nero:* Acts 25:8, 11–12, 21; 26:32; 27:24; 28:19

In chapter 2 Luke tells the story of Jesus's birth. He adds unique material, such as setting it in the days of Caesar Augustus's census, which sought to quantify Rome's power. But Rome will be subjugated by an infant born in a manger. Caesar is contrasted to lowly shepherds, who are the first to visit Israel's Savior. David was also a shepherd, and shepherding is often associated with the Messiah (1 Sam 17:15; Ezek 34:23). Angels appear to the shepherds as a mighty army announcing a new reign. Angels also have a militaristic role in Daniel, indicating the upheaval of nations (Dan 10:13). Their presence is also full of light, pointing to temple themes.

Jesus is brought to the temple as the firstborn son. Levites likewise function as a corporate "firstborn" representing the nation (Num 3:12). Jesus will be a light to the Gentiles, the redemption of Jerusalem. The aged Simeon and Anna prophesy over Jesus. Simeon was awaiting the consolation (*paraklēsis*) of Israel (Luke 2:25), which is the defining concept concerning Israel's restoration and return from exile: "Comfort, comfort [*paraklēsis*] my people" (Isa 40:1). As a young boy, Jesus is later found in his Father's house, introducing the theme of sonship. Jesus will be tested shortly as the Son of God. He understands his identity; his mission is about to be clarified.

JESUS INTRODUCED AND TESTED (3:1–4:13)

Luke returns to pairing John the Baptist and Jesus (Luke 3:1–20; 3:21–4:13), but he also places these events in a larger context of Roman and Jewish history and rulers (3:1–2). During the reign of Tiberius Caesar, while Pontius Pilate was governor, John came onto the scene preaching a baptism of repentance (3:3). John's presence fulfills the words of Isaiah of a voice calling from the wilderness to make a straight path so they can see the salvation of God (Isa 40:3–5). Only Luke includes the line from Isaiah that all flesh will see God's salvation, prefiguring the Gentile mission in Acts. Readers should note that the first two chapters were centered mainly on the temple. Now the scene has shifted to the wilderness. Jesus will return to the temple but not until the end of his ministry.

Jesus is baptized by John, indicating he is the Son of God. Luke includes more details about the people who came to John for baptism than the other Gospels. Those of high society, tax collectors, and soldiers come to John. John indicates he is simply preparing the way of Jesus, for while John baptizes with water, Jesus will baptize people with the Holy Spirit and fire (3:16). The fire indicates both judgment and cleansing: judgment for those who rebuff and cleansing for those who accept.

ANCIENT CONNECTIONS 3.4. JOHN
THE BAPTIST AND BAPTISM

Purification in water was an important ritual for Jews and especially to the community at Qumran. Many homes have been found to contain a *mikvah*, a small stone pool carved into the ground. The temple was also equipped with pools for cleansing before rituals. However, John's baptism in the Jordan mainly recalled Israel crossing the Jordan to enter the land of Canaan (Joshua 1–3). This and the Red Sea crossing became the main background image for their purification rituals.

Luke then provides a seventy-seven-name genealogy starting with Jesus and going back to Adam, the first son of God (3:23–38). Jesus is the universal Savior, the new Adam, and the true Son of God. Now Jesus will be tested as the Son of God, for the previous sons of God have failed (Luke 4:1–13). The Spirit leads Jesus into the wilderness, where he fasts for forty days, mirroring Israel's wilderness wandering. The devil tempts Jesus regarding his vocation. To subdue creation, he must cast the serpent from his presence as Adam should have in the garden. The final temptation, unlike in Matthew, appropriately takes place in Jerusalem at the pinnacle of the temple. Jesus knows his vocation is not about saving himself but following God's path to glory through suffering. He was sent to suffer with the downcast so he might lift them up again.

Galilee (4:14–9:50)

Jesus's inaugural Jubilee sermon in Nazareth encapsulates his ministry. In Nazareth Jesus reads from Isaiah, saying he has been anointed by the Spirit to proclaim good news to the poor. (The word for "anointed" in Greek is the verbal form of Jesus's title "Christ," or "the anointed one.") This good news concerns release, redemption, and Jubilee for the outcast (4:16–30). The rest of the Galilee narrative illustrates how Jesus proclaims freedom and reveals his identity. He drives out demons, heals, calls and trains disciples (men and women), welcomes centurions, and raises the dead. Jesus condemns the rich and the religious leaders while eating with sinners and tax collectors. Jesus's parables prove the Word will be accepted only by some. Peter then confesses Jesus is the Messiah, and Jesus is transfigured before the three disciples, but they do not understand this means Jesus must take up his cross.

ANCIENT CONNECTIONS 3.5. JUBILEE

Every seventh year the Israelites were to give the land a Sabbath rest (Lev 25:4–7). After the seventh Sabbath rest, there was to be the year of Jubilee (the fiftieth year). According to biblical regulations, Jubilee was to have a special impact on the ownership and management of the land of Israel (25:8–55). It was an economic reset whereby each person was to return his property to the original clan owner, free slaves, and let the land rest. All of this would prevent accumulation of land, render it hard to fall into absolute poverty, stop the flow of inequalities, and eventually do away with slavery.

GOOD NEWS FOR THE POOR (4:14–44)

Jesus returns to Galilee, where he will remain until Luke 9:51. He does so in the power of the Spirit after having passed the devil's test. He comes to his hometown, Nazareth, where he delivers his keynote speech (4:18–19). Jesus does not say to repent, for the kingdom of God is at hand, as in Matthew and Mark. He quotes from Isaiah 61, claiming he is the Spirit-filled anointed one. Luke links Jesus's baptism to his "anointing" by the Spirit more explicitly than the other Gospels (3:21; 4:1, 14, 18). As the anointed one he proclaims release to the captives, the blind, and the oppressed. This is the same kingdom message, but he emphasizes social dimensions. However, those in Nazareth only can see him as Joseph's son. Already readers know Jesus has proved he is God's Son. Therefore, he later reminds his people that Elijah and Elisha were also rebuffed by Israel and therefore sent outside Israel in their days to spread God's message of release. Readers are getting a sense of what the response to Jesus will be. The people are enraged at Jesus and try to kill him, but he escapes (4:16–30).

Jesus begins his work in earnest by driving out an unclean spirit and performing various healings in Capernaum. He has announced the releasing of captives; now he enacts this reality. While he was driven out of Nazareth by his own people, now he drives out demons in Capernaum. In the synagogue he performs his first exorcism, indicating the synagogue has become corrupt. They are not spreading the life-giving message of God. The demonic spirit recognizes Jesus as the Holy One of God, but Jesus's own people cannot see him for who he is. At Capernaum, Jesus heals Simon's mother-in-law and people with diseases. He cleanses the land as the Holy One of God (4:31–41; Isa 12:6; 17:7; 29:19; 47:4).

Jesus Establishes His Family (5:1–6:49)

Luke's next section is centered on Jesus establishing his family. He does this by calling followers to his side. Jesus says that instead of capturing fish, they will fish for people. This imagery not only comes from fishing but from warfare. Nations would use hooks to lead along conquered people to a new land (2 Kgs 25:7; Isa 37:29; Ezek 38:1–4). However, the disciples would follow Jesus's politic of persuasion rather than a politic of power. Peppered throughout the narrative are call stories as Jesus gathers a community around him.

Jesus calls Simon Peter (Luke 5:1–11). The story is longer than the other Gospels and tells of when Jesus had Peter let down the nets again and catch a large quantity of fish. This scene foreshadows the work Peter will do with Jesus and after Jesus leaves. James and John follow Jesus as well. Jesus then heals a man with leprosy, and the man also recognizes Jesus as Lord (5:12–16). Though large crowds follow Jesus, he often escapes to the desert to pray. Jesus then not only heals a man who is paralyzed but forgives his sins. This leads to sustained conflict with the Pharisees (5:17–6:11). They think Jesus blasphemes, making himself one with God. But Luke has already proved Jesus is the Son of God, the Holy One of God.

Another narrative section begins with Jesus calling the tax collector Levi (5:27–32). Levi hosts a great banquet for Jesus. Isaiah 25:6 says that God will host a great feast for all peoples, but the Pharisees and scribes are incensed that Jesus would associate with sinners. Jesus reiterates that he came for the lowly, sick, and sinners. The Pharisees ask why Jesus's disciples do not fast, but he tells them the time for fasting is not appropriate when the bridegroom is here (5:33–39). In other words, this is a unique time in salvation history. Things will not proceed as usual.

Jesus continues to define his true family by appointing his twelve disciples (6:12–16). Previously, Luke has recorded a few times individuals were called, but now Luke names the Twelve. While the Pharisees are filled with rage against Jesus, he establishes the new Israel. Jesus teaches his disciples what it means to be his follower. He calls the poor, hungry, and mourners blessed. He pronounces woes on the rich, full, and those who laugh. He presents the upside-down nature of the kingdom, telling them to love their enemies, be slow in judgment, and produce the kind of fruit that indicates a pure heart. If they do these things, they will be children of the God who is kind and merciful (6:35–36). This language echoes a variety of Old Testament texts but most importantly alludes to Exod 34:5–7, when God appears to Moses on Mount Sinai and declares he is a merciful and gracious God. Jesus's disciples will either build their lives and ministry on his words or on some other philosophy. They need a strong foundation to stand against the storm on the horizon.

REVELATION, PARABLES, AND THE TWELVE (7:1–9:50)

Jesus has taught his disciples, and now he continues to reveal himself and expand his family. In Capernaum he heals a centurion's servant (7:1–10). A centurion worked for Rome, Israel's overlord. But Jesus said he has not found such great faith even in Israel (7:9). Like Naaman, a Gentile official encounters the powerful work of Yahweh. Jesus also raises a widow's son from the dead (7:11–17). Jesus's work mirrors the ministry of the great prophets Elijah and Elisha (Mal 4:5–6). Elijah also meets a woman who is a widow, her son dies, and she recognizes Elijah is a man of God (1 Kgs 17:10–24). Elisha also raises a young boy to life (2 Kgs 4:32–37).[4] However, while Elijah and Elisha heal by the power of God, Jesus heals by the power of the Spirit who rests more fully on him.

These miracles raise the question of Jesus's identity. The pairing of John and Jesus comes together again. John wonders if Jesus is the "coming one" or if they should wait for another figure (7:19). This language of the "coming one" evokes Ps 118:26: "He *who comes* in the name of the LORD is blessed." Jesus replies with prophecies from Isaiah. He is their long-awaited King who restores all things: the blind receive their sight, the lame walk, those with leprosy are cleansed, the deaf hear, the dead are raised, and the poor are told good news (Luke 7:22; Isa 26:19; 29:18–19; 35:5–6; 42:7, 18; 61:1). Jesus explains John was a transitional figure. He was the last of the old age and introduced the new era. But this generation, like this wilderness generation, has not accepted God's word. They have rejected both John and Jesus.

After Jesus clarifies the type of Messiah he is, a woman confirms Jesus's identity by anointing him as king with perfume (Luke 7:36–50). While the other Gospels position this story as an anointing for burial, Luke narrates this as a great act of service and love. Luke focuses on unique aspects of this anointing. Jesus is anointed by a sinful woman in a Pharisee's house (7:39). Jesus is their hoped-for King, but he also challenges their social customs. God's family is defined by love and repentance, not social standing or wealth. This point is reiterated as Luke notes many women support Jesus's ministry (8:1–3). Luke is the only Gospel writer to comment on these

---

[4] Gladd, *Handbook on the Gospels*, 239 (see chap. 1, n. 13).

women, all of whom have been cured of evil spirits and diseases. They are new Eves, cleansed and remade.

Luke has pressed home Jesus's identity, but the question remains as to why so many do not accept him. Therefore, Jesus tells the parable of the sower, indicating the response to the kingdom will be varied (8:4–15). His words only enter receptive hearts. Jesus speaks in parables to clarify the division between insiders and outsiders. They need to listen carefully and be not only hearers but doers of his word to be a part of his family (8:16–21).

Some are hesitant to follow Jesus, and this theme continues as Jesus displays his authority over both the sea and the land. When Jesus calms the storm he tells them they lack faith, and they question who he is (8:22–25). When Jesus comes to the Gerasenes, he cleanses the land by casting out a demon (8:26–39). The unclean spirit recognizes Jesus as the Son of the Most High. Demons can see Jesus more clearly than his disciples. The title "Son of the Most High" emphasizes God as sovereign over all other powers in the world (Ps 18:13; 47:2).

ANCIENT CONNECTIONS 3.6. THE SEA IN THE OLD TESTAMENT

Jesus calms storms and walks on the water in Luke. The sea was the place of chaos, death, and rebellion in the Old Testament. God tames the sea and brings the dry land out from the sea in creation (Gen 1:6–10). The psalmist says the voice of the Lord is over the waters (Ps 29:3–10). The raging of the nations is compared to the sea (Isa 17:12–13). God tramples over the sea (Hab 3:8–15), rebukes it (Nah 1:4), and triumphs over it (Ps 74:10–17; 89:9–10; Isa 27:1; 51:9–10; Job 26:13). The sea is also a place of struggle for individuals (Ps 18:16; 69:14–15; 144:7). In the New Testament, Revelation portrays the sea as the source of evil and the place where the foreign nations will cause suffering for God's people (4:6; 12:18; 13:1; 15:2).

Jesus has now proven his power over Satan: the chaotic sea has been tamed, the dead have been raised, the unclean spirits have been banished, and diseases of death have been stopped. Now Jesus gives his disciples the same authority to conquer (Luke 9:1–6). They too will conquer the forces of darkness. Jesus show will show them not only his authority but his care. He spreads a banquet for God's people in the wilderness, imitating Moses and foreshadowing the eschatological banquet (9:10–17;

Exod 16:4; Isa 25:6–8). Earlier in the narrative flow than in the other Synoptics, Peter confesses that Jesus is the Messiah, the Son of God (9:18–20). His message to the poor and his vocation cohere, for his destiny is to be numbered with the transgressors (Isaiah 52–53). Jesus must lower himself like those to whom he ministers. He will become poor and the one who is cast out so he might be the Savior to all.

The disciples and the current generation misunderstand this sacrificial mission, so Jesus transfigures before Peter, John, and James, showing them the only way to exaltation is through suffering (Luke 9:28–36). Moses and Elijah appear beside him, indicating he fulfills the Law and the Prophets. Only in Luke do we overhear the topic of their conversation: Jesus's exodus in Jerusalem. The Elijah echoes continue as the narrative proceeds. Jesus is taken up (9:51; 2 Kgs 2:9–12), fire comes from heaven (9:54; 1 Kgs 18:20–40; 2 Kgs 1:9–13), and followers are warned not to look back from the plow (9:59–62; 1 Kgs 19:19–21).[5] The disciples might think everything is about to end after seeing the dazzling face of Jesus, but the episode immediately after this indicates there is still unbelief and more work to do (9:37–43; Deut 32:20–21). The disciples cannot drive out a demon, so Jesus calls them an unbelieving generation. They still do not understand that death will lead to life. Jesus needs to instruct his followers more. That is exactly what he will do as he travels toward Jerusalem.

Journey (9:51–19:27)

Luke spends more time on Jesus's journey to Jerusalem than any other Gospel writer. The section contains Luke's most unique material. In 9:51 Jesus sets his face toward Jerusalem. Two other times, the "journey to Jerusalem" will be mentioned (13:22; 17:11) and many other reminders follow (10:1, 38; 18:31; 19:1). Isaiah becomes the blueprint for Jesus's journey as Jesus now goes on the way out of exile (Isa 40:3–5). The focus on the journey is an apprenticeship. The first section focuses on Discipleship 101, the basics of what it means to follow Jesus (9:51–13:21). The next block warns the disciples about counting the cost, not becoming proud, and trusting God rather than money (13:22–17:10). On the last leg of the journey Jesus speaks of the coming kingdom, encouraging the disciples to receive the kingdom like a child and trust in Jesus's saving power (17:11–19:27). The journey to Jerusalem is the path to becoming Jesus's pupil.

---

[5] Hays, *Echoes of Scripture in the Gospels*, 202 (see intro., n. 8).

DISCIPLESHIP 101 (9:51–13:21)

Though Jesus's entire journey to Jerusalem concerns discipleship, a particular focus rests on this theme in the first section. Jesus molds the disciples into the type of followers Israel was meant to be. The first episode shows Jesus rejecting any type of ethnic superiority. While the disciples want to call down fire from heaven to consume Samaritans, Jesus rebukes them (9:51–56). He explains that following him will mean giving up much, and this includes their tribalistic thinking (9:57–62). Jesus then sends out the seventy (or seventy-two) to proclaim his message (10:1–24). Likely a textual variant is included here, because it recalls Genesis 10 and the Table of Nations, where God splits humanity into seventy-two (LXX) or seventy (MT) people groups (Gen 10:32). Jesus's followers will reclaim all nations for Yahweh, again hitting on the theme of inclusion. Much work remains to be done, and Jesus conveys they do not need much on their journey. They are like the wilderness generation, who only need God's presence. When the seventy-two return, Jesus tells them that he saw Satan fall like lightning from heaven (10:18). This recalls Isa 14:12, where the morning star falls from heaven. The disciples are dismantling Satan's kingdom because they are reversing the allotment of the nations to the spiritual powers (Deut 32:8). They have God's authority to trample snakes.

ANCIENT CONNECTIONS 3.7. THE TABLE OF NATIONS

The Table of Nations refers to the clans of Noah's sons, who spread over the earth after the flood (Gen 10:32). These genealogies trace the descendants of Noah's three sons—Shem, Ham, and Japheth. By sending his disciples to the same number, Luke indicates Jesus's disciples are welcoming all nations.

- From Shem will stem Abraham (Arphaxad).
- From Ham's progeny stems Egypt, Babylon, and Assyria (all of these will be nations set against Israel in the Scriptures).
- From Japheth came those from Europe and Asia (the Medes and Greeks).

The theme of hospitality to the "other" continues when Jesus tells a parable about loving their neighbors, famously called the parable of the good Samaritan (Luke 10:25–37). Jesus instructs them that neither ethnicity nor blood relations characterize his kingdom community. Rather, his people are marked by actions of love and mercy. The Good Samaritan story unifies this section as Jesus teaches them who their neighbor is. Jesus expands on what it means to be his disciple by pointing to a female. Mary sits at the Lord's feet and learns from him (10:39). This is what defines his family, not ethnicity or gender.

Jesus warns them that conflict will come with this controversial message of Jubilee release. When Jesus does good by casting out demons some say he does so by the prince of demons (Beelzebub). But Jesus says he drives out demons by the finger of God (11:18–20). In Exodus, Pharoah also recognizes the finger of God at work, but his heart is still hardened (8:19; 31:18; Deut 9:10). God's enemies remain stubborn despite signs from God's own hand. This time it is the Jewish leaders who are cast as Egypt opposing God's anointed one. The crowds even begin to demand signs from Jesus, but Jesus says only the sign of Jonah will be given to them, which refers to Jesus's greatest sign—his resurrection.

Because the Jewish leaders have rejected his message, Jesus pronounces woes on them. They love money, power, and fame (Luke 11:37–54). Jesus tells the disciples the leaders are hypocrites (12:1–12). Jesus's condemnation of the religious leaders leads to teaching on money, anxiety, and readiness for his return (12:13–48). The parable of the rich fool displays that people should be rich toward God. The next section is filled with illustrations indicating that those who refuse to submit to Jesus will be judged (12:39–13:9). Jesus says he did not come to bring peace but division. He warns them that destruction could come on them at any time and compares people to a fig tree. A barren fig tree will be cut down if it does not produce fruit.

Jesus closes this first section on discipleship by instructing his followers that the kingdom might not look mighty initially. It is like a small mustard seed, but it will grow. When it grows it will become a large tree that all the birds of the sky come to for rest. This paints the kingdom plan in new creation imagery (Gen 2:19; Ezek 31:6; Dan 4:12, 21). A new tree of life stands before them. The shocking thing is this tree will soon be covered in blood.

WARNINGS (13:22–17:10)

The middle section of Jesus's journey to Jerusalem continues the theme of discipleship but focuses more on warnings. The end is coming, and those who follow Jesus must be ready. Jesus sets the tone by saying his followers need to strive to enter through the narrow door (Luke 13:22–30). The way will not be easy; few will find it. Luke then indicates that Herod seeks to kill Jesus. Earthly rulers seek to knock people off the corridor of faithfulness, and Jesus laments Jerusalem's negative response to his ministry (13:31–35). They have not heeded the warnings of the prophets, but he still longs to gather them under his wings.

Jesus continues to warn and instruct his followers. He says they must not be like those who seek the best seats in a house. Rather, they should be clothed in humility (Prov 25:6–7). They must not be like those invited to the banquet but do not come. Jesus argues it will be costly to follow him (Luke 14:1–35). Though they might be offended, Jesus's ministry is one of welcoming and seeking after those on the highways and hedges, the lost sheep, lost coin, and the lost (prodigal) son (15:1–32). Jesus eats with sinners, he came for the sick, and he seeks after those who are wandering (Deut 14:28–29). He pursues people like someone who has lost a coin in their house.

He also welcomes those who return to him like the prodigal son. The prodigal son is not only about Jesus's acceptance of those who initially run from him, but also of those who respond in jealousy like the other brother. Jesus is looking straight at the Jewish leaders, warning them they should be rejoicing rather than complaining. Whether the prodigal son refers to wayward Israel, Gentiles, or outsiders is difficult to determine. Maybe the point is the prodigal son represents anyone who strays.

ANCIENT CONNECTIONS 3.8. THE PRODIGAL SON

The parable of the prodigal son (or as the CSB calls him, the "lost son") is famous, but important background information makes it come to life.

- It was shameful for a young son to request his inheritance from his father early and may have indicated he wished for his father's death.
- The son fled to a "distant country," which should probably be interpreted as Gentile territory. The son was leaving not only his home but his ancestral faith.
- Swine herding not only has implications for how far from Judaism the son has strayed but was also a lower-class vocation.
- Because the son has shamed the father, it would be expected for the father to refuse to meet the son and to disgrace him. Instead, the father runs to meet him.
- When the son returns, the father gives him sandals, a robe, and a ring. Sandals represent acceptance. (Servants and slaves went barefoot, and masters and their sons wore footwear.) A robe wrapped the son in fine clothes, bestowing the honor of his household on the son. Finally, a ring was a sign of authority and legal authentication that the son was part of the family.

The final warnings concern money and one's status in the kingdom (Luke 16:1–17:10). Jesus's followers must not be those who are unjust or love mammon. The kingdom is for those who give, not for the greedy. Jesus's parable of the dishonest manager is full of difficulties (16:1–13). Is this unjust or shrewd manager a virtuous model or a negative example? The point is people need to use their wealth, possessions, and connections all for the sake of the kingdom. No matter the view one takes on this manager, Jesus's message is clear: you cannot serve God and money. Earthly wealth should be used to build God's kingdom and not our own. If we are faithful with our earthly possessions, Jesus will entrust us with what is truly valuable. Worldly wealth is simply a test.

Jesus also tells the story of the rich man and Lazarus, which further develops the theme of money (16:19–31). A life devoted to pleasure and wealth is out of step with the kingdom. Moses taught the Israelites to open their hands to the poor (Deut 15:7–8). The rich man is failing to heed this call. The story shows the upside-down nature of the kingdom and identifies who are true children of Abraham (Luke 3:8–9). Lazarus goes to Abraham's side, while the rich man is tormented in Hades. One's position in life on earth does not determine one's position in the afterlife.

Jesus closes this second discipleship section in the journey to Jerusalem by warning people that if they cause other people to stumble, it would be better if they died. They should watch out for one another but forgive people if they repent. The disciples want their faith increased, and Jesus says they only need a little faith to do great things. Followers of Jesus need to remember they are only servants sent to do their duty.

Readiness (17:11–19:27)

The final part of Jesus's teaching on his slow trek to Jerusalem is centered on the coming kingdom. The disciples must be ready for his return. The Pharisees ask Jesus when the kingdom will come (17:20–37). Jesus answers the kingdom is already in their midst. The kingdom is where the king is. He warns the disciples he must leave, but he will soon return. They must be ready for his return and even be like the persistent widow. She kept asking the judge for justice, and he listened to her. Jesus says the disciples ought to pray in the same way (18:1–8). They must be humble and acknowledge their sin like a tax collector and unlike Pharisees, who look down on people for their own failings (18:9–14). Repentance, perseverance, and humility mark kingdom citizens.

Being ready also means being willing to sacrifice (18:18–30). Luke tells the story of the rich young ruler who has kept the law but was not willing to part with his riches. It raises the question of whether this rich man has kept the law or if he has broken the tenth commandment, which warns against coveting his neighbor's goods (Exod 20:17; Deut 5:21).[6] People who have wealth must be willing to give it up for Jesus, but those who have less will not have the same burden. Jesus himself embodies this kingdom mentality. He came from heaven to suffer in the place of others (Luke 18:31–34). Jesus demonstrates his care for others by healing a blind man (18:35–43).

The theme of sacrifice and money continues as Jesus meets Zacchaeus (19:1–10). Though Zacchaeus is a tax collector and a man of small physical stature, Jesus goes to his house. Zacchaeus needed to ascend a tree to see Jesus. Zacchaeus's repentance is evident by his pledge to give half of his possessions to the poor. Repentance includes contrition, confession, and satisfaction. Zacchaeus needed to ascend to see Jesus, but he descends to care for those below. He rights his wrongs, and Jesus proclaims that salvation has come to Zacchaeus's house.

Jesus then tells a parable of the ten minas (three years of wage), indicating growth in virtues must characterize his disciples while he is gone (19:11–27). A nobleman distributes ten minas to ten servants while he goes to a faraway country. Some invest the money; some do not. Those who are foolish with the money have the money taken away. The meaning of the parable is debated. It could be about being faithful while Jesus is away, but some argue it concerns a pagan ruler and contrasts this kingship to Jesus's. This section began with the presence of the kingdom and ends with a word about the delay of the kingdom. The kingdom is here and is coming; disciples of Jesus must be ready. The rich, proud, and powerful will have the most difficulty. But there is still hope for the humble and repentant.

Jerusalem (19:28–24:53)

Jesus finally enters Jerusalem as both a passive victim and a potent victor. The conflict has been heightening. Largely positive responses made up the introduction (1–4), Galilee had some opposition (4:14–9:50), and the Jerusalem journey displayed more hostility (9:51–19:27). Now Jerusalem crucifies its Savior. Jesus must bear not only the burdens of Israel but the whole world.

The passion and exaltation of Jesus are the climax of the various themes in Luke's Gospel. Luke begins his Gospel with a prayer in the temple; he concludes with a prayer in the garden and rejoicing in the temple. Luke opens with a focus on

---

[6] Hays, 209.

women; he closes with women spreading the news of resurrection. Luke begins with the poor; he concludes with the unimpressive disciples in Jerusalem. The Gospel begins with John the Baptist paving the way for forgiveness of sins; it ends with a command from Jesus to preach forgiveness of sins to the whole world. The beginning foreshadows the end.

JESUS CONFRONTS JERUSALEM (19:28–21:38)

Jesus enters Jerusalem. One would expect him to enter it with pomp and circumstance, but he comes into the city on the back of a donkey, fulfilling the prophecy from Zech 9:9. The crowds welcome him as a king, but the Pharisees are upset with the crowd and jealous of Jesus. When Jesus enters Jerusalem, he weeps over the city because of his great love for it (2 Kgs 8:11–12). Jesus knows the days of the city are numbered, and soon it will be destroyed by enemies. Then he goes into the temple and declares the Jewish temple corrupt. What was holy has turned into a den of thieves (19:28–46). Jeremiah also condemned the temple in the same way when Israel abandoned their loyalty to Yahweh (Jeremiah 7).

Because of Jesus's actions on entering Jerusalem, he is confronted with various questions and hostilities. First, he is asked where he gets his authority to do these things (20:1–8). Who is he to enter the city this way and declare these things about the temple? Jesus responds by turning the table and questioning them. He shows that his opponents are corrupt. They play politics, trying to both please the people and keep their positions of authority. They cannot answer Jesus, so neither will he answer them. But Luke's readers already know the Ancient of Days has given the Son of Man authority (Dan 7:13–14). Jesus then tells a parable about a vineyard owner, modeled after Isaiah 5 and directed at the leaders who question him (Luke 20:9–19). Israel is also compared to a vineyard in the Old Testament (Isaiah 5). These leaders want the vineyard for themselves; they do not understand they are hired hands. They have rejected the son of the vineyard owner. Only Jesus will become the cornerstone of this new community. This combines a quotation from Psalm 118 with an allusion to Dan 2:34–35. Jesus is both the *crushing* stone and the *corner*stone.[7]

Jesus continues to be questioned about the hot topics of the day, as in the other Synoptic Gospels. The leaders first ask him a question about authority, politics

---

[7] Gladd, *Handbook on the Gospels*, 284.

(Luke 20:20–26), and theology (20:27–40). Jesus confounds the religious leaders with his own query (20:41–44). They cannot understand the Scriptures because they can't see Jesus's true identity. Jesus asks them about Ps 110:1 and how they can say the Messiah is the son of David when David calls him Lord. How can David call one of his sons Lord? They cannot answer his question because they cannot see that Jesus fulfills their Scriptures. Therefore, Jesus proceeds to castigate their practices. He warns people of their pride. He says the poor widow gives more to God than them (Luke 21:1–4). Then, climactically, he foretells the destruction of their most holy place: the temple.

ANCIENT CONNECTIONS 3.9. RESURRECTION IN THE OLD TESTAMENT

It may be surprising that Sadducees do not believe in a resurrection, but two factors make this more understandable. First, in that time resurrection was not a widely held belief. Second, the Old Testament is not as clear on this reality as the New Testament. The Old Testament usually only refers to Sheol, the place of the dead (Gen 37:35; Num 16:33; Job 7:9; Ps 6:5). However, evidence of resurrection hope can be found in the Old Testament. Daniel 12:2 says, "Many who sleep in the dust of the earth will awake, some to eternal life, and some to disgrace and eternal contempt." Isaiah 26:19 also affirms, "Your dead will live; their bodies will rise. Awake and sing, you who dwell in the dust!" The psalmist notes that God will ransom his soul from Sheol (Ps 49:15) and God will bring people up from the depths of the earth again (71:20). Many also see a resurrection in Ezekiel's vision of dry bones springing to life (Ezek 37:7–10).

The disciples ask when these things will happen, and Jesus correlates two events: the end of history and the destruction of the temple. Luke 21:8–24 deals with the events leading up to the destruction of the temple in 70 CE. Verses 25–36 concern the arrival of the Son of Man. For both, signs will occur before the event. War, imprisonment, and betrayal will fill the earth. When Jerusalem is surrounded, the disciples should know the destruction of the temple is nearby. There will also be signs in heaven. They will see the Son of Man coming with the clouds of heaven as Daniel spoke of. At this point, they should know their redemption is close. Jesus warns them and encourages them to be watchful (21:29–38). His followers know how to tell when fruit is coming, so they should be ready for his return.

THE PASSION (22:1–23:56)

Jesus's death is set in the days of the Feast of Unleavened Bread and the Passover. The Passover images collapse and coalesce in Jesus. He is the unbroken lamb, the firstborn who is slain, the firstborn who is freed, and the light who leads Israel out of darkness. The Passover paints Jesus's death as a redemptive event, and maybe most importantly, this liberation comes about by the death of an innocent and unbroken lamb whose blood is sprinkled over the people. During this festival, the chief priests and the scribes look for a way to put Jesus to death. Judas decides he will sell his soul for money and power and looks for an opportunity to betray Jesus (Luke 22:1–6). Luke has consistently warned the greedy in his Gospel. Luke even says Satan entered Judas (22:3). Though Jesus defeated Satan, he still has the power to deceive, distort, and depress followers of God. By mentioning Satan at the beginning of the passion, Luke affirms the crucifixion has a deep spiritual dimension.

Luke then recounts how Jesus eats the Passover meal with his disciples (22:7–23). The meal functions as an interpretive grid over the events about to occur. Jesus takes the bread and the wine and says they symbolize his body and blood. Then he has his disciples eat and drink. A new covenant is being made like God made a covenant with Israel at Sinai (Jeremiah 31). Jesus is about to cover them in his own blood as he looks toward the cross. But the disciples are still like the Israel of old. They quarrel about who will be the greatest. Jesus reminds them that greatness is defined by servanthood and sacrifice. In fact, he tells Peter, the leader of the disciples, that even he will betray Jesus (22:24–34).

Jesus and the disciples go to the Mount of Olives and enter the garden. Here he prays the cup the Father has given him will be taken from him. But he also submits himself to the Father's will. An angel comes to him to strengthen him for his task, but he goes back and finds the disciples sleeping rather than praying (22:39–46). While Jesus is steady in his resolve, his disciples are sluggish and not ready for what is about to happen. Like Israel, they fail. Only Jesus will follow the Father's will and be a light to the nations. Suddenly, a mob led by Judas enters the garden, and they arrest Jesus. One of the disciples strikes out with the sword, but Jesus instructs him to put his sword away (22:47–53). Violence is not the way to the kingdom. Jesus could call down a legion of angels to his side and quickly win this battle. However, the kingdom will come only by sacrifice. The soldiers seize Jesus and lead him away.

Those who arrest Jesus begin to mock and beat him. Jesus fulfills the role of the innocent Servant in Luke. Now he will stand trial before the leaders of his own nation and even Rome itself. Jesus is brought before the Sanhedrin (the ruling class) and asked if he is the Messiah. Jesus tells them they will not believe him no matter what he says, but he does affirm that from now on, they will see the Son of Man seated at the right hand of the Father (22:63–71; Dan 7:13–14). The one brought low is ultimately the exalted one. They ask him if he is the Messiah, to which Jesus coyly says, "You say that I am" (22:70). Jesus confirms he is the Messiah but not the one *they* expect. They interpret this as an affirmation and declare he has blasphemed. Jesus has associated himself too closely with Yahweh. Jesus's opponents do not know half the truth.

In order to kill Jesus, they must bring Jesus before Pilate. Rome ruled the region, and Jews did not have the political right to carry out capital punishment. The religious leaders falsely witness about Jesus before Pilate, saying he is a political menace and misleading the nation (23:1–2; 1 Kgs 18:17). Pilate asks Jesus if he is the King of the Jews, and Jesus again says, "You say so" (23:3). Pilate knows the leaders are jealous, so he says he finds nothing wrong with Jesus. Two other times in this narrative Jesus will be declared innocent by Pilate (Luke 23:4, 14, 22). Later Herod (23:15), the thief (23:41), and the centurion (23:47) will affirm the same thing. A major point of Luke's passion narrative is Jesus's innocence (Isa 53:9–12).

When Pilate learns Jesus is a Galilean, he asks Herod Antipas to come see him because Herod rules the region of Galilee. Herod wants to meet Jesus and ask him many questions, but Jesus does not answer him. So, they dress Jesus up as a king and mock him. The true King is debased while the fraudulent king sits on his throne. Pilate calls the people together again and declares Jesus has done nothing wrong, but they cry out that he should be crucified. The crowds asks that Barabbas, a true insurrectionist, be released instead of Jesus. Pilate frees the revolutionary and sends the Prince of Peace to his death (23:6–25).

Jesus is crucified between two criminals, ironically pointing again to Jesus's innocence (23:32–49). It also fulfills the prediction from Isaiah that Jesus will be numbered with the transgressors (23:37; Isa 53:12). Despite the mistreatment, Jesus asks that his opponents would be forgiven, for they do not know what they do (Luke 23:34). This request appeals to a distinction in the Torah of intentional versus unintentional sins (Num 15:22–31).[8] Shockingly, Jesus affirms that crucifying him is a forgivable offense against God. One of the criminals screams at Jesus, but the other one sees Jesus for who he is, and Jesus promises that man that he will be in paradise with him. Paradise often refers to the garden of Eden (Gen 2:8), and here Jesus connects it to the presence of God. Jesus came to restore the garden.

---

[8] Hays, *Echoes of Scripture in the Gospels*, 211.

At noon, darkness covers the land, and the curtain of the sanctuary is torn in two. Darkness signals an apocalyptic event and even God's wrath. The temple curtain being torn in two indicates both judgment on the temple and the release of the expansive presence of God. A new covenant has come. Jesus entrusts his spirit in the Father's hand and breathes his last. The centurion does not say Jesus was the Son of God like in the other Gospels (Matt 27:54; Mark 15:39). This time he says Jesus was just or righteous (Luke 23:47). Luke's point is that Jesus is the innocent and righteous Servant of the Lord (Isa 53:9–12).

One of the righteous Sanhedrin members asks for Jesus's body so he might bury him. Deuteronomy 21 speaks of the requirement to bury the body of the executed so it does not defile the land (21:22–23). Yet Jesus's body will revive the land. Joseph takes Jesus's body down and lays it in a tomb cut in the rock. No person had ever been placed in this tomb, indicating Joseph's wealth. Isaiah 53:9 says the Suffering Servant was "assigned a grave with the wicked, but he was with a rich man at his death, because he had done no violence and had not spoken deceitfully." Some of the women who had followed Jesus note where Jesus has been laid and begin to prepare perfumes and spices for his body. The King of the Jews has died. His body now lies cold in a tomb and will soon begin to smell.

ANCIENT CONNECTIONS 3.10.
BURIAL IN THE OLD TESTAMENT

Burial identified which land was yours and claimed rights to land. God had promised Abraham land for his people, but when Sarah died, Abraham bought a burial plot (Genesis 23). Though God had not given him the land yet, buying this plot was an act of faith. In Genesis 47–49 Jacob desires to be buried in the land of his father rather than in Egypt. Jesus's burial was an act of claiming the earth as his and for his people.

EXALTATION (24:1–53)

Luke ends in a unique way. Unlike Mark, where the women run in fear; and Matthew, where the disciples are climactically sent off, in Luke, Jesus is found in a very normal way: walking, eating, and continuing to instruct his friends after his resurrection. The focus in the final chapter is how all of Jesus's life, including his death, resurrection, and ascension, fulfills the Scriptures.

On the first day of the week, some women followers of Jesus come to the tomb. They find the stone rolled away and go in to see the body, but it is gone. Two angels appear to them. These two angels mirror the cherubim on the mercy seat, indicating that Jesus can be equated with the living presence of God (Luke 24:1–8; Exod 25:18–22). The Gospel began with an angel appearing to Zechariah and Mary declaring new births. Now angels announce another new birth. Death has been defeated; Jesus is the living one who holds the keys to death and Hades (Rev 1:18).

The women return to the Eleven and tell them what has happened. They are the first proclaimers of the resurrection gospel. However, the men do not believe them. Peter wonders what has happened to Jesus's body, so he runs to the tomb and only finds the cloths in which they had wrapped Jesus's body (24:9–12). The scene shifts to the Emmaus road, where two disciples are walking and talking about the events. They had hoped Jesus was the one to *redeem* Israel (Luke 24:21). Earlier in the narrative, Zechariah praised God for visiting his people, making *redemption* for them, and raising the horn of salvation (1:68–69).

Jesus appears to these disciples on the road, but they do not recognize him. He gives them a lesson in the Scriptures, telling them that Moses, the Prophets, and the Psalms foretold these events. Luke sends all readers back to the beginning of the Scriptures for a reread (24:13–27). He uses an unusual tripartite division of the Scriptures (Moses, Prophets, and Psalms). The twofold description is more popular (Moses and the Prophets), but Jesus includes the Psalms as well. Some suppose the Psalms stand for the Writings as a whole, but it could be that the Psalms hold a particularly relevant key to understanding the suffering Messiah. As David suffered, so will the Messiah. Both Psalms 22 and 69 play prominent roles in the passion narrative. These psalms have Davidic associations, and therefore he is like David in that his friends betray him (Ps 55:12–14, 20–21) and in his silence before his accusers (62:1, 5). Jesus must explain this reality to show them the Scriptures foretold the cross.

Not until Jesus breaks bread with the two men do they recognize him, but he disappears from their sight. The words for breaking bread are nearly identical to what we find at the Last Supper (22:19). They cannot understand Jesus until they understand his death as a sacrament. The disciples go to find the Eleven and tell them what has happened (24:28–35).

At this point Jesus appears in the disciples' midst and declares peace to them. They think they are seeing a ghost, so Jesus has them touch him, and he even eats to display this is not a hallucination. Like the angel, and as Jesus did on the Emmaus road, he reminds them he told them these things and the Scriptures foretold these events would occur. But it is not the end of the story. The disciples need to wait in

Jerusalem, and they will receive power from on high (24:36–49). The message of repentance and forgiveness of sins through a Savior is to be proclaimed to the whole world by the Spirit. This is what Isaiah predicted: "Speak tenderly to Jerusalem and announce to her that her time of hard service is over, her iniquity has been pardoned, and she has received from the LORD's hand double for all her sins" (Isa 40:1–2). Jesus then climactically ascends into heaven. He blesses them as a priest who has entered the presence of God (24:50–51). Luke's whole story has moved in a U-shape. Jesus came from heaven and returned to heaven. One day he will return again.

Old Testament Connections

If Matthew is intentional and Mark is allusive, Luke possesses the most eloquence and dexterity in narrating Jesus's life in the garb of Israel's story. In the words of Richard Hays, Luke is symphonic.[9] Rather than interrupting the narrative with authorial commentary, he seamlessly weaves the Old Testament into his story. Many of the direct quotations are found in characters' mouths, making the narrative flow flawlessly. Additionally, Luke is fond of using allusions rather than direct quotations.

Though we could look at several themes, and the following is by no means exhaustive, Luke does have a particular interest in (1) Jubilee release, (2) the temple, and (3) the "least of these." All of these are sourced in the Jewish Scriptures as Luke demonstrates God has been true to his promises in the gift of his Son.

Luke and Jubilee Release

Luke paints Jesus's ministry as a Jubilee release based on Isaiah 61, Leviticus 25, and Deuteronomy 15. When Jesus opens the scroll in Nazareth and reads from Isaiah, he gives the outline of his ministry. The expressions "release to the captives" and "the year of the Lord's favor" refer to the Jubilee year (Luke 4:18–19; Isa 61:1): "The Spirit of the Lord is on me, because he has anointed me to preach good news to the poor. He has sent me to proclaim *release to the captives* and recovery of sight to the blind, to set free the oppressed, to proclaim *the year of the Lord's favor*" (emphasis added).

But before we examine Luke 4 in more detail, it is important to get a sense of what Jubilee entailed. Jubilee was the year at the end of seven cycles. Every seventh year, the Israelites were to give the land a Sabbath rest (Lev 25:4–7). After the seventh Sabbath rest, there was to be the year of Jubilee (the fiftieth year). The

---

[9] For more on Luke's style see Hays, 191–95, 275–80.

fiftieth year begins with the Day of Atonement, where the high priest enters the Holy of Holies and releases a goat to remove Israel's sins so God can dwell with his people (25:9).

According to biblical regulations, Jubilee was meant to have a special impact on the ownership and management of the land of Israel (25:8–55).

> "The fiftieth year will be your Jubilee; you are not to sow, reap what grows by itself, or harvest its untended vines. It is to be holy to you because it is the Jubilee; you may only eat its produce directly from the field.
>
> "In this Year of Jubilee, each of you will return to his property. If you make a sale to your neighbor or a purchase from him, do not cheat one another. You are to make the purchase from your neighbor based on the number of years since the last Jubilee. He is to sell to you based on the number of remaining harvest years." (25:11–15)

ANCIENT CONNECTIONS 3.11. THE WORD *JUBILEE*

The word *jubilee* comes from the Hebrew *ywbl*, which refers to the ram's horn. In Greek it is translated as *aphesis*, meaning release, liberation, freedom, or pardon. Half of the times that *aphesis* is used in the LXX it refers to the Jubilee. Though no record exists of the observance of this festival, there are numerous allusions (Deut 15:1–11; Neh 5:1–13; Isa 5:7–10; 61:1–4; Jer 34:8–9; Ezek 7:12–13; 46:17).

At the sound of a ram's horn, Israel was to consecrate the fiftieth year and proclaim freedom in the land. It was an economic reset where each person was to return his property to the original clan owner, free slaves, and let the land rest. All of this would prevent accumulation of land, rendering it hard to fall into absolute poverty. It would stop the flow of inequalities and curb slavery. The point of this was to remind Israel that "the land ultimately belongs to God. His people are but *resident aliens and settlers in the land*."[10]

Jesus employs Jubilee imagery (release of the captives and the year of the Lord's favor) and the term *aphesis* to summarize his ministry. Yet, for Jesus, release (*aphesis*) is not merely physical or social release but release from sins.

---

[10] Gordon J. Wenham, *The Book of Leviticus* (Grand Rapids: Eerdmans, 1979), 320 (italics in the original).

- In Mary's Magnificat she praises God for the child who will give "knowledge of salvation" through the "forgiveness [*aphesei*] of their sins" (Luke 1:77).
- John the Baptist also proclaims a baptism of repentance for the forgiveness (*aphesin*) of sins (3:3).
- Jesus tells the woman at Simon's house that her sins are released (*apheontai*) (7:47–49).
- Jesus instructs his followers to pray, "Forgive [*aphes*] us our sins, for we ourselves also forgive everyone in debt to us." (11:4).
- On the cross Jesus prays for the Father to forgive (*aphes*) those who have crucified him (23:34).
- Jesus says at the end of Luke's Gospel that "repentance for forgiveness [*aphesin*] of sins will be proclaimed in his name to all the nations, beginning at Jerusalem" (24:47).

All of these speak of *aphesis* as liberation from sins.[11] Some therefore argue Luke spiritualizes Jubilee.

However, the two uses of *aphesis* in Jesus's Nazareth speech indicate the social dimension is not lost (4:18, 19). Jesus quotes from Isaiah 61, saying he is the one who has been anointed "to proclaim release [*aphesin*] to the captives and recovery of sight to the blind, to set free [*aphesei*] the oppressed" (4:18). While some might argue that the other examples should determine how we interpret Luke 4, this chapter is *the summary* of Jesus's ministry. Luke 4:19 in particular resonates with the social realities of Jubilee. There he speaks of the "year of the Lord's favor." This is a direct connection to the Jubilee year.

How does one bring all these dimensions together? The story in 5:17–26 clarifies. Luke presents salvation as multidimensional. A lame man is brought to Jesus on a stretcher through a hole in the roof, and Jesus tells the man his sins are forgiven. The Pharisees and scribes are incensed. However, Jesus shows them he has authority to both forgive sins and make the man well again. So Jesus tells him to get up, and he does. He has provided release and freedom for this man at two levels: physical and spiritual. Yet the spiritual dimension receives the primary emphasis: "'But so that you may know that the Son of Man has authority on earth to forgive sins'—he told the paralyzed man, 'I tell you: Get up, take your stretcher, and go home'" (5:24).

Luke 5 illustrates that the forgiveness of sins and the social dimension are not opposed. They are joined. This corresponds to the Old Testament. We already saw

---

[11] Luke 4:39 and 13:10–17 speak of "release" from demonic oppression.

the Jubilee Year and the Day of Atonement coincide. For Luke, Jesus came to declare Jubilee release. This meant the pardon of sins, political freedom, economic liberty, demonic freedom, and social emancipation. In Jesus, the year of Jubilee arrived, in part. God's people were not politically free; they did not acquire economic liberty or social emancipation. But their sins were forgiven. In the new heavens and new earth, Jubilee—and all its social implications—will occur in full.

Luke and Temple Life

All of Israel's history revolves around divine presence and the temple. Appropriately, Luke has a particular focus on the temple. The fall ruptured communion with God; the goal is to recover this. Therefore, the tabernacle and temple are central to the Bible. In these places God dwelt with his people in a similar way in which God dwelt with humanity in the garden. In fact, many have noticed how the temple is patterned after an Edenic picture.[12]

	Garden	Tabernacle or Temple
Structure	The garden had a tripartite structure (Eden, garden, outer world).	The temple had a tripartite structure (Holy of Holies, Holy Place, courtyard).
Location	The entrance to Eden faced east (Gen 3:24) and was situated on a mountain (Ezek 28:14–16).	Israel's temple faced east and was on a mountain (Ezek 40:2, 6; 43:12).
Vegetation	The garden had vegetation, plants, and fruit trees (Gen 1:11–12; 2:9).	The temple had carvings of gourds, flowers, palm trees, lilies (1 Kgs 6:18, 29, 32, 35; 7:18–20).
Tree	The garden had the tree of life (Gen 2:9).	The tabernacle had the lampstand (Exod 25:31).
Water	A river flowed out of Eden (Gen 2:10).	A river flows from the eschatological temple (Ezek 47:1–12; Ps 36:8–9; Rev 21:1–2).

---

[12] Many of these correspondences are noted in G. K. Beale, *The Temple and the Church's Mission*, New Studies in Biblical Theology (Downers Grove, IL: InterVarsity Press, 2004).

Decorations	Precious stones, gold and onyx, are in the garden (Gen 2:11–12).	Precious stones are used to decorate the sanctuaries and priestly garments (Exod 25:7, 11, 17, 31).
Wisdom and law	In the center of the garden was the tree of the knowledge of good and evil, which led to wisdom (Gen 2:9).	The ark of the covenant in the most holy place contained the law and led to wisdom (Exod 25:16; 26:34).
Priest	Adam is described as a priest who will "work" and "keep" the garden (Gen 2:15).	The priest's task was to work and keep the temple (Num 3:7–8; 8:25–26; 18:5–6; 1 Chr 23:32; Ezek 44:14; 28:13).
God's presence	God walked back and forth in the garden (Gen 3:8).	The same word (walk; *halak*) is used to describe God's presence in the tabernacle (Lev 26:12; Deut 23:14; 2 Sam 7:6–7; Ezek 28:14).
Purpose	The purpose of the garden was rest (Gen 2:1–3).	The construction of the tabernacle culminates in rest (Exod 31:12–17).

The point of all this is to show that the temple represented Eden. Here the divine presence resided. Luke picks up on this temple theme in various ways, arguing Jesus fulfills the role of the temple. Jesus is God's presence; he will extend God's presence, thus creating the new garden. However, to do so, he must deal with the corruption and sin of the temple people.

Luke places his whole narrative under a temple frame. The Third Gospel is the only Gospel to begin in the temple and end in the temple. The story begins with Zechariah going into the temple to serve as priest when an angel appears to him (1:8–9). Luke's Gospel ends with this statement: "And they were continually in the temple praising God" (24:53).

Many of the early scenes also occur in or around the temple. While Zechariah is in the physical temple, Mary has the Holy Spirit overshadow her (1:35). This language recalls how God's glory overshadows the tabernacle (Exod 40:35). A new temple presence is here and within Mary's womb. Simeon is led to the temple when Jesus is dedicated (Luke 2:27), and Anna had not left the temple in many years and finally saw Jesus (2:37). We also have the shepherds' experience. They are in the dark, but an angel of the Lord stands before them, and the glory of the Lord shines around them (2:9). The bright light, glory language, and presence of the angels indicate temple themes.

The rest of Luke is also filled with temple scenes. Luke tells the story of Jesus's boyhood visit to the temple, which Jesus refers to as his Father's house (2:46, 49). Already Jesus understands the importance of the temple and his unique relationship with his Father. Unlike Matthew, Luke places Jesus's final temptation at the pinnacle of the temple (4:9). Here the devil tempts him to throw himself down from the temple, but Jesus asserts it is not right to test God.

In Luke 9:51 Jesus sets his face toward Jerusalem, where the temple resides. In fact, over 35 percent of Luke's Gospel is taken up with this journey (chapters 9–19). In 9:29–36 Jesus is transfigured before three of the disciples. His clothes become dazzling white like a priest. This narrative presents Jesus as God's very presence on the earth. As Jesus approaches Jerusalem, he predicts the destruction of the temple (chapter 21). When he arrives in Jerusalem, he goes into the temple, and instead of restoring it, he condemns it for its impurity. Jesus clears out the temple, his Father's house (19:45–46). Then when Jesus dies, the temple curtain is torn in two (23:45), and when Jesus ascends, the implication is that he ascends to the true temple (24:50–53).

What are we to do with all these temple references? By painting his narrative with temple hues, Luke presents Jesus as the locus of God's presence to the world. Jesus is the new Adam, priest, and temple who will extend God's presence and has brought new creation to earth. The temple references and their connection to Eden indicate Jesus's mission is to make the whole earth the temple again. This mission begins with Jesus being born and culminates in his death, resurrection, and ascension. Now the curtain is torn in two, making way for God's presence to fill all of creation.

Luke and the Least of These

The Old Testament demonstrates a pervasive concern for the marginalized. The Torah includes regulations for the protection of the poor. Exodus 23:6 says, "You must not deny justice to a poor person among you in his lawsuit." Deuteronomy 15:7–11 puts it this way:

> "If there is a poor person among you, one of your brothers within any of your city gates in the land the LORD your God is giving you, do not be hardhearted or tightfisted toward your poor brother. Instead, you are to open your hand to him and freely loan him enough for whatever need he has. Be careful that

there isn't this wicked thought in your heart. . . . Give to him, and don't have a stingy heart when you give, and because of this the LORD your God will bless you in all your work and in everything you do. For there will never cease to be poor people in the land; that is why I am commanding you, 'Open your hand willingly to your poor and needy brother in your land.'"

In fact, the Jewish tradition presents a threefold category of who to care for: the widow or fatherless, the foreigner, and the poor (Deut 24:19–21; Ps 146:9; Jer 7:6, 22:3; Zech 7:10). In addition, the prophets continually condemn those who oppress the poor. Isaiah castigates those who "add house to house and join field to field until there is no more room and you alone are left in the land" (Isa 5:8). Amos says those who oppress the poor and crush the needy will be taken away into exile by fishhooks (Amos 4:1–2). Later he continues saying that God will never forget the people who "trample on the needy and do away with the poor of the land, asking, 'When will the New Moon be over so we may sell grain, and the Sabbath, so we may market wheat? We can reduce the measure while increasing the price and cheat with dishonest scales. We can buy the poor with silver and the needy for a pair of sandals and even sell the chaff!'" (8:4–6). It is only proper, therefore, that Jesus cares for these three groups. This is especially evident in Luke's Gospel. Mary's words set the tone for the whole Gospel: "He has toppled the mighty from their thrones and exalted the lowly. He has satisfied the hungry with good things and sent the rich away empty" (1:52–53). These words echo the words of Hannah in 1 Samuel: "He raises the poor from the dust and lifts the needy from the trash heap. He seats them with noblemen and gives them a throne of honor" (2:8).

Jesus is thus the one who enacts this "great reversal." He announces that the poor are blessed (Luke 6:20). When Jesus enters the temple, he sees a poor widow dropping in two tiny coins. He tells the disciples she is the righteous one (21:1–4). Jesus also tells the story of the rich man and Lazarus (16:19–31). The rich man goes to Hades, but Lazarus sits beside Abraham. This is a warning against neglecting the needs of the poor. Zacchaeus, who makes restitution to the poor for his thievery, stands in contrast to this example (19:8).

Jesus also cares for the sick and lame. Both these groups would have been poor and would have to beg for a living. Jesus summarizes his ministry to John the Baptist as "the blind receive their sight, the lame walk, those with leprosy are cleansed, the deaf hear, the dead are raised, and the poor are told the good news" (7:22). He goes to Peter's mother-in-law and heals her of a fever (4:38–40). He says he was sent to go to the sick and sinners (5:31–32). Later, when Jesus tells the parable of the banquet, the master of the house tells the host to invite the poor, maimed, lame, and blind (14:13, 21). This parable occurs in no other Gospel.

Jesus also welcomes the foreigner in Luke. He heals a centurion's servant (7:1–10). He receives Samaritans and does not accept any notions of ethnic superiority. James and John ask if they can call fire down from heaven to consume the Samaritans, but Jesus turns and rebukes them (9:51–55). In the parable of the good Samaritan, Jesus points to the Samaritan (instead of a priest or Levite) as someone who was a good neighbor (10:29–37). Then, when passing again through Samaria, Jesus heals ten men with leprosy. Only one Samaritan man returns to thank him, and Jesus blesses him (17:11–19).

Additionally, Luke shows special attention to the widow and fatherless. In Luke 2 Anna, the widow, meets Jesus and thanks God for the redemption he is providing (2:36–38). Jesus tells the story of Elijah going to the widow at Zarephath in Sidon (4:26). When Jesus is in Nain, he touches a dead man and tells him to get up, and the man goes back to his mother (7:11–17). This man's mother was a widow. Jesus tells the parable of the persistent widow (18:1–8) and praises a poor widow for dropping two coins into the temple treasury (21:1–4).

Finally, Luke also has a particular focus on the involvement of women. His Gospel begins with Elizabeth and Mary. Then the prophetess Anna appears to praise the Lord for Jesus's arrival (2:36). Jesus also notes that Elijah was sent to a Gentile woman in Sidon (4:26). Luke is the only one to specifically name the women followers of Jesus (8:1–3). He tells the story of the woman who touched Jesus so that her flow of blood would stop (8:42–48), and he praises Mary for sitting at his feet while Martha performs the typical social duties of the day (10:38–42). Luke also uses women both at the cross and in post-resurrection reports (23:27; 24:1–3, 9–11). For Luke, women were central to Jesus's ministry.

All these stories from Luke display that Jesus came to reverse the fortunes of the poor, the foreigner, and the widow (Zech 7:10). He fulfills the commands of the Torah in caring for "the least of these." He performs what Israel was called to do all along. God's mission is to reverse things on the earth. Jesus begins the restoration project one individual at a time.

Gospel Connections

Like the other Gospel writers, a distinct emphasis on the gospel exists in Luke. While all the Gospels have harmony in terms of the core elements of the gospel, each writer provides a unique angle on the good news that cannot be contained by one image or metaphor. The gospel for Luke includes the confession that Jesus is Lord, the gospel as salvation, and the gospel is only good news because of Jesus's ascension.

The Gospel as Jesus Is Lord

In one sense, a good summary of the gospel is "Jesus is Lord." As N. T. Wright writes, "The gospel itself refers to the proclamation that Jesus, the crucified and risen Messiah, is the one, true and only Lord of the world."[13] Though this might seem like an insufficient description, it touches all aspects of life. What humanity needs is both a good king and God himself to come and redeem us. The confession "Jesus is Lord" affirms God has done this in his Son, Jesus Christ.

Luke is the only Gospel writer to regularly use "Lord" as a title for Jesus. *Lord* is the Greek word used by the Septuagint to translate the holy name of God (Yahweh) and Adonai (Lord or Master). Luke continues to use the name *Lord* to refer to Yahweh (1:6, 9, 15–16, etc.). However, he also includes instances when Jesus is referred to as Lord. (The italics in the following examples are mine.)

- Elizabeth says, "How could this happen to me, that the mother *of my Lord* should come to me?" (1:43).
- The angels say to the shepherds, "Today in the city of David a Savior was born for you, who is the Messiah, *the Lord*" (2:11).
- When Jesus sees a widow weeping over the death of her only son, Luke says, "When *the Lord* saw her, he had compassion on her and said, 'Don't weep'" (7:13).
- Mary is described as sitting at *the Lord's* feet (10:39).
- It is *the Lord* who turns and look at Peter (22:61).
- The women announce to the disciples that "*the Lord* has truly been raised" (24:34).

Jesus is the Lord but in two ways. He is both King and Master, but the term also indicates he is more than that. He himself is Yahweh embodied.

Luke picks up on this lordship language in his second volume, Acts, in two summative texts. While Luke recognizes Jesus *is* Lord, he also recognizes he *will be* Lord.

---

[13] N. T. Wright, Paul in Different Perspectives: Lecture 1: "Starting Points and Opening Reflections" (lecture presented at the Pastors' Conference at Auburn Avenue Presbyterian Church, Monroe, LA, January 3, 2005), https://ntwrightpage.com/2005/01/03/paul-in-different-perspectives/.

"He *will be* great and *will be* called the Son of the Most High" (Luke 1:32, emphasis added). This is indicated in Acts 2:36, when Peter's climactic conclusion to his Pentecost speech asserts that Jesus has become Lord: "Therefore let all the house of Israel know with certainty that God has made this Jesus, whom you crucified, both Lord and Messiah."

But how can the Lord be made Lord? This is not adoptionistic language. Rather, Luke tells the story of how Jesus was *appointed* as Lord from long ago (even before time began), *designated* in his life and baptism, and then *installed* as Lord at his ascension. As Ben Witherington explains, "It was not that Jesus became *someone* different from who he was before, but that he entered a new stage in his career, or assumed new roles after the ascension."[14] An epochal shift has taken place. The Lord was made Lord. He was Lord (Yahweh) before his birth, and now he is the *messianic Lord* who has accomplished God's will.

The gospel is therefore "Jesus is Lord" in a double sense. He is Lord in the sense that he is King and Master of the earth. For example, a "lord" stands over a slave (Matt 10:24–25; 18:25; Luke 12:36–37; Eph 6:5; Col 3:22). The term can also indicate ownership (Matt 15:27; Mark 12:9; Luke 19:33; Gal 4:1). While the Roman emperors Augustus and Tiberius rejected the title, Emperor Caligula found the title attractive. Nero is also described as "lord of the world" in an inscription. Domitian used the title *dominus et deus noster* (Our Lord and God).

But Jesus is also Lord in a second sense: he is one with God the Father. That is why the Apostles' Creed (120–50) confesses, "I believe in Jesus Christ, his [the Father's] only Son, our Lord." The Nicene Creed (381) says it this way: "We believe in God the Father almighty. . . . And in one Lord Jesus Christ, the only Son of God." The Chalcedonian Creed (451) asserts, "We . . . teach men to confess one and the same Son, our Lord Jesus Christ, the same perfect in godhead and also perfect in manhood."

The early church did not make up these affirmations, nor was this a later development, though it was a growing apprehension. Luke provides a myriad of clues that fuse Jesus's identity with Yahweh. After Jesus heals the Gerasene demoniac, Jesus tells him to go back to his house and tell all that *God* has done for him. The man went throughout the town telling how much *Jesus* had done for him (Luke 8:39). When Jesus rebukes an unclean spirit, the people are astonished at the greatness of God (9:43). Jesus's coming to earth is also described as a visitation in several Lukan passages (1:68, 78; 7:16; 19:44). The precursor text is when God "visited" his people

---

[14] Ben Witherington III, *The Acts of the Apostles: A Socio-Rhetorical Commentary* (Grand Rapids: Eerdmans, 1998), 149 (italics in the original).

in Egypt to release them from bondage to Egypt (Exod 4:31 ESV). Finally, Luke employs images for Jesus associated with God in the Old Testament. For example, when Jesus comes to Jerusalem, he wishes to gather his children as a hen gathers her chicks under her wings (13:34). This language is attributed to God in Deut 32:10–12, where it says that when God shielded Israel in the desert, he hovered over his young and spread his wings over them. Psalm 91:4 also speaks of how the Lord will cover his people in his feathers and under his wings.[15]

Therefore, Jesus is Lord in a double sense.[16] He is Lord in that he is King and Master of the universe. He is also Lord in the sense that he is of the same essence of the Father. Both are necessary for our salvation. Luke reminds us that the gospel is that Jesus is Lord.

The Gospel as Salvation

We tend to equate salvation with the gospel, but it is Luke who is particularly fond of describing Jesus's work under the banner of salvation. Luke employs *sōzō* or a related word forty-seven times in his two-volume work. While the term is used comprehensively in the Scriptures of Christ's redemptive work, it is often a military metaphor. In the Greek world, salvation means saving from one's enemies and the bestowal of blessings and gifts.[17] If justification is a judicial metaphor, regeneration is material, reconciliation is social, adoption is familial, sanctification is cultic, and redemption is economical, then salvation is martial. This is supported in the Old Testament.

In the Old Testament, salvation denotes deliverance, preservation, and rescue. The term first appears when God rescues Israel from Egypt. Moses calls the people in Exod 14:13 to stand firm and see the salvation God will accomplish for them. Yahweh then destroys Egypt in the sea and lets Israel walk on dry ground. In the song by the sea, the people sing, "The LORD is my strength and my song; he has become my salvation" (Exod 15:2).

As readers continue through the Old Testament, salvation continues to communicate deliverance from enemies. When Israel enters the land, Moses tells them they shall be saved from their enemies, referring primarily to the Canaanites (Num 10:9).

---

[15] Hays, *Echoes of Scripture in the Gospels*, 256–61.

[16] C. Kavin Rowe, *Early Narrative Christology: The Lord in the Gospel of Luke* (Grand Rapids: Baker, 2006).

[17] Some of the following material is reproduced from my book *The Mission of the Triune God: A Theology of Acts*, New Testament Theology (Wheaton, IL: Crossway, 2022).

Though the enemy has shifted from the Egyptians to the Canaanites, the idea is the same. Later, while Israel's main opponent is the Philistines, Hannah prays, "My heart rejoices in the LORD; my horn is lifted up by the LORD. My mouth boasts over my enemies, because I rejoice in your salvation" (1 Sam 2:1; see also Ps 3:8; 18:2). The prophets tell Israel to turn to God and be saved while in exile (Isa 45:22; 59:1). So, salvation means safety from enemies, whether from Egypt, the Canaanites, the Philistines, Assyria, or Babylon.[18]

However, in each of these instances, salvation was not only salvation *from* but salvation *to*. Israel was not only saved from Egypt but saved to a new covenant relationship with Yahweh. Israel needed to be saved from the Canaanites to continue their worship of Yahweh. Israel longed for salvation from Babylon so they could gather as a community again. Salvation and freedom are intimately linked. This Old Testament background frames Luke's concept of salvation. Salvation is a military idea centered on a ruler who comes and rescues his people by defeating their enemies so they can form a society in which their traditions are honored. Luke agrees with this prevailing meaning, but he also heightens it.

Luke affirms that salvation has this political sense. Mary praises God her Savior for the arrival of Jesus (Luke 1:47). She thanks God because he is in the process of reversing social positions. Zechariah similarly thanks God for raising up a horn of salvation for Israel (1:69). He defines this deliverance as "salvation from our enemies and from the hand of those who hate us" (1:71). The shepherds are told that in the city of David a Savior has been born (2:11). A Savior in the city of David would indicate a liberator of Israel. Simeon takes up Jesus in his arms while in the temple and identifies Jesus as the embodiment of salvation: "My eyes have seen your salvation" (2:30). John the Baptist quotes from Isaiah, saying he prepares the way of the Lord "and everyone will see the salvation of God" (3:6).

Other times salvation is put under the banner of healing. Jesus restores the shriveled hand of a man in the synagogue on the Sabbath. When the scribes and Pharisees are incensed, he asks, "Is it lawful to do good on the Sabbath or to do evil, to save life or to destroy it?" (6:9). When the woman who had suffered from bleeding for twelve years touches Jesus, Jesus turns to her and declares, "Your faith has saved you. Go in peace" (8:48). When the synagogue leader's daughter has died, Jesus turns to him and

---

[18] It is also clear that it is the Lord who saves. Deuteronomy 33:29 says the people are saved by the Lord. Even when salvation seems to come from secondary causes, the Scriptures show that the Lord saves. It is the Lord who raised up judges who saved Israel (Judg 2:16, 18; 3:9, 31; 6:14–15). People are powerless to save (Jer 14:9; Hos 13:10). If they return to the Lord, they will be saved (Isa 30:15).

says, "Only believe, and she will be saved" (8:50). When Jesus is crucified, the people stand there watching. They say, "He saved others; let him save himself" (23:35; see also vv. 37, 39).

Jesus also equates salvation with entering the kingdom of God. The rich young ruler comes to Jesus, and Jesus declares it is difficult for a rich man to enter the kingdom. The people ask, "Then who can be saved?" (18:26). Zacchaeus pledges to make restitution, so Jesus proclaims salvation has come to his house and then affirms the Son of Man came to seek and save the lost (19:9–10).

This analysis might suggest salvation in Luke is exclusively focused on a "this-worldly" reality, but this is only part of the picture and distorts the thrust of Luke's narrative. Zechariah not only speaks of salvation as deliverance from enemies but as the forgiveness of sins (1:77). At Simon's house, when the woman anoints Jesus's feet, he declares to her that her sins are forgiven (7:48). Then he tells her, "Your faith has saved you. Go in peace" (7:50). As one steps into Acts, Luke consistently ties salvation to the forgiveness of sins (Acts 2:38; 5:31; 10:43; 13:38; 15:9; 22:16; 26:18).

The most important facet for defining salvation is the way Jesus acts as Savior. He does not go after Rome. He does not seek Caesar's throne. He does not seek to destroy the enemies of Israel. Rather, his main mission as Savior is to go to the cross to heal and restore creation. The Savior saves by dying. At the Last Supper, Jesus indicates salvation will come by his body and blood, which will be poured out and sprinkled on his people (Luke 22:19–20). When he stands before Rome (Pilate), he does not seek to escape. He affirms he is the King of the Jews, but Pilate cannot find any reason to put him to death. Jesus's great work of salvation is done on the cross. He is vindicated when he rises from the dead and ascends to the Father.

Though the term *salvation* connoted physical deliverance in the Old Testament, the hope was connected to Israel's rescue from sin (Isa 43:25; 44:22; Jer 31:34). Therefore, while it seldom exclusively expresses a spiritual state, the common sense was of physical deliverance accompanied by spiritual blessings. The two always intertwine in the Old Testament, and Luke picks up that thread. Luke subverts the common notion that our enemies are only outside of us. The enmity begins within. Our fallenness is our fundamental problem. The anthropology and soteriology of Luke is no different from the rest of the New Testament. People need salvation because they are sinners and under the power of the evil one. The enthroned Messiah is thus the benefactor of salvation, the one authorized to give this gift.

Therefore, though interpreters should recognize this *spiritual* element, it would also be a mistake to wholly *spiritualize* it. Luke has a distinctly earthy and embodied view of salvation. Salvation includes healing. Salvation includes deliverance. As

Darrell Bock concludes, "Salvation in Luke is a broad concept. It is about comprehensive deliverance and restoration."[19] The result of salvation in Luke's writings is the reversal of social, spiritual, and physical status by incorporation into Christ.

The Gospel and the Ascension

Often when we describe the gospel, we speak only of Jesus's death.[20] But without Jesus's resurrection and exaltation the cross is a tragedy. While Luke is not the only one to speak of the ascension, he is the only Gospel writer to narrate the ascension. Luke narrates Jesus's ascension twice, once at the end of his Gospel and once at the beginning of Acts.

> Then he led them out to the vicinity of Bethany, and lifting up his hands he blessed them. And while he was blessing them, he left them and was carried up into heaven. After worshiping him, they returned to Jerusalem with great joy. And they were continually in the temple praising God. (Luke 24:50–53)

> After he had said this, he was taken up as they were watching, and a cloud took him out of their sight. While he was going, they were gazing into heaven, and suddenly two men in white clothes stood by them. They said, "Men of Galilee, why do you stand looking up into heaven? This same Jesus, who has been taken from you into heaven, will come in the same way that you have seen him going into heaven." (Acts 1:9–11)

While it might seem as though the Gospel of Luke does not seem to make much of the ascension since it occurs at the end, Luke actually makes the ascension a focal point. In fact, the rest of the New Testament "thinks and speaks from this point, with a backward reference" to the ascension of Jesus Christ.[21] One of the surest markers of the ascension is the title attributed to Jesus: Lord (Luke 1:17, 43, 76; 2:11; 3:4; 5:8, 12; 6:5, 46; 7:6, 13; 9:54, 59, 61; 10:1; etc.). Jesus is labeled "Lord" because he has been enthroned.

The ascension is the moment when Jesus is installed as the Son of Man from Dan 7:13–14. Several clues in Luke's literature indicate that this is Jesus's

---

[19] Darrell L. Bock, *A Theology of Luke and Acts*, Biblical Theology of the New Testament (Grand Rapids: Zondervan Academic, 2012), 237.

[20] Some of the following is taken from my book *The Ascension of Christ: Recovering a Neglected Doctrine* (Bellingham, WA: Lexham, 2020).

[21] Karl Barth, *Church Dogmatics* (Peabody, MA: Hendrickson, 2010), 4.15.2, 134.

enthronement ceremony. First, Luke says Jesus was carried up to heaven. Second, he notes a cloud took him out of their sight. Third, the disciples witnessed this reality. Fourth, the disciples worshipped during this event. In Daniel 7 the Son of Man also ascends with the clouds of heaven, Daniel witnesses it, and everyone worships the Son of Man. These intertextual references indicate it is the Son of Man, not the rulers of the earth (beasts), who sits on God's throne. They might seek power, but it is only given to the human one.

While Luke emphasizes Jesus's lordship in the ascension, he also points to Jesus's high priesthood by mentioning two details. First, Luke says Jesus blesses the disciples before he leaves. In the Old Testament, as the high priest left the tent of meeting, he would lift up his hands and bless the people (Lev 9:22–23). This was modeled after both Moses and Melchizedek, who blessed Israel and Abraham. Numbers provides the content of the priestly blessing: "May the LORD bless you and protect you; may the LORD make his face shine on you and be gracious to you; may the LORD look with favor on you and give you peace" (6:24–27).

Part of the gospel is Jesus blessing us as the true High Priest. He does this as his face shines in the transfiguration, but the transfiguration is an anticipation of the ascension. In Luke, God's blessing is regularly connected with his presence (1:42, 68–69; 2:28–32). Jesus is the new Aaron who extends his hands over the people and grants the peace of the Spirit. Jesus fulfills the Aaronic blessing by giving it.[22]

T. F. Torrance correctly connects the Lukan blessing with Pentecost: "Pentecost is the content and actualization of that high priestly blessing. [Jesus] ascended in order to fill all things with his presence and bestow gifts of the Spirit upon men."[23] The timing of the gift of the Spirit is important here. Only *after* Jesus ascends is he positioned to give his people the Spirit as the priest. The ascension marks the perfection of his work as priest.

Second, Luke details that Jesus was carried into heaven, and clouds covered him. This is modeled after Moses and Aaron, the first priests who ascended to God. In Exodus 24, God tells Moses to come up on the mountain while the rest of Israel should worship from afar: "Moses alone is to approach the LORD, but the others are

---

[22] Kelly M. Kapic, "Receiving Christ's Priestly Benediction: A Biblical, Historical, and Theological Exploration of Luke 24:50–53," *Westminster Theological Journal* 67, no. 2 (2005): 252.

[23] T. F. Torrance, *Space, Time and Resurrection* (London: T&T Clark, 2000), 118.

not to approach, and the people are not to go up with him" (v. 2). The text of Moses's meeting with God follows.

> So Moses arose with his assistant Joshua and went up the mountain of God. He told the elders, "Wait here for us until we return to you. Aaron and Hur are here with you. Whoever has a dispute should go to them." When Moses went up the mountain, the cloud covered it. The glory of the LORD settled on Mount Sinai, and the cloud covered it for six days. On the seventh day he called to Moses from the cloud. The appearance of the LORD's glory to the Israelites was like a consuming fire on the mountaintop. Moses entered the cloud as he went up the mountain, and he remained on the mountain forty days and forty nights. (24:13–18)

Moses's ascent was the pattern for the priestly service. Priests symbolically entered the highest heavens as they entered the Holy of Holies to meet with God and intercede for the people. Cherubim on the curtains indicated priests were approaching the heavens. Aaron is commanded to come inside the veil in an ordered way, for the Lord will appear in the cloud over the mercy seat. The cloud kept him from beholding the full glory of the Lord. He comes before the Lord with a sacrifice (Lev 16:3, 6–10, 25), dressed in a holy linen coat (16:4), bathed (16:4, 24), with incense before the Lord (16:12–13), and with blood sprinkled seven times on the mercy seat and the altar (16:14, 19). Exodus 28:29 informs readers that when the high priest enters the Holy Place, he bears the names of the sons of Israel on his breastpiece, thus indicating going before God on behalf of the people.

Jesus also ascends as the Priest, but his ascension is different. Rather than ascending to Mount Sinai or the Holy of Holies, he ascends to the heavens, the true temple. At the ascension Jesus begins to minister in the actual highest heavens. The Most Holy Place symbolizes the reality Jesus now fulfills at his ascension. Priests would offer their sacrifices on earth, but Jesus now offers his sacrifice in the true tent. And unlike the priests on earth, Jesus is holy, innocent, unstained, and separated from sinners (Heb 7:26). Luke has taken pains to communicate Jesus is righteous and innocent (23:4, 14, 22; 23:15, 40, 47), thus indicating he is the pure Priest.

While we tend to focus on the cross and resurrection, the ascension of Christ resolves the narrative. It is the climax when Jesus is installed as the great King and the true High Priest. The ascension reveals Christ's exaltation, finishes his work on the earth, guarantees his current sovereignty, and pledges his return. The ascension is the crown and climax to Christ's story.

Life Connections

God's people are commanded to care for the poor and marginalized. Luke challenges the idea that Christians could be the type who care about doctrine but do not care for their fellow citizens of earth. For Luke, the gospel message is tightly connected to the idea of enacting justice and loving those who are in need. When Jesus announces his message he describes it as good news *to the poor*, release *to the captives*, sight *to the blind* (4:18).

Jesus does not give a program or policy to follow, but the concept of moral proximity can be helpful for those seeking to walk in Jesus's footsteps. Jesus traveled around and healed those who were near to him. Likewise, Christians should enact care first and foremost with those to whom they are nearest. This starts in the nuclear family. Sexual, physical, and emotional abuse run rampant in homes, but those who are for social justice must address the enemy at home. Parents must care for their children in a way that does not threaten or scare them physically. Siblings should protect one another and not seek to take advantage of one another. We should be quick to protect the weak in our midst.

This idea of moral proximity should next find application in the church. Throughout the Bible, God's people are to do good to all, but especially to the household of faith (Gal 6:10). That is why in Acts we see the believers sharing their possessions and giving to the poor within their communities. The church is the first social safety net. This means when someone in your faith community goes bankrupt, the church should be there to help that person. Or when someone has a tragedy, the church should rally around him or her. It is easy to talk about caring for the world, but often the world is right next to us.

Some might think I am advocating for the rest of world to be ignored, but this is not the case. The larger population is in the next concentric circle of moral proximity. Christians are called to do good to all. This is why Christians were the first ones to start hospitals and schools. Christians can join any number of organizations to help with orphan care or to provide clean water, medical assistance, and education. Following in the tradition of Luke, we need to have a renewed vision for how we can use our resources for the good of humanity.

Luke reminds us that part of our witness includes doing good. Yes, the Gospels are to engender faith. However, as we trust Jesus, we listen to what he says about those who need help. Often our witness is stunted because we unintentionally communicate that we only care about people's minds rather than their whole being (Jas 1:27). Luke reminds us that Jesus came to save us in a holistic sense as we await that final day when everything will be made right.

Interactive Questions

3.1. What makes Luke unique compared to the rest of the Gospels?

3.2. What does Luke's prologue tell us about his work?

3.3. What are the themes of Luke's Gospel that the infancy narrative foreshadows?

3.4. What are some main Old Testament echoes that readers find in Luke?

3.5. How does Luke portray the marginalized?

3.6. How does the hope of Jubilee release function in Luke?

3.7. What is Luke's view of salvation?

3.8. What is the role of the temple in Luke?

3.9. Why does Luke include the unique material that he does after Jesus's resurrection?

Recommended Resources

Modern Commentaries

Bock, Darrell L. *Luke.* 2 vols. Baker Exegetical Commentary on the New Testament. Grand Rapids: Baker Academic, 1994–96.

Edwards, James R. *The Gospel according to Luke.* The Pillar New Testament Commentary. Grand Rapids: Eerdmans, 2015.

Garland, David E. *Luke.* Zondervan Exegetical Commentary on the New Testament. Grand Rapids: Zondervan Academic, 2011.

Green, Joel B. *The Gospel of Luke.* The New International Commentary on the New Testament. Grand Rapids: Eerdmans, 1997.

Johnson, Luke T. *The Gospel of Luke.* Sacra Pagina. Collegeville, MN: Liturgical Press, 1991.

Just, Arthur, Jr. *Luke.* Ancient Christian Commentary on Scripture. Downers Grove, IL: InterVarsity Press, 2005.

Marshall, I. Howard. *The Gospel of Luke.* The New International Greek Testament Commentary. Grand Rapids: Eerdmans, 1978.

Early Commentaries

Aquinas, Thomas. *Gospel of St. Luke Parts 1 and 2*. Catena Aurea. Vol. 3. New York: PCP, 2009.

Cyril of Alexandria. *Commentary on Luke*. Pickering, OH: Beloved, 2014.

Just, Arthur A. *Luke*. Ancient Christian Commentary on Scripture. New Testament III. Downers Grove, IL: InterVarsity Press, 2003.

Origen. *Homilies on Luke*. The Fathers of the Church. Vol. 94. Translated by Joseph T. Lienhard, S. J. Washington, DC: The Catholic University of America Press, 2009.

Special Studies

Alexander, Loveday. *The Preface to Luke's Gospel: Literary Convention and Social Context in Luke 1:1–4 and Acts 1:1*. Society for New Testament Studies Monograph Series. Book 78. Cambridge: Cambridge University Press, 2005.

Baltzer, Klaus. "The Meaning of the Temple in the Lukan Writings." *Harvard Theological Review* 58, no. 3 (July 1965): 263–77.

Bartholomew, Craig G., Joel B. Green, Anthony C. Thiselton. *Reading Luke: Interpretation, Reflection, Formation*. Scripture and Hermeneutics Series. Vol. 6. Milton Keynes, UK: Paternoster Press, 2005.

Bock, Darrell L. *A Theology of Luke and Acts: God's Promised Program, Realized for All Nations*. Biblical Theology of the New Testament. Grand Rapids: Zondervan Academic, 2012.

Chace, J. Bradley. *Jerusalem, the Temple, and the New Age in Luke-Acts*. Macon, GA: Mercer University Press, 1988.

Denova, Rebecca I. *The Things Accomplished Among Us: Prophetic Tradition in the Structural Pattern of Luke-Acts*. Sheffield, UK: Sheffield Academic Press, 1997.

Esler, Philip Francis. *Community and Gospel in Luke-Acts: The Social and Political Motivations of Lucan Theology*. Society for New Testament Studies Monograph Series. Book 57. Cambridge: Cambridge University Press, 1989.

Evans, Craig A., and James A. Sanders. *Luke and Scripture: The Function of Sacred Tradition in Luke-Acts*. Eugene, OR: Wipf and Stock, 1993.

Fitzmyer, Joseph A. *Luke the Theologian: Aspects of His Teaching*. Eugene, OR: Wipf and Stock, 1989.

Garrett, Susan R. *The Demise of the Devil: Magic and the Demonic in Luke's Writings*. Minneapolis: Fortress, 1990.

Green, Joel B. *The Theology of the Gospel of Luke.* New Testament Theology. Cambridge: Cambridge University Press, 1995.

Kimball, Charles. *Jesus' Exposition of the Old Testament in Luke's Gospel.* Journal for the Study of the New Testament Supplement 94. Sheffield, UK: Sheffield Academic Press, 1994.

Litwak, Kenneth. *Echoes of Scripture in Luke-Acts: Telling the History of God's People Intertextually.* New York: T&T Clark, 2005.

Moessner, David P. *Lord of the Banquet: The Literary and Theological Significance of the Lukan Travel Narrative.* Minneapolis: Fortress, 1989.

Neagoe, Alexandru. *The Trial of the Gospel: An Apologetic Reading of Luke's Trial Narratives.* Society for New Testament Studies Monograph Series. Book 116. Cambridge: Cambridge University Press, 2002.

Rowe, C. Kavin. *Early Narrative Christology: The Lord in the Gospel of Luke.* Grand Rapids: Baker Academic, 2006.

Senior, Donald. *The Passion of Jesus in the Gospel of Luke.* The Passion Series. Vol. 3. Collegeville, MN: Liturgical Press, 1989.

Strauss, Mark. *The Davidic Messiah in Luke-Acts.* The Library of New Testament Studies. Sheffield: Sheffield Academic Press, 1995.

Turner, Max. *Power from on High: The Spirit in Israel's Restoration and Witness in Luke-Acts.* Eugene, OR: Wipf and Stock, 2000.

Zwiep, Arie W. *The Ascension of the Messiah in Lukan Christology.* Novum Testamentum Supplements. Vol. 87. Leiden: Brill, 1997.

4

John

Outline[1]

1. The Book of Signs (1–12)
    a. Prologue (1:1–18)
    b. John the Baptist (1:19–51)
    c. Four Jewish traditions (2–4)
    d. Four Jewish feasts (5–10)
    e. Foreshadowing resurrection (11–12)
2. The Book of Glory (13–20)
    a. The Servant Messiah (13:1–30)
    b. Jesus's farewell speech (13:31–16:33)
    c. Jesus's high priestly prayer (17)
    d. The passion (18–19)
    e. The resurrection (20)
3. Epilogue (21)

---

[1] This outline is similar to and dependent on Raymond Brown, *An Introduction to the Gospel of John*, ed. Francis J. Moloney, The Anchor Yale Bible Reference Library (New Haven, CT: Yale University Press, 2003), 298–316.

THE APOSTLE JOHN IN THE NEW TESTAMENT

- John and his brother James were among the first disciples called. They were fisherman and sons of Zebedee (Mark 1:19–20).
- John belonged to the inner circle of Jesus's followers: Peter, James, and John (Matt 17:1; Mark 5:37; 13:3; 14:33; Luke 8:51; 9:28).
- James and John bore the nickname "Sons of Thunder" (Mark 3:17), indicating they were headstrong (Mark 10:35–41; Luke 9:51–55).
- John accompanied Peter early on in Acts (3:1–11; 4:1, 19–20). His brother James was the first apostle to die as a martyr (Acts 12:2), and John became known as one of the pillars of the church (Gal 2:9).

Author, Date, and Message

While the authorship of the Synoptic Gospels is debated, no other authorship is more disputed than the Fourth Gospel. Three main proposals are made. First, most throughout history have claimed the author is John, the son of Zebedee and disciple of Jesus. Second, some have claimed a certain individual named a certain "John the Elder" penned this work. Finally, some have said a Johannine community produced the Fourth Gospel.

The arguments for John, the son of Zebedee, are the following. First, according to the Synoptics John was one of the disciples (Matt 4:21; 10:2; Mark 1:19; 3:17; 10:35; Luke 5:10) and, maybe more importantly, one of the three in Jesus's inner circle who would have been an eyewitness to these events.

Second, within John's Gospel a literary character appears called "the disciple Jesus loved" (13:23; 20:2; 21:7; 21:20–23). Readers are told in the epilogue, "This is the disciple who testifies to these things and who wrote them down" (21:24). There are also remarkable similarities between John's Gospel, the epistles attributed to John, and Revelation. The internal evidence points to the author as the "disciple Jesus loved." This person is usually assumed to be John.

Third, the external evidence is virtually unanimous that John (the apostle and son of Zebedee) is the author. Irenaeus, Clement of Alexandria, and Tertullian all saw the apostle as the author. Irenaeus said, "John, the disciple of the Lord, who also had leaned upon His breast, did himself publish a Gospel during his residence at Ephesus in Asia."[2] Irenaeus's testimony is important because he was a student of Polycarp, who knew John the apostle.

---

[2] St. Irenaeus of Lyons, *Against the Heresies* (New York: Paulist Press, 2012), 3.1.1.

A few challengers to John the apostle as the author have arisen in the modern era. Some argue a certain John the Elder, an obscure elder at Ephesus, wrote the Fourth Gospel. This view stems from a statement by Papias, quoted by Eusebius, in which he mentions John the Elder.[3] Eusebius says Papias mentions two Johns. The former one he puts with Peter, James, and Matthew (and the other apostles). However, he puts another John, whom he calls the Elder, outside the apostles with Aristion. From this statement, many have argued a second John wrote the Gospel.

This argument has several good responses. First, D. A. Carson notes it is widely recognized that while Eusebius makes a distinction between "apostles" and "elders," Papias does not. In addition, John is designated an elder because he is a first-generation witness who is still alive.[4] Second, not until the nineteenth century did this challenge arise.

Others have argued that it was a Johannine community that wrote this Gospel and it was produced over a period of time. A single document that underwent several revisions might have served as the base. The problem with this view is that it is largely reconstructive guesswork based on minor hints. According to Raymond Brown, John reflects the preaching and teaching of Jesus's disciples around Jerusalem because of the emphasis on Jerusalem and the Jewish festivals. However, John could have focused on these places and events for many reasons. Therefore, the author is most likely John, the apostle and son of Zebedee.

Proposals for the date of John range from before 70 CE to the final quarter of the second century. The precise date is difficult to pinpoint, and even Carson notes that "almost any date between 55 CE and 95 CE is possible."[5] The main evidence people employ to date the Fourth Gospel is the following. First, since Peter's death is narrated retrospectively in 21:18–19, the Fourth Gospel was likely written after 65 CE. Second, John does not discuss the destruction of the temple, whereas the Synoptics include this. We cannot know for sure why, but some have supposed either it had not happened yet or enough time had elapsed that John didn't feel the need to mention it. Given such evidence, many argue the Fourth Gospel was published in the 80s.

---

[3] Eusebius, *Ecclesiastical History* (Cambridge, MA: Harvard University Press, 1926), III, 39.4–5.

[4] D. A. Carson, *The Gospel according to John*, The Pillar New Testament Commentary (Grand Rapids: Eerdmans, 1991), 69–70.

[5] Carson, 82.

DISCOURSES WITH INDIVIDUALS

1. Nathaniel (1:47–51)
2. Nicodemus (3:1–21)
3. Samaritan woman (4:7–26)
4. Martha (11:20–27)
5. Pilate (18:33–19:12)
6. Mary Magdalene (20:14–17)
7. Peter (21:15–22)

John and Luke are the only Gospel writers to explicitly include a purpose statement. John writes to persuade his readers to believe his testimony that Jesus is the Messiah, the Son of God. If they believe, they will have life in his name (20:31). The words *believe*, *life*, and *name*, and the concept of witness, all occur many times throughout John's work. John's Gospel is a witness to Jesus. He writes to compel belief in Jesus's actions and identity.

JOHN AND THE SYNOPTICS

Some have rejected the notion of any literary relationship between John and the Synoptics, but more recently it has been argued that John wrote with literary awareness of the Synoptics. Certain statements might indicate awareness such as "this was before John was put in prison" (3:24) and John explaining it was Mary who anointed the Lord with ointment (11:2). Additionally, John mentions the many other signs Jesus did (20:30–31).

The first thing someone who has read the Synoptics will notice is how unique John is compared to the other Evangelists. He tells stories no Synoptic writer includes. Jesus goes back and forth between Galilee and Jerusalem, while the Synoptics have Jesus mainly ministering in Galilee before proceeding to Jerusalem. Jesus's voice sounds different in that he has long discourses with individuals. John uses images to describe Jesus. He is the lamb; water of life; bread of life; light; good shepherd; true vine; the way, truth, and life. John has no parables, exorcisms, or teaching discourses, and he does not narrate Jesus's baptism, temptation, transfiguration, or even the Last Supper. John alone speaks of the Logos; he describes Jesus's message as eternal life rather than the kingdom of God. About 92 percent of John is not in the Synoptics.

IMAGES OF JESUS

1. Sacrificial lamb (1:36; Leviticus 16)
2. Water of life (4:14; Ezekiel 47)
3. Bread of life (6:35; Exodus 16)
4. Light into darkness (8:12; Gen 1:3)
5. Good shepherd (10:11; Ezekiel 34)
6. Resurrection life (11:25; Dan 12:1–3)
7. Way, truth, and life (14:6; Prov 6:23; 9:6)
8. Vine (15:5; Ezekiel 17)

However, John was also one of the most loved Gospels in the early church. John's Gospel soars with splendor. It begins before time. Before light and darkness. Before creation. The easy style and surface simplicity of John's Gospel conceal the depth and profundity of his writing. Metaphors and symbols abound and are always building on one another, acquiring more layers of meaning, and expanding. Oftentimes, John transforms or evokes images and symbols from the Old Testament. He is a master of irony, and his characters constantly say more than they intend. John the author constantly winks at his readers, asking them if they are following his deeper meaning.

Interpretive Overview

Even though John's Gospel is unique, it is still part of the Fourfold Gospel. Like the other Gospels, John tells the story of Jesus, narrating Jesus's ministry, death, and resurrection. One could view John's structure in many ways. The Gospel begins and ends similarly: it begins with the witness of John the Baptist (1) and ends with the witness of the disciple Jesus loved (21). John is particularly fond of the term *witness*, using it copiously in his Gospel and framing his narrative with the concept.

The first half of John concerns seven signs that Jesus performs pointing to the new creation (1–12). Amid these, Jesus transforms the meaning of four Jewish traditions and then four Jewish festivals. The first half ends with the greatest sign: Lazarus is raised from the dead, foreshadowing Jesus's resurrection.

Chapter 13 introduces the second half of John, the book of glory (13–20). It is called this because John views the cross and resurrection as Jesus's glorification. Unlike the Synoptics, John spends much of his time on Jesus's farewell speech (13–17). Jesus then goes to the garden where he is betrayed. At his trial he is condemned to die and then crucified as the Passover Lamb. Chapter 20 recounts Jesus's victory as it narrates Jesus's resurrection appearances. Jesus meets with various individuals, and John concludes with a statement about the purpose of his Gospel. The epilogue (21) confirms the testimony of the beloved disciple, restores Peter, and corrects a false report.

The Book of Signs (1–12)

The first half of John centers on Jesus's seven signs, but it begins with an affirmation of Jesus as the Word and John the Baptist as witness to Jesus. As Jesus's ministry begins, he performs seven signs: (1) he turns water into wine; (2, 3, 4) he heals three individuals; (5) he supernaturally feeds people; (6) he walks on the water; and (7) he raises from the dead. Structurally, the first half also breaks down into four Jewish traditions and four Jewish festivals.

THE SEVEN SIGNS IN JOHN 1–12

1. Water into wine (2:7–9)
2. Healing the official's son (4:50)
3. Healing the paralyzed man (5:8)
4. Feeding the 5,000 (6:11–12)
5. Jesus walks on water (6:19)
6. Healing the blind man (9:6–7)
7. Lazarus raised from the dead (11:43–44)

Chapters 2–4 follow Jesus as he transforms the meaning of four Jewish traditions (jars, temple, rabbi, well). Jesus fills six Jewish ritual purification jars with new wine (2:1–11), enters the temple and condemns it (2:13–25), teaches a rabbi about new birth (3:1–21), and talks to a Samaritan woman at a sacred well (4:1–26). This is not all that makes up these chapters, but they are unifying actions. The section begins and ends with a Cana reference (2:1; 4:46) and the first and second sign (2:11; 4:54).

Chapters 5–10 follow Jesus as he shows himself as the Messiah at four Jewish feasts and thereby transforms their meaning. No longer is the Cana reference used, but the section is bookended by a reference to colonnades (5:2; 10:23) and contains signs three through six.

Table 4.1: Festivals in John

Festival	Reference in John	Fulfillment
Passover	*2:13, 23*	*New temple*
One of the Jewish festivals—Feast of Trumpets? (Lev 23:23–25) (Sabbath)	5:1, 9	New rest
Passover	*6:4*	*New bread of life*
Tabernacles (Shelters/Booths)	7:2	New provision (water and light)
Dedication (Hanukkah)	10:22	New liberation
Passover	*11:55; 12:1; 13:1*	*New Lamb of God*

After these two sections comes a transition, but it is the ultimate sign (11:1–12:50). Jesus raises Lazarus from the dead. Jesus says to Martha that he is the resurrection and the life and that the one who believes in him will never die (11:25–26). Jesus then heads toward his death as he enters Jerusalem.

Prologue (1:1–18)

Mark begins with John the Baptist's ministry, Matthew goes all the way back to Abraham, and Luke rewinds to Adam in his genealogy. John surpasses them all. He takes a quantum leap back before time and space. John exists on a different plane than the other Gospels. He states what was happening "in the beginning."

In the beginning the Logos was with God, and the Logos was God. All things were created through the Logos (1:1–3). John picks up resonances from both Jewish and Greek traditions and combines them with Lady Wisdom (Prov 8:22–31). In Greco-Roman philosophy the Logos referred to divine reason that brought unity and order to the cosmos. But John will assert later that this Logos took on flesh and was the very Word that spoke through the prophets of old.

The most obvious echo is to Gen 1:1. The words "in the beginning" thrust readers back to the beginning of the Hebrew Bible. However, instead of saying, "In the beginning was God," John says, "In the beginning was the Word." The Word is both distinct from God and is God (1:1).

The narrative turns to John the Baptist but only in that he is a forerunner and witness to Jesus. The Baptizer is not about himself; he points to the light. Words such as *truth* and *witness* display a covenantal law-court theme taken from Isaiah 40–55.[6] John came to witness so all might believe in him. However, the responses to the light were not positive. He came to his own people, but they did not receive him. But those who did receive him became his children (1:6–13).

John testifies this Word, that was in the beginning, has now swooped down to earth. He became flesh and made his temple on the earth, and John has seen him (1 John 1:1). Though no one has ever seen God, Jesus has revealed him. Moses asked to see God, and in Jesus they now have revealed God. The opening eighteen verses introduce readers to most of the themes the apostle will pick up later: life, light, darkness, sending, knowing, believing, seeing, witnessing, rebirth, truth, and glory.

ANCIENT CONNECTIONS 4.1. THE LAMB OF GOD

The Lamb of God language reverberates back to Genesis 22 where God provided a lamb in the place of Isaac on Mount Moriah. It also recalls the Passover when a lamb's blood covered Israel's doorposts as protection (Exod 12:3, 7, 13). The Messiah is described by the prophet Isaiah as a lamb led to the slaughter who takes away the sin of many (Isa 53:7–12).

JOHN THE BAPTIST (1:19–51)

The rest of chapter 1 continues the theme of the Baptizer's witness to Jesus. John the Baptist is the new Elijah, the one who prepares the way; Jesus is the Lamb, who takes away the sin of the world. The Baptizer witnesses the Spirit descending on Jesus and testifies Jesus is the Son of God (1:19–34).

Andrew, Peter, and Philip also begin following Jesus. Philip finds Nathanael, and the narrative pauses (1:35–51). Nathanael becomes a paradigm for restored Israel coming to recognize their King (1:49). When Jesus sees Nathanael coming, he declares he is an Israelite in whom there is no deceit. It was Jacob who was a deceiver and took away Esau's blessing (Gen 27:35). Zephaniah predicts that the remnant of Israel will tell no lies and a deceitful tongue will not be found in their mouths

---

[6] Andrew T. Lincoln, *Truth on Trial: The Lawsuit Motif in the Fourth Gospel* (Grand Rapids: Baker Academic, 2000).

(Zeph 3:13). Jesus then states he saw Nathanael under the fig tree before Phillip called him. The prophets speak of restored Israel all sitting under their own fig tree (Mic 4:4; Zech 3:8–10).

Jesus's response to Nathanael brings the first chapter to a climax. Jesus is the Word, Life, Light, Lamb, and Son of God. But he is also Jacob's stairway (*sullam*) to heaven and Daniel's Son of Man. Jesus says Nathaniel "will see heaven opened and the angels of God ascending and descending on the Son of Man" (John 1:51).[7] Jesus is the bridge between heaven and earth. Daniel's Son of Man will travel on this stairway or highway. By identifying himself as Jacob's ladder Jesus indicates he is both the bridge between God and man and the locus of God's presence.

Four Jewish Traditions (2–4)

In the Cana section (2:1; 4:46) Jesus performs two signs and encounters four Jewish traditions (jars, temple, rabbi, well) and transforms their meaning. Jesus displays he is the reality to which they all point. The old has gone; the new has come. These signs are performed so people will believe in him, but the signs, as in Egypt, do not convince all (Ps 106:7).

First, Jesus goes to a wedding party, where six jars for ritual purification become containers for new wine (2:1–11). At this wedding feast the wine runs out, which is a huge social faux pas, but in the symbolism of John's Gospel it indicates the old era was ending and the new had come. Jesus changes the water into wine. By filling these jars with wine Jesus indicates that the old order was being fulfilled by something greater. Six jars are used because that is one less than seven, the number for completion. By performing this sign Jesus points to the great banquet where the wine will flow liberally (Jer 31:12–15; Hos 14:7; Joel 3:18; Amos 9:13–14). The hour has not come completely, but Jesus displays it is here in part through him. Jesus is the messianic bridegroom (Matt 22:1–14; 25:1–13), but he is even more, because "the Lord of Armies will prepare for all the peoples a feast of choice meat, a feast with aged wine, prime cuts of choice meat, fine vintage wine" (Isa 25:6). John notes this is the first of the miraculous signs that Jesus does. The last sign will also include water, blood, and purification themes (John 19:34).

---

[7] Genesis 28:12 uses this word *stairway* to refer to Jacob's ladder. However, the root *sll* means to lift up or exalt, and it appears in a few key Isaiah texts. Israel is called to make a straight "highway" (*mesillah*) in the desert (Isa 40:3). God will build a "highway" (*mesillah*) for his people (62:10).

Second, Jesus enters the temple and clears it with a whip (John 2:13–25). The temple was the center of the universe for Jews; it was where the presence of God was located. The Messiah was meant to restore true temple worship. However, when Jesus enters the temple, he finds corruption (Zech 14:21; Mal 3:1, 3). People are selling and trading. This would have been common, but the traders must have been taking advantage of the poor. Jesus is furious. He drives out these robbers and turns over tables. Jeremiah also gave a prophetic denouncement of temple corruption in Jeremiah 7, and therefore Jesus stands in a long line of prophets. John even notes the disciples remembered what the psalmist said: "Zeal for your house has consumed me" (Ps 69:9). Jesus desires pure worship, a theme repeated in John's Gospel (John 4:23). The Jews ask Jesus by what authority he does these things. Jesus replies with a cryptic statement about destroying the temple and raising it back up in three days. The disciples later understand he is referring to his body (2:18–22). Jesus is not only the messianic bridegroom; he is also the new temple (Ezekiel 40–48). His body is pure and is the locus of God's presence.

THE TEMPLE CLEANSING IN JOHN

Though the Synoptics tell the story of Jesus cleansing the temple at the end of their work, John places it at the beginning. Whether there are two temple cleansing episodes or just one is debated. Jesus, as a faithful Jew, would have traveled to Jerusalem multiple times and not only once as the Synoptics portray it. Therefore, Jesus, as John narrates it, would have gone back to Jerusalem early in his ministry and not simply at the end. However, the Synoptics portray Jesus as going to his death in part because of his temple action (Matt 26:61; 27:40; Mark 14:58). This means it more likely would have occurred toward the end of his ministry, but John moves it toward the beginning because it is programmatic for understanding Jesus. However, it is also possible that two temple cleansings occurred.

The third Jewish tradition Jesus transforms is that of a Rabbi. In John 3 Jesus confounds the teacher Nicodemus, showing he is Israel's one true teacher. Nicodemus needs more teaching and, most importantly, to be born from above. Like the previous episodes, Nicodemus is both a real and symbolic figure who represents the Jewish leadership. Nicodemus, a Pharisee, comes to Jesus at night. Already readers have learned Jesus is light; he dispels darkness. Nicodemus is impressed by Jesus's signs, but Jesus says that unless Nicodemus is born from above, he cannot see the kingdom of God. Nicodemus is confused because he thinks Jesus is talking about physical birth (being born again). Already the first three stories have indicated that Jesus presses into the deeper meaning of wine, the temple, and now what it means to be born again. Jesus corrects Nicodemus and even questions whether he is a teacher since he does not understand these things. Nicodemus and the rest of the Jewish leadership need to be born again from above. The prophet Ezekiel prophesied that in the latter days the Spirit will give them a new heart (Ezek 36:24–27). This is not something they can do on their own; it needs to be done to them. Then Jesus points out he himself is from above, saying, "No one has ascended into heaven except the one who descended from heaven—the Son of Man" (John 3:13; Dan 7:13–14).

ANCIENT CONNECTIONS 4.2. MEETINGS AT WELLS IN THE OLD TESTAMENT

- After Hagar fled from Sarah, an angel of the Lord appeared to her at a well (Gen 16:6–14).
- Abraham's servant stopped at a well and met Rebekah there (24:10–21).
- Jacob met Rachel at a well, where she came to water her father Laban's flock of sheep (29:1–11).
- Moses met his future wife, Zipporah, at a well when she came with her sisters to water their father's flock (Exod 2:15–22).
- Saul met young women who were on their way to draw water while he was searching for his father's donkeys (1 Sam 9:3–12).

Finally, as Jesus passes through Samaria, he goes to a sacred well and displays that he is the true and living water to a Samaritan woman (John 4). Samaritans were viewed as half-breeds because they had intermarried with the Canaanites. This is Jacob's well (Gen 28:12–13). Her appearance at the well at "noon" (4:6) may be meant to contrast with Nicodemus coming at "night" (3:2). Jesus converses with her, which is shocking itself as Jews do not associate with Samaritans and men do not speak to women alone like this. But Jesus is the bridegroom, and the woman eventually rejoices in his words (Ps 45:2, 10–15). Jesus cares for her as the Lord cared for his bride (Ezekiel 16). The conversation centers on a well and the water coming from it. Like before, Jesus uses the water from the well to press into deeper truths. He tells the woman he can give her living water that will satisfy her thirst forever and will spring up in eternal life. Ezekiel speaks of water flowing from the temple and giving life to the earth (47:1–12; Isa 35:6; Jer 2:13; Zech 14:8), and Revelation asserts a river of the water of life flows from the throne of God and the Lamb (Rev 22:1). Samaritans will not worship on their mountain, and neither will Jews. They will all worship through Jesus.

ANCIENT CONNECTIONS 4.3. SAMARIA

Samaritans were treated as half-breeds by Jews or even foreigners (Luke 17:18). To eat with a Samaritan was said to be like eating pork. Their daughters were seen as unclean. The background to the relationship between Jews and Samaritans goes back to 1 Kings 12 and the rebellion of the northern kingdom against the southern kingdom. Omri ended up building the city of Samaria (1 Kgs 16:24), which became the capital of the northern kingdom, and Jerusalem was the capital of the southern kingdom. Both the north and the south were exiled, but those who remained in the land intermarried with Canaanites. When the exiles came back, they sought permission from Alexander the Great to build a temple on Mount Gerizim, and they had their own form of the Pentateuch. The Samaritans therefore had a different capital, customs, and temple.

When the disciples return, the metaphor switches from water to food (John 4:27–42). They urge Jesus to eat. But once again, Jesus sees all of life as symbolic. He gets life from obeying the Father, and they must look to the world, for the harvest is plentiful. For John, all these physical images have a deeper meaning. The old jars, temple, teaching, baptisms, sacred wells, and food could not provide true life. Life only comes through the Son of God. He provides this life as he heals the official's son in Cana—the second sign (4:54). The jars of purification, the temple, the Jewish teaching, and the wells all point to him.

ANCIENT CONNECTIONS 4.4. JEWISH FESTIVALS

Feasts and festivals were common parts of ancient religion. Leviticus 23 detailed Jewish festivals, and Deuteronomy 16 their pilgrimage festivals.

- *Sabbath* was the most frequently observed festival. It occurred weekly, monthly, every seven years, and every fifty years. It included feasting, rest from work, and extra sacrifices. It was based on the pattern shown at creation and redemption in the exodus (Exod 20:9–11; Deut 5:12–15).
- *Passover* was celebrated once a year (fourteenth day of Abib) to commemorate God's election and grace when he redeemed his people from Egypt. The angel of the Lord passed over the houses of Israel that had blood on the doorposts. The feast included a lamb and unleavened bread. People were to dress as if they were ready for travel.
- *Shelters* commemorates the wilderness wanderings after Israel left Egypt. It lasted seven days and included sacrifices and living in tents to recall the wilderness wandering. (Other Bible translations refer to this festival as the Feast of Tabernacles or the Feast of Booths.)
- *Hanukkah* commemorated the cleansing of the temple in the Maccabean revolt. It was celebrated for eight days and was called the *Festival of Lights* because, as the story goes, when the temple was rededicated, even though there was only enough oil for one day, the menorah remained lit for eight days.

Four Jewish Feasts (5–10)

Although John has already mentioned a few festivals (2:23; 4:45), in chapter 5 a particular festival cycle begins (John 5:1; 6:4; 7:2, 8, 10–11, 14, 37; 10:22). In this section Jesus is portrayed as completing four Jewish feasts (Sabbath, Passover, Shelters, and Hanukkah) while also performing signs two through six. Jesus's actions and words toward these festivals produce conflict, but he shows he is the reality to which these calendar cycles point.

On the Sabbath, Jesus heals a lame man—the third sign (5:8). This lame man has been afflicted for thirty-eight years, possibly reflecting the thirty-eight years Israel wandered in the wilderness (5:8; Deut 2:14). This man stands as a symbol for a needy Israel, whom Isaiah said would one day leap like a deer (Isa 35:6). John notes that Jesus went up to Jerusalem for a Jewish festival. We are not exactly sure what festival this is. The important thing is that this healing intentionally occurred on the Sabbath (John 5:9). The healing occurs at a pool called Bethesda (house of outpouring). The man always attempted to enter the pool when the waters were stirred because people believed an angel came down at a certain time and stirred the water to heal people (5:4, 7). Yet Jesus heals him and tells him to pick up his mat and walk. Instead of rejoicing in the lame man's healing, the Jews are furious because, according to their traditions, it is not lawful to pick up mats on the Sabbath.

This whole episode prompts a long discourse on what the Sabbath is and who it is meant for. Jesus responds by pointing to his relation as Son to the Father. He says, "My Father is still working, and I am working also" (5:17). God is always working, and therefore Jesus can work too because, as the Son of God, he participates in God's unique work (5:18). Jesus is the Lord of the Sabbath. Jesus then asserts he is not able to do anything except through the Father's authority. The Jews pore over the Scriptures, but they miss that it is all pointing to Jesus. They are holding onto the shadows rather than embracing the reality. If they believed Moses, they would believe Jesus. As Carson notes, this narrative shows that as the water from the purification pots could not produce the wine of the new kingdom, and as the water from Jacob's well could not satisfy ultimate thirst, so the promises of superstition had no power to transform.[8] Jesus upholds the true meaning of the Sabbath.

The next festival John mentions is Passover (6:4). Several Mosaic echoes occur. Jesus multiplies bread and fish and feeds the 5,000, recalling Israel's manna in the wilderness. This is the fourth sign. He goes up on the mountain (6:3), it is during the Passover celebration (6:4), the language of "test" is employed because Israel was also tested in the wilderness yet failed (6:6), and the Jews begin to grumble (6:41). These actions portray Jesus as the new Moses. God has promised a coming prophet (Deut 18:15–18) and a new exodus (Isa 43:15–19; Jer 23:7; Hos 2:14–15; Mic 7:14–15). As Moses fed the people in the wilderness with bread from heaven (Exod 16:4, 12, 15) now the true prophet feeds his people on the mountain with bread from heaven. The Moses typology continues as Jesus next comes walking to the disciples on the sea. While Moses had led them through the sea, Jesus can walk *over* the sea—the fifth sign (John 6:19; Job 9:8). Jesus teaches them that while Moses gave them bread from heaven, his Father gives them the true bread from heaven (John 6:32–33). Jesus is the bread of life, and whoever eats of him and drinks of him will have everlasting life. This language not only reaches back to the wilderness manna but also alludes to the fact that bread was contained in the temple. The first sin in the garden was also related to eating (Genesis 3). The fall came by eating; redemption will also come by consumption.

---

[8] Carson, *The Gospel according to John*, 242–43.

ANCIENT CONNECTIONS 4.5. FESTIVAL OF SHELTERS RITUALS

- *Water ritual:* According to early Jewish tradition, a priest would fill a golden pitcher with water from the pool of Siloam on the Feast of Tabernacles and bring it to the water gate, where he would pour it into one of two silver bowls. The other bowl was filled with wine, and then both were poured out on the altar (*m. Sukkah* 4.9–10).
- *Light ritual:* Priests would light four large menorahs at the temple so that every courtyard in Jerusalem was lit up (*m. Sukkah* 5.3).

The third festival, the Festival of Shelters (John 7:1–10:21), is mentioned in 7:2. This festival commemorated the wilderness wanderings after Israel left Egypt. Jews would gather to remember God's provision in the wilderness by pouring out water and kindling lights. Every day during the feast the priests would draw water from the pool of Siloam and pour water and wine into the bowls with holes on the altar of the temple. The water would spill over the altar, recalling God's provision of water in the wilderness. The temple was also lit by four large menorahs, meant to recall the pillar of fire that accompanied the Israelites in the wilderness. These actions anticipated Zech 14:7–8, where the prophet said there would be a continuous day and living waters would flow out of Jerusalem. The narrative begins with Jesus going to the temple and teaching. Jesus asks why the Jewish leaders are trying to kill him and asserts he will be with them only a short time. On the last and most important day of the festival Jesus compares himself to water: "If anyone is thirsty, let him come to me and drink" (John 7:37). This is an important remark because in the wilderness the people drank from the rock at Marah, Elim, and Massah (Exod 15:22–25, 27; 17:6–7; Num 20:1–13). The people respond by being divided about who Jesus is.

Jesus not only declares he is their living water but says, "I am the light of the world. Anyone who follows me will never walk in darkness but will have the light of life" (John 8:12). The Festival of Shelters not only celebrated the water in the wilderness but the pillar of fire at night that kept them warm. Jesus now declares he is their light. The Pharisees again question Jesus's testimony, but Jesus says the Father testifies about him. He will be lifted up (Isa 53:12). Then they will know that *he is*, a clear allusion to the name Yahweh gives to Moses in Exod 3:14—"I AM WHO I AM." Jesus predicts his departure and encourages his disciples to "continue in [his] word" (John 8:31). If they know the truth, the truth will set them free. Again, this language has resonances with the Festival of Shelters because the wilderness generation also had the Torah (word), but they did not keep it. In Egypt they were enslaved by a foreign nation; in the wilderness they were enslaved by their own sin. Sin manifests itself in systems and the self. If the Son sets them free, they are free indeed.

JOHN 8 AND YOUR BIBLE

In most English Bibles, John 7:53–8:11 is put into brackets because it is absent from the original manuscripts. Many church fathers omitted this narrative in their comments and pass immediately from 7:52 to 8:12. It was included in earlier English versions, and most view it as a true story from Jesus's ministry but not something originally in John's work. In fact, a few later manuscripts place this story after Luke 21:38, while others place it after John 7:44, 7:36, or 21:25. Additionally, numerous phrases, expressions, and constructions are found nowhere else in John's style of writing. Therefore, the passage seems true to the tradition of Jesus (there is little reason to doubt the event occurred) but not integral to John's narrative nor a part of Scripture.

Jesus performs the sixth sign by healing a man born blind (9:1–41) and then declares he is the Good Shepherd (10:1–21). Both these narratives allude to the Festival of Tabernacles. The wilderness generation wandered about blindly. Moses said those who forsake God's covenant will at noon grope as a blind person (Deut 28:29). However, Jesus is their Good Shepherd who will lead his people beside still waters (10:1–21). Moses was also the shepherd of God's people (Num 27:17) who led them to waters in the wilderness. But Israel suffers under worthless shepherds.

The final festival is the Feast of Dedication (Hanukkah; John 10:22–42). Historically, this celebrated the rededication of the temple by Judas Maccabeus in 164 BCE. As Jesus walks into temple the expectation is high. Will he rededicate the temple again like the Maccabean family? The Jews even surround Jesus and ask him if he is the Messiah. Already Jesus has detailed he is the Good Shepherd (10:14, 22–30), indicating that he is the new restorer of Israel in the mold of David (Ezek 34:23–24). However, he claims even more than that. Jesus asserts that he and the Father are one (John 10:30). Jesus can fulfill all the festivals because he is God himself. This angers the Jews; they pick up stones to kill him. If he is not going to do what they want, if he is going to blaspheme, they will rid themselves of him. Jesus again reiterates that he and the Father are one. They seek to grab him, but he escapes from their grasp. Jesus has claimed he is much more than their Messiah; he is from the Father, and the Father is in him. He is the Son of God.

ANCIENT CONNECTIONS 4.6. THE MACCABEAN REVOLT

The Festival of Dedication was based on an event that took place in the Maccabean Revolt (166–135 BCE). Antiochus IV, the Syrian ruler, sought to turn Israel into a Hellenistic state and even entered the temple and dedicated an altar to Zeus in the Holy Place (abomination of desolation). He attempted to eradicate Judaism. Out of this desecration grew a rebellion called the Maccabean Revolt. This family refused to perform pagan sacrifices and gathered an army of rebels to fight the Syrians. After fighting for some time, the Maccabees liberated the temple in 164 BCE, three years after the desecration by Antiochus Epiphanes. They cleansed the temple and reinstated Jewish sacrifices. This became the Feast of Dedication (also called the Festival of Lights, or Hanukkah). You can read about this story in 1–2 Maccabees.

Foreshadowing Resurrection (11–12)

Antagonism has been increasing. Now Jesus's seventh sign solidifies division, but it also foreshadows his greatest sign: the resurrection. Jesus hears his friend Lazarus is sick, but he decides to stay two more days. He then tells his disciples he is on the way to wake Lazarus up. Like the rest of the characters in John, the disciples interpret this in an earthly way, but Jesus's language exposes the secrets of the universe. When Jesus arrives, Martha runs to Jesus saying that Lazarus already died. Jesus affirms he is the resurrection and life. Then Jesus, being deeply moved, comes to the tomb and calls for Lazarus to come forth. The dead man is raised, prefiguring Jesus's own death and resurrection (11:1–44). In both narratives there are tombs (John 11:38; 20:1), removal of a stone (11:39; 20:1), and death for several days (11:39; 20:1). The body is wrapped in strips of linen (11:44; 20:5), a cloth is wrapped around the head (11:44; 20:7), and the resurrection causes belief (11:45; 20:29).[9] Jesus's body must also go into the ground to sprout new life.

---

[9] Gladd, *Handbook on the Gospels*, 357 (see chap. 1, n. 13).

However, while this sign causes many to believe in Jesus, it also results in his opponents plotting how to kill him (11:45–57). The Jewish leaders are afraid of both losing their position and the wrath of the Romans. The high priest Caiaphas says it is better that one man dies than the nation. He says this to support Jesus's death, but the deeper meaning is that Jesus is going to die *in the place* of the nation. This inadvertent and ironic prophecy not only foreshadows Jesus's resurrection but also his substitutionary death.

In chapter 12 Jesus goes to Bethany, where he is anointed for his burial (12:1–8). Everything in John's narrative now leans toward the cross. The words *fragrance* and *perfume* recall the various sacrifices in the temple (12:3; Exod 29:18; 30:25). Jesus's body is anointed to be the cornerstone in the temple. Jesus leaves Bethany and finally enters Jerusalem. He comes on the Passover festival, indicating that his entrance will be a new redemption by blood. However, he does not come on a warhorse but on a donkey. He comes to die. His entrance causes division, and some praise him, while others plot to kill him. Jesus says this is all according to the Father's will. The Son of Man came for this hour, to be glorified and lifted up (Isa 53:12). He came into the world to draw all people to himself, to repel the darkness, to save the world. If they believe in him, they believe in the Father. But the leaders are blind, for they love the glory of man more than the glory of God. Jesus quotes from Isa 6:10, saying their eyes have become blind and their hearts hard. They have become like Pharaoh, whose heart was hard and whose land was filled with darkness. God will provide redemption, but some might find themselves in the sea rather than on dry ground (12:9–50).

The Book of Glory (13–20)

The book of glory centers on the glory Jesus receives by dying and being raised from the dead. Unlike the Synoptics, John spends a long time on Jesus's farewell speech to his disciples (13–17). Jesus acts as the servant Messiah as he washes the disciples' feet (13), promises them the Holy Spirit on his departure (14), encourages them to have union with the Son (15), and warns them about end-time suffering (16). In Jesus's high priestly prayer, he intercedes for his followers, pleading for unity (17).

After this, Jesus goes to the garden where he will be betrayed (18–19). He goes to trial before the high priest and Pilate. He is condemned to die and be crucified. However, Jesus is clearly in control of his destiny. His death is his choice and the hour of his glorification. Chapter 20 recounts this victory as John narrates Jesus's resurrection appearances. John concludes with a statement about the purpose of his Gospel. The epilogue that follows this section (21) corroborates the testimony of the beloved disciple.

The Servant Messiah (13:1–30)

The first half of John covered several years of Jesus's ministry. The next seven chapters describe Jesus's last twenty-four hours: the last night and Jesus's final words with his disciples. John slows down the narrative for Jesus's death, the crucifixion, and his resurrection.

Before the Passover meal with the disciples, John does not recount the institution of Communion; instead, he narrates Jesus becoming a common servant, showing the world how he will cleanse it. At the Last Supper he takes off his outer clothing and begins to wash his disciples' feet (13:1–20). This was a slave's task, but Jesus shows them that to be great they must become servants. He is about to exemplify the greatest act of self-emptying of all time. The prophet Isaiah tells of a coming "righteous servant" who will submit himself to death (Isa 53:11–12). This washing is also symbolic as Jesus ties it to cleanliness. He came to purify them. Both an ethical aspect and a sacramental component exists to this cleansing. Jesus's service is to be emulated, but it ultimately points to the cross. When Jesus commands his disciples to "wash one another's feet" (John 13:14) he tells them to be "little suffering servant figures."[10] The whole Gospel began with John baptizing in the wilderness, and many narratives have to do with purification and water (1:33; 2:6; 3:5; 4:14, 23; 7:38; 9:7; 19:34).

However, Jesus asserts that one of them is not clean. Jesus foretells that one of the disciples will betray him (13:10–11). He quotes from Ps 41:9, which in its original context describes the oppression of David. Judas has become a typological betrayer of the Davidic servant. Psalm 41 explains that not only those on the outside oppress the Messiah, but there is an enemy from the inside: "Even my friend in whom I trusted, one who ate my bread, has raised his heel against me" (41:9). David himself was betrayed by those closest to him (Saul and Absalom), and Jesus's life fulfills this Davidic design.

ANCIENT CONNECTIONS 4.7. FICTIVE KINSHIP IN JOHN

Fictive kinship is the creation of family relationships that do not exist by blood ("fictive" means "made up"). Covenant relationships in the Old Testament created familial relationships. John's Gospel emphasizes both the believing communities' relationship to Jesus and one another under the banner of fictive kinship. Believers share in a common birth (John 1:12–13). Believers are born of water

---

[10] Gladd, 364.

and Spirit (3:3, 5–6). Believers are children of light (12:36). Christians are called to love one another (13:34). Christians are called to share goods (17:10) and have harmony among themselves (17:11, 21). Jesus also uses this category for his opponents. They are children of the devil, not Abraham (8:39–41).[11]

JESUS'S FAREWELL SPEECH (13:31–16:33)

As Jacob, Moses, Joshua, David, and Paul gave farewell addresses, so does Jesus (Genesis 49; Deuteronomy 33; Joshua 24; 1 Chronicles 28–29; Acts 20). However, these figures did not resurrect. Jesus will rise from the grave and send the Holy Spirit so he can always be with them. Jesus assures, comforts, and consoles his disciples in light of his coming departure. As Gladd argues, the purpose of the farewell speech is given in John 16:33:[12] "I have told you these things so that in me you may have peace. You will have suffering in this world. Be courageous! I have conquered the world."

The first section of Jesus's farewell discourse concerns his departure. He begins by instructing his disciples to love one another. Jesus is going away, and one of the greatest temptations is to fight among themselves. But the best evangelistic strategy is a compelling community: "By this everyone will know that you are my disciples, if you love one another" (13:35). This makes them the true loving Torah community (Lev 19:18). Though Peter wants to imitate Jesus, Jesus tells him he will deny him three times before he leaves (13:36–38). The theme of Jesus's departure continues as Jesus speaks of the place to which he is going: his Father's house to prepare rooms for his family. This language alludes to making rooms in the temple (John 14:1–4; Exod 15:17; Isa 2:2). Jesus leaves to prepare their place in God's presence.

Thomas wants to know where Jesus is going and the way to get there. Jesus affirms he is the way, truth, and life (John 14:5–7). The "way" comes from Isa 40:3 and speaks to the return from exile. "Truth" is more philosophical and points to the trial motif in John's Gospel (John 1:14, 17; 5:33; 8:32, 40, 44; 15:26; 16:7; 18:38). "Life" is a new creation theme John uses consistently (1:4; 3:15–16; 4:14; 5:24; 20:31). Philip asks Jesus to see the Father and Jesus affirms they have seen the Father in Jesus (14:8–11).

The discourse switches from Jesus's relationship to the Father to the sending of the Spirit at his departure (14:15–31). When Jesus leaves, he will send the *parakletos* to them. The word *parakletos* is translated in various ways: helper, comforter,

---

[11] See deSilva, *Introduction*, 436–38 (see chap. 1, n. 3).
[12] Gladd, *Handbook on the Gospels*, 366.

counselor, or advocate. Later, John will describe the Spirit as one of "truth" (14:17), but a comforting tone is also present. The term is likely multifaceted. The point is that Jesus will not leave them as orphans. He will give them his own Spirit, and the Holy Spirit will remind them of everything Jesus has taught.

THE *PARAKLETOS*

The term *parakletos* occurs only in the Johannine writings, but its precise meaning is debated. It is applied to the Holy Spirit in John 14–16 and to Jesus in 1 John 2:1. The etymology of the term suggests it means "one who has been called in to help." In this sense, "helper" or "intercessor" is a good translation. Some argue it is a legal term and therefore "advocate" is a more proper translation, but the word had a more general meaning than being a technical legal term. The argument for a law-court meaning must be derived from the context in which the word is employed more than the word itself.

The second portion of the farewell discourse concerns believers' union with the Son (15:1–16:4). The key image is agricultural. Jesus says, "I am the true vine" (15:1). The Father is the gardener, and believers are the branches. This imagery is pulled from the Old Testament, where Israel is depicted as a vine (Ps 80:9–20; Isa 5:1–7; Jer 8:12–14). If they stay close to Jesus, if they get nourishment from his word, then they are one with him. Abiding in him is necessary because persecution will come (John 15:18–27). If the world hated Jesus, they will also hate those who follow him. This opposition from the world has been noted by John from the beginning (1:9, 29; 3:16–17, 19; 4:42; 12:31). It also reaches all the way back in the Old Testament to the war between the seed of the serpent and the woman (Gen 3:15). The one who hates believers hates Jesus, and if they hate Jesus, they hate the Father. Yet even in their animosity they fulfill the Scriptures: "They hated me for no reason" (John 15:25). This likely comes from Ps 35:19 and 69:4, where David laments those who oppose him. Again, Jesus is painted as the Suffering Servant and his disciples as mini–suffering servants. However, the Spirit will come and be their *parakletos*.

The third section of the farewell discourse dwells on the suffering that is to come (16:1–33). Jesus instructs the disciples about the coming suffering so they might not fall way. In the Old Testament the nation "fell away" from God in the wilderness, during the conquest and when they did not listen to the prophets. The prophets already predicted persecution would increase toward the end (Jer 30:7; Ezekiel 38–39; Dan 11:36–45; 12:10). Yet Jesus has promised his disciples the Spirit. Jesus is going away so that the Spirit can come. It is better if he goes away, for when the Spirit comes, he will convict the world since he is the Spirit of truth. In the Old Testament this convicting means bringing guilt and shame that leads to repentance (2 Sam 7:14; Prov 3:11). Though Jesus has many things to say to his disciples, the Spirit will also teach them. When Jesus leaves they will mourn and wonder why they can no longer see him. However, Jesus says their sorrow will be turned to joy. Anything they ask in the Father's name will be given to them (John 16:22–24).

Jesus closes the farewell discourse by speaking of himself as the conqueror of the world (John 16:25–33). Though Jesus has spoken in figures of speech, one day he will speak to them plainly. There is a sense in which all of Jesus's teaching has been in figures of speech. John has clued us in to the deeper meaning many times: Jesus came from the Father, and he is returning to the Father. He has told them all these things that they may have peace. He has foretold about his departure. He has spoken about how they need to have union with him because he has union with the Father. He has comforted them with news of the coming Holy Spirit. He has reiterated the impending persecution. They will have suffering in the world, but Jesus has conquered the world. He is victorious so they are victorious (1 John 2:13–14; 4:4; 5:4; Rev 2:7; 11:7; 12:11; 13:7; 21:7). They have no reason to fear.

JESUS'S HIGH PRIESTLY PRAYER (17)

Jesus's high priestly prayer is modeled after the priests in the Old Testament who would go before the Father and intercede for the people. Abraham interceded for Sodom and Abimelech (Gen 18:22–23; 20:7, 17), Moses interceded for Israel on multiple occasions (Exod 32:9–14; Deut 9:20–29; Num 14:13–19), Amos asked God to pardon Israel (Amos 7:1–2), and Ezekiel wrestled with God arguing his reputation would be at stake if he destroyed them (Ezek 9:8–11; 11:13–16). Jesus therefore steps into a long tradition of intercessory prayer, and he does so as the true High Priest and Prophet. All the previous saints pleaded for peace between God and man. However, Jesus's request is singular because he is one with the Father. Jesus's requests are based on trinitarian truths. Three sections make up Jesus's prayer: Jesus prays for himself (John 17:1–5), the disciples (vv. 6–19), and the church (vv. 20–26).

Jesus begins by stating the hour has come. The "hour" in John refers to Jesus's death and resurrection (17:1; see 2:4), but it also more generally speaks about the inauguration of the last days when there will be much tribulation (Jer 20:23–24; Dan 8:17, 19; 11:35, 40, 45; 12:1; Joel 4:1; Zeph 1:7). Jesus prays that the Father would glorify the Son in that hour, and he prays for honor at the cross because the cross will also be his moment of shame. A great reversal needs to take place. Jesus prays that he might be glorified so that the Father might be glorified. As the Son is glorified, so is the Father (John 17:1–5).

Jesus then prays for his disciples (17:6–19). Priests would glorify God in their service but also intercede for God's people. Jesus prays for the disciples' protection and sanctity in the world. They are not "of" the world but "of" the Son, and the Son is "of" the Father. Jesus has guarded them, and he prays that they continue to be guarded. This theme can be seen in the Synoptics when Jesus prays for Simon that his faith might not fail (Luke 22:31–32). Yet Jesus acknowledges the "son of destruction" has been lost (17:12). This is in reference to Judas, but this label also characterizes him as one of many to come. The prophet Daniel foretold a figure who would persecute God's people but be destroyed (7:25; 8:24–25; 9:26–27; 11:30–35; 12:10), and Paul speaks of a "mystery of lawlessness" still working in the world (2 Thess 2:7). Jesus prays in light of lawlessness that they might be sanctified by the truth. Already John has consistently used images pointing to Jesus as the Sanctifier of his church (John 1:33; 2:6; 3:5; 4:14, 23; 7:38; 9:7; 19:34).

Finally, Jesus prays for the church (17:20–26). He prays not only for his disciples but all who will hear their words. His prayer for future disciples is twofold. First, he prays that they may be one (17:20–23). Different ethnicities, socioeconomic statuses, and cultures need to come together under the name of God. He bases this unity on the oneness of the Father and Son. The bond between the Son and the Father is the paradigm for the church. Since he is in the Father and they are in him, they can be completely one. Second, he prays that they may come to where he is and see his glory. Jesus has made known to them the Father, and he requests that the love that is in the Trinity might be in them as well (17:24–26).

THE PASSION (18–19)

The hour of glory has now come. The final part of John's story begins and ends in a garden (18:1; 19:41). Jesus is betrayed in the garden but affirms that he must drink the cup the Father has given him to establish the new garden-city. One might think the garden will be a place of rest, but as in Eden, an enemy has slithered in. Judas brings in soldiers to arrest Jesus. However, Jesus foresees everything and is not surprised (18:2–14).

The law-court theme is one of the primary elements in this section. While people think Jesus is under examination, it is the world who is in litigation under Jesus's judgment. In the garden, when they ask who Jesus of Nazareth is, Jesus declares his final "I am" statement. At these words the soldiers fall backward. They cannot stand before the burning bush (18:5–6; Exod 3:14). Jesus demonstrates he is in complete control by two more actions: first, he tells the soldiers to let the disciples go, and then he commands Peter to put his sword away after he has cut off the right ear of one of the high priest's servants. Jesus will drink the cup the Father has filled for him (John 18:8–11).

THE TRIALS IN THE GOSPELS

The four Gospels together reveal four trials.
- Unofficial trial with Annas (John 18:13–24)
- Official trial with the Sanhedrin/Caiaphas with preliminary indictment (Matt 26:59–66; Mark 14:55–64) and then formal indictment (Luke 22:66–71)
- Herod Antipas's hearing of Jesus's case (Luke 23:6–12)
- Roman trial with Pilate (Matt 27:11–26; Mark 15:1–15; Luke 23:1–25; John 18:28–19:26)

Trial scenes come next. First Jesus goes before the Jews (John 18:12–27) and then before Rome and Pilate (18:28–19:16). Soldiers take Jesus before Annas, the father-in-law of Caiaphas, the high priest. John slyly notes this is the same Caiaphas who said it is better for one man to die than the whole nation. Annas and Caiaphas think they are in charge, but they are merely pawns on God's chess board. Peppered between these narratives is Peter's threefold denial of Jesus. While Jesus stands before the illustrious, Peter cannot even stand before a servant girl who asks him if he is one of Jesus's disciples. Jesus's faithfulness is contrasted to Peter's unfaithfulness. When Annas questions Jesus, Jesus asserts that his teaching has been done in public; he has not hidden anything.

After Jesus meets with Caiaphas, he is sent before Pilate (18:28–19:16). The whole world—both Jews and Gentiles—puts Jesus on trial. Pilate wants to keep the peace in Jerusalem, especially during the Passover, so he asks what Jesus has done. The Jewish leadership claims Jesus is a criminal. But Pilate perceives it is an issue of their own law, so he tells them to deal with him. Pilate asks Jesus if he is the King of the Jews. Jesus replies by stating his kingdom is not of this world, for if his kingdom was, he and his disciples would fight (18:36). For many, Jesus's statement confirms that he is only interested in building a spiritual kingdom, a reign in the hearts of mankind. But we must be careful to notice what Jesus does *not* say. He does not deny being a king. He does not say the world is not the sphere of his kingdom. By saying his kingdom is not "of this world," Jesus affirms his kingdom has a different source, nature, and means. Jesus was not sidestepping politics; he was asserting a different kind of politic. His kingdom does not follow earthly rules; its character is otherworldly, and it will not come as or when they expect. His kingdom is unique. After this, Pilate gives the Jews a choice to release Jesus or Barabbas. Barabbas was a Zealot, a revolutionary who sought to overthrow Rome by force. The Jews want the Zealot freed and the Prince of Peace crucified (18:39–40). They reject a Messiah who tells his people to sheath their swords.

Pilate takes Jesus and has him flogged. The soldiers dress him up as a king and slander him. When the chief priests and temple leaders see Jesus mocked, they shout to have him crucified. They want nothing of this bloody-silent king. Pilate is afraid because Jesus claims to be the Son of God (19:1–8). In the pagan world, gods came down in human form. Pilate wonders if Jesus is one of these gods. The pagan ruler has a better sense of Jesus than the Jewish leaders. Pilate tries to question Jesus more, but Jesus will not answer him. Pilate reminds Jesus of his governmental authority, but Jesus replies that Pilate's authority has only been given to him. The Father is the true sovereign. Pilate tries to release him, but the Jews assert that they have no king but Caesar. It is a tragic moment. The Jews have rejected their Messiah and pledged their loyalty to Babylon. Pilate hands Jesus over to be crucified. The darkest hour has come (19:9–16).

After the trial, John describes the crucifixion (19:16b–37). Jesus willingly goes to the cross to suffer. Every detail is part of God's plan, for on the cross Jesus is confirmed to be the Messiah, the Son of God. Though Pilate hands Jesus over to be crucified, it is evident Jesus delivers himself over (6:71; 13:11, 21; 19:11; Isa 53:12). While the Synoptics tell of Simon carrying Jesus's cross, John says Jesus bears his own cross (19:17). This emphasizes three themes: Jesus's obedience to his Father's plan, the suffering of Jesus, and Isaac carrying his own wood to the place of sacrifice (Gen 22:6). The soldiers bring Jesus to the Place of the Skull. This is the place of death. But the death of Jesus will be the crushing of Satan's skull (Gen 3:15; cf. Judg 9:53). On death's doorstep Jesus defeats death (1 Cor 15:55). John then simply recounts Jesus's crucifixion between two criminals (19:18). The lead-up has been intense, but John states the truth plainly for all to see. Jesus was crucified. It is a simple historical fact but also the deepest spiritual reality the world has ever seen. Humanity will spend the rest of eternity meditating on this reality and never plumb the significance of the cross.

John then spends a significant amount of time on what happens with Jesus's clothes (19:23–24). It is an odd detail to focus on. However, the way John describes Jesus's clothes signifies that Jesus is the High Priest. His garment is woven (Exod 28:2), and the priest is not to tear it (Lev 21:10). Jesus is a new Joseph and a priestly figure. John says the dividing of Jesus's clothing fulfills the Scriptures (Ps 22:18). John then turns from objects to people around the cross (John 19:25–27). He notes the women standing nearby and then recounts how Jesus entrusts John, the disciple Jesus loved, to Mary and Mary to John. While it shows Jesus's care for them, a deeper meaning exists. The statement, "Here is your Son," has a double meaning: it directs our attention to Jesus as the unique Son of God. After this, Jesus asks for a drink, an action that also fulfills the Scriptures (Ps 69:21). They give him sour wine on a hyssop branch (19:28–30). A hyssop branch was more suitable for sprinkling than drinking, and this reference may echo the sprinkling of Jesus's blood as the Passover lamb (Exod 12:22). Jesus then declares, "It is finished." He has completed his mission. The victory of God is at hand. The reconciliation of the world is accomplished. The rout of the devil is complete.

After Jesus dies, the soldiers come to break his legs to let him die faster. But Jesus has already expired, so they do not break his legs. The Passover lamb also had to be unblemished and unbroken (19:31–37; Exod 12:46; Num 9:12; Ps 34:20). The soldiers pierce Jesus's side and blood and water come out. The world is cleansed and restored by blood and water. As Adam's side gave life to Eve, so Jesus's side gives birth to the church in baptism and the Eucharist. Water flows from the temple and Eden to give life to all (John 3:5; 4:10–15; 7:38; 13:5). The piercing also fulfills Zech 12:10, where it says they will look on the one they have pierced. Jesus's death was not a random accident. It was not another rebel being nailed to a Roman cross. The Son of God came down to earth, and the world has rejected him. They saw the light and loved the darkness. But he loved the world so overwhelmingly that he took on the darkness so God's light might shine forever.

As noted earlier, the final scene begins and ends in a garden (John 19:38–42). Joseph of Arimathea comes and removes Jesus's body. Nicodemus also comes and anoints Jesus's body. The implication is that Nicodemus has turned from darkness to light. They took Jesus's body and prepared it as they prepared the Passover lamb. They lay Jesus in a garden tomb. From this garden new life will sprout. The new Eden, the new gardener, the new humanity is about to come forth.

THE RESURRECTION (20)

Darkness cannot overcome the light. On the first day of the new age, Mary Magdalene comes to the tomb. She finds the tomb empty and tells the disciples. Peter and John, the author of this Gospel, run to the tomb and find Jesus's burial cloths folded, but he is gone (20:1–10). No robber would have folded the clothes. Something else has happened, but they still do not understand that Jesus must rise from the dead. John therefore tells a series of stories of Jesus appearing to his followers.

First, Jesus shows himself to Mary. Mary stays in the garden weeping, and she sees who she thinks is the gardener (20:11–18). Jesus is the new Adam in the garden; he tends his new creation by giving life. Mary recognizes Jesus when he calls out her name. Jesus's sheep listen to his voice (10:3) for he is the great shepherd (10:11). Second, Jesus appears to his disciples, declaring peace to them (20:19–23; Num 6:24–26). Even though they abandoned him, even though Peter denied him, Jesus still receives them. His grace and forgiveness surpass what they can imagine. Then Jesus commissions them and breathes the Holy Spirit on them (20:22). This recalls creation, when God breathed life into Adam and made him a living being (Gen 2:7; Ezek 37:9). Likely, this breath is an anticipatory installment of the Spirit. The disciples get a foretaste of what is to come at Pentecost. Third, Jesus appears to Thomas (John 20:24–29). Thomas was not with the disciples when Jesus came. He doubts and says he will not believe until he is able to touch Jesus's scars. Therefore, Jesus appears to Thomas and tells him to touch his scars, saying, "Don't be faithless, but believe" (20:27).

This final comment leads John to note the purpose of the book (20:30–31). John has written all these things so that we too might believe. John is a witness to Jesus. He wants us to touch Jesus's side and hands through his words. By reading, we see Jesus's signs, we see his death, we see his promises, we see his resurrection. By seeing these we acknowledge Jesus is the Messiah, the Son of God. If we believe, we have life in him.

Epilogue (21)

The epilogue is possibly written by another author. In terms of the content, Jesus appears one more time to his disciples, who are back at their old profession—fishing. They do not recognize him at first, like Mary and Thomas. But Jesus reveals himself. Jesus has foresight to fill their nets with fish, and they eat together on the shore (21:1–14). This verifies Jesus's "physical" resurrected body. It also has a deeper meaning as they eat "fish and bread," echoing the feeding of the 5,000 in John 6.

Peter is then restored from his threefold failure with a threefold command to feed Jesus's flock. It is a commissioning scene, but the emphasis is on reinstatement. Jesus tells Peter the kind of death he will die. When he grows old, they will stretch his hands out, and he will be crucified. Peter needs to still follow Jesus all the way to his own cross (21:15–19).

The next story turns to John, the disciple Jesus loved and the author of the Gospel. Peter asks about John's death. Jesus replies that if he wants John to remain until Jesus comes, that is up to God's plan. John might have a different destiny than Peter. The author notes that the rumor that John would not die had spread. But that is not what Jesus meant. Rather, he spoke hypothetically, saying the end of John's life is none of Peter's business (21:20–23). John's death does not put in doubt his own testimony or Jesus's words.

The final verses affirm John's testimony is true (21:24–25). Yet "true" does not mean "comprehensive." Jesus did many things that John did not write down. John wrote these things down so that people might believe Jesus is the Lamb of God. He is the Word made flesh. He is the Lord of glory.

JOHN 21 AND AUTHORSHIP

John 21:24 says, "This is the disciple who testifies to these things and who wrote them down. We know that his testimony is true." The author of this chapter seems to separate himself from "the disciple who testifies to these things." However, John also refers to himself in the third person (13:23; 20:3). I lean toward viewing the epilogue as a separate author for the following reasons.

- The final chapter is stylistically different from the rest of the book.
- The entire Gospel has had a consistent focus on Jesus, but chapter 21 focuses on Peter and the beloved disciple.
- Already we have read the purpose of the Gospel (20:31), which is a fitting conclusion.

Three questions therefore arise: Who wrote it, why, and what authority does it hold for readers?

- First, we do not know who wrote it, but most think it was some of John's disciples who added this ending after John's death.
- Second, they included the ending to affirm John's testimony, not contradict it. They needed to squelch the rumor that Jesus said John would not die (21:23).
- Finally, every manuscript tradition contains this epilogue, so it is best to consider it as Scripture.

Old Testament Connections

John employs the Old Testament in a unique way. He includes relatively few direct citations, but the Jewish Scriptures are still the bedrock of his thinking. If Matthew is explicit with his fulfillment quotations, Mark is elusive and mysterious, and Luke weaves the Old Testament seamlessly into his story, then John employs images and symbols from the Old Testament.[13] Jesus is the Lamb, Shepherd, Water, Bread, Light, Life, Way, and Vine.

John beckons readers to "come and see" Jesus through signs and symbols. It would be impossible to cover all the images John recycles. Therefore, I have chosen three that John uniquely accentuates in comparison to the Synoptics. According to John, Jesus is the new creation and the new temple, and he is portrayed as on a cosmic trial.

John and the New Creation

John's conviction is that Jesus is the Messiah, the Son of God, who reinstates the new creation. Jesus renews a damaged world and completes creation's purposes. This new beginning has truly commenced in Jesus, but it has not been completed.[14]

Evidence for this theme is found in John's first words: "in the beginning" (*en archē*). This phrase recalls the first words of Genesis and decorates the life of Jesus as a new start. New creation echoes continue as John describes Jesus as the Word, life, and light. All these words are linked to Genesis. First, God creates by his word in Genesis. Ten times Genesis 1 says, "And God said." Second, by God's word life sprouts (Gen 1:11–28). Third, light is the first thing God created in Genesis (1:3–5, 14–18). In Genesis 2, God breathes the breath of life into the man, making him a living being (2:7). By beginning with Genesis allusions, John signals not only that Jesus was the agent and subject of all creation; he will now be the one who brings this story to culmination.

These themes thread their way through John's work. To punctuate this, John ends his Gospel speaking of how life is found in Jesus: "These are written so that you may believe that Jesus is the Messiah, the Son of God, and that by believing you may have *life* in his name" (John 20:31, emphasis added). The repeated use of "life" at the beginning and end creates an *inclusio* to all of John's Gospel. Jesus came to restore life on the earth. He is the new creation.

---

[13] These descriptions of the different ways the Gospel writers employ the Old Testament is reliant on Richard Hays, *Echoes of Scripture in the Gospels* (see intro., n. 7).

[14] Much of this material is also found in J. K. Brown, "Creation's Renewal in the Gospel of John," *Catholic Biblical Quarterly* 72 (2010): 275–90.

The new creation refrain is indicated by other images as well. Jesus consistently describes himself as water or bread (4:10; 6:35). Water and bread were understood in the first century as "sources" of life. Human beings depend on water and bread for life. Additionally, in the Old Testament water is a key image for the life God gives. Water goes forth from Eden in Genesis to irrigate the world (2:10); water is life in the desert (Exod 15:25, 27; 17:6; Isa 48:21); water is a picture of salvation and the Spirit in Isaiah (12:3). In Isaiah 44:3, God says, "For I will pour water on the thirsty land and streams on the dry ground; I will pour out my Spirit on your descendants." In Ezekiel, water flows from the temple (47:1–2).

Bread is also a picture of the life God gives in the Old Testament. God tells Adam he will eat bread until he returns to the ground (Gen 3:19). Israel ate unleavened bread on the Passover (Exod 12:8) and manna in the wilderness (16:35), and bread was in the tabernacle (25:30). God promised to bless Israel with bread and water if they serve him (Exod 23:25). Food was a sign of God's blessing (Isa 30:23; 51:14); the lack thereof was God's curse (Jer 38:9; Lam 1:11; Amos 4:6). Bethlehem was the "house of bread," and it was fitting Jesus was born there (John 7:42).

Bread sustains life and is linked to God's covenantal relationship with his people. This is why Jesus describes himself as the true bread from heaven, for he "gives life to the world" (6:33). Jesus is the living bread, the completion of the bread theme from the Old Testament.

New creation themes can also be seen in the temporal frame John employs. Jesus's ministry begins and ends with a calculated week, thus framing Jesus's ministry with the six days of creation. The first week comes in chapters 1–2, which ends with his reference to the "third day" (2:1). This time stamp has confused interpreters, but the previous temporal markers make the third-day reference clearer.[15]

Table 4.2: The Six Days of Creation in John

1:19–28	Day 1
1:29	Day 2 (the next day)
1:35	Day 3 (the next day)
1:43	Day 4 (the next day)
2:1	Day 6 (on the third day, two days later)

---

[15] Gladd, *Handbook on the Gospels*, 320; Edward W. Klink III, *John*, Zondervan Exegetical Commentary on the New Testament (Grand Rapids: Zondervan Academic, 2016), 160.

Jesus appropriately provides more wine at Cana on the sixth day. He provides life to those at a wedding feast that also looks forward to the messianic banquet (Isa 25:6).

The last week of Jesus's life is calculated in a similar way. John 12:1 says, "*Six days before* the Passover, Jesus came to Bethany where Lazarus was, the one Jesus had raised from the dead" (emphasis added). The last half of John is marked by Passover references, and the whole narrative leads toward the Passover when Jesus is crucified. The reference in 12:1 marks the last week of Jesus in a six-day frame.

John asserts Jesus came to bring about seventh-day rest. The emphasis on seven abounds in John. There are seven signs, seven "I am" statements, seven witnesses to Jesus, seven feasts, seven discourses, and seven references to Jesus's hour. In 20:26 Jesus speaks to his disciples after eight days, maybe equating the eighth day with the renewed creation. All these time stamps designate Jesus as the new creation.

Finally, new creation images can be seen in the passion and resurrection narratives. Both the passion and resurrection scenes revolve around a garden (18:1; 19:41). Mary confuses Jesus with the gardener (20:15). Adam typology is implied when Pilate declares, "Behold the man!" (19:5 ESV). Pilate ironically depicts Jesus as the second Adam. Confirming this is Jesus's crown of thorns. Jesus takes Adam's curse upon himself (19:5).

On the cross Jesus says, "It is finished," alluding to the completion of God's work on the seventh day (19:30; Gen 2:2). When Jesus is stabbed in the side, water and blood flow out to the world like water flowed from Eden (John 19:34; Gen 2:10). Jesus's resurrection then takes place on the first day of the week (John 20:1, 19). Re-creation begins at resurrection. Jesus also performs a new creation act when he breathes on the disciples and gives them the Holy Spirit (20:22; Gen 2:7; Ezek 37:9).

John sees Jesus as the new creation. Jesus is the new Adam who establishes the new garden and gives life to the world. If the mission of God is to bring healing and renewal to all of creation, the wellspring of this project is Jesus.

John and the Temple

Closely related, but distinct from Jesus being the new creation, is John's portrayal of Jesus as the new temple. Temple images weave their way through John's Gospel but are most explicit when Jesus enters the temple in John 2:13–25. Jesus does so on the Sabbath and drives out those who buy and trade. He quotes the Scriptures and then says, "Destroy this temple, and I will raise it up in three days" (2:19). The author John steps in with his own commentary and declares that the disciples understood Jesus was speaking about his body only *after* he had been raised from the dead (2:22). John gives his audience a hint: a deeper meaning exists to Jesus's words and actions. Jesus's body is the true temple. His earthly actions have heavenly meaning.

In other parts of John, Jesus identifies himself with water, light, and bread. All these images are temple related. Light is linked with the temple in a myriad of ways. Preceding but paving the ground for the tabernacle, God creates light in Genesis (1:3), he reveals him as a smoking fire pot to Abraham (Gen 15:17), a burning bush to Moses (Exod 3:2), a pillar of fire at night to the wilderness generation (13:21), and on Mount Sinai to Israel as smoke and fire (19:18; 24:17; Heb 12:18–21). Fire then burned inside the tabernacle on the lampstand (Exod 40:38; Lev 24:1–9) and temple (2 Chr 7:1). The lampstand recalled Israel's history and reminded Israel of God's presence. Therefore, when Jesus says he is the "light of the world" he claims to be God's temple presence (John 1:4–9; 3:19–21; 8:12; 9:5; 12:35–36). The true meaning of the light was Jesus all along.

Bread is also connected with the temple. Before the institution of the tabernacle and temple, bread is a symbol of God's provision. Melchizedek brings bread to Abraham as a priestly act (Gen 14:18). Abraham also presents bread to God when the three visitors come to him (18:6). In the Passover, Israel prepares unleavened bread before their journey (Exod 12:8). Before Sinai God rains down bread from heaven (16:4). Appropriately, therefore, God commands Israel to put the bread of presence on the table in the tabernacle and temple for all time (25:30; Lev 24:1–9). When Jesus says he is the "bread of life" he lets the world know the true meaning of the bread all along: Jesus is the bread (John 6:35, 48, 51).

Water is also correlated with the temple. At creation God separated the waters and created the land (Gen 1:6). This reality is repeated as Israel goes through the waters at the Red Sea (Exod 14:16). God then provides water for Israel in the wilderness (15:25; 17:6). These events are reenacted in the temple rituals as the Levites wash in water before they enter the Lord's presence (29:4; 30:18–20; 40:12, 30; Lev 8:6). Most of the sacrifices are also to be washed with water (1:9, 13; 6:28; 14:5–9). The temple ceremonies ritualized passing through water before meeting with God, who would then provide water for the people's nourishment. Later, the prophet Ezekiel says that out of the eschatological temple will flow water to the whole earth.

> Then he brought me back to the entrance of the temple and there was water flowing from under the threshold of the temple toward the east, for the temple faced east. The water was coming down from under the south side of the threshold of the temple, south of the altar. Next he brought me out by way of the north gate and led me around the outside to the outer gate that faced east; there the water was trickling from the south side. (Ezek 47:1–2)

Jesus takes up these images saying unless someone is baptized with water and Spirit, they cannot see the kingdom of God (John 3:5). He claims to be living water to the Samaritan woman (4:10, 14). Maybe most importantly, Jesus asserts that the one who believes in him will have water flowing from him (7:38). This verse could be understood to mean that water will flow from the believer, but it also could be read that the water flows from Jesus. Perhaps the two do not have to be opposed. These words occur at the Festival of Tabernacles, indicating Jesus identifies himself with Ezekiel's temple from which waters flow to the world. The water is a shadow; the reality is Jesus.

John's encyclopedia of temple references continues. When Jesus tells Nathanael he is the ladder to heaven in 1:51, this signifies that Jesus is the temple, for the temple was the gateway to heaven. When Jacob sees the ladder, he appropriately names the place Bethel, meaning "house of God." This is the gate of heaven (Gen 28:17). Jesus is the new gate and ladder to heaven.

Another temple image comes from John's passion. John locates Jesus's crucifixion on the day of preparation for the Passover (John 19:14). The time stamp aligns Jesus's death with the slaughter of the Passover lambs. This point is reiterated by John when the Roman soldiers refrain from breaking the legs of Jesus on the cross, fulfilling Exod 12:46 and Ps 34:19–20, where it says not to break the bones of a lamb on the Passover. Jesus is the temple's true Passover lamb.

It is no wonder that John begins his Gospel by asserting that the Word became flesh and "dwelt" (*skēnoō*) among God's people (John 1:14) The related noun form is employed for the tabernacle, the forerunner for the temple (Exod 25:9; 26:1). John, like the rest of the New Testament authors, affirms Jesus is not only the true temple; he is everything in the temple. He is the priest, lamb, sacrifice, water, bread, and light who has made his dwelling with humanity. God's presence has come to earth in the body of Jesus.

John and the Cosmic Trial

Another Old Testament theme unique to John is a cosmic trial. Jesus is put on trial, but John makes clear it is Jesus who judges the world. The script is flipped. Andrew Lincoln has argued that some of John's favorite terms—*witness, judgment, truth,* and *see*—all have judicial connotations.[16] John seems to have borrowed this law-court

---

[16] Andrew T. Lincoln, "Trials, Plots and the Narrative of the Fourth Gospel," *Journal for the Study of the New Testament* 17, no. 56 (1995): 3–30.

theme from Isaiah 40–55, which contains eight courtroom trial scenes between Yahweh and Israel or the nations.

Isaiah 43 is a key example of the courtroom motif. Yahweh calls for the nations to gather. Then he calls for his witnesses, the people of Israel, to come forth. Will Israel testify that God alone is God? That God is their Savior (43:11)? Will they be true witnesses in the courtroom? Isaiah says Israel is blind and deaf. The solution to Israel's unfaithfulness is that a servant will come and be the true witness (chapters 52–53). He will come before the court and truly testify.

John takes up this theme and presents Jesus's public ministry under the banner of a trial. Jesus is Isaiah's servant and God's true witness. The Jewish leaders and others dispute with Jesus. But a twist occurs. This trial is two sided. As in Isaiah, while Israel thinks they can put God on trial, God puts them on trial. In John, while the world supposes they put Jesus on trial, John signals that Jesus will be the true judge of the earth (5:30; 8:16; 12:48). The world is under prosecution.

The trial motif occurs in each of John's five main sections. In the prologue (1:1–18) John the Baptist is introduced as a witness who comes to testify about the light (1:6–8, 15). The noun *witness* and the verb *testify* are the same word in Greek (*martureō*). A form of this word occurs four times in the first eighteen verses. John stands as a courtroom witness to Jesus to vindicate the veracity of his claims.

The second section of John's Gospel is also framed by this courtroom language (1:19–12:50). The Baptizer's first words are introduced with "This was John's testimony" (1:19). Then the first half of John concludes with Jesus speaking about himself as the light (12:46). If anyone hears his words and does not keep them, his word will judge them on the last day (12:48). Jesus says John testifies to the truth (5:33), and if they continue in Jesus's words, they will know the truth and the truth will set them free (8:32).

In this second section the devil is also contrasted to Jesus because the devil is a liar, and the truth is not in him (8:44). Jesus says judgment has come on the world because light has come but people loved the darkness. Throughout the second section Jesus speaks of different witnesses to him. Jesus testifies to himself (8:14), and his works testify to him (5:36), as does the Father (8:18) and the Scriptures (5:39). The Baptizer is also joined by the Samaritan woman who spreads her testimony (4:39), and the crowds testify about Jesus raising Lazarus (12:17). Jesus not only has witnesses and testifies to himself, but he acts as the judge. The Father has given judgment to the Son (5:22, 30; 8:16).

The third portion of John's Gospel also includes a trial motif (13:1–17:26). In the farewell discourse, Jesus refers to the Spirit as the Paraclete (*paraklētos*). This could also be translated as Advocate, one who has been called in to help. Though the term is not always used in a legal sphere, it mirrors the Latin legal term *advocatus,* meaning a person of high social standing who speaks on behalf of a defendant in the court of law before a judge.[17] A *paraklētos* is like an attorney.

Because the term occurs in this section during the trial, the legal sense is likely included. Most contexts speak of the Paraclete with reference to the final judgment. The Paraclete will speak before God on behalf of humans (14:16, 26; 15:26; 16:7). The Spirit will convict the world about sin, righteousness, and judgment (16:8). Jesus says he himself is the truth (14:6), and the Spirit is the truth (14:17; 15:26; 16:13).

In the fourth segment of John's Gospel Jesus stands on trial, but he reverses the sentence (18:1–20:31). It is the world that is on trial and judged. Jesus defends his innocence (18:20–23), challenges the authority of Pilate (18:34), and confirms he came to bear witness to the truth (18:37–38). Pilate asks what truth is. The trial unmasks both Pilate and the Jewish leadership. Both are seeking to preserve their power and do not try Jesus fairly. The battle between truth and power is resolved on the cross. Jesus is the embodiment of truth, and with truth is all power. Jesus says to Pilate that he would have no authority unless it was given to Pilate (19:11). Only after Jesus dies and his side is pierced does the author step in and affirm his testimony is true (19:35). Truth flows to the world through an unjust sentence.

John's epilogue closes with a twofold reference to the testimony of the beloved disciple (21:1–25). "This is the disciple who *testifies* to these things and who wrote them down. We know that his *testimony* is true" (21:24, emphasis added). The last chapter also has the disciples witnessing Jesus's resurrection. Peter is rehabilitated so he can continue to witness about Jesus. Peter has already faced a trial and will face an even greater one.

Table 4.3: The Cosmic Trial Motif in John's Gospel

Prologue (1:1–18)	John the Baptist witnesses to Jesus.
Signs of Jesus (1:19–12:50)	Jesus's own works witness to him.
Final sayings of Jesus (13:1–17:26)	The Father and Paraclete witness to Jesus.
Passion of Jesus (18:1–20:31)	Jesus puts the world on trial.
Epilogue (21:1–25)	The disciples witness to the truth of Jesus.

---

[17] Lochlan Shelfer, "The Legal Precision of the Term 'Παράκλητος,'" *Journal for the Study of the New Testament* 32, no. 2 (2009): 131–50.

All this amounts to the fulfillment of the cosmic trial that began in Isaiah. Jesus came as the chief witness and judge. He is righteous Israel and the promised servant from Isaiah who truly testifies of God. People also witness about Jesus. While some put Jesus on trial, they are under judgment. If they do not receive Jesus's testimony, they will be judged.[18] The true servant who testifies of God has come.

Gospel Connections

Unlike the Synoptic Gospels, John never uses the term *gospel*. That does not mean the concept is not present. The narrative of Jesus's life is the gospel, which is why this book was early on called "The Gospel according to John." As already discussed, John approaches Jesus's life distinctively compared to the other Gospels. The same holds true for how John describes the gospel. Therefore, I will explain three different aspects of John's presentation of the gospel: (1) the gospel and the Trinity, (2) the gospel as eternal life, and (3) the gospel as grace and truth.

The Gospel and the Trinity

Too often when people explain the gospel, they only speak about Jesus. John instructs that this is not sufficient. The gospel cannot truly be spoken of without reference to the triune God: the Father, Son, and Spirit. According to John, Jesus and the Spirit's missions correspond to the inner life of the triune God.

The eternal generation of the Son and procession of the Spirit in eternity are extended in God's acts on the earth to save humanity. The three persons of the Godhead are united in the mission to redeem humanity and bring them into the presence of God. The Son's sending is based on the Father's action and both then send the Spirit. Without the Trinity there is no gospel. This is evident in John in a few ways.

First, "Jesus derives his mission from the Father and is entirely dependent on him in carrying it out."[19] To put this another way, the Father *sends* while the Son is *sent*. We must not neglect God the Father in our proclamation of the good news. The first chapter of John asserts the Son is the *monogenes* of the Father (1:14). Jesus is *from* the Father, eternally begotten from him. Thus, it is fitting that the Son becomes flesh.

---

[18] Lincoln, "Trials, Plots and the Narrative of the Fourth Gospel," 14.

[19] Andreas J. Köstenberger and Scott R. Swain, *Father, Son and Spirit: The Trinity and John's Gospel*, New Studies in Biblical Theology (Downers Grove, IL: IVP Academic, 2008), 151.

This language of the Father sending the Son is repeated continually in John (5:23, 36–37; 6:44, 57; 8:16, 18; 12:49; 14:24; 20:21). John also affirms that the work of Jesus stems from the Father. Jesus says he is working because the Father is working (5:17, 19). The Father raises the dead, and the Son is able to give life as well (5:21). The Father gives judgment to the Son (5:22). As the Father has life in himself, so does the Son (5:26). The Father gives the Son works to accomplish (5:36). No one comes to the Son unless the Father draws him or her (6:44). There is no gospel of the Son without the sending and working of the Father.

Second, John reminds readers that while Jesus is the Sent One, returns to the Father, and glorifies the Father, he also has absolute unity with the Father. Some might think the first part leads to a sort of subordinationism, but Jesus asserts he is also one with the Father. John 1:1 says the Word is not only with God but is God. In John 14:11 Jesus asserts, "I am in the Father and the Father is in me." Jesus says that if people hate him, they hate the Father (15:23). Jesus affirms that he is not alone, for the Father is with him (16:32). The Son also gives what he receives. As the Father loves the Son, he also loves his disciples (15:9). As the Father sends the Son, so he sends the disciples (20:21). As the Father and Son have unity, so Jesus prays that his disciples might have unity (17:11, 21). Not only is the Son sent from the Father, but he and the Father are of the same essence.

Third, John reminds us there is no gospel without the Spirit. The Spirit is also sent from the Father and Son to teach, illuminate, and give life. As the Son descends from heaven, so the Spirit rests on Jesus (1:32–33). The idea that the Father sends the Spirit is supported by John 14:26: "But the Counselor, the Holy Spirit, whom the Father will send in my name . . ." Jesus also asserts that he sends the Spirit: "When the Counselor comes, *the one I will send to you* from the Father . . ." (15:26, emphasis added). If Jesus does not leave, he says, then the Spirit does not come: "It is for your benefit that I go away, because if I don't go away the Counselor will not come to you. If I go, *I will send him to you*" (16:7, emphasis added). The Spirit "proceeds" (*ekporeuomai*) from the Father and the Son (15:26). In the Nicodemus narrative Jesus says that unless one is born of the water and Spirit, one cannot see the kingdom of God (3:5–8). To be born from above is to be regenerated. In John 6:63 not only Jesus gives life, but the Spirit also gives life. In John 14–16 the Spirit is especially identified with his teaching and illuminating function. He is the Spirit of truth (14:16; 15:26), and he will teach the disciples all things (14:26; 16:13).

John's Gospel reminds us that without the Trinity, without the missions of the Son and Spirit, there is no gospel. Too often gospel presentations are devoid of a trinitarian theology. However, the three persons of the Trinity work inseparably. They are of the same essence, and while they have different missions, they have a united will. According to John, the Father, Son, and Spirit together offer good news.

The Gospel as Eternal Life

While the Synoptic Gospels usually describe the content of the gospel in terms of the kingdom of God, John transposes this to "life" or "eternal life."[20] The gospel, according to John, is that humanity in Christ will participate in God's life. They will become immortal. John begins with this statement about Jesus (all italics in the verses in this section have been added for emphasis): "In him was *life*" (1:4). John ends his Gospel by stating that he has written all this so people might have eternal *life* (20:31). In the middle of the Gospel Jesus declares he is the resurrection and the *life* (11:25). As many people's favorite verse, John 3:16 says, "For God loved the world in this way: He gave his one and only Son, so that everyone who believes in him will not perish but have *eternal life*."

John relegates kingdom language to three verses: 3:3, 5; 18:36. The close relationship between eternal life and the kingdom of God can be found in Jesus's conversation with Nicodemus.

- "Truly I tell you, unless someone is born again, he cannot see the *kingdom of God*." (3:3)
- "Just as Moses lifted up the snake in the wilderness, so the Son of Man must be lifted up, so that everyone who believes in him *may have eternal life*" (3:14–15)

While the kingdom of God and eternal life overlap and have some similarities, it is important to note the differences as well. The conceptual range for life speaks more to images of creation, rebirth, resurrection, immortality, and philosophy. Kingdom, on the other hand, is more concrete and speaks of authority, rule, and empire.[21] Kingdom insinuates political hopes, while life has more philosophical and anthropological

---

[20] The Synoptics do employ the terms *life* and *eternal life*. For example, see Matt 19:16–17: "Just then someone came up and asked him, 'Teacher, what good must I do to have eternal life?' 'Why do you ask me about what is good?' he said to him. 'There is only one who is good. If you want to enter into life, keep the commandments.'" See also Matt 19:23–29; Mark 9:43, 45, 47; 10:17–30; Luke 18:24–30.

[21] Thanks to my student Mark Kelly for pointing out many of these differences in an unpublished class paper and through conversations. Much of the following is dependent on his work.

resonances. While overlap exists between the terms, it is also true that John's evocative world is much different from the Synoptics.

This does not mean that John pulls his ideas primarily from somewhere outside of the Old Testament, but it is also true that many philosophies during Jesus's time attempted to present a way of life that led to an ideal state of being.[22] Aristotle called the ideal state of being *eudaimonia* and presented a thorough set of ethics to develop virtues to get there. During the ministry of Jesus, Stoicism was a rival tradition.[23] Stoics were concerned with how to arrive at the ideal state of being, which they believed involved self-sufficiency and virtue, allowing one to be happy despite circumstances and various external realities. According to Seneca, the biggest external threat to one's happiness is the opposite of life: death.

Philo, a Hellenistic Jew, represents a slightly different philosophical school from the Stoics. Philo "platonized" the Old Testament in an effort to show its philosophical viability.[24] For Philo, the end goal was less about *eudaimonia* and more about ascending to God through the Logos—Logos being the image of God. All this indicates that John seems to have been conversant and aware of the philosophical discourses of his day. He transposes gospel language into a philosophical frame. Readers can learn much from John's presentation of the gospel as eternal life.

First, John thinks it appropriate to translate concepts from one culture to another. This does not mean that life is not in the Jewish tradition. John is willing to note where systems overlap and to describe the gospel in philosophical garb, but he always asserts Christianity is the superior system.

Second, John is not fearful of describing the gospel in a variety of ways. For John, the gospel is about the good life. It is about flourishing in God's creation. Eternal life does not merely mean "quantity of life but quality of life."[25] However, this eternal life only comes from above. It cannot be found here on this earth except in the heavenly Son.

Third, John presses into the ethical component of the gospel by representing it as life. Philosophy was about beliefs but also about the art of living. The gospel is not

---

[22] The only time "eternal life" is used in the Old Testament is in Dan 12:2: "Many who sleep in the dust of the earth will awake, some to eternal life, and some to disgrace and eternal contempt."

[23] C. Kavin Rowe, *One True Life: The Stoics and Early Christians as Rival Traditions* (New Haven, CT: Yale University Press, 2016).

[24] Daniel Boyarin, "The Gospel of the *Memra*: Jewish Binitarianism and the Prologue to John," *Harvard Theological Review* 94, no. 3 (2001): 243–84.

[25] Marianne Meye Thompson, "Eternal Life in the Gospel of John," *Ex Auditu* 5 (1989): 37.

simply a message but a way of life. It includes virtues and character formation. As Marianne Thompson states, "Eternal life is life lived from God's perspective, by God's own values."[26]

Finally, in John, life is found only in Jesus: "In him was life" (1:4). Life cannot be found in these other philosophies, systems, or even in ethics. Life is found in a person. For John, eternal life connotes the totality of salvation. It is an all-encompassing term and only found in the triune God.[27]

John's presentation of the gospel as eternal life is unique. The phrase has resonances with the Jewish tradition, specifically Moses's promises of life or death for covenantal actions (Deut 30:15–20), but it also speaks into the wider Greco-Roman culture and the philosophies of the day. The gospel transcends culture and challenges all other conceptual schemes.

The Gospel as Grace and Truth

Often when we consider the gospel, we do not begin our discussions with the character of God. John is explicit in tying his Gospel to God's nature. Jesus can save because of who he is. In John's prologue he makes a statement about Jesus that can be passed over quickly. John asserts, "The Word became flesh and dwelt among us. We observed his glory, the glory as the one and only Son from the Father, *full of grace and truth*" (1:14, emphasis added). Three verses later John reaffirms that the law was given through Moses: "grace and truth came through Jesus Christ" (1:17). Grace and truth are both affirmations about God's nature and Johannine ways to describe how the gospel came.

John is fond of the word *truth* (*alētheia*), employing it twenty-five times. "Grace" (*charis*), on the other hand, appears only four times in the space of four verses (1:14–17). However, as pointed out earlier, John seems to see these terms in tandem.

John links these terms because he is dependent on Exod 34:6–7. After God has proclaimed his name (Yahweh), he goes on to give a description of his nature. This is supplementary to what Moses got in Exod 3:14 when God declared, "I AM WHO I AM." In Exodus 34 God reveals more: "The Lord—the Lord is a compassionate and gracious God, slow to anger and *abounding in faithful love and truth*, maintaining

---

[26] Thompson, 51.
[27] Thompson, 51.

faithful love to a thousand generations, forgiving iniquity, rebellion, and sin. But he will not leave the guilty unpunished, bringing the consequences of the fathers' iniquity on the children and grandchildren to the third and fourth generation" (34:6–7, emphasis added). The italicized words in Hebrew are *hesed* and *emet. Hesed* can be translated as "gracious," and *emet* means "truth." This pair of words occurs throughout the Old Testament to describe God's nature (2 Sam 2:6; 15:20; Ps 25:1; 86:15; 89:14).

John asserts Yahweh's character is displayed in Jesus. *Charis,* or grace, is simply another term for a gift or favor. According to John, God's gift is found in a person: Jesus Christ. In both John 1:14 and 16 grace and truth are linked to the idea of fullness. Yahweh was described in Exodus as abounding in grace and truth. Jesus is likewise abundant grace and truth. We receive grace from God's abundance. This communicates the superabundance and sufficiency of God's grace. Jesus is the fullness of grace, the fullness of God's gift. Nothing else is needed.

John also asserts that Jesus is the fullness of truth. God does not merely possess truth; he is truth. Jesus says to Nicodemus that whoever lives by the truth comes to the light (3:21). To the Samaritan woman, Jesus says that people must worship in Spirit and truth (4:24). Jesus emphasizes that John testified to the truth (5:33), and the truth will set people free (8:32). The devil does not stand in the truth (8:44), and Jesus is the way, the truth, and the life (14:6). The Spirit is also the Spirit of truth (14:17; 15:26; 16:13). Jesus also affirms that God's word is truth (17:17). At the end of John's Gospel, Pilate asks Jesus, "What is truth?" (18:38). The same question confronts readers of John's Gospel.

Most would assume truth is related to propositions or that which accords to fact or reality. However, the Bible affirms that truth is found in a person and the term has ethical connotations. Jesus is the fullness of truth by nature; that is why he displays faithfulness to his people. The ethical component flows from the ontological reality.

John more specifically ties this truth to the death of Jesus. Grace and truth are found in Jesus because, as Jesus says to Nicodemus, God truly does love the world because he sent his only begotten Son (3:16). Grace and truth are found in his death on behalf of the world.

The gospel, for John, is based on God's character. Grace and truth, the very things Yahweh declared about himself, are found in Jesus. The world is loved by God, and this is proved by Jesus coming to earth. Jesus is God's gift to the world. God offers fullness of grace and truth in Jesus. This is consistent with God's nature in the Old Testament, but now God has made his dwelling with humanity in the person of Jesus. His love for the world is undeniable.

Life Connections

The Gospel of John abounds with ethical imperatives, but only two will be mentioned here. John's Gospel is a call both to contemplate God in the face of Jesus Christ and to witness to what we have seen. These two realities are integrally connected.

When Nathanael asks Philip whether anything good can come out of Nazareth, Philip tells him, "Come and see" (1:46). In one sense, the whole Gospel of John is a call to come and see. John reminds us that the central thing we all need in life is to see God. Heaven is the pattern for earth, and seeing God puts everything in its ordered place. The Gospel of John is a call to contemplate God. To do so we must commit ourselves to looking to Jesus in the Scriptures.

John teaches us that we see God in the face of Jesus Christ: "No one has ever seen God. The one and only Son, who is himself God and is at the Father's side—he has revealed him" (1:18). When Philip asks to see the Father, Jesus replies, "The one who has seen me has seen the Father" (14:9). And we see the face of Jesus Christ in the Scriptures. While we see Jesus in all the Scriptures, the Gospels are particularly bright.

We are to, as Jesus says, "behold" (*idou*). Sometimes this is translated as "listen." It is better to understand it as a term of sight. John 12:15 says, "Behold, your king is coming, sitting on a donkey's colt" (ESV). Pilate says, "Behold the man!" (19:5 ESV). The Bible starts and ends with this theme. Adam and Eve enjoyed fellowship with God as they walked in the garden with him. In Revelation God comes down from heaven to dwell again with his people. The goal of the entire biblical storyline is to see the face of God and contemplate him for the rest of eternity.

Second, the Gospel of John is not only a call to behold but a summons to testify. We tell others about the one we have encountered in these pages. John the author is a witness of these things. So are John the Baptist and the Samaritan woman. The Gospels are written because this message was to be preserved *in order to be* spread to the world. When we read the Gospels, we are reminded of the universe's secrets: God took on flesh, died on behalf of humanity, and was raised from the dead. To spread this message is why we exist.

We are to speak of what God has done in this world. Jesus was a historical figure who has come to remake all things. Our task is not only to believe him but to let others know about him. Like John, we witness to Jesus being the Messiah, the Son of God. If people believe, they have life in his name (20:31). We therefore tell our neighbors, coworkers, rideshare drivers, friends, and family. We are to tell others of this Jesus found in the Gospels.

This book has been a project in trying to convince you of the importance, beauty, and centrality of the Gospels. May we ever return to this deep well, for in them we find the one who is "living water" (4:10–14) and the hope of the world.

Interactive Questions

4.1. In what ways would it matter if John the apostle was not the author of the Fourth Gospel?

4.2. What are some ways in which John differs from the Synoptics?

4.3. Describe the difference in John's theology compared to the Synoptics.

4.4. How does Jesus interact with the Jewish traditions in John? Is it better to say that he fulfills them or that they have become obsolete? What difference does it make?

4.5. How is Jesus's death presented in John?

4.6. How does John employ the Old Testament in comparison with the Synoptic Gospels? Give some examples.

4.7. Why does John use the term *eternal life* instead of *the kingdom of God*?

4.8. Explain the importance of the trial motif in John and how it affects our reading.

4.9. How can you obey the summons to witness to Jesus?

Recommended Resources

Modern Commentaries

Barrett, C. K. *The Gospel according to John.* 2nd ed. London: SPCK, 1978.

Carson, D. A. *The Gospel according to John.* The Pillar New Testament Commentary. Grand Rapids: Eerdmans, 1991.

Hoskyns, Edwyn Clement. *The Fourth Gospel.* London: Faber and Faber Limited, 1940.

Keener, Craig S. *The Gospel of John: A Commentary.* 2 vols. Peabody, MA: Hendrickson, 2003.

Klink, Edward W. *John.* Edited by Clinton E. Arnold. Grand Rapids: Zondervan Academic, 2016.

Lincoln, Andrew. *The Gospel According to St. John*. Black's New Testament Commentaries. Peabody, MA: Continuum, 2006.

Michaels, J. Ramsey. *The Gospel of John*. The New International Commentary on the New Testament. Grand Rapids: Eerdmans, 2010.

Morris, Leon. *The Gospel according to John*. The New International Commentary on the New Testament. Grand Rapids: Eerdmans, 1995.

O'day, Gail R. *John*. Louisville: Westminster John Knox Press, 2006.

Ridderbos, Herman. *The Gospel of John: A Theological Commentary*. Grand Rapids: Eerdmans, 1997.

Schnackenburg, Rudolf. *The Gospel according to St. John*. 3 vols. Translated by Kevin Smyth. London: Burns & Oates, 1968.

Thompson, Marianne Meye. *John: A Commentary*. Louisville, KY: Westminster John Knox Press, 2015.

Early Commentaries

Aquinas, St. Thomas. *Commentary on the Gospel of John*. 2 vols. Translated by Fr. Fabian R. Larcher, O.P. Lander, WY: The Aquinas Institute for the Study of Sacred Doctrine, 2013.

Augustine of Hippo. *Tractates on the Gospel of John*. 5 vols. Translated by John W. Rettig. Washington, DC: The Catholic University of America Press, 1988–1995.

Calvin, John. *John*. The Crossway Classic Commentaries. Wheaton, IL: Crossway, 1994.

Chrysostom, John. *Commentary on Saint John the Apostle and Evangelist*. Homilies 1–47. The Fathers of the Church. Translated by Sr. Thomas Aquinas Goggin. Washington, DC: Catholic University of America Press, 2000.

———. *Commentary on Saint John the Apostle and Evangelist*. Homilies 48–88. The Fathers of the Church. Translated by Sr. Thomas Aquinas Goggin. Washington, DC: Catholic University of America Press, 1959.

Cyril of Alexandria. *Commentary on John*. 2 vols. Ancient Christian Texts. Translated by David Maxwell. Downers Grove, IL: IVP Academic, 2013–15.

Theodore of Mopsuestia, *Commentary on the Gospel of John*. Ancient Christian Texts. Translated by Marco Conti. Downers Grove, IL: IVP Academic, 2010.

Special Studies

Bauckham, Richard. *Gospel of Glory: Major Themes in Johannine Theology*. Grand Rapids: Baker Academic, 2015.

————. *The Testimony of the Beloved Disciple: Narrative, History, and Theology in the Gospel of John.* Grand Rapids: Baker Academic, 2007.

Culpepper, R. Alan. *Anatomy of the Fourth Gospel: A Study in Literary Design.* Minneapolis: Fortress, 1983.

Frey, Jörg. *The Glory of the Crucified One: Christology and Theology in the Gospel of John.* Translated by Wayne Coppins and Christoph Heilig. Waco, TX: Baylor University Press, 2018.

Köstenberger, Andreas J. *A Theology of John's Gospel and Letters.* Biblical Theology of the New Testament. Grand Rapids: Zondervan Academic, 2009.

Köstenberger, Andreas J., and Scott R. Swain. *Father, Son and Spirit: The Trinity and John's Gospel.* New Studies in Biblical Theology. Nottingham, UK: Apollos, 2008.

Morris, Leon. *Studies in the Fourth Gospel.* Grand Rapids: Eerdmans, 1969.

Porter, Stanley E. *John, His Gospel, and Jesus: In Pursuit of the Johannine Voice.* Grand Rapids: Eerdmans, 2015.

SUBJECT INDEX

A

Aaron, 58, 150–51
Abel, 53, 58
abomination of desolation, 69, 86–87, 173
Abraham, 1, 10, 21, 23–25, 31, 57–59, 78, 125, 128, 134, 142, 150, 163, 167, 176, 178, 188
Acts, 86, 110–11, 115, 118, 144, 148–49, 152, 158
Adam, 1, 10, 27, 45, 48–49, 83, 88, 104, 112, 114, 119, 140–41, 163, 182–83, 186–87, 198
Ahaz, 60
Alexander the Great, 11, 168
Amos, 142, 178
Ancient of Days, 87, 130
Andrew, 75, 164
angels, 25, 45, 47, 87, 91, 94, 115, 118, 132, 135, 140–41, 144, 165, 167, 169
Anna, 118, 140, 143
Anti-Marcionite Prologue, 68–69
Antiochus IV (Epiphanes), 11, 173
aphesis, 137–38
apocalyptic, 44, 47, 53, 87, 134
apostolicity, 4
Aristotle, 195
audience, 19–20, 55, 70, 111, 188
Augustus, 101–2, 117–18, 145
authority, 4–5, 11–12, 23, 30, 32–33, 38–40, 42–44, 46–47, 49, 73–76, 78–82, 84–85, 87, 89, 103, 123, 125, 127, 130, 138, 166, 170, 181, 184, 191, 194
authorship, 18–19, 158, 184

B

Baba Batra, 50
Babylon, 10–11, 53, 93, 125, 147, 181
banquets, 18, 42, 88, 121, 123, 127, 142, 165, 187
baptism, 27–28, 39, 51, 73–74, 95, 118–20, 138, 145, 160, 168, 182
Barabbas, 89, 104–5, 133, 181
Barnabas, 68
beatific vision, 59
Beatitudes, 29, 44
Bethany, 6, 88, 149, 174, 187
Bethesda, 169
Bethlehem, 25–26, 51, 186
blasphemy, 46, 78, 89
blessing, 25, 29, 54, 146, 148–50, 164, 186
blindness, 32, 34, 56, 70, 82, 84–85, 97–98, 120, 122, 129, 136, 138, 142–43, 152, 162, 172, 174, 190
blood, 30, 35, 37, 46–47, 53–54, 76, 79–80, 88, 91, 96, 99, 104, 125–26, 132, 143, 148, 151, 164–65, 169, 174–75, 182, 187
Bock, Darrell, 149
born from above/born again, 166–67, 193–94
Brown, Raymond, 159
Burridge, Richard, 8

C

Caesar, 43, 91, 101–2, 117, 148, 181
Caesarea Philippi, 38, 82–83
Caiaphas, 174, 180

calendar, 45, 100, 169
Caligula, Gaius, 69, 101, 117, 145
Cana, 162, 165, 168, 187
Canaanite woman, 38, 58
Capernaum, 75, 80, 96, 102–3, 120, 122
Carson, D. A., 159, 170
census, 118
centurion's servant, 31, 122, 143
characters, 8–9, 71, 136, 161, 173
children, 26, 34, 40–41, 51, 53, 114, 121, 128,
    146, 152, 164, 176, 197
church
    and canon, 4–6
    and Christ, 37–40
    and Gospels, 2–3
    moral proximity, 152
    unity, 179
Clement, 6, 18, 68
confession of Peter, 38–39
convicting, 178
council of Ephesus, 3
creation, 10, 12, 14, 28, 32, 36, 40, 48, 79, 119,
    123, 141, 148, 161, 169, 175, 183, 185–88,
    194–95
creeds, 2–3
cross, 13–14, 38–39, 46–47, 52, 57, 71–72,
    82–83, 88–91, 96–97, 99, 103–6, 113, 119,
    132, 135, 138, 143, 148–49, 151, 161, 174–
    75, 178, 181–82, 184, 187, 189, 191
culture, 7, 11, 27–28, 62, 70, 100, 116, 179,
    195–96
Cyril of Alexandria, 3
Cyrus, 49, 61

D
Daniel, 36–37, 131, 150, 179
darkness, 1, 47, 74–75, 78, 83, 88, 91, 97, 100,
    102, 116–17, 123, 132, 134, 161, 164, 166,
    171, 174, 182, 190
dating, 20, 111
David, 1, 10, 21, 23–26, 32, 34, 42–43, 50, 52,
    57–58, 60, 78, 86, 89, 116, 118, 131, 135,
    144, 147, 172, 175–77
Day of Atonement, 137, 139
deafness, 56, 70, 97, 122, 142, 190
death, 13, 21–23, 27–28, 30–32, 37, 41, 45–48,
    53–54, 56–59, 68–69, 76, 78–80, 82–83,
    88–91, 98–103, 105, 113, 123–24, 127, 132–
    35, 141, 144, 148–49, 159, 161, 163, 166,
    173–75, 178, 181–84, 189, 195–97, 199
Decapolis, 97
demon possession, 32
destruction of Jerusalem, 20, 111

destruction of the temple, 43–47, 53, 69, 86–87,
    131, 141, 159
devil, 27, 38, 103, 105, 119–20, 141, 176, 182,
    190, 197
discipleship, 2, 13, 18, 22, 61–63, 82–83, 124–
    26, 128
divorce, 29, 40–41, 84
dove, 27, 73–74

E
Egypt, 10, 20, 26, 41, 57, 59, 96, 99, 125–26,
    134, 146–47, 165, 169, 171–72
elders, 37, 42, 151, 159
Elijah, 34, 39, 52–54, 74–75, 81, 84, 115, 120,
    122, 124, 143, 164
Elisha, 31, 53–54, 81, 120, 122
Elizabeth, 115–16, 143–44
emet, 197
Emmaus road, 113, 135
Epistles, 2, 19, 55–56
Erasmus, Desiderius, 3
Essenes, 43
eternal life, 12, 40, 84, 131, 160, 168, 192,
    194–96, 199
ethics, 40, 195–96
eudaimonia, 195
Eusebius, 68, 159
evangelicals, 12, 55
evangelism, 33
Eve, 10, 48, 83, 182, 198
exile, 10, 24–26, 28–29, 52–54, 57, 73, 93–94,
    98, 118, 124, 142, 147, 168, 176
Exodus (book), 28, 45, 47, 54, 93, 99, 126, 197
exodus (event), 59, 73, 96, 169
exorcism, 13, 71, 79, 84–85, 102–3, 120, 160
eyewitness, 5, 19, 68, 110, 114–15, 158
Ezekiel, 7, 25, 35, 44, 47, 52–53, 131, 167–68,
    178, 188–89

F
faith, 2, 7, 13–15, 24, 38, 62, 79, 81, 85, 105,
    115, 122–23, 127–28, 134, 147–48, 152, 179
false witness, 46, 89
family, 7, 10–11, 24–26, 28, 33–35, 37–38,
    48, 73, 78–81, 105, 121–23, 126–27, 152,
    172–73, 175–76, 198
fasting, 30, 77, 121
Feast of Tabernacles, 169, 171
Feast of Unleavened Bread, 132
Festival of Dedication, 172–73
festivals, 88–89, 99, 132, 137, 159, 161–63,
    168–72, 174
firstborn, 24, 118, 132

fishing, 36, 121, 183

forgiveness, 20, 40, 77, 97, 104, 130, 136, 138, 148, 183

four Gospels, 1–9, 19, 49, 180

fulfillment, 9, 21–23, 55, 57, 60, 71, 110–11, 163, 192

fulfillment quotations, 21, 25, 31, 48, 50, 52, 60, 185

G

Gabriel, 116

Galilee, 26, 28, 47, 52, 72, 74, 84, 114, 119–20, 129, 133, 149, 160

garden of Eden, 10, 74–75, 83, 133, 139–41, 179, 182, 186–87

Gemara, 50

gematria, 24

genealogy, 20, 24–25, 38, 49, 54, 57, 72, 112, 114, 119, 163

Genesis, 25, 36, 47, 49–50, 53–54, 57–58, 185–86

Gennesaret, 81

Gentiles, 18, 24, 26, 31, 33–34, 38, 40, 47–48, 52, 61, 81, 111, 114, 118, 127, 180

Gerasenes, 123

Gethsemane, 88

Gladd, Benjamin, 39–40, 176

God

    authority, 5, 74, 89, 125

    character, 27, 196–97

    contemplation, 198

    eternal generation of the Son, 192

    Father, 3, 14, 27, 30, 35, 42, 45, 49, 61–62, 71, 73, 75, 88, 91, 99, 118, 132–34, 138, 141, 145–46, 148, 168, 170–74, 176–81, 190–94, 196, 198

    and genealogies, 25

    grace, 197

    and humanity, 10

    and Israel, 10

    Jesus Christ, 23, 39, 60–61, 73, 84, 95, 140, 197

    Logos, 163

    and Luke, 141

    nature, 36, 196–97

    presence, 11, 28, 40, 60–61, 84, 125, 133–36, 140–41, 165–66, 176, 188–89, 192

    procession of the Spirit, 192

    and Scripture, 2

    seeing, 59–61, 82, 118, 164, 198

    truth, 197

God-fearers, 111

Golgotha, 91

gospel (message), 2, 58, 152

Great Commission, 21, 61

Greco-Roman culture, 27–28, 100–101, 116, 196

Gregory of Nyssa, 14

H

Hannah, 116, 142, 147

Hanukkah, 163, 169, 172–73

hardening, 36, 126

Hays, Richard, 92, 136

healing, 3, 13, 28, 30–32, 51, 54, 70, 75–78, 82, 84–85, 98, 103, 113, 120, 129, 147–48, 162, 169–70, 172, 187

heaven, 12, 14, 21–22, 27–30, 36, 38–40, 43, 46–49, 61–63, 74, 84, 87, 91, 124–25, 129, 131, 136, 143, 149–50, 165, 167, 170, 186, 188–89, 193, 198

Hellenization, 11

Herod, 11, 22, 26, 51–52, 75, 81, 113, 126, 133, 180

hesed, 197

historical context, 7, 19

historical development of the Gospels, 4–5

Holy One of God, 75, 96, 120–21

Holy Spirit, 5–6, 25, 27, 34, 52, 73, 76, 78, 86, 95, 97, 111–12, 114, 118–20, 122, 136, 140, 150, 164, 167, 174, 176–78, 183, 186–87, 189–94, 197

honor-shame culture, 27–28

hope, 1, 11–15, 21, 25, 34–35, 41, 53–54, 57–58, 61, 74, 95–96, 129, 131, 135, 148, 153, 194, 199

hospitality, 33, 44, 125

household code, 40

humanity, 1, 10, 14, 71, 114, 125, 139, 144, 152, 181–82, 189, 192, 194, 197–98

hypocrisy, 62, 81, 126

hyssop branch, 182

I

Immanuel, 21, 25, 48, 59–60

Intertestamental Period, 11

Irenaeus, 5–7, 18, 20, 68, 92, 110, 158

Isaac, 24, 49, 164, 181

Isaiah, 25, 31, 34–35, 38, 52–53, 60, 74–75, 85, 93–95, 97–99, 118, 122, 124, 133, 136, 142, 147, 164, 169, 175, 190

Israel

    and Christ, 2–3, 26, 54, 59

    covenant, 10, 94

    enemies, 12, 23, 146–48

    and God, 10

hope, 35–36
Jubilee, 137
and kingdom of God, 12–13
land, 7, 12–13, 24, 35, 120, 137
and Luke, 136
and Mark, 92–95
and Matthew, 48–54
monarchy, 10
and the nations, 10, 104, 111
parables, 42–43
Passover lamb, 99
promised land, 10, 25
salvation, 146–47
and Seleucids, 11
shepherd, 58
story, 10–11

J

Jacob, 25, 49, 57–59, 75, 134, 164–65, 167, 170, 176, 189
James, 39, 41, 75, 83–84, 88, 121, 124, 143, 158–59
Jerusalem, 11, 20, 41, 43–44, 49, 53, 58, 60, 72, 81–82, 84–85, 96, 98, 111–14, 116, 118–19, 124–26, 128–31, 136, 138, 141, 146, 149, 159–60, 163, 166, 168–69, 171, 174, 180
Jesus Christ
    and Abraham, 24
    abandonment, 88, 91
    anointing, 88, 120, 122
    arrest and trials, 45–46, 82, 86, 89, 132, 179
    ascension, 149–51
    authority, 30, 32, 43, 49, 73–82, 85, 123, 130
    baptism, 27–28, 39, 51, 73–74, 95, 120, 160
    birth, 22–24, 45, 48, 50, 57, 72, 115, 118, 145
    bread, 52, 88, 132, 135, 160–61, 163, 170, 185–86, 188–89
    breaking bread, 88, 135
    bridegroom, 121, 165–67
    burial, 88, 99, 134, 174, 183
    calling, 28, 31–32, 75, 77, 80, 121, 124
    and centurion, 31, 47, 91, 102, 119, 122, 133–34, 143
    and church, 17, 37, 40, 179
    clothes, 84, 141, 181
    coming one, 122
    commission, 47, 49
    and community, 39–40, 58, 79
    cornerstone, 61, 86, 130, 174
    covenant, 37
    and creation, 32

crucifixion, 31, 45–46, 82, 89–91, 99, 111, 113, 129, 132–33, 138, 144–45, 148, 162, 174–75, 181, 184, 187, 189
and Daniel, 36
death, 13, 28, 31, 41, 45–46, 56–57, 82–83, 88, 90, 98–100, 102, 113, 132–33, 135, 141, 149, 163, 166, 174–75, 178, 181–83, 189, 197, 199
and demons, 32
departure, 171, 174, 176, 178
and disciples, 15, 23, 28–29, 32–33, 37–38, 45, 47, 49, 58–61, 75–79, 81, 86, 88–89, 102, 105, 121–23, 125, 129, 132, 159, 171, 173–80, 183, 187, 193
Egypt, 26
and Elijah, 52–54
enters Jerusalem, 41–44
enthronement, 89, 150
and ethnic superiority, 125, 143
and exodus, 94
face, 1, 61, 124, 198
faith in, 14, 62
family, 24, 78–80
farewell speech, 161, 174, 176–78
and Father, 145–46
feeding, 38, 81, 97, 162, 183
and fig tree, 41, 53, 85, 126, 165
and foreigners, 143
foot washing, 175–76
forgiveness, 32, 46, 77, 103–4, 121, 138, 183
and Gentiles, 31, 38, 81, 114, 118, 180
glorified, 174, 178–79
God, 23, 39, 60–61, 73, 84, 95, 140, 197
good shepherd, 57–58, 160–61, 172
and gospel, 56–57
and Gospels, 3
healings, 13, 31
high priesthood, 150
high priestly prayer, 178–79
and Holy Spirit, 27
honor, 28
humility, 41
"I am," 171, 179, 187
identity, 27, 41, 72–73, 86, 104
Immanuel, 21, 25, 48, 59–60
insiders and outsiders, 79–80, 123
and Israel, 2–3, 26, 54, 59
Jacob's ladder, 165
and Jews, 11, 23, 26, 37
and Joshua, 51–52
judgment, 43–45
King, 12–13

Lamb, 45, 163–64, 184
last days, 13, 35, 44–45, 57, 86, 88, 178
and law, 29–30
legs broken, 182
liberator, 27, 96, 98, 147
life, 168, 185
light, 171, 185
Lord, 144–46
message, 11–13
Messiah, 2–3, 11, 13, 21, 23, 25–26, 34–35,
    37–39, 43, 46, 52–53, 55, 57–59, 71–72,
    82–86, 89, 105, 111, 118–19, 122, 124,
    131, 133, 135, 144–45, 148, 160, 162,
    164, 166, 172–75, 181, 183, 185, 198
messianic secret, 83, 85
ministry, 5, 13, 28, 36, 75, 81, 93, 114, 122,
    127, 136, 138, 143, 161–62, 172, 175,
    186, 195
miracles, 31, 74, 102
mission, 32, 38, 73, 78, 97, 141
and Moses, 50–51
and Nazareth, 26, 37, 52, 80, 102, 114,
    119–20, 136, 138, 179
not of this world, 180
oral traditions, 4, 81
parables, 35–37
and Paul, 55
and Peter, 38
and Pharisees, 29, 32, 34, 37–38, 40, 43–44,
    77–78, 81, 84, 121–22, 128, 130, 138,
    147, 166, 171
piercing, 182–83
and politics, 23, 42, 101–2, 121, 130, 133,
    139, 181
the poor, 40
power, 31–32, 72, 74, 79–80
prayer, 45, 138, 178–79, 193
predictions of death, 82
presence, 3, 28, 61, 97
prophet, 39
and purity laws, 76
rejection, 33–35
return, 14, 28, 44
royal procession, 41
and the Sabbath, 34–35
sacrifice, 55, 57
and Satan, 32, 34, 45, 47, 73–74, 78, 80, 95,
    103, 123, 125, 132, 181
Savior, 1, 7, 13–14, 77, 88, 111, 113–14, 116,
    118–19, 124, 129, 136, 144, 147–48
Servant, 1, 33, 71, 132, 134
Servant-King, 82, 91
the seventy-two, 125

the sick and lame, 142–43
signs, 126, 167, 183
and sin, 14
social memory, 4–5
and Solomon, 43
son of David, 1, 23–25, 31–32, 41, 50, 52,
    57–58, 85, 116, 131
Son of God, 1, 3, 5, 13, 20, 25, 37, 46–47,
    55, 71, 73–74, 84–86, 91, 102, 105,
    114, 118–19, 121, 124, 134, 145, 160,
    164–65, 168, 170, 173, 181–83, 185,
    198
Son of Man, 34, 46–47, 71, 83–84, 87, 89,
    91, 99, 104, 130–31, 133, 138, 148–50,
    165, 174, 194
Son of the Most High, 103, 116, 123, 145
and storm, 31
substitute, 14, 84, 103–4
suffering, 23, 38–39, 82, 88–91, 181
Suffering Servant, 1, 27, 30–31, 97–100,
    134, 177
teachings, 4, 14
and temple, 41–42
temptation, 27
transfiguration, 35, 74, 83–84, 150, 165
truth, 176
the Twelve, 18, 54, 80, 88, 121–23
union with, 177
unity with the Father, 193
victorious, 178
warrior, 32, 96
water, 27, 32, 37, 51–52, 59, 73, 75, 80–81,
    95, 103, 118, 123, 160–62, 167, 171,
    182, 185–89, 193
water into wine, 162, 165
the way, 176, 185
weeps, 113, 130
and widows, 122, 142–44
and Wisdom tradition, 50
wonder worker, 71, 96
word, 36
worship, 166
Yahweh, 80
Jesus traditions, 2
Job, 62, 80
John
    author, 158–59
    believing, 160
    book of glory, 161, 174
    book of signs, 162–63
    cosmic trial, 189–92
    courtroom, 190
    cross, 161, 174–75, 181–82, 189, 191

crucifixion, 175, 181, 189
cultures, 195
date, 159
death of Jesus, 175, 178, 181–83, 189, 197, 199
disciple Jesus loved, 75, 158, 161, 182, 184
epilogue, 162, 183–84
eternal life, 194–96
ethics, 195–96
farewell speech of Jesus, 161, 174, 176–78
Father, 192–93
fictive kinship, 175–76
garden, 179, 182–83, 187
God's nature, 196–97
and gospel, 192–97
grace, 196
Holy Spirit, 177
the hour, 178
"in the beginning," 163, 185
irony, 161
and Judaism, 165–73
kingdom, 160, 167, 189, 193–94, 199
law-court theme, 164, 179–80, 189–90
life, 160
Logos, 160, 163, 195
name, 160
new creation, 185–87
and Old Testament, 161, 175, 177–78, 185–92, 195, 199
parakletos, 176–77, 190
prologue, 163–64
purpose statement, 160
resurrection, 161–63, 173–75, 178, 182–83, 187, 191, 194
seven, 162, 187
signs, 161–62, 165, 167–70, 172–74, 183, 187, 191
Son, 192–93
structure, 161–62
symbolism, 161, 165, 185, 188
and Synoptics, 115
temple, 159, 162, 164–68, 185, 187–89
temple cleansing, 166
temporal frame, 186
testifying, 198
trial, 161–62, 174, 176, 180–81, 189–92, 199
Trinity, 192–94
truth, 196
uniqueness, 160
witness, 160
Word, 163–65, 184–85, 189, 193, 196
John Mark, 67–68

John the Baptist, 27, 33–34, 37, 42, 56, 72–74, 80, 84, 104, 114, 118–19, 130, 138, 142, 147, 161–64, 190–91, 198
Jordan River, 27, 95
Joseph (father of Jesus), 22, 25, 120
Joseph of Arimathea, 134, 182
Joseph (patriarch), 26
Josephus, Flavius, 101
Joshua, 25, 51–52, 151, 176
Jubilee, 113–14, 119–20, 126, 136–39, 153
Judaism
    and Christ, 11, 23, 26, 37
    and John, 165–73
    and Mark, 70
    and Matthew, 19
    and Samaritans, 168
    sects, 43
    story, 11
    traditions, 165–68
Judas, 21, 45–46, 88–89, 132, 175, 179
Judea, 26, 84
justice, 25, 29–30, 34, 52, 62, 95, 97, 111, 128, 141, 152

K

keys to the kingdom, 38
kingdom of God, 12, 30, 52, 72–73, 75, 80, 88, 95, 120, 148, 160, 167, 189, 193–94, 199
King James Version, 91

L

Laertius, 8
Lamb of God, 45, 163–64, 184
lame man, 138, 169–70
last days, 13, 35, 44–45, 57, 86, 88, 178
law, 10, 19, 21, 29, 50–51, 59, 62–63, 76–77, 86, 111, 128–29, 140, 164, 177, 179–80, 189–91, 196
Lazarus, 113, 128, 142, 161–63, 173, 187, 190
leadership, 5, 10, 22, 42, 44, 53–54, 82–83, 166–67, 180, 191
Legion, 96, 103
leprosy, 30–32, 56, 75–76, 121–22, 142–43
Levi, 18, 77, 121
light ritual, 171
literacy, 7, 19
literary context, 8
Lives, 8, 19
living water, 167–69, 171, 189, 199
love, 3, 13–15, 29, 62, 105, 121–22, 125, 130, 174, 176, 179, 196–97
Luke
    allusions, 136–37

ascension, 149–51
audience, 111
author, 110
birth stories, 115–16
certainty, 111
date, 111
discipleship, 125–26
enthronement of Jesus, 150
exaltation, 113, 124, 129–30, 134–36
exodus of Jesus, 124
and foreigners, 142–43
genealogy, 114, 119
Gentile, 110–11
God's presence, 125, 133–36, 140–41, 150
high priesthood of Jesus, 150
innocence of Jesus, 133
introduction, 114
and Isaiah, 118–19
Israel, 136–37, 139
journey to Jerusalem, 113–14, 124–26, 128
Jubilee, 136–39
kingdom, 113, 116, 121, 123–24, 128–29, 132, 148
lordship, 144–46
and Mark, 111–13, 115, 120, 134, 136
and Matthew, 115, 119–20, 134, 136, 141
Messiah, 111, 118–19, 122, 124, 131, 133, 135, 144–45, 148
and New Testament, 110, 148–49
Old Testament, 136–43
passion, 129–30
Passover, 132
and Paul, 110–11, 114
the poor, 113–14, 119–22, 124, 128–31, 136, 141–43, 152
prologue, 111, 114–15
purpose statement, 160
rereading Scripture, 135
resurrection, 126, 130–31, 134–35, 141, 143, 149, 151, 153
salvation, 146–49
salvation history, 114, 121
Savior, 111, 113–14, 116, 124, 129, 136, 144, 147
Scriptures, 134–36
Servant, 132, 134
story, 115
symphonic, 136
temple, 111, 114–16, 118–19, 129–31, 134, 136, 139–43, 147, 149, 151, 153
warnings, 126–28
weeping of Jesus, 130
widows, 112–13, 122, 128, 131, 142–44

women, 113, 122–23, 130, 134–35, 143–44

M

Maccabean Revolt, 11, 169, 173
magi, 20, 26, 114
Malachi, 11, 93–94
mammon, 128
man with an unclean spirit, 75
marginalized, 31, 113, 141, 152–53
Mark
    atonement, 104
    audience, 70
    author, 68–69
    authority, 73
    brevity, 70
    controversy stories, 76–78
    cosmic conflict, 71, 73–74
    cross, 71–72, 82–83, 88–91, 96–97, 99, 103–6
    date, 20, 68–69
    death of Jesus, 71, 78, 82–83, 88–90, 98–100, 102
    episodic, 72
    and gospel, 54–61
    healer, 96–97
    historical present, 70–71
    hodos, 97
    "immediately," 70–71, 94–95
    impurity, 76
    introduction, 74
    and Isaiah, 74–75, 85, 93–95, 97–99
    and Israel, 92–95
    and Judaism, 70, 75–77, 79, 81, 89, 92, 98, 101, 106
    kingdom, 72–73, 75–76, 78–85, 88–89, 95, 101–3
    liberator, 96–98
    longer ending, 92–93
    and Luke, 68–69, 71–72
    and Matthew, 19–20, 68–73, 77, 92–93, 106
    Messiah, 71–72, 82–86, 89, 105
    messianic secret, 83
    miracles, 74, 76–77, 80, 91, 99, 102–3
    new exodus, 92–101
    and Old Testament, 70, 92–100
    Passover, 99–100
    and Peter, 68, 72–73, 75, 82–83, 88–89
    political victory, 100–102
    priority, 68
    prologue, 82–83, 93–95, 97
    resurrection, 71, 75, 82, 86, 89, 91
    revelation stories, 74
    and Rome, 70, 73–74, 89–90, 100–103, 106

Son of God, 73
story, 70–71
structure, 96–98
substitution, 103–5
suffering, 82
Suffering Servant, 97–100
supernatural victory, 100, 102–3
trust, 105–6
warrior, 96
wonder worker, 71, 96
marriage, 40, 43, 86
Mary, 25–26, 47, 67, 112, 116, 126, 135, 138,
    140, 142–44, 147, 160, 182
Mary Magdalene, 47, 160, 182–83, 187
Matthew
    and Abraham, 21, 23–25, 31, 57–59
    audience, 20
    author, 18
    birth of Jesus, 23–25, 45, 48, 50, 57
    chronological order, 22
    conclusion, 45–48
    cross, 38–39, 46–47, 52, 57
    date, 19–20
    death of Jesus, 22–23, 27–28, 31, 41, 45–48,
        56–57
    discipleship, 61–62
    discourses, 23
    fulfillment, 57–59
    genealogy, 24–25
    Good Shepherd, 57–58
    introduction, 23–26
    and Israel, 48–54
    Jewish, 19–21, 23–24, 26, 30, 33, 37–38, 41,
        43, 46, 50–51
    and Luke, 22–23, 115
    and Mark, 19–20, 22–23, 55
    message, 21–22
    and Moses, 50–51
    narratives, 22–23
    new creation, 27, 34, 49
    and New Testament, 18
    and Old Testament, 21, 48–54
    story, 48–50
    teachings, 22
    title, 18
Melchizedek, 150, 188
mercy, 33, 58, 62, 116, 125, 135, 151
miracles, 31–34, 51–52, 59, 71–72, 74, 76–77,
    80, 91, 99, 102–3, 122
Mishnah, 50
mission, 26, 32–34, 38, 47, 61, 73, 78–81, 83,
    97–98, 103, 110–11, 118, 124, 141, 143,
    148, 182, 187, 192

mission to the Gentiles, 33
moral impurity, 30–31, 76
moral proximity, 152
Moses, 8, 10, 21, 23, 28–30, 37, 39–40, 44, 48,
    50–52, 54, 58–60, 63, 78, 81, 83–84, 88–89,
    94, 96, 99, 121, 123–24, 128, 135, 146,
    150–51, 164, 167, 170–72, 176, 178, 188,
    194, 196
mountains, 24, 28, 38–39, 51, 59–60, 83–84, 99,
    111, 139, 150–51, 168, 170
Mount of Olives, 86, 88, 132
Mount Sinai, 10, 51–52, 54, 59, 83–84, 121,
    151, 188
mystery, 33, 35–36, 79, 91, 179

N
Naaman, 31, 122
narrative analysis, 8
Nathanael, 164–65, 189, 198
Nazareth, 26, 37, 52, 80, 102, 114, 116, 119–20,
    136, 198
Nero, 69, 117, 145
new covenant, 28, 37, 45, 48, 59, 78, 88, 99, 132,
    134, 147
New Testament
    and Alexander the Great, 11
    and Gospels, 2
    and Luke, 110
    Matthew, 18
    the sea, 123
Nicene Creed, 3, 145
Nicodemus, 160, 166–67, 182, 193–94, 197
Noah, 49, 125
Noah's sons, 125
noncanonical gospels, 5–6
northern kingdom, 168

O
Old Testament
    bread, 186
    burial, 134
    cosmic trial, 189–92
    and discipleship, 62
    fulfillment, 26
    and gospel, 100
    and Gospels, 2
    images, 146, 161, 185
    and John, 161, 185–92
    and Luke, 136–43
    and Mark, 70, 92–100
    and Matthew, 21, 48–54
    ordering, 49–50
    and Philo, 195

the poor, 141–43
resurrection, 131
salvation, 146–47
the sea, 123
story, 1
symbols, 185
water, 186
wells, 167
Olivet Discourse, 44, 86
Origen, 18, 68
orthodoxy, 4

P

Palestinian rulers, 117
Papias, 18, 68, 159
parables
    the banquet, 142–43
    and Christ, 35–37
    and disciples, 37
    dishonest manager, 113, 128
    faithful and unfaithful servant, 45
    Good Samaritan, 70, 112–13, 125–26, 143
    Israel, 42–43
    kingdom, 35
    landowner and vineyard, 42–43
    master and servants, 45
    mystery, 35
    prodigal son, 113, 127–28
    the sower, 36, 79, 123
    ten minas, 129
    ten virgins, 45
    two sons, 21, 42
    vineyard owner, 98, 130
    wedding banquet, 42
    workers in the vineyard, 40
paradise, 133
paralytic man, 32, 77
passion predictions, 98, 100
Passover, 45, 88, 96, 98–100, 132, 162–64,
    169–70, 174–75, 180, 182, 186–89
patronage, 7, 116
Paul, 20, 55, 57, 68, 100, 103, 110–11, 114, 176,
    179
peacemakers, 29, 40, 53
Pentecost, 87, 111, 145, 150, 183
people of God, 21, 28, 33, 53
persecution, 32–33, 61, 69, 177–79
Persia, 10–11, 46, 49
Peter, 6, 13, 19–20, 22, 38–40, 46, 68, 72–73, 75,
    82–83, 88–89, 111, 113, 119, 121, 124, 132,
    135, 144–45, 158–60, 162, 164, 176, 180,
    182–84, 191
Peter's denial of Jesus, 180

Peter's mother-in-law, 31, 75, 142
Pharisees, 21, 29, 32, 34, 37–38, 40, 43–44,
    77–78, 81, 84, 121, 128, 130, 138, 147, 171
Philo, 8, 101, 195
philosophy, 12–13, 122, 163, 194–95
Philostratus, 8
Pilate, Pontius, 21, 46, 89, 99, 101–2, 104, 113,
    117–18, 133, 148, 160, 174, 180–81, 187,
    191, 197–98
plot, 2, 8–9, 56, 71, 78
Plutarch, 8, 101
point of view, 8–9
Pompey, 11, 101, 117
poor, the, 7, 40, 56, 71, 95, 111–14, 116, 119–22,
    124, 128–31, 136, 141–43, 152, 166
Powell, Mark Allan, 22, 70
praetorium, 90
prayer, 30, 32, 45, 57–58, 61, 67, 75, 88, 98, 115,
    121, 128–29, 132, 138, 147, 174, 178–79, 193
Priene, 100
priesthood, 2, 11, 150
Prince of Peace, 133, 181
prophets, 10–11, 25, 30, 35, 44, 53–54, 58–59,
    84, 86, 95, 122, 126, 142, 147, 163, 165–66,
    177
proselytes, 111
protoeuangelion, 57
Psalms, 50, 135
purification, 73, 75, 94, 119, 162, 165, 168, 170,
    175
purity laws, 76, 106

Q

Q (sayings source), 115
Qumran, 119

R

Rachel, 26, 167
Rahab, 24, 38
Ramah, 26
ram's horn, 137
reading the Gospels, 7–9
Red Sea, 31, 51, 119, 188
repentance, 28, 34, 75, 118, 120, 122, 128–29,
    136, 138, 178
resolution, 1, 9
resurrection, 12–13, 22–23, 27, 31, 43, 45, 48,
    54, 56, 71, 75, 82, 86, 89, 91, 126, 130–31,
    134–35, 141, 143, 149, 151, 153, 161–63,
    173–75, 178, 182–83, 187, 191, 194
revelation, 3, 5, 74, 82–83
Revelation, book of, 31, 56, 123, 158, 168, 198
rich man and Lazarus, 128, 142

rich young ruler, 84, 105, 128, 148
righteousness, 27–29, 37, 62, 95, 191
ritual, 26, 30, 76, 91, 119, 162, 165, 171
ritual impurity, 30–31, 76
Roman emperors, 117
Roman triumph, 90–91
Rome, 7, 10–11, 19–20, 43, 68, 70, 73–74,
    89–90, 100–103, 106, 111, 113, 118, 122,
    132–33, 148, 180–81

S

Sabbath, 34, 47, 52, 76–78, 120, 136, 142, 147,
    163, 169–70, 187
Sabbath rest of the land, 136–37
sacrifice, 10, 24–25, 55, 57, 88, 90–91, 99,
    101–2, 128–29, 132, 151, 169, 173–74, 181,
    188–89
Sadducees, 38, 43, 131
salvation, 12, 14, 46, 60–61, 77, 94, 114, 116,
    118, 121, 129, 135, 138, 144, 146–49, 153,
    186, 196
Samaria, 26, 143, 167–68
Samaritans, 33, 125, 143, 167–68
Samaritan woman, 14, 160, 162, 167, 189–90,
    197–98
Sanhedrin, 45, 132, 134, 180
Satan, 32, 34, 45, 47, 57, 73–74, 78, 80, 95, 103,
    123, 125, 132, 181
scribes, 18, 20, 29–30, 32, 37, 44, 58, 77–78, 81,
    85, 91, 103, 121, 132, 138, 147
Scripture. *See also* New Testament; Old
    Testament
    canon, 4–6
    fulfillment, 45
    and God, 2
    and Gospels, 1
    Luke, 134–35
    rereading, 135
    story line, 2
    whole, 9
sea, the, 10, 31, 36, 75, 79–81, 96, 103, 123, 146,
    170, 174
self-authentication, 5
Seneca, 195
Septuagint, 11, 144
Sermon on the Mount, 20, 22, 28, 54, 70
serpent, 10, 57, 119, 177
Sertorius, Quintus, 101
service, 41–42, 122, 136, 151, 175, 179
setting, 8–9
shalom, 14, 33
Sheol, 47, 131

shepherd, 1, 25, 35, 44–45, 57–58, 72, 88,
    96, 112, 114, 118, 140, 144, 147, 160, 172,
    183
sign of Jonah, 38, 126
signs of the times, 87
Siloam, 171
Simeon, 118, 140, 147
Simon of Cyrene, 90
sin, 10, 14, 28–29, 40, 74, 78, 99–100, 103–4,
    128, 140, 148, 164, 170, 172, 191, 197
social dimension, 120, 138–39
source criticism, 115
southern kingdom, 168
spiritualization, 138
Stoicism, 195
story
    and gospel, 55
    Gospels, 1–3, 8–11
    Israel, 10–11
    Judaism, 11
    Luke, 115
    Mark, 70–71
    Matthew, 48–50
    Old Testament, 1
    reading, 9
    Scripture, 2
Synoptic Problem, 69
Syrophoenician woman, 81

T

table fellowship, 31, 77
Table of Nations, 125
Talmud, 50–51
tax collector, 14, 18–19, 76–77, 113, 118–19,
    121, 128–29
taxes, 18, 43
temple, 7, 10–12, 23–25, 29–30, 35, 41–45,
    47–49, 52–54, 60–61, 69, 75, 78, 82, 85–88,
    98, 111–12, 114–16, 118–19, 129–31, 134,
    136, 139–43, 147, 149, 151, 153, 159, 162–
    74, 176, 181–82, 185–89. *See also* destruc-
    tion of the temple
Tertullian, 158
testing, 38
Thomas, 176, 183
Tiberius Caesar, 117–18, 145
tomb, 1, 21, 32, 47, 103, 134–35, 173, 182–83
Torah, 12, 21, 23, 28–30, 35, 37, 43, 50–51, 53,
    59, 62, 84, 89, 110, 133, 141, 143, 172, 176
Torrance, T. F., 150
twelve disciples, 18, 32, 51, 121
Tyre, 38, 81

V

Vespasian, 101
vineyard, 40, 42, 85–86, 98, 130
virtue, 13–15, 44, 129, 195–96

W

water ritual, 171
Watts, Rikki, 93
wealth, 27, 40–41, 67, 105, 122, 128–29, 134
wedding at Cana, 165, 187
wells, 167–68
whole Gospels, 8
widow's son, 112, 122
wilderness, 27, 31, 33, 35, 37–38, 51, 59, 73–75,
    93–95, 97, 114, 118–19, 122–23, 125, 169–
    72, 175, 177, 186, 188, 194

Witherington, Ben, 145
witness, 7, 81, 86, 89, 133, 152, 159–62, 164,
    183, 189–92, 198–99
woes, 34, 44, 53, 121, 126
women, 7, 24, 47, 79, 91, 112–13, 119, 122–23,
    130, 134–35, 143–44, 167, 182
Wrede, William, 83

Z

Zacchaeus, 113, 129, 142, 148
Zealots, 43
Zebedee, 158–59
Zechariah, 53, 115–16, 135, 140, 147–48

X-ray picture of the Volkswagen shows convincingly
ere could be no more logical or effective way of
; space and weight. The engine and transmission
is right over the rear axle; accordingly the power
gine can be transmitted directly — without a pro-
ft — to the drive wheels, which are always under
load to give them traction. So, too, the ample
e space between back seat and engine is in
right location. The spare wheel is within easy

the fr...
ment behind re...
of course the body...
With this arrangement of the...
of gravity is always low — ...
passengers — and more to ...
A high degree of ... is ...
electrically ... at a level ...

Matt Meyer

DEDICATION

This book is dedicated to the memory of my two Volkswagen Beetles who fell victim to fire. This book is also dedicated to Volkswagen collectors worldwide who share the joy of the little car.

ACKNOWLEDGMENTS

Without the help of two extremely nice men, Mark Johnson and Reinhard Sokoll, this book would not have been possible. Mark lives in England, has an ever-growing collection of around two thousand Volkswagen Beetle models, and runs a mail order business, VW Toys and Models, specializing in tracking down harder to find models. You may contact VW Toys and Models via email at Mandt.johnson@btinternet.com. Reinhard lives in Germany. Until the category was removed from the record books in 1999, Reinhard Sokoll was a Guinness Book of World Records record holder, having the most Volkswagen Beetle models. Reinhard's collection of 5,674 (yes you read that right) models is housed in the Das Kafermodell Museum, which he established. An amazing four rooms, floor to ceiling, are filled with Volkswagen Beetle models. This surreal sight may be seen at the museum's web site at www.kaefermodell-museum.de. Mark and Reinhard, I thank you for all of your help and hospitality.

I would also like to thank the following people: Nigel Mynheer from Christies of London for supplying information. Bob Parker for sharing his photos and knowledge on Hot Wheels. Charlie Mack for sharing his photos and knowledge on Matchbox toys. Jeff Snyder for guiding me through the process of building the book. All of the other great people at Schiffer Publishing responsible for making the book beautiful. My aunt Lenore for the camera. All of my friends and family for their support. And last but not least, I'd like to thank my father and mother (Jim and Pat) for their ongoing support throughout the completion of this book.

Special thanks to Mark Johnson, shown here in front of just a small portion of his collection.

Special thanks to Reinhard Sokoll, shown here in front of one corner o his amazing Kafermodell Museum.

CONTENTS

Introduction _____ 8

Chapter One: Beetles™ of the 1930s and 1940s __ 10

Chapter Two: Huki® _____ 19

Chapter Three: Beetles of the 1950s and 1960s __ 22

Chapter Four: Japanese Tin Toys _____ 27

Chapter Five: Herbie™ _____ 32

Chapter Six: Functional Beetles _____ 46

Chapter Seven: Ceramic Beetles _____ 52

Chapter Eight: Characters in Beetles _____ 57

Chapter Nine: Beetle Transformers™ _____ 61

Chapter Ten: Corgi® _____ 64

Chapter Eleven: Franklin Mint® _____ 69

Chapter Twelve: Micro Machines™ _____ 72

Chapter Thirteen: Hot Wheels® _____ 76

Chapter Fourteen: Lledo® _____ 83

Chapter Fifteen: Maisto™ _____ 90

Chapter Sixteen: Matchbox® _____ 93

Chapter Seventeen: Sunnyside™ _____ 100

Chapter Eighteen: Tonka® _____ 102

Chapter Nineteen: Vitesse™ and Wiking™ _____ 104

Chapter Twenty: Beetles Made of Plastic _____ 107

Chapter Twenty-one: Beetles Made of Metal ___ 119

Chapter Twenty-two: Rarities _____ 133

Bibliography _____ 137

Price Guide _____ 138

INTRODUCTION

It has been nearly seventy years since Ferdinand Porsche built the first prototype of what we now call a Beetle™. Over these seventy years, it has turned into a worldwide phenomenon, touching nearly everyone's life in some way. Besides making its way onto roads in every country around the world, the Beetle can be found on products from cookie jars to underwear, not to mention toys. There have been thousands of toys and models made over the years modeled after the Beetle, so many it's next to impossible to list or collect them all. With this in mind, I wondered where to begin and what to include in a book like this. I decided to include Beetles™ often seen at flea markets, antique stores, and on the internet along with some older and more rare examples. This book is meant to be used as a guide, showing an array of Beetles of various materials, sizes, and ages. In compiling this book, I have literally traveled the world photographing collections, so please enjoy.

The origins of Volkswagen® Beetle toys and models go as far back as the beginnings of the actual car. Probably the most well known beginning would be the five KDF models built at the Porsche® Apprentice School Workshop in Stuttgart-Zuffenhausen in 1938. A well known photograph shows Ferdinand Porsche pointing out to Hitler the rear portion of the model. These are amazing models with removable bodies, opening doors, bonnets, and engine compartments containing engines that are highly detailed, right down to the spark plugs. Each model rides on a detailed chassis with a working rear suspension and steering. To top it all off, the interior of each model has upholstered seats and a carpeted floor. On February 29th, 1996, one of these models was auctioned off at Christies of London for an amazing 38,000 pounds (57,000 dollars).

Today, Volkswagen Beetle toys may be found just about anywhere from flea markets to fluffy boutique stores. I've found the best place to purchase Volkswagen toys is at Volkswagen car shows. There are always a few booths containing nothing but toys. If a Volkswagen collector's paradise is what you have in mind, then the annual Volkswagen and Porsche toy and literature show is the ticket. Held in Irvine, California, this is an entire show filled with Volkswagen models. The internet is also a wonderful place to locate Volkswagen toys; but, if hands on is more of your style, nothing beats a good flea market or antique store.

BUILDING & MAINTAINING A BEETLE COLLECTION

Overall, there is a lack of knowledge on the dealer's part when it comes to Volkswagen Beetle toys, which can be both good and bad. I often see the most common of Beetle models with outrages price tags. When inquiring of the dealer why the price is so high, the most common response I receive is, "Because the car is cute." If only I had a dime for every time I've heard that I would be, well, able to buy a sandwich. The moral of the story is, don't buy a Volkswagen Beetle toy just because it's there. Yes, they are cute and hard to resist, but, just remember that there are an abundance of them out there. If you pass one up, it is likely there will be another in nicer condition for less. Be smart and don't fall into the "because the car is cute" trap. On the other hand, a dealer may under mark a Beetle for a lack of knowledge. When this happens, it is always fun and exciting. Just remember to play it cool and talk the dealer down a few dollars more.

When collecting Volkswagen Beetle toys, it is very important to know the history of the actual car. On numerous occasions at flea markets and antique shows, I've seen toy Beetles with huge, square rear windows and thick bumpers marked "1950's tin toy $40.00." If you know the history, it is easy to say that this toy is not likely to be from the 1950s since the Beetle had an oval rear window up until 1958 and thick bumpers didn't enter the scene till the late sixties. It is also important to realize that a split rear window does not necessarily mean that a Beetle model is old. It is far more likely that it just rolled out of the toy factory. Early split window toys have the tendency to have an elongated form and will look old and used due to play; after all, such toys are more than fifty years old. In comparison, newer split window models tend to replicate the exact dimensions of the actual car, making the model far less elongated. Early split window toys have survived over the years but are few and far between. A wonderful place to locate them is the internet at auction sights such as eBay.

When buying over the internet, it is essential to make sure the toy you are about to purchase or bid on is an original. The easiest way to tell is if the toy has the original box. However, because this is not the norm, be sure to ask the seller lots of questions, such as "How did you acquire the toy?" or "How long have you owned the toy?" Usually, if it looks too good to be true, it is!

After parting with your hard earned cash in order to build a fabulous Volkswagen collection, it is probably a good idea to take care of the little cars. They can be displayed in any way your heart desires; however, keep the cars out of direct sunlight to prevent fading and in a place with a stable temperature and little moisture. Temperature and moisture changes can cause the metal to deteriorate and even rust. It is important not to forget about your little friends. Shifting your display once in a while is a great idea not only to keep the collection fresh to the eye but to provide an opportunity for dusting as well. I personally like to take my cars down off the shelf and play with them, pretending I own a giant Volkswagen restoration garage. However, most experts look down on this practice of playing with the cars, for oils and acids from your hands can cause damage over time. One way to prevent this problem is to wash your hands before handling your Beetles. Decals are very easily damaged, so it is best to keep your fingers off of them. It is essential that if the Beetle requires batteries to never leave the batteries in the toy. The battery terminals will corrode, as will the battery, causing damage to the car. It is also a good idea to keep the toy out of its original box. Most older boxes were printed on highly acidic stocks, which can turn decals on the car yellow or even eat through rubber tires. If you feel the need to store the Beetle in the original box, it is a good idea to first place a plastic bag around it to act as a liner.

If you find, or have found, that your Volkswagen collection has grown so large that you are out of shelf space, you have a few options. One, build another shelf. Two, store some of your Volkswagens and occasionally rotate them onto display just as large museums do. The main priority when storing Volkswagens long term is to protect them. Wrap the cars in tissue, not bubble wrap. Bubble wrap promotes sweating and can harm decals. Small plastic bags and individual plastic cases, both available at hobby stores, are other options for storage. When storing, it is best to keep the weight off of the tires. Placing the car on its side is the best option. An attic or damp basement is no place for a Volkswagen, so be sure to find a dry environment with a stable temperature to store them.

Like everything else in our world, toy Volkswagens get dirty. Small amounts of water or glass cleaner can be used to clean the Beetle; but, remember when it comes to water, the less used the better. A small toothbrush works nicely to get into all of the little cracks and crevices. After washing the toy, make sure that all parts of the car are dry before placing it back on the shelf. If the showroom floor shine is what you have in mind, car wax is a great option. Yes, the same stuff you use on your real life Beetle can also be used on your toys. It is always smart to do a test on a small portion of the toy before cleaning or waxing the entire car. With an ocassional cleaning, the value of your collection will be maintained, as will the happiness of your Beetles.

Although your collection of Volkswagens seems quite safe sitting on the shelves, tomorrow is a new day and you never know what it will bring. No matter how small or large your collection, it is important to consider insurance. If nothing else, consult with your current insurance agent to see if the collection is all ready covered. I learned the hard way and found out my collection wasn't covered after my house burned to the ground. It is wise to keep photographs and accurate records of your collection. Do not store the photos or records in your house, for they are no good once they've been turned into ashes. Storing them at your office or a relative's home is a great idea.

Pricing can be a tricky thing with the many variables involved such as age, condition, and rarity. The prices shown in the captions of this book reflect the Beetle as if it were in mint condition. The price guide at the end of the book shows the price in both mint and poor condition. These prices are meant to be used as a guide to assessing prices of Beetles. There is always the question of how much an original box adds to the value. If the box is in good condition, it can add over a third to the overall value. Boxes can also add a lot to a collection in that some are more interesting than the toys themselves. When it comes to blister packs, such as the ones that Hot Wheels® are packaged in, pricing becomes a bit different. The value of a newer model kept in its original blister pack is only increased by three to five percent. However the values of early Beetles still in the original blister packs can nearly triple.

In putting this book together, I was reminded that the Volkswagen community is comprised of some of the nicest people in the world. It doesn't come as a surprise, after all, anyone involved with the lovable little cars would have to have a kind and patient side. Many people happily supplied information and to them I say thank you. This book on the "people's car" is truly the people's book, so if you have any additional information please feel free to share.

CHAPTER ONE
BEETLES™ OF THE 1930S & 1940S

Prewar FCar made by Volk
ca. 1938. $950.

Front view of FCar.

Black example of prewar FCar made by Volk™, ca.1938. $950.

Prewar Liquor bottle made by Bodirsky™, ca. 1938. Clear glass with black
plastic lid, 4.5" in length. The bottle became one cm longer after the war. $275.

Prewar driver made by Distler™, ca. 1938. Tin plate with a clockwork motor. Keyhole on the side of the car, marked "Made in Germany" on the bottom, 9" in length. $915

Postwar version of the prewar driver made by Distler, ca. 1947. Tin plate with a clockwork motor. Keyhole on the side of the car marked Made in Germany on the bottom, 9" in length. $315.

A prewar Kafer sedan/convertible made by CKO™ standing for Manufacture of Georg Kellerman, ca. 1938. Tin with the ability to flip from a convertible into a sedan by pressing a button above the rear bumper, 6" in length. $600.

The CKO Kafer sedan/convertible shown as a sedan before its transformation.

The CKO Kafer sedan/convertible shown as a convertible after its transformation.

Kafer sedan/convertible made by CKO, ca. 1950. Bottom of car stamped "Made in U.S. Zone Germany", 6" in length. $400.

Made by Marklin™, ca. 1939. Chassis stamped "Marklin 9" and "Made in Germany". The bumper is marked "KDF", 4" in length. $110.

Front view of the Marklin KDF car.

Made by Karl Bub™, ca. 1940 through 1945. Metal marked KB on the bottom, 2.5" in length. $40.

FH-126 made by Horndlein™, ca. 1946. Tin plate litho, 5" in length. $150.

Made by Tipp and Co.™ of Germany, ca. 1948. Tin plate litho and is part of a track set, marked "Made in U.S. Zone Germany" on the bottom, 3.5" in length. $150.

Made by Tipp and Co. of Germany, ca. 1948. One piece tin plate with clock work motor and marked "Made in U.S. Zone Germany". The small hole on the side of the car is for a toy fuel pump. $150.

Made by Arnold™ of Germany, ca. 1953. Plastic body with cut out windows on tin chassis. Friction motor with no interior. $175.

Made by George Fischer™ of Germany, ca. late 1940s. One piece tin lithograph marked "Made in U.S. Zone" on the bottom, 23" in length. $135.

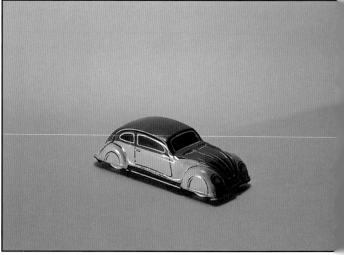

Two Volkswagens made by Arnold, ca. 1953. $175.

Made in Germany, ca. late 1940s. Tin plate litho with "Made in U.S. Zone Germany" printed on the deck lid, 4" in length. $140.

Made by Wiking™, ca. 1948 through 1950. One piece plastic with cut out windows. Removable plastic seats, gas tank, and engine, allowing toy to be taken apart and put back together, 4" in length. $75.

Made by Pramela of Germany, ca. 1949. Die cast with clockwork motor made in red, black, green, and unpainted. The tab in front is for steering, 4.5" in length. $230.

Unpainted example of the Pramela™ Volkswagen.

Made by Volkswagen in the Wolfsburg factory, ca. late 1940s. As a result of a lack of work, factory employees were instructed to make these models. They come in many color variations, with some being mounted on a piece of wood, 5" in length. $150.

An unpainted mounted example of the Beetle made by Volkswagen, ca. late 1940s. $150.

Made by Gama, ca. 1945. $250.

Made by Gama, ca. 1945. $250.

One particular Volkswagen that is highly sought after by ollectors is the Huki KdF Wagen. These extremely hard to ɪd toys come with a pretty price tag, with the average price ɪarting at $150 and going as high as $350 for a mint condi-ɔn model. That equates to over one hundred dollars per ch. The company was owned by HUbert KIenberger, hich is how the Huki name came to be. Huki was located Nuremberger, Germany, which was the main toy district Germany. The Huki KdF Wagens are easily identified with ɪe letters "HK" found on the license plate followed by a ɪree digit number identifying the model. These tin plate ɪys have a detailed lithograph design featuring a rear spit window, semaphores, and peoples faces in the windows. The earliest Huki KdF Wagen is the HK 403, which was pro-duced from the late 1930s to the early 1940s. It is gray in color and very rare. More commonly found are the post war HK 391, HK 392, and HK 393 models. These models came in many color variations with combina-tions of many different features such as two and four door models, key-wound motors, and some with brakes. Found on the HK 392 and HK 393 just above the license plate are one of three markings stating where it was made. These are not easy models to locate, so be prepared to pay the price.

ɪki #391, ca. late 1940s. Tin plate litho on tin chassis. Brown and light ɪeen two-tone with two doors. No motor, brake, or markings, 3" in ɪgth. $225.

Front view of Huki #391, ca. late 1940s.

Huki #392, ca. 1950. Tin plate litho on tin chassis. Cream and red two-tone with four doors. Marked "Made in Western Germany" above license plate, 3" in length. $125.

Huki #393, ca. late 1940s. Tin plate litho on tin chassis. Red and cream two-tone with two doors. Key wound motor labeled "Made in Western Germany" above license plate, 3" in length. $175.

Huki #393, ca. late 1940s. Tin plate litho on tin chassis. Cream and red two-tone with two doors. Marked "Made in Western Germany" just above the license plate, 3" in length. $175.

Huki #393, ca. late 1940s. Tin plate litho on tin chassis. Tan and light green two-tone with two doors. Key wound motor with brake labeled "Made in U.S. Zone Germany" above the license plate, 3" in length. $175.

Made by Arnold of Germany, ca. 1953. Tin plate body with Litho interior depicting a pre-1952 era Volkswagen, 8.5" in length. $175.

Made by Voss™, ca. early 1950s. One piece plastic body with cut out windows, 3". $60.

Made by Wuco™, ca. early 1950s. One piece plastic body stamped "Made in Germany" on the inside with accompanying metal garage, 2". $40.

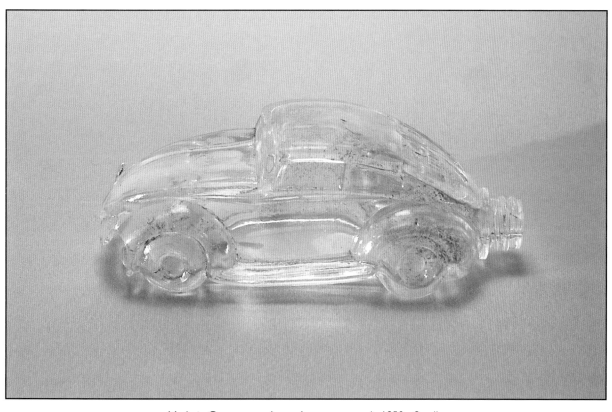

Made in Germany, maker unknown, ca. early 1950s. Small split window glass bottle with black plastic cap, 3". $35.

Made by DUX™, ca. 1950 through 1954. Tin plate and clock work motor with forward and reverse. Chassis is stamped "DUX Made in Germany," 4.5". $110.

Front view of DUX Volkswagen.

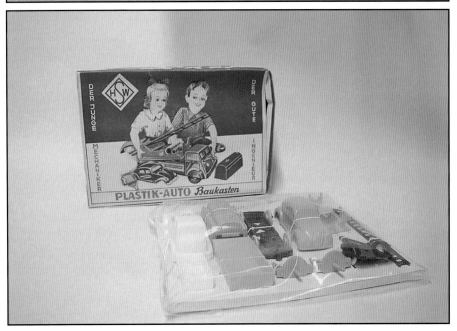

Plastic Auto Backasten made by HSW™, ca. 1952. $125.

Gummi-Auto made by Stehal™ of Western Germany, ca. late 1950s through the early 1960s. Rubber, 6" in length. $50.

Oval window Beetle, maker unknown, ca. 1950s. Hard metal, 3" in length. $35.

Made by Tudor Rose™ of England, ca. 1960s. Soft plastic, 8.5" in length. $40.

Cigarette dispenser, ca.1960s. Wood with removable slot in roof to insert cigarettes, 9" in length. $70.

Made by CIJ of France, ca. 1960s. Die cast, 4.5" in length. $65.

Made by Barclay, ca. 1960s. Metal shown in original package, 2.5" in length. $15.

CHAPTER FOUR
JAPANESE TIN TOYS

In the economic chaos following World War II, Japan's toy manufactures looked for a new type of toy in order to compete in a toy market already dominated by Germany and the United States. Their solution was to develop a small electric motor powered by household batteries. The new electric motor could perform many new functions, and perform them longer than traditional spring driven toys. The Japanese toy designers created hundreds of toys based on automobiles, including the Volkswagen Beetle. These Japanese toys were of very high quality and fine detail. The major goal of the designers was to make them look as close to the real thing as possible. The toys became very popular around the world, especially in the United States. The Japanese dominated the toy market for the next thirty years.

These toys do require some special care if they are to be kept in good condition and in working order, for after it stops working the value drops dramatically. In order to keep the toys loose, they should be operated periodically and may be sprayed with a light lubricant. Batteries should never be left within the cars and the battery contacts should always be kept clean. Car wax is a great option for keeping the outside of the car looking new; however, it is wise to first test the wax on a small portion of the car to make sure the paint isn't being softened or removed. Light surface rust can usually be removed with a careful polishing, but if the rust is deep within the metal, there's not much that can be done. Do not repaint the car, for this dramatically drops the value, making it worth next to nothing.

Made by Taiyo™, ca. 1960s. Tin, 9.5" in length. $75.

Fire chief made by HC™, ca. 1970s. Tin, 14" in length. $110.

Made by Yonaeawa™, ca. 1994. Tin labeled "Made in Japan", 5.5" in length. $20.

Made by Yonaeawa, ca. 1994. Tin with wind up motor labeled "Made in Japan", 3" in length. $16.

Made by Bandai™, ca. 1965. Tin with opening sunroof, doors, and hood. Man inside and electric lights in the front, 10" in length. $110.

Made by Bandai, ca. 1960s. Battery run, made of tin with clear deck lid and detailed interior, 10" in length. $85.

Made by Bandai, ca. 1960s. Tin with electric lights in the front. Opening sunroof and hood, 15" in length. $135.

Made by Bandai, ca. 1970s. Tin, 10" in length. $75.

Santa Express made by Toys Club™, ca. 1995. Tin with rubber wheels and labeled "Made in Japan". $25.

Made by Eindo™, ca. 1970s. Tin marked "Made in Japan", 4" in length. $35.

Battery run Volkswagen convertible, ca. early 196(Tin, 9" in length. $250.

Made by Modern Toys™, ca. 1970s. Tin, 10"
in length. $150.

Tin wind up, ca. early 1960s. Tin with
racing stripe and "28" on the roof.
Labeled "T.T. Made in Japan" on the
rear of the car, 4" in length. $35.

Made by Nomura Toy™, ca. 1982.
Plastic, 2" in length. $5.

CHAPTER FIVE
HERBIE™

Probably the most famous Volkswagen Beetle of all, Herbie has a very special place in the hearts of Volkswagen collectors and enthusiasts alike. Because in 1969 Disney® wasn't the marketing super giant it is today, there are very few official Herbie collectables. Luckily for the Herbie collector, many unofficial Herbie toys were manufactured by many different companies. Some of the more notable ones are the Taiyo™ "Bump-N-Go," the Tekno™ Herbie, and more recently the Solido™ Herbie, which is next to impossible to find due to overwhelming demand. Herbie has made a bit of a comeback lately, making his way back into the Disney product line. These new items can be found at Disney Stores throughout the country. The outlook for Herbie collectibles looks bright with Disney currently working on a script for a new Herbie feature.

Herbie made by Taiyo, ca. 1970s. Metal and battery run, 13" in length. $150.

Made by Politoys of Italy for Walt Disney, ca. 1978. Metal and able to pull apart in the middle to mimic the effect in the *Love Bug* movie, 4" in length. $75.

Made by Polistil for Walt Disney, ca. 1970s into the early 1980s. Metal and able to pull apart in the middle to mimic the effect in the *Love Bug* movie, 4" in length. $60.

Herbie made by Tekno of Denmark, ca. 1969. Metal. $130.

Herbie die cut and fold made by Walt Disney, ca. 1980. Cardboard, 5.5" length. $25.

Reverse side of Herbie cut out.

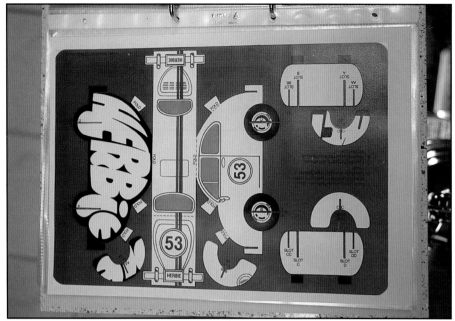

Die cut pattern for Herbie, 8.5" x 11". $30.

Remote control Herbie made by Duchic Spielsbug, ca. early 1980s. Battery operated and made of white plastic, 8.5" in length. $35.

Model kit made by Revell, ca. 1985. White plastic, 7" in length. $30.

Made by Schuco, ca. 1988. White metal wind up, 5" in length. $25.

Made by Matchbox, ca. 1988. Metal, 3.5" in length. $20.

Herbie Gross In Fahrt made by Minichamps, ca. 1995. Metal, 4" in length. $25.

Made by Minichamps, ca. 1995. Metal, 4" in length. $20.

Volkswagen auto museum Herbie made by Wiking, ca. 1996. Very limited numbers of this model were made and were only available through the Volkswagen Auto Museum in Wolfsburg, making it very rare in the United States. Plastic, 2" in length. $25.

Herbie made by Schuco Piccolo. Metal, 2" in length. $15.

Herbie made by Solido, ca. 1997. Metal, 9" in length. $55.

Herbie Gross In Fahrt made by Vittesse. Metal, 3.5" in length. $40.

Herbie made by Vittesse. Metal, 3.5" in length. $40.

Herbie made by Sunnyside, ca. 1998. White metal, 6" in length. $10.

Herbie made by Sunnyside, ca. 1998. White metal, 5" in length. $8.

Herbie convertible made by Sunnyside, ca. 1998. White metal, 5" in length. $7.

Herbie beanbag key chain made by the Disney Store, ca. 1999. Fabric, 4" in length. $12.

Opposite pa
The Love Bug comic book printed by Weste
Publishing, ca. 1969. With each Herbie movie
comic book was printed containing the story. The
comic books are hard to find in good conditi
making them very collectible. $

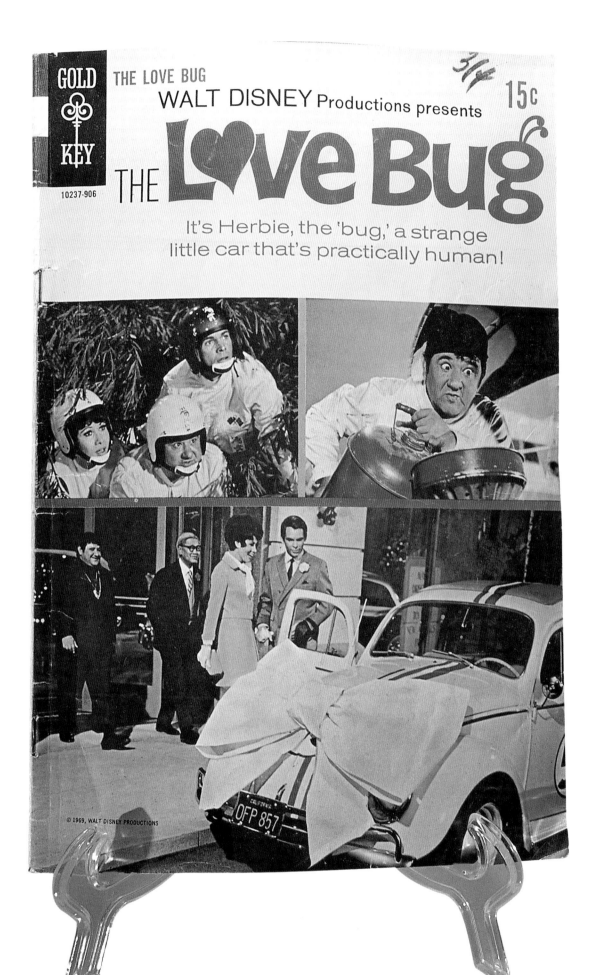

Herbie Rides Again comic book printed by Western Publishing, ca. 1974. $15.

Herbie Goes to Monte Carlo comic book printed by Western Publishing, ca. 1977. $10.

The Love Bug book printed by Scholastic, ca. 1969. With each Herbie movie that came out, a book was printed containing the story. These books are fairly common but are still great Herbie collectibles. $10.

Herbie Rides Again book printed by Scholastic, ca. 1974. $7.

Herbie Goes to Monte Carlo book printed by Scholastic, ca. 1977. $7.

Herbie Goes Bananas book printed by Scholastic, ca. 1980. $6.

Herbie Goes to Monte Carlo Disney Decade Coin, ca. 2000. $8.

CHAPTER SIX
FUNCTIONAL BEETLES

Over the years, the Beetle has been incorporated into many products from clocks to phones. Although these Beetles were not meant to be exact models or toys, they are still of great interest to collectors, for each of them carry out a different and unique function. It would be next to impossible to list all of the functional Beetles that have been made over the years, so I've attempted to show some of the more commonly found examples.

Beetle clock, ca. 1998. Silver, 3" in length. $40.

Beetle cassette player, ca. 1998. Plastic, 5" in length. $20.

Alarm clock made by Contact Design™, ca. 1997. Plastic, 5" in length. $40.

Beetle pencil holder, ca. 1988. Plastic, 5"
in length. $10.

Candy container, ca. 1999. Plastic, labeled
"buggy candy", 2.5" in length. $3.

Key chain, ca. 1998. Foam, 2.5" in
length. $5.

Christmas tree ornament made by Department 56™, ca. 1998. Hand blown glass, 6" in length. $25.

Christmas tree ornament, ca. 1997. Plastic, 3" in length. $7.

Christmas tree ornament made by Maisto, ca. 1999. Die cast metal and plastic, 4" in length. $10.

After shave container made by Avon®. This clear Avon Beetle was made in Mexico and is very hard to find in the United States. Glass, 6" in length. $30.

After shave container made by Avon. Glass, 6" in length. $10.

Made by E and J Mining Memories™ out of British coal, ca. 2000. Coal 4.5" in length. $35.

Volkswagen Beetle Phone made by Polyflame Concepts™, ca. 1997. Plastic, 8" in length. $40.

Candy containers, ca. 1990s. Clear plastic, 4.5" in length. $6

Silver Beetle on wood stand, 3" in length. $50.

Beetle table lamp made by Globe Electric Company™, ca. 2000. Glass with metal base, 8" in length. $24.

Coin operated children's ride located in the Automuseum Volkswagen™.

CHAPTER SEVEN

CERAMIC BEETLES

At times, ceramic Volkswagen Beetles can be very frustrating to the collector since the maker is usually unknown, making it hard to place an age and value on the model. I've attempted to show an array of models to hopefully clear up this fuzzy area. These ceramic models tend to be on a large scale and are often times functional, serving as salt and pepper shakers, book ends, or teapots. These are very fragile models, so it is essential before buying to examine for cracks or chips. If the crack or chip is large enough and visible, it reduces the value to next to nothing.

Cracks or chips that are not visible, such as those located on the underside of the model, still reduce the value but not as much as visible chips and cracks. Chips and cracks tell a lot about the integrity of the model as well as how it has been treated in the past.

Ceramic Bank, 8" in length. $18.

Ceramic bank with mice, 6" in length. $12.

Frog and Duck ceramic banks, 7" in length. Also available with a mouse or cat driving. $10 each.

Ceramic salt and pepper shakers, 4" in length. $8.

Ceramic Volkswagen convertible made by Colne Valley™, 13" in length. $40.

Ceramic Volkswagen made by Colne Valley, 13" in length. $40.

Ceramic Volkswagen, 12" in length. $30.

Ceramic book ends, 8" in length. $25.

Ceramic book ends, 11" in length. $25.

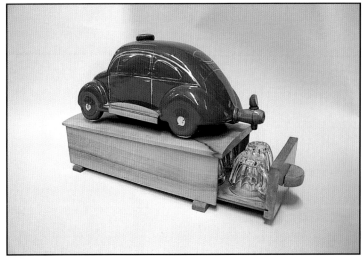

A rare ceramic decanter made by Allemagne™ of France, 12" in length. $125.

Ceramic teapot shown in blue, 8" in length. $60.   Ceramic teapot shown in yellow, 8" in length. $60.

A very rare ceramic teapot, ca. 1982. There are only a few known   Bottom view of the teapot.
examples of this highly detailed teapot, 9" in length. $150.

CHAPTER EIGHT

CHARACTERS INBEETLES

Mickey Mouse® in Beetle made by Masudaya™ for Walt Disney, ca. 1983. Plastic wind up, 6" in length. $30.

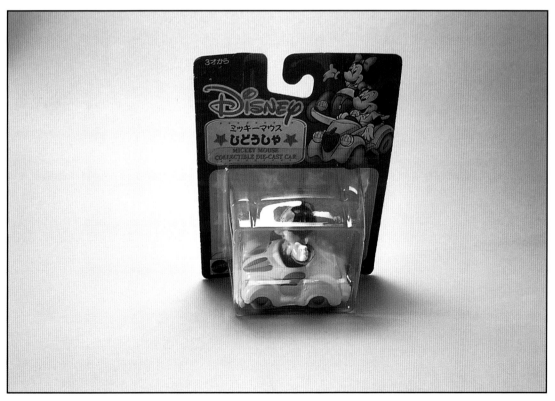

Mickey Mouse in Beetle made by Mattel® for Walt Disney, ca. early 1990s. Metal, 3" in length. $12.

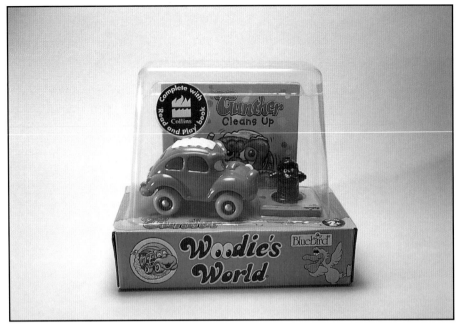

Woodies World Beetle made by Bluebird Toys™, ca. 1996. Contains plastic model of Gunther the Beetle along with story book, car 4.5" in length. $12.

Snoopy® in Beetle made by ESCI™. Metal, 3" in length. $28.

Christmas troll in Beetle made by Russ™, ca. early 1990s. Plastic, 2.5" in length. $5.

Ghostbusters transforming Beetle, ca. 1987. Plastic marked "1987 Columbia Pictures® Made in Mexico" on the bottom, 9" in length. $30.

Ghostbusters Beetle transformed into a ghost.

Garfield® driving a Volkswagen made by Ertl®, ca. 1990. Blue metal with Garfield in red cap and scarf, 3" in length. $13.

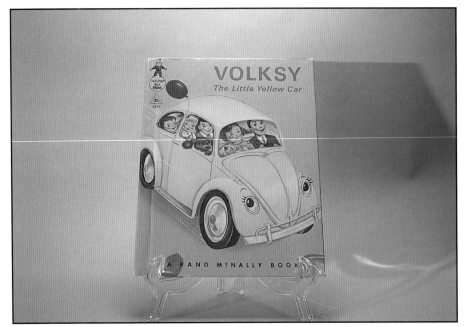

Volksy the Little Yellow Car™ printed by Rand McNally®. A very hard to find book featuring Volksy the Volkswagen. $40.

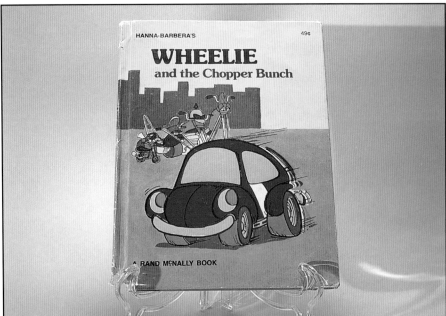

Wheelie and the Chopper Bunch™ printed by Rand McNally. $10.

Candy container made by Disney, ca. 2001. Clear plastic with characters heads in windows, 5" in length. $6.

The Volkswagen Beetle was part of the *Transformers* cartoon from the very beginning, in the form of "Bumblebee™." Bumblebee acted as a messenger and a spy, with some of his strengths including great fuel efficiency and adaptability to water environments. His weakness was being the physically weakest of all Transformers. The similarities between a real Beetle and Bumblebee are quite obvious. The Transformers line of toys included Bumblebee. As the popularity of the cartoon grew, many knock off Bumblebee toys appeared. How does one know if they have an original Transformer toy? Quite simple, an authentic Transformer contains the Transformer holographic decal on the roof the toy.

Bumblebee transformer made by Bandai™, ca. 1984. Plastic, 2" in length. $10.

Gold Transformer Beetle made by Bandai, ca. 1985. Plastic, 3" in length. $8.

Gold Beetle transformed into robot.

Transformer Beetle made by Bandai, ca. 1984. Metal and plastic, 4" in length. $35.

Volkswagen transformer, maker unknown, ca. mid-1980s. Plastic, 3.5" in length. $15.

Robo Machines™ Volkswagen Beetle transformer. Bandai replica, ca. 1986. Metal, 4" in length. $25.

Corgi (named after the Welsh dog) is one of Britains best known model makers and has been producing models for over 40 years. Created by the Mettoy Company, the name Corgi was chosen for its strong association with the Royal Family. The Corgi line was launched in 1956, modeled after the British automobiles of the time, each toy selling for an amazingly low 25 cents. Over the years, the Corgi line grew as did the complexity of the models. With spring suspension, opening hood and trunk, and diamond jeweled headlights, the popularity of these quality models grew. In the past forty years, Corgi has produced models of nearly every car and truck, along with numerous Volkswagen Beetles.

Slam Bam Sam made by Corgi, ca. mid-1970s. Yellow and red plastic with remote control, 7" in length. $35.

Slam Bam Sam made by Corgi, ca. mid-1970s. Black and red plastic with remote control, 7" in length. $35.

Polizei made by Corgi, ca. 1973. Metal, green with white fenders and light on top, 3.5" in length. $24.

Police Beetle made by Corgi, ca. 1970. White metal with black striped trunk and blue light on top, 3.5" in length. $14.

Corgi Jr. Whizzwheels made by Corgi. Metal body with plastic roof rack, 3" in length. $14.

Corgi Jr. Whizzwheels made by Corgi. Metal body with engine in the front, 3" in length. $14.

Corgi Jr. Whizzwheels made by Corgi. Metal body with flower sticker on the roof, 3" in length. $10.

Police Corgi Jr. Whizzwheels made by Corgi. Metal body with "police" sticker on the sides and light on roof, 3" in length. $10.

Opposite page

Top: Front view of Camio Collection Volkswagens made by Corgi. Metal available in many colors, 3.5" in length. $18 each.

Bottom: Rear view of Camio Collection Volkswagens made by Corgi. Metal available in many different colors, 3.5" in length. $18 each.

Camio Collection Rice Krispies promotional made by Corgi, ca. 1994. Yellow metal body, 3.5" in length. $30.

Max Wax promotional made by Corgi, ca. early 1990s. Black metal with "Max Wax" painted on top and sides in yellow and red, 3.5" in length. $15.

Motoring Memories Volkswagen made by Corgi, ca. early 1990s. Metal body labeled "Corgi" on bottom, 3.5" in length. $10.

Volkswagen 1200 Saloon made by Corgi, ca. 1990s. Metal body labeled "Corgi" on the bottom, 3.5" in length. $10.

CHAPTER ELEVEN

FRANKLIN MINT®

It is really every Volkswagen collectors dream to have a Franklin Mint Beetle in their collection, and for good reason. These Beetles are comprised of over 100 separate parts and are assembled and painted by hand. These 1:24 scale models are true to life with working features and stand out as some of the nicest Volkswagen Beetle models ever made.

1967 Cabriolet made by Franklin Mint, ca. early 1990s. $110.

1967 Sedan made by Franklin Mint, ca. early 1990s. $110.

1967 Sedan made by Franklin Mint, ca. early 1990s. $110.

1967 Flower Power Sedan made by Franklin Mint, ca. 1998. $110.

1967 Polizei Beetle made by Franklin Mint, ca. 1999. $125.

Micro Machines set #10
Volkswagens made by
Galoob™, ca. 1996. $14.

Micro Machines set #9
Volkswagens made by
Galoob, ca. 1997. $10.

Micro Machines Coolest Cars set made
by Galoob, ca. 1994. $10.

Splint window Micro Machines
Volkswagen made by Galoob, ca.
1990. Plastic with pull back motor, 1"
in length. $7.

Grey Micro Machines Volkswagen sedan made by
Galoob, ca. 1994. Plastic, 1.25" in length. $6.

73

Yellow hippie Micro Machines Volkswagen convertible made by Galoob, ca. 1995. Plastic, 1.25" in length. $6.

Two-tone green and tan sedan Micro Machines Volkswagen made by Galoob, ca. 1996. Plastic, 1.25" in length. $5.

Green Micro Machines Volkswagen convertible made by Galoob, ca. 1996. Plastic, 1.25" in length. $5.

Micro Machines Volkswagen made by Galoob, ca. 1996. Plastic, .5" in length. $3.

Talking Volkswagen made by Galoob, ca. 1998. Two buttons on the side make the car say seven different sayings from "It's off to the beach dude" to "Cool". Headlights light up as the mouth moves. Plastic, 8" in length. $17.

The Volkswagen Beetle has been part of the Hot Wheels line from the very beginning. In 1968 Mattel® released 16 cars to comprise the Hot Wheels line, one of which was #6220, the Custom Volkswagen. Hot Wheels torsion bar suspensions, low friction wheel bearings, and small price tags pushed sales of the line well beyond expectations. Factories in the United States and Hong Kong produced each model in many different colors, including magenta, purple, pink, gold, brown, red, aqua, light blue, blue, olive green, light green, and green. From its beginnings, Hot Wheels has grown, introducing new models each year. Many versions of the Volkswagen Beetle have been produced over the years with various paint schemes. These models are most commonly found out of the package, which are what the prices shown here reflect.

#6220 Custom Volkswagen shown in brown, ca. 1968. Metal with opening sun roof, 2" in length. $50.

#6220 Custom Volkswagen shown in metallic purple, ca. 1968. $50.

#6471 Evil Weevil, ca. 1971. Metal with opening sun roof labeled with one through nine on the side, 2" in length. $65.

#7620 Volkswagen, ca. 1974. Orange metal with no sunroof. Yellow, black, and white stripes, 2" in length. $400.

Incredibly rare Herfy's Promo in the package, ca. 1976. Orange metal with Beetle on the roof labeled "Herfy's" on the sides, 2" in length. $225.

#9548 Baja Bug, ca. 1984. Red metal labeled "Blazin Bug" in purple or blue, 2" in length. $25. "Blazin Bug" in yellow: $35.

#5907 Baja Bug, ca. 1984. Red metal with yellow and white trim labeled, "Baja Bug," 2" in length. $30.

#2542 Baja Bug, ca. 1984. White metal labeled "Blazin Bug" in purple, 2" in length. $15.

JC Whitney promotional Baja Bug. Yellow metal with black and white checker pattern on the sides labeled "JC Whitney", 2" in length. $25.

#453 VW Bug, ca. 1989. Purple metal with green, yellow, and orange geometric shapes, 2" in length. $8.

#2149 VW Bug, ca. 1989. Red metal with blue, yellow, and white flames, 2" in length. $20.

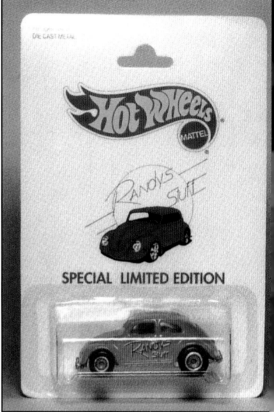

#11810 Special Limited Edition Randy's Stuff Beetle. Neon pink labeled "Randy's Stuff", 2" in length. $50.

#13280 Volkswagen, ca. 1995. Pink metal, 2" in length. $5.

Race Team Series II Baja Bug, ca. 1996. Blue metal with red, yellow, and white racing trim, 2" in length. $5.

#15240 Volkswagen, ca. 1996. Metallic Blue metal with yellow, green, and purple sunrise, 2" in length. $4.

#18776 Volkswagen, ca. 1998. White metal labeled "Bug'n' Taxi" on the sides, 2" in length. $4.

Surf' N Fun series VW Bug, ca. 1999. Metallic blue with green, white, and blue flowers labeled "Olas del Sol," 2" in length. $3.

Artistic License series VW Bug, ca. 1998. White metal with red, green, and blue graphics, 2" in length. $3.

Baja Bug, ca. 1999. Blue metal with bug graphics, 2" in length. $3.

Founded in 1983 by Jack Odell, Lledo (Odell spelled backwards) is one of the few die-cast manufacturers in England. Odell's goal was to produce high quality, die-cast models at an affordable price. The early Lledo models consisted of motor vehicles from the 1920s to the 1940s and are of little interest to Volkswagen collectors. However, the Lledo Beetle was launched in 1995. Lledo models became very popular in the promotional market by distinguishing the general release lines from the promotional lines. Promotional Beetle lines were cars produced that featured the logos of particular companies or clubs that were purchased and used by those organizations for promotional purposes whereas the general lines were vehicles sold straight to toy outlets with no special logos. This was a good thing for Beetle collectors because over the years there have been numerous Lledo promotional Beetles for many different company's and clubs. These promotional Volkswagens carry a much higher value than the general lines. In all, there has been a total of 120 different Volkswagen Beetles produced by Lledo.

Custom Classic pink Beetle made by Lledo, ca. mid-1990s. Pink metal with oval window, 3.5" in length. $18.

West of Scotland VW Club promotional Beetle made by Lledo, ca. mid-1990s. White metal with West of Scotland VW Club logo on the roof, 3.5" in length. $25.

PSI International Messe promotional Beetle made by Lledo, ca. 1996. White metal with PSI international Messe logo on the side, 3.5" in length. $25.

Ville d' Eu made by Lledo, ca. mid-1990s. Red metal, 3.5" in length. $20.

Campbells promotional made Lledo, ca. early 1990s. White metal with Campbells soup cans graphic on side and top of car, 3.5" in length. $35.

Campbells promotional made by Lledo, ca. early 1990s. Red and white two-tone metal with white Campbells soup cans graphic on side and top of car. Only five were ever made with this paint scheme, making it very rare, 3.5" in length. $125.

Hamleys Toy Store Beetle made by Lledo, ca. mid-1990s. Silver metal with "Hamleys" written on the sides, 3.5" in length. $16.

Minnie the Minx promotional made by Lledo, ca. early 1990s. Yellow metal with Minnie the Minx graphic on the sides, 3.5" in length. $20.

Maymurds Winegums promotional made by Lledo, ca. early 1990s. Black metal with Winegums logo painted on the sides, 3.5" in length. $20.

Das Kafermodell Museum promotional made by Lledo, ca. early 1990s. Black metal with Kafer Museum logo on the sides. Only 500 were made 3.5" in length. $35.

Das Kafermodell Museum promotional made by Lledo, ca. early 1990s. Red metal with Kafer Museum logo on the sides. Only 500 were made, 3.5" in length. $35.

Das Kafermodell Museum promotional made by Lledo in celebration of being admitted to the Guiness Book of World Records, ca. 1997. Light and dark blue two-tone with Das Kafermodell Museum information printed on top of the car, 3.5" in length. $25.

Das Kafermodell Museum promotional made by Lledo in celebration of being admitted to the Guiness Book of World Records, ca. 1997. Dark and light blue two-tone with Das Kafermodell Museum information printed on top of the car, 3.5" in length. $25.

Die cast Collection Volkswagen made by Lledo, ca. early 1990s. Red metal, 3.5" in length. $18.

Die cast Collection Volkswagen made by Lledo, ca. early 1990s. Yellow metal, 3.5" in length. $60.

Millionth Beetle made by Lledo, ca. early 1990s. Gold metal on plastic stand, 3.5" in length. $20.

H. Samuel Motoring Gems promotional made by Lledo, ca. early 1990s. Blue metal, 3.5" in length. $18.

Radio Times of BBC Radio promotional made by Lledo, ca. early 1990s. Orange metal, 3.5" in length. $18.

Coronation Street promotional made by Lledo, ca. early 1990s. Orange metal, 3.5" in length. $18.

Polizei and Feuerwehr Vanguards made by Lledo, ca. early 1990s. Metal body with metal chassis marked Vanguards, 3.5" in length. $23.

Convertible Vanguards Beetles made by Lledo, ca. mid-1990s. Metal body with metal chassis marked Vanguards, 3.5" in length. $23.

1951 Volkswagen Sedan made by Maisto, ca. 1995. Metal body with opening doors, trunk, and hood, 9" in length. $34.

1951 Volkswagen Convertible made by Maisto, ca. 1995. Metal body with opening doors, trunk and hood, 9" in length. $30.

1951 Volkswagen Convertible made by Maisto shown in light blue, ca. 1995. $30.

Pepsi Cola 1951 Volkswagen Convertible made by Maisto, ca. 1995. Metal body with blue and white two-tone paint. Pepsi Cola graphics on all sides of the car, 9" in length. $40.

1967 Volkswagen sedan made by Maisto, ca. 1996. Metal body with opening doors, hood, and trunk, 9" in length. $25.

1967 flower power Volkswagen made by Maisto, ca. 1999. Metal body with opening doors, hood, and trunk. Painted with flowers, hearts, and swirls, 9" in length. $20.

Motor Works twin pack made by Maisto, ca. 1999. Metal body labeled Maisto on bottom, 3" in length. $3.

Special edition Beetle made by Maisto, ca. 1999. Metal body labeled Maisto on bottom, 3" in length. $3.

Volkswagen 1300 made by Maisto, ca. 1997. Metal body, labeled Maisto on bottom, 3" in length. $3.

Volkswagen 1300 made by Maisto, ca. 1997. Metal body with plastic base, wheels, and interior, 3" in length. $3.

There would never have been any Volkswagen Beetles made by Matchbox had it not been for a chance meeting of Leslie Smith and Rodney Smith in the English Royal Navy. The two friends shared a vision of one day having their own engineering factory. After World War II, the two pooled their money and bought surplus die-casting machinery from the government, along with an old tavern, giving birth to the company named Lesney. Lesney produced its first toy in 1948, but it was in 1953 that small scale toys were introduced. The name matchbox comes from the toys being packaged in small matchbox type boxes.

These miniature cars were successfully produced with little trouble up until the late 1960s, when Hot Wheels were introduced, creating heavy competition for the Matchbox car. The 1970s were filled with many hurdles and the company began to branch off into other areas of toy production, such as doll making. By 1982, Lesney Products suffered under a $15 million dollar loss for the year and eventually went bankrupt. The company was bought out by Universal Toys, which in turn was bought out by Tyco Toys, Inc. in the early 1990s. In 1997, Mattel Toys bought out Tyco Toys for $755 million dollars and took control of both Hot Wheels and Matchbox cars. Through all of the turbulence, the Matchbox car continued to be produced, supplying the market with some very interesting Volkswagen Beetles.

Matchbox 25-B3 Volkswagen 1200 Sedan, ca. 1960.
Silver blue body with plastic wheels, 2" in length. $90.

Matchbox 15-A Volkswagen 1500, ca. 1969. Shown with a cream body and "137" decals on the sides, 2.5" in length. $25.

Matchbox 15-A Volkswagen 1500, ca. 1969. Shown with the harder to find red body. "137" decals on the side, 2.5" in length. $35.

Matchbox 31-B Volksdragon, ca. 1971. Red with yellow interior and eyes decal, 2.5" in length. $15.

Matchbox 11-B Flying Bug, ca. 1972. Red body with heart shaped hood, 2.5" in length. $20.

Flying bug on left with squared hood versus the heart shaped hood on the right.

Matchbox 43-B Dragon Wheels, ca. 1972. Green exterior with chrome interior, 2.5" in length. $18.

Matchbox Big Blue, ca. 1972. Blue exterior with chrome interior, 2.5" length. $18.

Roman Numeral Series VI-A1 Flying Beetle, ca. 1978. Orange metal, black windows with driver, 2" in length. $20.

Roman Numeral Series VI-A2 Lady Bug, ca. 1978. Black metal with flames and yellow interior, 2" in length. $20.

Matchbox 15-C Hi Ho Silver, ca. 1981. Silver metal with black base. Labeled "Hi Ho Silver", 2" in length. $12.

Matchbox 46-D1 Hot Chocolate, ca. 1981. Black metal with white roof stripes and brown sides, 2" in length. $12.

atchbox 49-D Sand Digger, ca. 1983. Black base, green body painted and Digger," 2.5" in length. $5.

Matchbox 49-D Dune Man, ca. 1983. Black base with red body painted "Dune Man," 2.5" in length. $5.

Copy of Matchbox, maker unknown, ca. 1984. Plastic, 2.5" in length. $4.

Matchbox WD-3-A Goofy's Beetle, ca. 1979. Yellow body with black ears attached to shoulders, 3" in length. $25. Yellow body with blacks ears not attached to shoulders: $75.

Matchbox connectable VW Dragster, ca. 1989. Plastic with the ability to pull apart in the middle, 2.5" in length. $6.

A Matchbox replica, made by Playmakers, ca. 1990. Plastic, 2.5" in length. $4.

Matchbox heritage collection. Metal, 4"
in length. $6.

Coca Cola Volkswagens made exclusively for
Target by Matchbox, ca. 1998. A 1962
Volkswagen Beetle and Volkswagen Concept 1,
oth red with the Coca-Cola logo on the sides of
the cars, each 2.5" in length. $20 for the set.

962 Volkswagen Beetle made by Matchbox, ca.
2000. Orange with black ragtop on the roof,
labeled "X Treme Mission" on the sides, 3" in
length. $3.

Sunnyside #4701. Volkswagen convertible, ca. 1993. Metal body with stripe coming down the side and pull back motor. Available in many different colors along with a sedan version, 4.5" in length. $7.

Sunnyside #4727. Volkswagen police car, ca. 1996. Metal body with light on top and pull back motor, 4.5" in length. $6.

Sunnyside #5702. Volkswagen sedan, ca. 1998. Metal body with pull back motor. Available in many different paint and color schemes, 5" in length. $5.

Sunnyside #5708. Volkswagen convertibles, ca. 1998. Metal body with pull back motor. Available in many different paint schemes and colors, 5" in length. $5.

Sunnyside #7707. Oval window Volkswagen, ca. 1994. Metal body with opening doors available in many different colors, 6" in length. $11.

Sunnyside #9701. 1967 Volkswagen Beetle, ca. 1999. Metal body with opening doors, trunk, and hood, 9" in length. $14.

Long before Tonka Toys produced any Volkswagens, they were named Mound Metalcraft Co. and operated out of the basement of a small schoolhouse in Mound, Minnesota. Mound Metalcraft produced hoes, rakes, and shovels with toy production as only a small portion of the company. In 1946 Mound produced two toys, a steam shovel and a crane, which started a long history of successful, quality toy production. In 1955, Mound Metalcraft Co. changed its name to Tonka Toys, Inc., named after Lake Minnetonka, where the plant was located. Over the past fifty-five years, Tonka has become a world-wide company and in 1991 became part of Hasbro, Inc®. Over the years, Tonka has produced a total of 230 million toys on average, using 5.1 million pounds of sheet metal per year. Tonka Volkswagen Beetles are very common, so it is best to wait and find examples that are in good to mint condition, instead of parting out with hard earned cash for a Tonka that is well played with and rusted

Beetle Sedan made by Tonka, ca. 1960s. Metal body and base labeled "Tonka" on the bottom, 8" in length. $60.

Toes Volkswagen made by Tonka, ca. 1960s. Metal body and base labeled "Tonka" on the bottom, 8" in length. $45.

Large motor Volkswagen made by Tonka, ca. 1970s. Metal body with base labeled "Tonka" on the bottom, 8" in length. $40.

Made by Tonka, ca. 1970s. Plastic body available in many different colors with metal base, 3" in length. $15.

Ladybug Beetle made by Tonka, ca. 1980s. Plastic yellow body with "Ladybug" decals on the sides and trunk, 3" in length. $8.

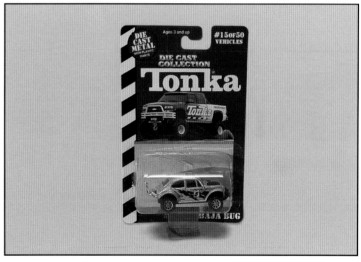

Baja Bug made by Tonka, ca. 2000. Die cast metal body, 3" in length. $4.

Vitesse was founded in 1982 and is currently situated in northern Portugal. The Volkswagen Beetles produced by Vitesse are some of the nicest on the market. They are entirely hand crafted and consist of more than 80 different parts. Some of the parts are so small, tweezers are required to attach them. Vitesse has set up two company's over the years to help produce the models. Compasso, founded in 1989, for engineering and tooling, and Seridecal, founded in 1993, for the production of high precision silk screen printing.

Vitesse has the ability to produce and replicate just about any known car. Although these Beetles come with a pretty high price tag, they are some of the most accurate models available.

Wiking, located in Germany, has been producing models for over sixty years. First producing models in metal, Wiking later changed to plastic. Over the years, Wiking has produced many Volkswagen Beetles, some dating as far back as 1948.

L164 Sedan 1200 made by Vitesse. Red metal with VW logo on the trunk and "261" on the sides, 3.5" in length. $30.

Michelin Beetle made by Vitesse. Yellow metal with Michelin man on top of the car and logo painted on the sides, 3.5" in length. $30.

Kaferwagen made by Vitesse. Metal with red and silver paint, 3.5" in length. $30.

Kaferwagen made by Vitesse. White metal, 3.5" in length. $30.

Cabriolet made by Wiking. Plastic, 2" in length. $12.

Cabriolet with people made by Wiking, ca. 1972. Plastic, 2" in length. $7.

VW 1200 made by Wiking. Plastic, 2" in length. $10.

VW 1200 made by Wiking, ca. 1996. Plastic, 2" in length. $10.

Volkswagen sedan made by Wiking. Plastic, 2" in length. $9.

AutoMuseum Edition VW 1200 made by Wiking. Only available through the auto museum in Wolfsburg, Germany, making this a rare Wiking, 2" in length. $24.

Super Power Buggy made by Action Toys™, ca. mid-1980s. Plastic, battery run, 8" in length. $15.

AutoMuseum Volkswagen made by AMW Automodelle, ca. 2000. Plastic, 2" in length. $25.

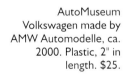

Made by Blue Box™. Orange plastic, 6" in length. $20.

Adjustable Beetle made by Combi Play™, ca. 1999. Hard plastic available in many colors, 5" in length. $4.

Hap-p-Kid Dancing Beetle made by Dickie Spielzeug™, ca. 2000. Yellow plastic with battery run motor, moves up and down, 3.5" in length. $8.

Early Learning Center™ Volkswagen, ca. late 1980s. Blue plastic with red wheels. $8.

Opposite page
Top: Made by BC Toys™, ca. mid-1980s. Yellow plastic with battery run motor. Control switches on top of the car, 8" in length. $20.

Bottom: Cartoon Beetle made by Blackfoot™. Yellow plastic with red interior, 36" in length. $20.

Sedan made by EKO™, ca. 1964. Plastic, 2" in length. $7.

Made by Estrela™, ca. 1985. All plastic parts with racing stickers, 13" in length. $20.

Made by Frankonia™, ca. 1984. Yellow plastic with no interior, 6" in length. $15.

Split window Beetle made by Heinz Trober GmbH and Co.™, ca. 2000. Black plastic with button on top. When pushed, the Beetle makes the noises of starting, accelerating away, and honking, 3.5" in length. $10.

Made by Joustra™, ca. 1988. Pink plastic with yellow, 9" in length. $15.

Smash up Buggem made by Kenner®, ca. 1972. Plastic, motor run by pulling plastic cord out of the Beetle, 7" in length. $25.

Volkswagen sedans made by Lego®, ca. 1964. Plastic, 3" in length. $20 each.

Volkswagen made by Lego. Housed in the Volkswagen Auto Museum in Wolfsburg, Germany, this highly detailed Beetle is made from Lego bricks and has an opening hood with engine inside. Not an easy task to build the rounded form of the Beetle out of square bricks, 36" in length.

Rear view of the Lego Volkswagen.

Volkswagen Cabriolet made by Lego. Also housed in the Volkswagen Auto Museum in Wolfsburg, Germany, and made from Lego bricks. Highly detailed with accurate Cabriolet proportions, 36" in length.

Stompers 4 by 4 Volkswagen made by Schaper MFG. Co.™, ca. 1982. Battery run motor with on/off switch on the bottom of the car, 3.5" in length. $20.

Stompers 4 by 4 Volkswagen, ca. 1997. Battery run motor with hi and low switch on the sides of the car, 3.5" in length. $8.

Volkswagen Beetle made by Strombecker™, ca. 1985. Blue plastic with red interior, 6" in length. $10.

Tomme Tappee™ Volkswagen. Red plastic with removable figure, 5.5" in length. $12.

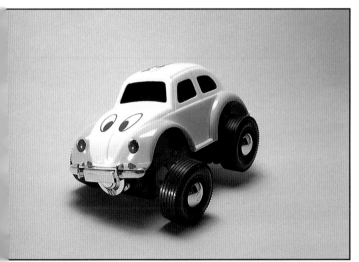

Dancing Beetle made by Tomy™, ca. 1998. Battery run, popping and popping around as it moves, 5" in length. $15.

Crashing Beetle made by Toy Tech™, ca. 2000. Plastic with pull back motor. When front bumper hits something, the doors and trunk pop open while the driver gets ejected out of the car, 4.5" in length. $7.

Volkswagen Beetle made by Viking Toys™ of Sweden, ca. 1998. Plastic, 3" in length. $3.

Recycled Volkswagen Beetle made by Volkswagen, ca. 1999. Made in Germany by melting down actual Volkswagen parts and pouring the liquid into a mold. Available in many colors labeled "Volkswagen Recycling" on top of the car. Very hard to find in America, 4.5" in length. $30.

Recycled Volkswagen Beetle made by Volkswagen, ca. 2000. Made in Germany by melting down actual Volkswagen parts and pouring liquid into mold. Battery run with blinking head lights, tail lights, and side lights. Blue plastic labeled "Volkswagen Recycling" on top, 4.5" in length. $35.

Lucky Red Taxi Beetle, ca. 1994. Plastic, 7.5" in length. $8.

Walking Volkswagen with feet, ca. early 1980s. Orange plastic with wind up motor labeled "Made in Hong Kong No. 128" on the bottom, 3" in length. $15.

Friction powered Beetle made in Hong Kong. Clear pink plastic with friction powered motor in the rear, 6" in length. $10.

Plastic Dancing Beetle. Battery run motor. Lights up, plays music, and hops and pops around as it moves, 5" in length. $10.

Boom boom drummer Beetle. Yellow plastic with wind up motor. Beats drum as it moves, 6" in length. $10.

Rabbit Volkswagen Beetle, ca. 1980s. Friction powered. As car moves, the rabbit's head turns and the characters in the bubble move, 6.5" in length. $7.

Tomato in Beetle. Clear plastic with red plastic tomato inside. Marked "Made in Germany" on bottom, 3.5" in length. $3.

Red Beetle, maker unknown. Hard plastic, 5" in length. $8.

Volkswagen Beetle cabriolet, maker unknown. Yellow plastic, 2" in length. $9.

Volkswagen Beetle cabriolet, maker unknown. Blue plastic, 1.5" in length. $4.

Volkswagen Beetle sedan, maker unknown. Green plastic labeled "Germany" on the bottom, 2" in length. $6.

Volkswagen Beetle sedans, maker unknown.
Plastic, 2" in length. $3.

Monster 4 by 4 Beetle, maker unknown, ca. 1997.
Plastic with pull string motor. $6.

Flip Beetle, maker unknown. Pull back motor and
as car moves forward it flips over, 5" in length. $4

CHAPTER TWENTY-ONE

BEETLES MADE OF METAL

1955 Kafer-Beetle made by Burago™, ca. 1998. Metal with
opening doors, trunk, and hood, 9" in length. $40.

Metro Police made by Dandy Tomica™. Yellow metal, 3.5" in length. $25.

Number 181 Volkswagen Beetle made by Dinky, ca. 1964. Grey metal, 4" in length. $60.

1964 export sedan made by Dinky™, ca. 1971. Blue metal, 4" in length. $30.

Happy Birthday Beetle made by Edocar™, ca. 1996. Red metal with "Happy Birthday" painted on the sides, labeled Edocar on the bottom, 3" in length. $7.

Opposite page

Top: Beetle sedan made by Darda™, ca. 1999. Metal with clear plastic bottom and very fast pull back motor, 3" in length. $10.

Bottom: Beetle sedan made by Darda, ca. 1995. Metal with clear plastic bottom and very fast pull back motor, 3" in length. $15.

Always Coca Cola Beetle made by Edocar, ca. 1994. Pink metal with Coca Cola® logo on the top and purple arrows on the sides. Labeled Edocar on the bottom, 3" in length. $11.

Coca Cola Beetle made by Edocar, ca. 1995. Yellow metal with "Coca Cola" written in red on the top and sides of the car. Labeled Edocar on the bottom, 3" in length. $11.

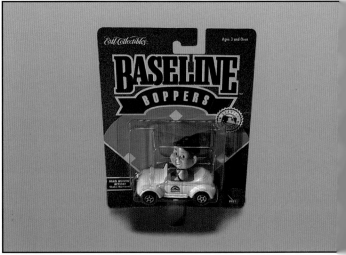

Dutch Beetle Club promotional made by Edocar. Black metal with Dutch Beetle Club logo in white on the sides of the car, 3" in length. $14.

Baseline Boppers made by Ertl, ca. 1994. White Volkswagen convertible with bopping head figure. Available in all major league teams, 3" in length. $12.

Volkswagen sedan made by Ertl, ca. 1992. Red metal marked Ertl on the bottom, 3" in length. $8.

I love New York Beetle made by Harvey Hutter and Co.™, ca. 1996. Metal body with "I Love NY" painted on the top, 4" in length. $10.

Made by Husky™. Metal, 3" in length. $12.

Unpainted Bug Bomb in package made by Johnny Lightning™, ca. 1995. Metal, 3" in length. $15.

Bug Bomb made by Johnny Lightning, ca. 1995. Metal, 3" in length. $9.

1303 VW Beetle Cabriolet made by Joluef Evolution™, ca. 1997. Metal body highly detailed with plastic parts, 3.5" in length. $25.

Made by Kintoy™, ca. 1998. Metal body with pull back motor available in many color and paint variations, 2" in length. $3 each.

Made by Kintoy, ca. 1998. Metal body with pull back motor available in many color and paint variations, 3.5" in length. $5.

"Flower Smile" Beetle made by Kintoy, ca. 1998. Metal body with pull back motor, 3.5" in length. $5.

Sedans made by Lesney®. Metal body with metal wheels and opening hood, 3" in length. $10 each.

Toys Club Volkswagens made by Mattel®. Metal body with plastic surfboard, 3.5" in length. $12 each.

GNR Volkswagen made by Metosul™ of Portugal, ca. 1989. Metal body, 3.5" in length. $12.

Made by Metosul of Portugal, ca. 1989. Metal body, 3.5" in length. $12.

Made by Metosul of Portugal, ca. 1989. Metal body, 3.5" in length. $12.

1951 VW 1200 made by New-Ray™, ca. 1997. Metal body with plastic base and wheels, 3.5" in length. $8.

Argus Miniature promotional Beetle made by Norev™. Orange metal, Argus Miniature logo on the sides, 3.5" in length. $25.

Made by Playart™. Metal body available in many colors, 3" in length. $12.

Taxi cab Beetle made by Praline, ca. 1987. Metal body, 3.5" in length. $9.

Various Volkswagens made by Praline™, ca. 1987. Metal body, 3.5" in length. $9.

Minichamps split window made by Pauls Model Art™, ca. 1997. Die cast model on plastic base, 3.5" in length. $30.

Ragtop Beetle made by Rio™. Die cast model on plastic base, 3.5" in length. $25.

Volkswagen Cabriolet and Wohnwagen made by Schuco Piccolo™, ca. 2000. Solid metal models, 2" in length. $20.

Sport weekend set made by Simba™, ca. early 1990s. Volkswagen cabriolet with pull back motor and trailer with boat, 8" in length. $15.

Volkswagen Beetle made by Siku™, ca. 1999. Metal body, 2.25" in length. $4.

Volkswagen Beetles made by Siku, ca. 1994. Metal body, 2.25" in length. $6.

Close up of Beetle made by Siku, ca. 1994. Metal body, 2.25" in length. $6.

Coca Cola Beetle made by Solido™, ca. 1995. Red metal body with opening doors and trunk, 9.5" in length. $65.

Coca Cola Beetle made by Solido, ca. 1996. White metal body with red fenders and opening doors and trunk, 9.5" in length. $40.

Volkswagen Beetle made by Tootsie Toy™. Metal body with no interior, 2" in length. $8.

Volkswagen Sedan made by Tootsie Toy®. Metal body on plastic base with "Tootsie Toy Racing" stickers on the side, 3" in length. $12.

Volkswagen Sedan made by Voiture™, ca. 1995. Tin body with friction powered motor, 5" in length. $12.

Volkswagen 1303 made by Welly™, ca. 1994. Metal body with pull bac motor, 4" in length. $6.

Made by Yat Ming™, ca. 2000. Metal, 3.5" in length. $10.

KFC kid's meal toy made by Yat Ming. Metal, 2" in length. $8.

Chicago taxi cab Beetle, ca. 1997. Metal with pull back motor, labeled "Chicago" on the top, 4" in length. $8.

Bug Bomb Beetle made by Zyll Enterprise Ltd.™, ca. 1993. Metal body with plastic wheels labeled "Bug Bomb" on the sides, 3" in length. $6.

New York City taxi and police set, ca. 2000. Metal bodies with plastic base, 3" in length. $7 for the set.

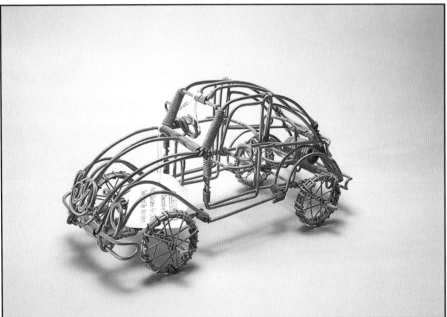

Metal wire Volkswagen, maker unknown. 8" in length. $20.

Made in South Africa out of bug spray cans, ca. 2001. No two are alike, 6" in length. $25.

CHAPTER TWENTY-TWO

RARITIES

This Beetle was made by Volkswagen in the Wolfsburg factory in the late 1940s. As a result of the factory having a lack of work, the employees were assigned to produce these models. The models were produced in a variety of colors and measure 3" in length. This particular model has steel wheels which makes it one of six in the world. Because of this, this Beetle is one of the rarest of the rare.

Made by Staufen Porcellan™ of Germany, these models measure 6" in length and were produced for Volkswagen's 50th anniversary. Only 2000 were made, which were distributed within the Wolfsburg factory to the higher-ups. Unless you know one of the big shots at the factory, this model is next to impossible to find, which is why it is one of the rarest of the rare.

This Vittesse™ model was specially made by the Beetle Shop in Paris to celebrate the Volkswagen Model Club's 20th anniversary. This particular model is number 24 of 35. That's right, only 35 were made, making this one of the rarest of the rare.

Opposite page
Top: This wooden Beetle was made at a hospital in Konigslutter, Germany. With fully opening doors and trunk, this model measures 21" in length. However, after figuring out that the curves of the Beetle and wood contradict each other, the design was abandoned after the completion of just two models. One lives in a collection in Germany while the other is out there somewhere, making it one of the rarest of the rare.

Bottom: Rear portion of the wooden Beetle.

This one-of-a-kind giant red Beetle was made by Volkswagen in the Wolfsburg factory on a scale of one to four. It was used in the factory during the 1960s to test wind resistance as well as paint color. This one-of-a-kind Volkswagen was never intended to be a collectable, but for obvious reasons every collector would love to have this one, making it one of the rarest of the rare.

This Beetle was made in 1993 and is one of eight in the world. It was made in Germany by AMW Automodelle™ and was a promotional piece for the maker as well as a magazine. With only eight made, it wasn't much of a promo, but makes it one of the rarest of the rare.

BIBLIOGRAPHY

Evans, David. "Thirty Years of the Love Bug." *VW Trends*, June 2000: 71-78.

Flament, E. *Numero Special VW Coccinelles.* Le Pecq, France: Argus de la Miniature, No. 174, July/August 1995.

Gilmore, Robert and Arai, Akihiro. "Huki Volkswagen Toys are Highly Collectible and Sought-After." *Dune Buggies and Hot VWs,* November 2000: 90-91.

Mack, Charlie. *The Encyclopedia of Matchbox Toys.* Atglen, Pennsylvania: Schiffer Publishing Ltd., 1999.

Mynheer, Nigel. "The First Beetle." *Model Collector*, March 2000: 22-25.

Parker, Bob. *The Complete Book of Hot Wheels.* Atglen, Pennsylvania: Schiffer Publishing Ltd., 1998.

Stephan, Elizabeth. *O'Brien's Collecting Toy Cars and Trucks.* Iola, Wisconsin: Krause Publications, 2000.

PRICE GUIDE

Manufacturer	Year Made	Beetle Year & type	Additional Information	Material	Color	Scale	Price/Mint Condition	Price/Poor Condition
ACTION TOYS	1985	1972 Beetle	"SUPER POWER BUGGY", battery run	Plastic		1/18	$15	$
ALLEMAGNE		1960 Beetle	Decanter	Ceramic	Brown	1/18	$125	$3
AMW	1995	1972 Beetle		Plastic	Green, Almond	1/87	$12?	$
AMW	1994	1972 Beetle	"ADAC STRASSENWACHT" printed on car	Plastic	White, Yellow	1/87	$12	$
AMW	1995	1972 Beetle		Plastic	Red	1/87	$12	$
ARNOLD	1953	1951 export Beetle 1100		Plastic	Red	1/19	$175	$6
ARNOLD	1957	1951 export Beetle 1100		Plastic	Green	1/19	$75	$2
AVON		1979 Beetle 1200	Perfume Bottle	Glass	Varies in color	1/30	$22	$
BANDAI	1965	1963 Beetle	"ADAC STRASSENWACHT"	Tin	Yellow	1/16	$215	$7
BANDAI	1965	1957 Beetle	"POLITIE", light on the roof.	Tin	Black	1/16	$215	$7
BANDAI		1963 Beetle export		Tin	Red	1/8	$360	$18
BANDAI		1963 Beetle export		Tin	Red	1/12	$285	$14
BANDAI		Karmann Cabriolet		Tin		1/24	$145	$7
BANDAI		Beetle 1303	Remote control Beetle, "BEETLE"	Plastic	Yellow	1/37	$30	$
BANDAI	1984	Standard Beetle	Bumblebee transformer	Plastic	Red. Yellow. Gold	1/55	$10	$
BANDAI	1984	1974 Beetle	Transformer	Plastic & metal	Yellow	1/32	$35	$
BC TOYS		Standard Beetle	Battery run motor	Plastic	Yellow	1/20	$20	$
BIP		Standard Beetle	"BEETLE CANDY" written on the roof of car	Plastic	Varies in color	1/70	$3	$
BERKINA	1994	1964 Beetle 1200		Plastic	Red, Blue,green, & beige	1/87	$12	
BERKINA	1995	1964 Beetle 1200	Firemans car	Plastic	Red and black	1/87	$12	$
BERKINA	1995	1964 Beetle 1200	"POLIZEI" printed on car.	Plastic	Dark green	1/87	$12	
BLACKFOOT		1972 Beetle	Cartoon Beetle	Plastic	Yellow	1/12	$20	
BLUEBIRD	1996	Standard Beetle	Gunther from Woodies World	Plastic	Purple	1/24	$12	
BLUE BOX		1965 Beetle		Plastic	Orange	1/30	$12	
BURAGO	1998	1955 Beetle	opening doors, trunk, & hood	Die cast metal	Various colors	1/18	$40	
CENTURY	1986	1949 Beetle 1100		Metal	Grey	1/43	$42	$
CIJ	1954	1953 Beetle 1200	"AR" on base of license plate	Die cast metal	Grey, green	1/43	$90	$
CIJ	1955	1953 Beetle 1200		Die cast metal	Cream, gray, green	1/43	$85	$
CKO	1938	1938 Beetle/Cabriolet	Flip top with driver	Tin		1/28	$400	$1
CKO	1957	1957 Beetle 1200		Tin	Gold	1/35	$40	$
CKO	1958	1957 Beetle	Police car	Tin	Dark green	1/35	$50	$
COLNE VALLEY		1972 Beetle		Ceramic	Various colors	1/12	$40	
COMBI PLAY	1999	1969 Beetle	Adjustable rear wheels	Plastic	Pink. Red.	1/32	$4	
CONTACT DESIGN	1997	1973 Beetle Cabriolet	Alarm clock	Plastic	Red	1/30	$40	$
CORGI	1965	1964 Beetle 1200	East African safari with chrome chassis	Die cast metal	Orange	1/43	$65	$
CORGI	1970	1967 Beetle	"POLICE" printed on car, chrome chassis	Die cast metal	White & black	1/43	$32	$
CORGI	1973	1967 Beetle	"POLIZEI"	Die cast metal	Green, white	1/43	$24	
CORGI	1970	1967 Beetle	Flower Power	Die cast metal	Red	1/43	$30	
CORGI	1973	1967 Beetle	Green chassis, white seats	Die cast metal	Red	1/43	$24	
CORGI	1975	1967 Beetle	White chassis, beige seats	Die cast metal	Orange	1/43	$24	
CORGI	1977	1967 Beetle		Die cast metal	Blue	1/43	$19	
CORGI	1970	1968 Beetle	Corgi Junior series "POLICE"	Die cast metal	White & black	1/60	$14	
CORGI	1970	1968 Beetle	Corgi Junior series, seats yellow or red	Die cast metal	Green	1/60	$14	
CORGI	1970	1968 Beetle	Corgi Junior series, roof rack, red seats	Die cast metal	Beige	1/60	$14	
CORGI	1971	1968 Beetle	Corgi Junior series, roof rack, yellow seats	Die cast metal	Red	1/60	$12	
CORGI	1991	1951 Beetle	Camio Collection	Die cast metal	Red and blue	1/56	$18	
CORGI		Standard Beetle	Slam Bam Sam, remote control	Plastic	Yellow, red	1/24	$35	
CORGI	1993	1968 Beetle	"MAX WAX" promotional	Die cast metal	Black, red, yellow	1/43	$15	
CORGI	1994	1968 Beetle	Rice Krispies promotional	Die cast metal	Yellow	1/43	$30	
CORGI	1993	1968 Beetle	Motoring memories	Die cast metal	Yellow	1/43	$10	
DANDY TOMICA		Standard Beetle	Metro police	Die cast metal	Yellow	1/43	$25	
DARDA		1963 Beetle	Decorated with flower, friction motor	Plastic	Colors vary		$6	
DEPARTMENT 56	1998	1969 Beetle	Skis on rear of car	Glass	Red	1/30	$25	
DICKIE SPIELZEUG	2000	1972 Beetle	Hap-p-Kid Dancing Beetle, battery run	Plastic	Yellow	1/43	$8	
DINKY-MATCHBOX	1989	1951 Beetle	Made in Macau	Die cast metal	Blue, gray	1/43	$15	
DINKY-MATCHBOX	1992	1951 Beetle	Made in China	Die cast metal	Red, gray	1/43	$14	
DINKY-TOYS	1956	1953 Beetle		Die cast metal	Gray, blue, green	1/45	$60	
DINKY-TOYS	1962	1953 Beetle		Die cast metal	Dark blue	1/45	$60	
DINKY-TOYS	1966	1953 Beetle	Assembled in South Africa	Die cast metal	White, blue	1/45	$450	$
DINKY-TOYS	1967	1953 Beetle	Plastic wheel rims	Die cast metal	Blue	1/45	$75	

Manufacturer	Year Made	Beetle Year & type	Additional Information	Material	Color	Scale	Price/Mint Condition	Price/Poor Condition
DINKY-TOYS	1967	1953 Beetle	Yellow plastic wheel rims	Die cast metal	Yellow & black	1/45	$185	$60
DINKY-TOYS	1979	1964 Beetle	Ivory seats, assembled in Chile	Die cast metal	Blue	1/43	$75	$20
DINKY-TOYS GB	1973	1964 export Beetle	Gray seats, one piece mold	Die cast metal	Yellow & black	1/43	$70	$30
DISNEY	2001	Standard Beetle	Candy container with characters heads in windows	Plastic	Clear	1/24	$6	$1
DISNEY	1999	1963 Beetle	Herbie beanbag key chain	Fabric	White	1/24	$12	$3
DISTLER	1939	1938 Type 60	Spring wound motor, small hubcap	Sheet metal	Green	1/36	$950	$285
DISTLER	1947	1938 Type 60	Spring wound motor, small hubcap	Sheet metal	Red	1/36	$315	$110
DISTLER	1950	1938 Type 60	Spring wound motor, large hubcap	Sheet metal	Red	1/36	$240	$80
DUCHIC SPIELSBUG	1982	1963 Beetle	Remote control Herbie, battery operated	Plastic	White	1/18	$35	$10
DUX	1950	1949 Beetle	Spring wound motor	Plastic	Plum	1/36	$160	$50
DUX	1954	1953 Beetle	Spring wound motor	Plastic	Dark red	1/36	$110	$30
DUX	1954	1953 Beetle	Kit. Spring wound motor	Plastic	Metallic blue	1/36	$110	-
DUX	1960	1960 Beetle	Spring wound motor	Plastic	Orange	1/36	$50	$20
E AND J MINING MEMORIES	2000	1952 Beetle	Copy of Lledo model	Coal		1/42	$35	$8
EDOCAR	1992	1972 Beetle 1303		Die cast metal	Red, white	1/55	$6	$2
EDOCAR	1991	1972 Beetle 1303	Decorated with flowers	Die cast metal	White	1/55	$6	$2
EDOCAR	1993	1972 Beetle 1303	"HAPPY BIRTHDAY" chassis engraved "1988"	Die cast metal	Red	1/55	$6	$2
EDOCAR	1993	1972 Beetle 1303	Chassis engraved "1989"	Die cast metal	Red	1/55	$6	$2
EDOCAR	1994	1972 Beetle 1303	"COCA-COLA"	Die cast metal	Yellow	1/55	$11	$3
EDOCAR	1994	1972 Beetle 1303	"ALWAYS COCA-COLA, ATLANTA, MIAMI"	Die cast metal	Pink	1/55	$11	$3
EDOCAR	1991	Baja Bug	"SURFWAY"	Die cast metal	Pale orange	1/55	$6	$2
EDOCAR	1994	Baja Bug	"COCA-COLA IS THE MUSIC"	Die cast metal	Yellow	1/55	$11	$3
EDOCAR	1994	1972 Beetle 1303	Dutch Beetle Club promotional	Die cast metal	Black	1/55	$14	$3
EKO	1964	1957 Beetle		Plastic	Beige, red	1/88	$7	$2
ERTL	1992	1975 Beetle		Die cast metal	Red	1/66	$8	$2
ERTL	1994	1975 Beetle Cabriolet	Baseline Boppers, bopping head figure	Die cast metal	White	1/50	$12	$3
ERTL	1990	Beetle Cabriolet	Garfield figure in car	Die cast metal	Blue	1/66	$13	$4
ERTL	1992	1975 Beetle	Marked "Ertl" on the chassis	Die cast metal	Red	1/66	$8	$2
ESCI		Karmann Cabriolet	With Snoopy	Die cast metal	Blue	1/43	$28	$8
ESCI		Karmann Cabriolet	With Snoopy, "POLICE"	Die cast metal	Orange	1/43	$8	$2
ESTRELA	1985	1962 Beetle	"33"	Plastic	Orange	1/16	$20	$4
FRANKLIN MINT		1967 Beetle		Die cast metal	Yellow	1/24	$110	$45
FRANKLIN MINT		1967 Beetle		Die cast metal	White	1/24	$110	$45
FRANKLIN MINT		1967 Cabriolet		Die cast metal	Red	1/24	$110	$45
FRANKLIN MINT	1998	1967 Beetle	Decorated with flowers		Orange. Blue. Green. Pink	1/24	$110	$45
FRANKLIN MINT	1999	1967 Beetle	"POLIZIE", light on roof		Green, white	1/24	$125	$55
FRANKONIA	1984	1962 Beetle	No interior	Plastic	Yellow	1/30	$15	$4
GALOOB	1990	1951 Beetle	Pull back motor	Plastic	Red, white, black	1/90	$7	$2
GALOOB	1994	1967 Beetle		Plastic	White	1/90	$6	$1
GALOOB	1995	1967 Beetle Cabriolet	Decorated with flower	Plastic	Yellow	1/90	$6	$1
GALOOB	1996	1967 Beetle		Plastic	Green, tan	1/90	$5	$1
GALOOB	1996	1967 Beetle Cabriolet		Plastic	Green	1/90	$5	$1
GALOOB	1996	Standard Beetle		Plastic	Purple	1/110	$3	$1
GALOOB	1998	1969 Beetle	Talks, yellow surf board on roof	Plastic	White, turquoise	1/18	$17	$5
GAMA	1969	Beetle 1302		Die cast metal	Metallic green	1/63	$16	$4
GAMA	1972	1972 Beetle		Die cast metal	Yellow orange	1/43	$30	$8
GAMA	1972	1972 Beetle	"POLIZEI"	Die cast metal	Dark green	1/43	$30	$8
GAMA	1974	1972 Beetle	With boat	Die cast metal	Metallic orange	1/43	$25	$5
GAMA		1972 Beetle	Black interior, Chassis stamped "898"	Die cast metal	White	1/43	$25	$2
GAMA	1958	1957 Beetle		Die cast metal	Ivory, blue, red, yellow, green	1/46	$60	$8
GAMA	1964	1957 Beetle	fire vehicle	Die cast metal	Red	1/46	$40	$8
GLOBE ELECTRIC	2000	Standard Beetle	Table lamp	Glass	Yellow	1/18	$24	$8
HARVEY HUTTER	1996	1973 Beetle	"I LOVE NY"	Die cast metal	White	1/43	$10	$2
HASBRO-TAKARA		Standard Beetle	Transformer	Plastic	Yellow	1/83	$8	$2
HEINZ TROBER GmbH	2000	1951 Beetle	Makes accelerating & honking noises	Plastic	Black	1/43	$10	$2
HORNDLEIN	1946	Beetle sedan	Litho faces, brake	Tin	Blue	1/30	$150	$30
HUKI		1963 Karmann Cabriolet	Friction motor	Sheet metal	Yellow	1/29	$160	$45
HUSKY	1968	1968 Beetle 1300	"POLICE", red seats	Die cast metal	White, black	1/60	$16	$6
HUSKY	1968	1968 Beetle	Roof rack with baggage	Die cast metal	Blue	1/60	$16	$6
JNF	1939	1938 Beetle type 60	Spring wound motor, Made in Germany	Die cast metal	Red	1/36	$300	$120
JNF	1945	1938 Beetle type 60	Spring wound motor, Made in Germany US Zone	Die cast metal	Dark blue	1/36	$260	$100
JNF	1950	1938 Beetle type 60	Spring wound motor	Die cast metal	Blue	$150	$60	
JOHNNY LIGHTNING	1995	Standard Beetle	Two engines	Die cast metal	Red, turquoise, yellow, & no paint		$9	$3

Manufacturer	Year Made	Beetle Year & type	Additional Information	Material	Color	Scale	Price/Mint Condition	Price/Po Conditi•
JOLUEF EVOLUTION	1997	Beetle Cabriolet 1303		Die cast metal	White	1/43	$25	
JOUSTRA	1988	Open roof Beetle	Decorated with water skier	Plastic	Pink, yellow	1/19	$15	
JOUSTRA	1988	Open roof Beetle	"VW" logo, "MOTOR SPORT", friction motor	Plastic	Metallic blue, black	1/19	$15	
KARL BUB	1938	1938 Beetle type 60		Die cast metal	Dark red	1/70	$50	$
KARL BUB	1945	Beetle Sedan	No rear window, marked "KB"	Die cast metal		1/66	$40	$
KENNER		Standard Beetle		Plastic	Orange	1/27	$15	
KENNER	1972	1969 Beetle	Smash up Buggem, pull cord motor	Plastic	Blue	1/24	$25	
KINTOY	1994	1973 Beetle 1303	"FUN CAR", friction motor	Plastic	Metallic blue	1/75	$5	
KINTOY	1995	1973 Beetle 1303	"HI BEETLE", friction motor	Plastic	Red	1/75	$5	
KINTOY	1998	Standard Beetle	"FLOWER SMILE", pull back motor	Die cast metal		1/75	$5	
LEGO	1958	1957 Beetle		Plastic	Salmon	1/38	$140	$
LEGO	1956	1953 Beetle		Plastic		1/86	$20	
LEGO	1964	1960 Beetle		Plastic		1/86	$20	
LESNEY		1959 Beetle	Metal wheels, opening decklid	Die cast metal	Blue	1/66	$10	
LLEDO	1995	1951 Beetle		Die cast metal	Blue	1/43	$18	
LLEDO	1995	1951 Beetle		Die cast metal	Green	1/43	$18	
LLEDO		1951 Beetle	"WEST OF SCOTLAND VW CLUB"	Die cast metal	White	1/43	$25	
LLEDO	1996	1951 Beetle	"PSI INTERNATIONAL MESSE"	Die cast metal	White	1/43	$25	
LLEDO		1951 Beetle	Campbells promotional	Die cast metal	White	1/43	$35	$
LLEDO		1951 Beetle	Campbells promotional	Die cast metal	Red	1/43	$125	$
LLEDO		1951 Beetle	"HAMLEYS"	Die cast metal	Grey	1/43	$16	
LLEDO		1951 Beetle	"MINNIE THE MINX"	Die cast metal	Yellow	1/43	$20	
LLEDO		1951 Beetle Cabriolet	"WINEGUMS"	Die cast metal	Black	1/43	$20	
LLEDO		1951 Beetle	"DIE CAST COLLECTION"	Die cast metal	Red	1/43	$18	
LLEDO		1951 Beetle	"DIE CAST COLLECTION"	Die cast metal	Yellow	1/43	$60	
LLEDO		1951 Beetle	Millionth Beetle	Die cast metal	Gold	1/43	$20	
LUCKY		1968 Beetle	"POLICE"	Plastic	Blue	1/32	$6	
MAISTO	1995	1951 export Beetle		Die cast metal	Black	1/18	$34	
MAISTO	1995	1951 export Beetle		Die cast metal	Gray	1/18	$34	
MAISTO	1995	1951 export Beetle		Die cast metal	Green	1/18	$34	
MAISTO	1995	1951 Karmann Cabriolet		Die cast metal	Black	1/18	$30	
MAISTO		1973 Karmann Cabriolet		Die cast metal	Green	1/36	$12	
MAISTO	1995	1951 Karmann Cabriolet	"PEPSI"	Die cast metal	White, blue.	1/18	$40	
MAISTO	1996	1967 Beetle		Die cast metal	Yellow, green, red.	1/18	$25	
MAISTO	1999	1967 Beetle	"FLOWER POWER"	Die cast metal	Red	1/18	$20	
MAISTO	1999	1973 Beetle		Die cast metal	Pink. Blue. Red.	1/66	$3	
MAISTO	1999	1973 Beetle Cabriolet	Christmas ornament	Die cast metal & plastic		1/32	$10	
MAJORETTE	1971	1971 Beetle		Die cast metal	Green	1/55	$6	
MAJORETTE	1974	1971 sunroof Beetle	Windows tinted amber	Die cast metal	Red. Blue metallic. Yellow. Black	1/55	$5	
MAJORETTE	1979	1971 sunroof Beetle	Windows tinted blue, "VW"	Die cast metal	Gray	1/55	$6	
MAJORETTE	1973	1971 open roof Beetle 1302	with boat and trailer	Die cast metal		1/55	$7	
MARKLIN	1939	1938 Beetle type 60	"KDF" on the license plate	Die cast metal	Red. Gray. Green	1/70	$110	
MARKLIN	1953	1938 Beetle type 60		Die cast metal	Red	1/87	$35	
MARKLIN	1938	1938 Beetle type 60	"KDF" on the bumper, metal wheel rims	Die cast metal	Dark gray	1/38	$450	$
MARKLIN	1945	1938 Beetle type 60	"KDF" on the bumper, chrome metal wheel rims	Die cast metal	Blue	1/38	$400	
MARKLIN	1955	1953 export Beetle	Chassis stamped "MARKLIN made in Germany"	Die cast metal	Yellow. Olive green. Blue		$100	
MARKLIN	1960	1960 export Beetle	Chassis stamped "8005 MARKLIN Volkswagen Made in Western Germany"	Die cast metal	Gray. Green. Red. Yellow. Olive green.	1/43	$70	
MASUDAYA	1983	Beetle Cabriolet	Wind up motor, Mickey Mouse figure in car	Plastic	Red	1/30	$30	
MATCHBOX	1972	Standard Beetle	Flying Bug	Die cast metal	Red	1/55	$20	
MATCHBOX	1978	Standard Beetle	Flying Beetle	Die cast metal	Orange, black	1/55	$20	
MATCHBOX	1968	1967 Beetle 1500	No. 137 on sides, towing hitch	Die cast metal	White	1/60	$25	
MATCHBOX	1969	1967 Beetle 1500	No. 137 on sides, towing hitch	Die cast metal	Metallic red	1/60	$35	
MATCHBOX	1972	1967 Beetle 1500	No. 137 on sides, towing hitch	Die cast metal	Metallic red	1/60	$35	
MATCHBOX	1960	1957 Beetle	Non tinted windows, gray plastic wheels	Die cast metal	Metallic blue	1/65	$30	
MATCHBOX	1961	1957 Beetle	Green tinted windows, gray plastic wheels	Die cast metal	Metallic blue	1/65	$30	
MATCHBOX	1962	1957 Beetle	Green tinted windows, silver gray wheels	Die cast metal	Metallic blue	1/65	$30	
MATCHBOX	1971	Standard Beetle	Volks-Dragon, yellow interior, pink tinted windows	Die cast metal	Red	1/59	$15	
MATCHBOX	1973	Standard Beetle	Volks-Dragon, yellow interior, non tinted windows	Die cast metal	Red	1/59	$15	
MATCHBOX	1973	Standard Beetle	31c, pink tinted windows	Die cast metal	Red	1/59	$8	
MATCHBOX	1978	Standard Beetle	Lady-Bug, with flames	Die cast metal	Black	1/59	$8	

Manufacturer	Year Made	Beetle Year & type	Additional Information	Material	Color	Scale	Price/Mint Condition	Price/Poor Condition
MATCHBOX	1981	Standard Beetle	Hi Ho Silver	Die cast metal	Silver, black	1/59	$18	$4
MATCHBOX	1972	Standard Beetle	Dragon Wheels	Die cast metal	Green	1/54	$18	$4
MATCHBOX	1973	Standard Beetle	43a	Die cast metal	Green	1/54	$3	$1
MATCHBOX	1975	Standard Beetle	43a, gray bottom	Die cast metal	Green	1/54	$3	$1
MATCHBOX	1981	Standard Beetle	"BIG BLUE"	Die cast metal	Metallic blue	1/54	$6	$2
MATCHBOX	1982	Standard Beetle	"HOT CHOCOLATE"	Die cast metal	Black	1/54	$6	$1
MATCHBOX	1983	Standard Beetle	"SAND DIGGER"	Die cast metal	Metallic green	1/59	$3	$1
MATCHBOX	1979	Beetle Cabriolet	"Made in Hong Kong"	Die cast metal	Yellow	1/60	$11	$3
MATCHBOX	1980	Beetle Cabriolet	"Made in Hong Kong"	Die cast metal	Yellow	1/60	$10	$2
MATCHBOX	1982	Beetle Cabriolet	"Made in Macau"	Die cast metal	Yellow	1/60	$11	$4
MATTEL	1984	Baja Beetle	"BLAZIN BUG", Good-Year tires	Die cast metal	White	1/90	$4	$1
MATTEL	1968	Standard Beetle	Custom Beetle	Die cast metal	Various Colors	1/60	$50	$10
MATTEL	1971	Standard Beetle	Evil Wevil	Die cast metal	Blue	1/60	$65	$15
MATTEL	1984	Baja Bug	"BLAZIN BUG", white wheel rims	Die cast metal	Black	1/60	$35	$8
MATTEL	1988	Baja Bug	"BLAZIN BUG", chrome wheel rims	Die cast metal	White	1/60	$15	$4
MATTEL	1990	Standard Beetle	Getty promotional	Die cast metal	Green	1/60	$15	$4
MATTEL		Baja Bug	"HOT BUG RACING"	Die cast metal	Pink	1/60	$7	$2
MATTEL	1989	Standard Beetle	Green, yellow, & orange geometric shapes	Die cast metal	Purple	1/60	$8	$2
MATTEL	1989	Baja Bug	Blue, yellow, and white flames	Die cast metal	Red	1/60	$20	$5
MATTEL	1995	Standard Beetle		Die cast metal	Pink	1/60	$5	$1
MATTEL	1996	Baja Bug	Race Team series II, with racing trim	Die cast metal	Blue	1/60	$5	$1
MATTEL	1996	Standard Beetle	Yellow, green, & purple sunrise	Die cast metal	Metallic blue	1/60	$4	$1
MATTEL	1998	Baja Bug	"BUG n' TAXI"	Die cast metal	White	1/60	$4	$1
MATTEL	1999	Standard Beetle	"OLAS DEL SOL", Surf'N fun series	Die cast metal	Metallic blue	1/60	$3	$1
MATTEL	1998	Standard Beetle	Artistic License series	Die cast metal	White, red, green	1/60	$3	$1
MATTEL	1999	Baja Bug	Bug graphics	Die cast metal	Blue	1/60	$3	$1
MATTEL	1990	Standard Beetle	Mickey Mouse figure in car	Die cast metal	Yellow	1/60	$12	$3
MATTEL		1974 Beetle	Toys Club, with Surfboard	Die cast metal	Red	1/43	$12	$3
MC-TOY		1972 Beetle		Die cast metal	Metallic Blue	1/55	$6	$2
MC-TOY		1973 Cabriolet	Pull back motor, made in Hong Kong	Die cast metal	Black. White. Beige. Pink.	1/36	$6	$2
MC-TOY		1973 Karmann Cabriolet 1303	Pull back motor	Die cast metal	Yellow	1/36	$6	$2
MC-TOY		1973 Karmann Cabriolet 1303	Pull back motor, "LOVE", decorated with flowers	Die cast metal	Pink	1/36	$6	$2
MC-TOY		Baja Bug		Die cast metal	Violet blue	1/118	$5	$2
MC-TOY		Baja Bug	"BAJA"	Die cast metal	White	1/55	$5	$2
MERCURY	1959	1953 Beetle	Black chassis, chrome wheel rims, black tires	Die cast metal	Blue	1/48	$80	$25
METOSUL	1968	1967 Beetle		Die cast metal	Black. Blue. Yellow.	1/45	$12	$5
METOSUL	1988	1967 Beetle 1200	"POLICE", antenna	Die cast metal	Blue	1/45	$17	$5
METOSUL	1989	1953 Beetle	"GNR"	Die cast metal	Gray	1/45	$15	$6
METOSUL		1967 Beetle 1200	"GNR", antenna, smooth wheel rims	Die cast metal	Dark green	1/45	$15	$6
METOSUL	1989	1967 Beetle		Die cast metal	Red	1/45	$12	$3
MINICHAMPS	1995	1950 Beetle convertible		Die cast metal	Black, gray	1/43	$30	$8
MINICHAMPS	1995	1950 Beetle		Die cast metal	Gray	1/43	$30	$8
MINISTYLE	1993	Beetle with two front ends		Die cast metal	Gray	1/43	$50	$15
MINISTYLE	1993	Beetle with four doors		Die cast metal	Black	1/43	$35	$14
MINISTYLE	1994	Beetle pick-up		Die cast metal	Black	1/43	$40	$14
MINISTYLE	1994	Standard Beetle	Rolls Royce front end	Die cast metal	Red	1/43	$35	$14
NEW-RAY	1997	1951 Beetle 1200 Cabriolet	Top Down, plastic chassis	Die cast metal	Blue	1/43	$8	$2
NOREV	1962	1960 export Beetle	"VW 113", "No. 62", chrome plastic wheel rims	Plastic	Blue-gray	1/43	$11	$2
NOREV	1972	1960 Beetle	"VW 1300"	Plastic	Yellow, green, or orange	1/43	$25	$3
NOREV	1995	1963 Beetle 1200	750SB/62a, "ARGUS MINIATURE NUMERO SPECIAL COX"	Die cast metal	Orange	1/43	$30	$8
ONTRADE		Standard Beetle	Friction motor, "FANCY BEETLE"	Plastic	White, dark blue	1/32	$10	$2
PEPE		1953 export Beetle	Friction motor, cream wheel rims with red hubcaps	Plastic	Cream	1/19	$12	$5
PLAYART		1968 Beetle		Die cast metal	Yellow	1/41	$12	$6
POLISTIL	1977	Beetle 1300	Five spoke wheel rims	Die cast metal	Metallic blue. Metallic green	1/43	$12	$5
POLISTIL	1978	Beetle 1303 Cabriolet		Die cast metal		1/25	$15	$6
POLISTIL	1971	1962 Beetle	Herbie, "No. 53"	Die cast metal	White	1/32	$55	$17
POLISTIL		1963 Beetle	Herbie, pulls apart in the middle	Die cast metal	White	1/43	$60	$15
POLITOYS	1966	1963 export Beetle		Plastic	Metallic blue. Gray. Beige	1/41	$45	$17
POLITOYS	1978	1963 Beetle	Herbie, pulls apart in the middle	Die cast metal	White	1/43	$75	$15
POLYFLAME CONCEPTS	1997	1967 Beetle	Telephone	Plastic		1/18	$40	$10

Manufacturer	Year Made	Beetle Year & type	Additional Information	Material	Color	Scale	Price/Mint Condition	Price/Po· Conditi·
PRALINE	1985	1952 export Beetle 1100		Plastic	Gray. Red. Black. Blue.	1/87	$6	
PRALINE	1986	1952 export Beetle 1100	"POLIZEI"	Plastic	Dark green	1/87	$6	
PRALINE	1986	1952 export Beetle 1100	Taxi	Plastic	Black	1/87	$6	
PRALINE	1987	1952 export Beetle 1100	Postal vehicle	Plastic	Yellow	1/87	$9	
PRALINE		1952 Beetle 1100 convertible		Plastic	Metallic green, black. Metallic blue, black	1/87	$9	
PRALINE		1952 Beetle 1100 convertible	"MAKE LOVE NOT WAR", decorated with flowers	Plastic	Pink, black	1/87	$9	
PRAMETA	1939	1938 Beetle type 60		Die cast metal		1/38	$230	$
REVELL	1965	1962 Beetle convertible	Model kit, No. 53	Plastic	-	1/24	$35	
RIO		1947 Beetle		Die cast metal	Green, maroon	1/43	$18	
RIO		1950 Beetle cabriolet		Die cast metal	Black, Blue, beige	1/43	$18	
RIO		1953 Beetle		Die cast metal	White	1/43	$18	
RUSS	1990	Beetle Cabriolet	Troll figure in car, wind up motor	Plastic	Red	1/50	$5	
SABRA	1970	1962 export Beetle		Die cast metal	Dark blue. Black. Yellow. Orange. Red	1/43	$40	$
SCHAPER MFG	1982	1972 4 by 4 Beetle	Battery run motor	Plastic	Blue	1/43	$20	
SCHUCO	1956	Beetle 1200	Piccolo series	Die cast metal	Red. Dark green.	1/90	$40	
SCHUCO	1958	Beetle 1200	Piccolo series, "POLIZEI"	Die cast metal	Green, white	1/90	$35	
SCHUCO	2000	Beetle Cabriolet	Piccolo series with wohnwagen	Die cast metal	Green	1/90	$20	
SCHUCO	1973	1972 Beetle 1302S	Micro-Models series	Die cast metal	Metallic blue, dark red	1/66	$12	
SCHUCO	1960	1960 Beetle	1046a	Die cast metal	Brick red. Blue	1/40	$75	$
SCHUCO	1960	1960 Beetle	3040a	Die cast metal	Green, white	1/40	$75	$
SIKU	1955	1953 Beetle		Plastic	Blue. Beige. Orange. Blue-gray.	1/60	$110	$
SIKU	1964	1960 Beetle		Die cast metal	Blue, beige	1/60	$20	
SIKU	1975	1973 Beetle		Die cast metal	Metallic blue. Yellow. Gold	1/60	$10	
SIKU	1976	1969 Beetle Cabriolet	Trailer hitch	Die cast metal	Yellow	1/59	$6	
SIKU	1993	1973 Karmann Cabriolet	White or black interior	Die cast metal	Dark blue	1/43	$7	
SIKU	1999	1973 Beetle		Die cast metal	Various colors	1/43	$4	
SIMBA	1990	1973 Karmann Cabriolet	Pull back motor, trailer with speed boat	Die cast metal	Pink	1/43	$15	
SOLIDO		1957 Beetle Convertible	Top up	Die cast metal	Maroon	1/17	$30	
SOLIDO	1990	1949 Karmann Cabriolet	Top down	Die cast metal	Black, white	1/17	$32	
SOLIDO	1990	1949 Karmann Cabriolet		Die cast metal	Black, beige. Metallic maroon.	1/17	$30	
SOLIDO	1991	1949 Beetle		Die cast metal	Green	1/17	$32	
SOLIDO	1991	1949 Beetle	Customized	Die cast metal	Gray. Red. Black	1/17	$32	
SOLIDO	1991	1949 export Beetle	"POLITIE", lights, antenna	Die cast metal	Black	1/17	$40	$
SOLIDO	1991	1949 export Beetle	"MICHELIN"	Die cast metal	Dark yellow, blue	1/17	$40	$
SOLIDO		1949 Karmann Cabriolet	Limited series	Die cast metal	Maroon, beige top	1/17	$35	
SOLIDO	1994	1949 Karmann Cabriolet	"SUCHARD"	Die cast metal	lilac, white	1/17	$45	$
SOLIDO		1957 Beetle Cabriolet	"NIVEA CREME"	Die cast metal	Ivory	1/17	$45	$
SOLIDO		1949 export Beetle	"ADAC STRASSENWACHT"	Die cast metal	Dark yellow	1/17	$40	$
SOLIDO		1949 export Beetle	"DRINK COCA-COLA ICE-COLD"	Die cast metal	Yellow	1/17	$40	
SOLIDO		1949 export Beetle	"ADV & SALES DIVISION COCA-COLA BOTTLING CO."	Die cast metal	Red	1/17	$45	$
SOLIDO		1957 Beetle Cabriolet	"ADV & SALES DIVISION COCA-COLA BOTTLING CO."	Die cast metal	Red	1/17	$55	
SOLIDO		1957 Beetle Cabriolet	1967 Monte Carlo rally car No. 177.	Die cast metal	Gray, black	1/17	$30	
SOLIDO	1996	1962 Beetle	"THE PAUSE THAT REFRESHES COCA COLA"	Die cast metal	White, red	1/18	$40	
SOLIDO	1997	1963 Beetle	Herbie	Die cast metal	White	1/17	$55	$
SS	1986	Beetle Cabriolet	"BOB and JEAN"	Plastic	Yellow	1/46	$6	
SS	1993	Beetle Cabriolet	#4701, pull back motor	Die cast metal	Many color variations	1/32	$7	
SS	1994	1956 export Beetle		Die cast metal	Metallic blue. Gray. White. Red. Pink.	1/24	$11	
SS	1996	1972 Beetle	#4727, "POLICE", "HIGHWAY PATROL", light on roof	Die cast metal	Green, black	1/43	$6	
SS	1998	1972 Beetle	#5702, pull back motor	Die cast metal	Many color variations	1/32	$5	
SS	1998	1972 Beetle Cabriolet	#5708, pull back motor	Die cast metal	Many color variations	1/32	$5	
SS	1999	1967 Beetle	#9701	Die cast metal	Black. Turquoise.	1/18	$14	
STOMPERS	1998	1974 Beetle	Battery run motor	Plastic	Black, yellow	1/40	$8	
STROMBECKER	1985	1972 Beetle	Red interior	Plastic	Blue	1/30	$10	
TAIYO		1954 Karmann Cabriolet		Sheet metal		1/18	$310	
TAIYO	1972	1963 Beetle	Herbie replica, battery run motor	Tin	White	1/16	$150	
TEKNO	1955	1953 Beetle		Die cast metal	Beige. White. Green. Red. Metallic blue	1/50	$110	
TEKNO	1955	1953 Beetle	"POLIZEI"	Die cast metal	White, black	1/50	$150	
TEKNO	1958	1957 Beetle		Die cast metal	Blue. Beige. Red.	1/43	$130	

Manufacturer	Year Made	Beetle Year & type	Additional Information	Material	Color	Scale	Price/Mint Condition	Price/Poor Condition
TEKNO	1960	1960 Beetle	Silver base	Die cast metal	White. Black.	1/43	$110	$30
TEKNO	1962	1960 Beetle	Chrome wheel rims	Die cast metal	Black. White	1/43	$90	$20
TEKNO	1962	1960 Beetle	"POLIZEI"	Die cast metal	Green	1/43	$90	$20
TEKNO	1964	1960 Beetle	"DEUTSCHE BUNDESPOST" on the doors, silver chassis	Die cast metal	Yellow-orange	1/43	$80	$12
TEKNO	1969	1960 export Beetle	Chrome wheel rims, No. 53 on the doors, box says "HERBIE THE LOVE BUG"	Die cast metal	White	1/43	$130	$30
TIPPCO	1938	1938 Beetle type 60	With motor	Sheet metal	Blue	1/50	$330	$50
TIPPCO	1939	1938 Beetle type 60		Sheet metal		1/40	$300	$50
TIPPCO	1948	1947 Beetle 1100		Sheet metal		1/40	$150	$30
TIPPCO	1938	1938 Beetle type 60	Electric motor	Sheet metal		1/50	$320	$50
TOMME TAPPEE		Removable figure		Plastic	Red	1/28	$12	$3
TOMICA-DANDY			"BEETLE", chrome wheel rims, black chassis marked "F11"	Die cast metal	Yellow	1/43	$26	$2
TOMICA-DANDY		1974 Beetle	Rolls Royce front, gray wheel rims, gray chassis	Die cast metal	White	1/43	$28	$2
TOMICA-DANDY		1974 Beetle	"POLIZEI", chrome wheel rims & bumpers, gray chassis marked "F21"	Die cast metal	White, green	1/43	$28	$2
TOMICA-DANDY		1974 Beetle	"POLICE", with two lights on roof, gray wheel rims, gray chassis marked "F21"	Die cast metal	Black, white	1/43	$28	$2
TOMICA-DANDY		1974 Beetle	"RACING", roof rack with two motorcycles	Die cast metal	Gray	1/43	$28	$3
TOMICA-DANDY		1971 Beetle 1302	Police vehicle with light on roof	Die cast metal	Red, white	1/60	$6	$1
TOMY	1998	1974 Beetle	Battery powered motor, decal of eyes	Plastic	Yellow, white	1/32	$15	$4
TONKA		1965 Beetle	"TONKA" stamped on the chassis	Die cast metal	Red. Black. Blue. Green.	1/18	$60	$15
TONKA		1965 Beetle	"TONKA" stamped on the chassis, "TOES"	Die cast metal	Red	1/18	$45	$10
TONKA		1965 Beetle	Large engine, "TONKA" stamped on the chassis	Die cast metal	Green	1/18	$40	$10
TONKA		1972 Beetle	Metal chassis	Plastic	Green. Orange. Red. Yellow.	1/50	$15	$4
TONKA		1974 Beetle	"LADYBUG"	Plastic	Yellow, red.	1/66	$8	$2
TONKA	2000	1974 Baja Bug		Die cast metal	Grey	1/66	$4	$1
TOOTSIETOYS	1960	1957 Beetle		Die cast metal	Metallic	1/27	$62	$27
TOOTSIETOYS	1960	1957 Beetle		Die cast metal	Green	1/54	$47	$23
TOOTSIETOYS		1968 open roof Beetle		Die cast metal	Dark red	1/32	$20	$6
TOOTSIETOYS		1967 Beetle	"TOOTSIE TOY RACING", plastic chassis	Die cast metal	Yellow	1/66	$12	$3
TOOTSIETOYS		1963 Beetle	No interior or chassis	Die cast metal	Various colors	1/66	$8	$2
TOY TECH	2000	1972 Beetle	Pull back motor, driver ejects out of roof	Plastic		1/30	$7	$2
TUDOR ROSE	1964	1952 Beetle	No interior	Plastic	Yellow. Blue.	1/20	$40	$10
VANGUARDS	1994	1952 Beetle	"POLIZEI"	Die cast metal	White, green.	1/43	$23	$5
VANGUARDS	1994	1952 Beetle cabriolet		Die cast metal	Light blue	1/43	$23	$5
VIKING	1998	1972 Beetle		Plastic	Blue	1/50	$3	$1
VITESSE		1962 Beetle	"MICHELIN"	Die cast metal	Yellow, blue	1/43	$32	$9
VITESSE		1949 Karmann Cabriolet	"JUST MARRIED", made in Portugal	Die cast metal	Lilac	1/43	$32	$9
VITESSE	1994	1945 Beetle pick up	Ambulance	Die cast metal	Blue	1/43	$32	$9
VITESSE		1949 export Beetle	"POLIZEI", two light on roof, made in Portugal	Die cast metal	White, black	1/43	$32	$9
VITESSE		1945 Beetle 1100	Made in Portugal	Die cast metal	Black	1/43	$29	$7
VITESSE		1949 export Beetle	"POLIZEI", two lights on roof, made in Portugal	Die cast metal	White, green	1/43	$29	$7
VITESSE		1949 export Beetle	"DEUTSCHE POST", made in Portugal	Die cast metal	Yellow	1/43	$29	$7
VITESSE		1949 export Beetle	"TRULLY NOLEN", eyes, nose, tail of mouse, made in Portugal	Die cast metal	Yellow	1/43	$23	$7
VITESSE		1949 Karmann Cabriolet	"JUST MARRIED", bride & groom in car, black interior, made in Portugal		Red. White	1/43	$32	$9
VITESSE		1949 Karmann Cabriolet	"PEACE AND LOVE", with driver, made in Portugal	Die cast metal	Pink, gray	1/43	$23	$7
VITESSE		1962 export Beetle	Rally Safari 62, made in China	Die cast metal	Maroon	1/43	$23	$7
VITESSE		1962 export Beetle	"THE UNITED STATES OF AMERICA", US dollar, made in China	Die cast metal	White	1/43	$32	$9
VITESSE	1994	1962 Beetle Cabriolet	"HERBIE 53"	Die cast metal	White	1/43	$32	$9
VITESSE		1962 Beetle Cabriolet	1964 Monte Carlo rally car No. 61, antenna, made in China	Die cast metal	Gray	1/43	$29	$7
VITESSE		Beetle	"PINK-FLOYD"	Die cast metal		1/43	$32	$9
VITESSE		Beetle 1200 Sedan	L164, "VW" and "261"	Die cast metal	Red	1/43	$30	$7
VOITURE	1995	1969 Beetle	Friction motor	Tin	Red. Yellow.	1/30	$12	$3
VOLKSWAGEN	1949	1948 Beetle		Metal	Many color variations	1/32	$150	$30

Manufacturer	Year Made	Beetle Year & type	Additional Information	Material	Color	Scale	Price/Mint Condition	Price/Poor Condition
VOLKSWAGEN	1999	1972 Beetle	"VOLKSWAGEN RECYCLIING"	Plastic	Various colors	1/32	$30	
VOLKSWAGEN	2000	1972 Beetle	"VOLKSWAGEN RECYCLING", flashing lights	Plastic	Blue	1/32	$35	$
VOSS	1952	1951 Beetle		Plastic	Yellow. Grey	1/43	$60	$
WELLY		1974 Beetle 1303	"STAR LIGHT", pull back motor	Die cast metal	Black	1/36	$8	
WIKING	1948	1947 Beetle	Removable body, seats, engine, & gas tank.	Plastic	Clear	1/43	$75	$
WIKING	1955	1955 Karmann Cabriolet	With driver & passenger	Plastic	Blue-gray. Dark Green.	1/87	$14	
WIKING	1959	1957 Beetle		Plastic	Black. Gray. Red. Brown. Orange.	1/87	$12	
WIKING	1973	1972 Beetle 1302		Plastic	Red. Blue. Green.	1/87	$8	
WIKING	1995	Beetle 1200		Plastic	Gray	1/87	$7	
WIKING	1994	Beetle 1200	"DEUTSCHE BUNDESPOST"	Plastic	Yellow	1/87	$7	
WIKING	1994	1949 export Beetle	Taxi No. 3	Plastic	Black	1/87	$7	
WIKING	1994	1949 export Beetle	Auto-Museum Volkswagen	Plastic		1/87	$7	
WIKING	1995	1973 Karmann Cabriolet		Plastic	Blue,black top	1/87	$7	
WIKING	1962	1960 Karmann Cabriolet		Plastic	Gray. Green. Black. Red. Blue.	1/40	$120	$
WIKING	1963	1963 Karmann Cabriolet		Plastic	Blue. Olive green. Gray	1/40	$100	$
WIKING	1971	1971 Karmann Cabriolet		Plastic	Gray. Dark red. Blue. Beige.	1/40	$45	$
WIKING	1950	1949 Beetle 1100	With driver	Plastic	Clear	1/40	$275	$
WIKING	1958	1956 Beetle		Plastic	Olive green. Red. Blue. Black.	1/40	$130	$
WIKING	1970	1970 Beetle		Plastic	Red. Orange. Blue. Green. Gray.	1/40	$45	$
WIKING	1995	1971 Beetle 1302		Plastic	Dark blue	1/40	$18	
WUCO	1950	1948 Beetle	Tin garage	Plastic	Blue. Cream.	1/60	$40	$
YATMING	1995	1966 Beetle 1500	Road tough series	Die cast metal	Yellow. Blue. White.	1/18	$24	$
YATMING		1966 Beetle	KFC promotional, "KFC"	Die cast metal	Green	1/66	$8	
YATMING	2000	1967 Beetle Cabriolet		Die cast metal	Blue	1/43	$10	
YONAEAWA	1994	1971 Beetle	"CHIEF", "MADE IN JAPAN"	Tin	Red, white	1/30	$20	
YONAEAWA	1994	1967 Beetle	"POLICE", wind up motor	Tin	White, black	1/50	$16	
ZYLL ENTERPRISE LTD	1993	Monster Beetle	"Bug Bomb"	Die cast metal	Orange	1/50	$6	
Maker Unknown		1973 Beetle 1303	Lighter	Die cast metal	Blue, chrome	1/50	$5	
Maker Unknown	1990	Standard Beetle	Chocolate	Chocolate		1/32	$15	
Maker Unknown		Standard Beetle	Electric clock, roof rack with surfboard	Plastic	Black	1/24	$16	
Maker Unknown		Standard Beetle	"BEETLAND" lighter	Plastic	White	1/30	$8	
Maker Unknown		Standard Beetle	Four feet supporting the car, wind up motor, feet walk	Plastic	Orange	1/52	$10	
Maker Unknown		Standard Beetle	"FIRE CHIEF", friction motor	Sheet metal	Red, white	1/55	$11	
Maker Unknown		Standard Beetle	Eraser	Eraser	Yellow. Green	1/83	$5	
Maker Unknown		Standard Beetle	"FLIP OVER", pull back motor		Orange. Red	1/52	$8	
Maker Unknown		1973 Karman Cabriolet	"I LOVE VW", antenna	Plastic	Black, gray	1/16	$20	
Maker Unknown		Standard Beetle	"CHIEF", friction motor	Sheet metal	Red	1/33	$9	
Maker Unknown		Standard Beetle	"RESCUE", friction motor	Sheet metal	Blue	1/33	$9	
Maker Unknown		Standard Beetle	With Bugs Bunny	Ceramic	Pink	1/32	$11	
Maker Unknown		Beetle 1303	Cookie jar	Ceramic	Dark blue	1/13	$20	
Maker Unknown		Standard Beetle	"NEW YORK TAXI"	Ceramic	Yellow	1/27	$15	
Maker Unknown		Standard Beetle	With clown	Ceramic	White	1/38	$10	
Maker Unknown		1957 Beetle	"TAXI"	Plastic	Black, yellow	1/43	$30	
Maker Unknown		1974 Beetle	Friction motor, as car moves forward it flips over	Plastic	Yellow	1/52	$4	
Maker Unknown		Standard Beetle	Metal wire Volkswagen	Wire	Silver	1/18	$20	
Maker Unknown		Standard Beetle	Made in South Africa	Recycled Aluminum cans	Green, red, white	1/24	$25	
Maker Unknown	1997	1968 Beetle	Chicago taxi cab, "CHICAGO"	Die cast metal	Yellow	1/32	$8	
Maker Unknown	2000	1974 Beetle	New York taxi & New York police car set		Yellow. Blue	1/55	$7	
Maker Unknown	1994	1970 Beetle	Lucky red taxi Beetle	Plastic	Red	1/18	$8	
Maker Unknown		Standard Beetle	Tomato in Beetle, marked "made in Germany"	Plastic	Clear	1/38	$3	
Maker Unknown		Standard Beetle	Wind up motor, drummer beats drum as car moves	Plastic	Yellow	1/24	$7	
Maker Unknown	1982	Standard Beetle	Rabbits head turns as car moves	Plastic	Red	1/18	$7	
Maker Unknown		1955 Beetle cabriolet		Plastic	Yellow	1/100	$9	
Maker Unknown		Standard Beetle	Bank	Ceramic	Various colors	1/18	$18	
Maker Unknown		Standard Beetle	Bank with mice driving	Ceramic	Blue	1/24	$12	
Maker Unknown	1996	1972 Beetle	Salt and pepper shakers	Ceramic	Various colors	1/32	$8	
Maker Unknown		Standard Beetle	Book ends	Ceramic	Yellow, green	1/18	$25	
Maker Unknown		Standard Beetle	Teapot	Ceramic	Yellow. Green. Red. Blue	1/18	$60	
Maker Unknown	1984	1974 Beetle	Transformer	Die cast metal & plastic	Gold	1/32	$15	
Maker Unknown	1995	Standard Beetle	Candy container	Plastic	Clear	1/24	$6	
Maker Unknown	1999	Standard Beetle	Candy container, "BUGGY CANDY"		Red. Yellow	1/55	$3	
Maker Unknown	1988	Standard Beetle	Pencil holder	Plastic	White	1/24	$10	
Maker Unknown	1998	Standard Beetle	Key Chain	Foam	Various colors	1/50	$5	
Maker Unknown	1997	Standard Beetle	Christmas tree ornament with Santa	Plastic	Red. Blue	1/43	$7	